OXFORD CLASSICAL MONOGRAPHS

*Published under the supervision of a Committee of the
Faculty of Literae Humaniores in the University of Oxford*

D0420756

The aim of the Oxford Classical Monographs series (which replaces the Oxford Classical and Philosophical Monographs) is to publish books based on the best theses on Greek and Latin literature, ancient history, and ancient philosophy examined by the Faculty Board of Literae Humaniores.

Between Geography and History

Hellenistic Constructions of the
Roman World

KATHERINE CLARKE

CLARENDON PRESS · OXFORD

*This book has been printed digitally and produced in a standard specification
in order to ensure its continuing availability*

OXFORD
UNIVERSITY PRESS

Great Clarendon Street, Oxford OX2 6DP

Oxford University Press is a department of the University of Oxford.
It furthers the University's objective of excellence in research, scholarship,
and education by publishing worldwide in

Oxford New York

Auckland Cape Town Dar es Salaam Hong Kong Karachi
Kuala Lumpur Madrid Melbourne Mexico City Nairobi
New Delhi Shanghai Taipei Toronto
With offices in
Argentina Austria Brazil Chile Czech Republic France Greece
Guatemala Hungary Italy Japan South Korea Poland Portugal
Singapore Switzerland Thailand Turkey Ukraine Vietnam

Oxford is a registered trade mark of Oxford University Press
in the UK and in certain other countries

Published in the United States
by Oxford University Press Inc., New York

ISBN 978-0-19-924826-1

For Chris

Preface

This book started its official life as an Oxford D.Phil. thesis, written at St. John's College and Christ Church. As a student at St. John's I benefited enormously from the expert guidance and inspirational teaching of Michael Comber and Nicholas Purcell. Both have continued to provide support in all kinds of ways; and it was while I was an undergraduate at St. John's that the seeds of the idea to research ancient geography and conceptions of the wider world were sown in my mind.

I was enabled to undertake research in the first place by postgraduate funding from the British Academy. The award of a Senior Scholarship at Christ Church in Michaelmas 1995, followed by a Junior Research Fellowship in 1997, provided the ideal, even idyllic, conditions for the final stages and completion of both thesis and book—a friendly and comfortable environment, and freedom from financial worries. For this, and above all for the warm welcome which I received, in particular from Alan Bowman, Richard Rutherford, Peter Parsons, and Dirk Obbink, I am extremely grateful. My three years at Christ Church have been a source of great pleasure.

Naturally the project has changed since the initial stages, often in unexpected directions. Having set out to study spatial conceptions in antiquity, I encountered Strabo's *Geography*, and decided that its startling historical content would make a more interesting topic. However, I have returned to incorporate many of the spatial notions which I thought I had left behind. In order to understand what kind of work Strabo was writing, I was drawn back to tackle the question of spatial models and their transformation. So, I have had the good fortune to pursue simultaneously the project that I first proposed, as well as the one on which I finally settled.

In the course of the book's development, I have been greatly helped by the comments and suggestions of many scholars, whose generous assistance has greatly enhanced my work at all stages. The list is too long for all to be mentioned by name, but I would like to thank in particular: Peter Derow, for his help with my work on Polybius; Donald Russell, for reading, commenting on, and greatly improving my chapter on Posidonius; Jack Langton, for introducing me to the modern geographical bibliography, which transformed my approach; Don Fowler, for his help with the first chapter; the participants in the Ancient History Work-in-Progress Seminar, where the combination of energy and tolerance provides a perfect forum in which to try out unformed ideas. Judith Pallot, James Ryan, and Eric Swyngedou helped with discussion of modern geographical approaches. I have been delighted to unearth and benefit from the comments of Strabonian enthusiasts overseas, in particular Daniela Dueck and Yuval Shahar. Peter Wiseman and Chris Pelling examined the work as a D. Phil. thesis and their many suggestions for its future life were a great help. Simon Hornblower and Oswyn Murray were extremely generous with their help as my 'Graduate Advisers'; the latter also oversaw the transformation from thesis into book, and contributed greatly with bibliography, ideas, and an excellent eye for the broader picture.

However, I save my greatest debts until last. My supervisor, Fergus Millar, contributed expertise, encouragement, generosity, and enthusiasm for the project, and has been a constant source of support. I should also like to thank my mother for painstakingly proof-reading the work, and for much else besides. Finally Chris, for innumerable discussions, for the time-consuming, but invaluable, task of reading the entire manuscript in minute detail and making many illuminating observations and criticisms, for providing moral support at every stage, and for everything else that he has been to me throughout the whole period of my research.

Contents

List of Abbreviations

The following abbreviations have been used throughout.

AJA	*American Journal of Archaeology*
AJP	*American Journal of Philology*
ANRW	*Aufstieg und Niedergang der Römischen Welt*
AR	Dionysius of Halicarnassus, *Roman Antiquities*
CISA	*Contributi dell'Istituto di Storia Antica*
Class. Phil.	*Classical Philology*
CQ	*Classical Quarterly*
E–K	L. Edelstein and I. G. Kidd (eds.), *Posidonius*, 3 vols.: *I. The Fragments; II(i). Testimonia and Fragments 1–149; II(ii). Fragments 150–293* (Cambridge Classical Texts and Commentaries, 13 and 14; Cambridge, Cambridge University Press, 1972 and 1988)
FGrH	F. Jacoby (ed.), *Die Fragmente der griechischen Historiker* (15 vols.; Berlin, 1923–30; Leipzig, 1940–58)
GGM I	C. Müller (ed.), *Geographici Graeci Minores, i* (Paris, Firmin-Didot, 1855)
GRBS	*Greek, Roman and Byzantine Studies*
Italia Antica	G. Maddoli (ed.), *Strabone e l'Italia Antica* (Perugia, Università degli Studi, 1988)
JHS	*Journal of Hellenic Studies*
JRS	*Journal of Roman Studies*
LSJ	H. G. Liddell and R. Scott, with H. S. Jones and R. McKenzie, *A Greek–*

	English Lexicon, rev. 9th edn. (Oxford, Clarendon Press, 1996)
Making Sense of Time	T. Carlstein, D. Parkes, and N. Thrift (eds.), *Making Sense of Time* (Timing Space and Spacing Time I; London, Arnold, 1978)
PCPS	*Proceedings of the Cambridge Philological Society*
Purposes of History	H. Verdin, G. Schepens, and E. de Keyser (eds.), *Purposes of History: Studies in Greek Historiography from the 4th to the 2nd Centuries B.C.* (Studia Hellenistica 30; Leuven, Dack and Dessel, 1990)
R-E	A. Pauly and G. Wissowa, *Real-Encyclopädie der classischen Altertumswissenschaft*
Strabone I	F. Prontera (ed.), *Strabone. Contributi allo studio della personalità e dell'Opera I* (Perugia, Università degli Studi, 1984)
Strabone II	G. Maddoli (ed.), *Strabone. Contributi allo studio della personalità e dell'Opera II* (Perugia, Università degli Studi, 1986)
TAPA	*Transactions and Papers of the American Philological Association*
TIBG	*Transactions and Papers of the Institute of British Geographers*

I

Geographical and Historiographical Traditions

'Where are you going from here?' Gilles asked.

'South, to Sartène and Bonifacio.'

'Bonifacio is a very pretty place. You know Homer's *Odyssey*? Bonifacio is where the Laestrygonians live.'

That was beautiful, that he referred to the distant little port, not for a good restaurant or a luxury hotel or its fortress or a trivial event, but as the place where a group of savage giants had interfered with Ulysses. When it comes to literary allusions you can't do much better than use the authority of the *Odyssey* to prove that your home town was once important. In Gibraltar Sir Joshua Hassan had jerked his thumb sideways towards the Rock and said to me 'That's one of the Pillars of Hercules'.[1]

IDENTIFYING THE ISSUE

Theroux's modern account of a journey around the Mediterranean perfectly illustrates the interaction between geography and history, in which the world of the present day is best described by reference to its remote past, and in which the temporal aspect of a place forms an integral part of the spatial description. The example is an extreme one—covering a span of several millennia—but particularly apposite, given the predominance of the Homeric epics in the formation of views about the world in antiquity. It is my aim to explore the relationship between two fields of study which we have come to regard as the separate disciplines of geography and history. Although I have started with a self-conscious modern example of the inextricable link between the two, the tendency both in the modern academic subjects and in our dealings with ancient

[1] P. Theroux, *The Pillars of Hercules: A Grand Tour of the Mediterranean* (London, 1995), 136–7.

writers is to classify works and their authors as belonging to one or other category. It seems quite acceptable to state that Strabo was a geographer and Polybius a historian, and it is likely that those titles will remain. However, I should like to raise the issue that in practical, literary, and philosophical terms, geography and history overlap considerably, making it necessary for us to question the ease with which we classify ancient works and authors according to genre.

I shall discuss throughout this book various ways in which ambiguity in definitions of geography and history is apparent in texts from the late Hellenistic period, and I shall be advocating much broader, inclusive, and overlapping historiographical and geographical traditions. My main author, Strabo, produced two works which highlight the nature of the issue. The *Geography* of Strabo contains a vast proportion of material which we would term historical, and which I shall analyse in chapter V. However, Strabo also wrote a *History*, which he clearly considered worth distinguishing from the *Geography*. The *History* is now lost except for nineteen fragments, and its survival would have provided at least a partial answer to my question.[2] If we were to know how a single author chose to write both a historical and a geographical work, we should make some progress along the road towards understanding how at least one ancient mind perceived these fields. Baldly stated, the problem arising from ancient texts is as follows.

We have evidence for separate geographical and historical works, for which we must account. But the contents, organizing principles, and character of these works are often very similar. On the one hand, I shall ask what makes Strabo's account of the whole known world, including the past of almost every place described, 'geographical', as opposed to either Diodorus' contemporary 'historical' account of the known world from the earliest times to the present day, or Strabo's

---

[2] For the extant fragments of Strabo's *History* see *FGrH* 91. At 11. 9. 3 of the *Geography* Strabo explains that 'having said many things about the Parthian customs in the sixth book of the *Histories* . . . I shall pass them by here, so as not to appear to repeat myself' (εἰρηκότες δὲ πολλὰ περὶ τῶν Παρθικῶν νομίμων ἐν τῇ ἕκτῃ τῶν ἱστορικῶν ὑπομνημάτων βίβλῳ . . . παραλείψομεν ἐνταῦθα, μὴ ταυτολογεῖν δόξωμεν). The problem could not be more plainly visible. The same kind of material seems to have been applicable to both works, but they were at the same time kept distinct.

own historical project. On the other, I shall argue that generic fluidity was built into the historiographical tradition from the start, and that the late Hellenistic period, a time of new horizons and re-evaluation of the world, was naturally characterized by works of a broad and comprehensive scope.

I hope that asking such questions may yield rewards in several ways. Firstly, it may enhance our appreciation of the 'geographical' aspects of 'historical' works, such as that of Polybius. Secondly, I argue in chapter III that a broader conception of the nature of geography and history in antiquity also encourages a reappraisal of our approach towards fragmentary works, such as those of Posidonius, and challenges some of the assumptions which have underpinned their reconstruction. Thirdly, an exploration of these issues may lead to new ways of understanding the enormous geographical project undertaken by Strabo, rather than continuing the traditional approaches of searching for his sources, or testing the accuracy of his description alongside modern maps. Much of the existing literature on ancient works has tended not to explore in depth the complexities of the relationship between geography and history. The topic has sometimes been thought satisfactorily treated merely by noting the contribution made to our understanding of specific historical events by a knowledge of topography. Although this is one important aspect of the relationship, it by no means exhausts the possibilities.

By contrast, the ambiguous position of geography as a modern academic discipline has resulted in serious attempts by modern geographers to define their subject both in terms of its own tradition and against other fields of study, in particular history. It seems justified to apply to the ancient material some of the issues and arguments raised in these debates, partly because the beginnings of the modern geographical tradition developed against an awareness of the ancient predecessors, and partly because the explicit and implicit issues which emerge from the ancient texts coincide with many of the modern debates, and can thus be helpfully elucidated by them. While the initial impetus to look at the modern disciplines has sprung, in my case, from reading ancient authors such as Strabo, those modern debates in turn attune us to further complexities in the ancient material. However, this

should not be a one-way flow of ideas, and a study of the
ancient sources in the light of the arguments of modern
geographers can contribute to refining some of *their* assertions,
with the result that both the ancient and modern studies are
enriched. For these reasons I intend to consider some of the
modern discussions about geography and history, before turning to the ancient sources. I certainly do not aim to provide a
complete synthesis of modern geographical thought and its
development through time, a feat which would far exceed the
limitations of this project. Instead, I have selected certain
themes which seem to be of relevance to an understanding of
ancient intellectual history, and to some of the literary texts
which were the products of that thought.

The nature of my project means that it is impossible to adopt
a purely linear approach. The ancient material has affected my
interest in the modern debates, and the questions raised in
those debates have in turn affected my reading of the ancient
sources. Everything is interconnected and difficult to order. I
leave it to Polybius to provide the formulation of the way in
which this introductory chapter both foreshadows and is
informed by the ideas discussed throughout the whole book:

How can one begin a thing well without having grasped beforehand in
one's mind the completion of the project, and without knowing how
and in relation to what and why one strives to do it? And again how is
it possible to summarize events properly without reference to the
beginning, and understanding whence, how, and why the final situation was reached? So we should consider that beginnings stretch not
only to the middle, but to the end, and both writers and readers of
universal history should pay the greatest attention to them. And this I
shall now try to do.   (5. 32. 3–4)

GEOGRAPHY AND HISTORY: THE
DEVELOPMENT OF TWO DISCIPLINES

Historie without geographie like a dead carkasse hath neither life nor
motion at all . . . geographie without historie hath life and motion, but
at randome, and unstable.[3]

[3] From P. Heylyn, *Microcosmus*; see R. A. Butlin, *Historical Geography:
Through the Gates of Space and Time* (London, 1993), 2. Heylyn (1599–1662)
was an ecclesiastical writer and Fellow of Magdalen College, Oxford.

That geography and history together encompass our entire experience of the world was asserted by Defoe in *On Learning*.[4] One modern historian, Meinig, has formulated the relationship more fully. 'Geography and history are rooted in the basic stuff of human existence. As fields of study they are analogous, complementary, and interdependent. Their relationship is implied by such common terms as space and time, places and events—pairs that are fundamentally inseparable. What differentiates geography and history is the proportionate emphasis each gives to these terms.'[5] This is the reality in both practical and literary terms, and yet, both in antiquity and now, geography and history have existed distinctly, but rather uncomfortably, side by side. It is interesting, given this interdependence, that historians have, in general, felt less bound to justify and define their subject than have geographers.

Meinig's contribution to recent attempts to relate geography and history to each other is significant, but limited. He states that they 'are not the study of any particular set of things, but are a particular way of studying anything'.[6] This accounts for some of the difficulties encountered over some fragmentary Hellenistic texts, where subject matter does not seem to indicate any clear division between geographical and historical works. Although some might argue that geography and history stress different themes, this view has not been prominent in recent discussions. In other words, Meinig's concern with the manner of relating material, rather than with the subject matter itself, leads us in a direction which is commonly acceptable. Meinig's limitation, however, is that he does not express a view as to what are the particularly 'historical' and 'geographical' ways of studying.

Various suggestions have been put forward for what distinguishes geography from history. The development of the modern subject-distinction is interesting in its own right,

[4] See J. N. L. Baker, *The History of Geography* (Oxford, 1963), 158. Defoe claimed that 'in Geography and History he had all the world at his fingers' ends'.

[5] D. W. Meinig, 'The Continuous Shaping of America: A Prospectus for Geographers and Historians', *American Historical Review*, 83 (1978), 1186.

[6] Ibid. 1187.

although many of the intricate arguments about the nature of
time and space in their various forms and configurations may
seem either irrelevant, or so far removed from the ancient texts
as to be worthless, or simply misconceived and wrong. However, since we inevitably come to the ancient texts with generic
preconceptions which are influenced, if only indirectly, by
these arguments, it is important to examine them in some
detail. In any case, many of the ideas and definitions involved
can offer interesting and unexpected insights on the ancient
sources. Two major models emerge, and I treat these in turn:
firstly, a four-part analogy 'geography : space : : history : time',
and secondly the model 'geography : present : : history : past'.

I turn first to the model associating geography with space
and history with time. The dominant account of the evolution
of geography and history as disciplines characterized in this
way may be summarized as follows. In the opinion of many
modern geographers, Kant was the first to devote significant
thought to the philosophical notions of time and space, and his
work was dependent on the Newtonian advance of conceptualizing time and space as absolute and abstract qualities,
which existed independently of the world and its events.[7] From
this time on, geography and history evolved as distinct fields of
study, and Kant was himself the first to lecture on geography as
a university subject.[8]

The introduction to Kant's *Physische Geographie* is regularly
cited for the formulation of his ideas on geography, history,
time, and space. Like Defoe he asserted that 'geography and
history fill up the total span of our knowledge; geography that
of space, and history that of time' ('Geographie und Geschichte
füllen den gesammten Umfang unserer Erkenntnisse aus; die

[7] S. Kern, *The Culture of Time and Space: 1880–1910* (London, 1983),
however, qualifies the connection, contrasting Newtonian absolute and
objective time and space with Kant's subjective abstractions.
[8] It is noteworthy that the argument starts so late. Although the beginnings
of the modern geographical tradition were characterized by a consciousness of
the classical past, as in the works of Samuel Johnson, later attempts to trace
the development of two separate subjects often reach back only as far as the
Enlightenment period. Kant's geographical papers are found in F. W.
Schubert (ed.), *Immanuel Kants Schriften zur physischen Geographie* (Leipzig,
1839). Chapter XIII of this volume contains the *Vorlesungen über Physische
Geographie* (1802), to which I shall refer simply as the *Physische Geographie*.

Geographie nämlich den des Raumes, die Geschichte aber den der Zeit') (§4). He had earlier in the same chapter defined geography as description according to space, and history according to time: 'So, history is differentiated from geography only in respect of space and time. The first is, as stated, an account of events which follow one after the other, and is related to time. But the other is an account of occurrences which take place alongside each other in space.'[9]

I argue later that Kant's role as pioneer of certain concepts has been overestimated, to the detriment of thinkers from antiquity; but his influence on the debates concerning the two subjects is undeniable. The notion of geography as spatial and history as temporal has been taken up and discussed by modern geographers.[10] These definitions have also been upheld with regard to ancient authors, for instance by the Strabonian scholar, Prontera, who argues that geography differs from history 'because here the dimension of space is predominant over that of time' ('perché in essa la dimensione dello spazio domina . . . su quella del tempo').[11] Prontera insists on a continuum of time–space dominance along which history and geography may be placed, which seems much more satisfactory than a straight dichotomy. But, the broad identifications of geography with space and of history with time are relatively satisfactory in abstract terms, and they are characterizations

[9] 'Die Historie ist also von der Geographie nur in Ansehung des Raumes und der Zeit verschieden. Die erste ist, wie gesagt, eine Nachricht von Begebenheiten, die auf einander folgen, und hat Beziehung auf die Zeit. Die andere aber ist eine Nachricht von Begebenheiten, die neben einander im Raume vor sich gehen.' For Kant's schematization of geography and history in this way see *Physische Geographie*, §4; also J. A. May, *Kant's Concept of Geography and its Relation to Recent Geographical Thought* (Toronto, 1970), 124.

[10] Notably by R. Hartshorne in his influential book, *The Nature of Geography: A Critical Survey of Current Thought in the Light of the Past* (Lancaster PA, 1939). Hartshorne has been seen as heavily influenced by Kant, in so far as he upheld Kant's distinction between time and space. See N. Smith, 'Geography as Museum: Private History and Conservative Idealism in *The Nature of Geography*', in J. N. Entrikin and S. D. Brunn (eds.), *Reflections on Richard Hartshorne's* The Nature of Geography (Washington, 1989), 91–120.

[11] F. Prontera, 'Prima di Strabone: Materiali per uno studio della geografia antica come genere letterario', in *Strabone I*, 252.

which I shall follow implicitly from time to time in my discussion of various authors. The model is, however, beset with problems related to the fact that the world is experienced against both space and time simultaneously. This entails the most obvious objection, namely that history must take place in a spatial context and geography must be temporally located in so far as it changes through time. Geography and history both require a spatial and a temporal context.

Furthermore, the introduction of the notion of experience, as opposed to abstractions, means that care is required with each side of the analogy in indicating precisely what kind of time and space is being referred to. Within the space–time model there are problems with both the identification of 'geography' with 'space' and that of 'history' with 'time'. I treat these now in turn.

The belief in abstract and absolute space was held, as I have mentioned, by such influential geographers as Hartshorne, whose view has been summarized as being that 'events, objects and processes do not constitute space, but happen "in space"'.[12] Some modern geographers have strongly asserted the existence of abstract space in the form of geometry: 'Geometry is explicitly an abstraction from real physical bodies at the same time as it describes the structure of space.'[13] It has often been suggested that abstract space, like abstract time, was a product of Enlightenment thought, and alien to antiquity. Gurevich, in his important work on medieval culture, draws what I feel is too sharp a distinction between the ancient and modern mind-set in this regard, viewing abstract concepts as the preserve of the modern world.[14]

Support for his view can be found not only among modern geographers, such as Harvey, who has suggested that maps and calendars were almost an innovation of the Enlightenment, but also, more surprisingly, among some ancient historians. Brodersen, in a seminar on the map of Agrippa, posited the view that this map came in the form of a list of places, rather than a

[12] Smith, 'Geography as Museum', 109.

[13] See N. Smith, *Uneven Development: Nature, Capital and the Production of Space* (Oxford, 1984), 70.

[14] A. J. Gurevich (trans. G. L. Campbell), *Categories of Medieval Culture* (London, 1985), 26 and 29.

graphic representation of the world, starting from the debatable premise that abstract space did not exist for the Romans.[15] One wonders, if this view were correct, what we should make of explicit references to drawn maps in ancient sources. Herodotus, as so often, provides an example in the bronze plaque (χάλκεον πίνακα) displayed in 499 BC to the Spartans, and on which 'a depiction of the entire world (γῆς ἁπάσης περίοδος) had been engraved, with the whole sea and all the rivers' (5. 49). Another famous fifth-century example is the map of the world referred to by Strepsiades in Aristophanes' *Clouds*, and on which Athens, the area of Attica, Euboea, and Sparta could be picked out.[16] Again the word used is περίοδος ('geographical representation'), nicely illustrating the fact that these graphic depictions were parallel to verbal descriptions of the earth from Hecataeus onwards.[17] Geometrical abstract space is attested not only in literary references to drawn maps, but also in the Hellenistic theoretical writings of Hipparchus and Polybius.

However, alongside the abstract space of geometry and drawn maps, it is clear that we must take into account the experienced space of the world. I shall discuss this in more detail below (pp. 25–8), but note simply at the moment that arguments over abstract and experienced time and space are also relevant to the various systems devised for their formal representations. We can hardly contemplate enterprises in which the world was depicted in geographical and historical works, without also considering the different organizational strategies which they used. Formalizing a scheme for terrestrial space in abstract terms perhaps reached its peak with the

[15] *Contra*, R. Moynihan, 'Geographical Mythology and Roman Imperial Ideology', in R. Winkes (ed.), *The Age of Augustus* (Providence, 1985), 149–52, discusses the shape of Agrippa's map, without questioning that it was a graphical representation. On the nature of Greek cartography, see C. Jacob, 'Carte Greche', in F. Prontera (ed.), *Geografia e geografi nel mondo antico: Guida storica e critica* (Rome, 1983), 49–67.

[16] Aristophanes *Clouds* 206: αὕτη δέ σοι γῆς περίοδος πάσης. ὁρᾷς; ('Here you have a depiction of the whole world. Do you see?') The last word makes perfectly clear the visual nature of the depiction.

[17] But caution should be exercised. The use of the same terminology for written and visual depictions (γράφειν, περίοδος) can lead to confusion. Herodotus 4. 36, on those who draw depictions of the earth (γῆς περιόδους γράψαντας), could just as readily refer to written accounts as to visual maps, the usual assumption.

Geography of Ptolemaeus, in which places were described, not in terms of their relationship to the places immediately surrounding them, but with reference to a grid which covered the whole world.[18] But alongside that, we should recall the periplus tradition in which places were sited largely in relation to each other rather than to an externally imposed grid, and where the experienced nature of space was paramount. I shall have more to say about both of these traditions in chapter IV. So, the interchangeability of 'geography' with 'space' requires further consideration as to whether abstract space, or experienced space, or both are intended.

Similarly, the association of 'history' with 'time' is problematic. Some historians have written about history and historiography as temporally determined, with no explicit discussion of the nature of the time to which they refer. Breisach, for example, notes that history springs from the fact that 'human life is subject to the dictates of time' and that 'history deals with human life as it "flows" through time'.[19] He then goes on to treat individual historians and the various chronological systems they used to demarcate the course of history. But can the experienced time of 'human life' be equated with the measured time of chronological systems? And are different kinds of time mutually exclusive?

One problem is that no single method of conceptualizing and measuring time has been found commonly acceptable to all peoples. There is no overall consensus on the nature of time and the best method for its calibration. The introduction of GMT by act of Parliament in 1880 entailed a radical move

[18] The objectivity often attributed to Ptolemaeus' project should, however, be qualified. He derived much of his information from travel reports, which he called ἱστορία περιοδική ('knowledge acquired through travel', 1. 2). Note also that Ptolemaeus' account of Taprobane and eastern India is rich in ethnographic material, making false any assertion that he was not interested in 'lived-in' space. Given this strand in Ptolemaeus' thought, the implicit contrast that is drawn by G. H. T. Kimble, *Geography in the Middle Ages* (London, 1938), 182, between his approach and that of geographers in the Middle Ages, when the map was 'a somewhat elastic framework within which subjects of popular, rather than scientific, interest could be delineated', should be questioned.

[19] E. Breisach, *Historiography: Ancient, Medieval, and Modern* (Chicago, 1983), 2.

away from the previously more local nature of time in Britain, in a way which was necessitated by the development of a national communications system. No countrywide system could function while villages only a few miles apart were still not in synchronism. It is noteworthy that Christ Church in Oxford still operates five minutes behind GMT, in order to reflect its precise location to the west of Greenwich. The parallel with the difficulties of co-ordination facing ancient authors who attempted to write universal accounts involving lands which used different time-systems is clear.

The most radical attempt to impose a universal time-system in Greek historiography was the development of the Olympiadic system, attributed by Bickermann to Timaeus or Eratosthenes.[20] Both wrote treatises on Olympic victors, and Timaeus had gone on from his calculations to innovate in using the Olympiad as 'the basic unit of chronological punctuation in a complex historical work'.[21] Thenceforth it became the basis of all Greek chronology and its acceptance is not hard to understand. There was simply no other system available to those who wished to write an account of more than a confined region, for which a local dating-system would suffice. Dionysius of Halicarnassus' use of Olympiadic time was specifically designed as a bridge across different time-systems. He wrote a work on chronology showing 'how one may make the Roman times conform with the Greek' (*AR* 1. 74. 2).[22] Thucydides' attempt to link his own narrative into as many external time-systems as possible at the start of Book 2 illustrates the difficulty of having no universally applicable chronology:

[20] E. J. Bickermann, *Chronology of the Ancient World* (London, 1968), 75–6. There seems to be some debate over which of the two should be ascribed the honour of having first developed the use of Olympiads as a system of reckoning. Timaeus was clearly chronologically prior, but it seems that Eratosthenes did much to take the system forward. On Timaeus' chronological research see T. S. Brown, *Timaeus of Tauromenium* (Berkeley, 1958), 10–14.

[21] See S. Hornblower (ed.), *Greek Historiography* (Oxford, 1994), 46.

[22] See C. E. Schultze, 'Dionysius of Halicarnassus and Roman Chronology', *PCPS* 41 (1995), 192–214. One of the purposes of his chronological work was to prove that the principles of Eratosthenes were sound.

The thirty years' truce which was entered into after the reconquest of Euboea lasted for fourteen years. In the fifteenth year, the forty-eighth year of Chrysis being priestess at Argos, when Aenesias was ephor at Sparta, and two months before the end of the archonship of Pythodorus at Athens, six months after the battle at Potidaea, at the very beginning of the spring, [a Theban force attacked Plataea]. (2. 2. 1)

Polybius, like Dionysius, clearly reaped the benefits of the chronological work of Timaeus and Eratosthenes in the third century, in spite of his repeated criticisms of the former. Dating by eponymous magistrates was far too localized to be useful in a work of his scope, but the system of Olympiads and the various synchronisms computed by the chronologists were ideally suited to his project. As Pédech states, the first had the advantage of providing an absolute chronology; the second was valuable in the composition of a universal history which had to relate to each other the events of different countries.[23] It is arguable that not even the system of Olympiads was 'absolute', being anchored to a set of events imbued with human significance. However, in so far as it was largely unconnected with the narrative which it was being used to date, and involved straightforward numerical counting both of and within an invariable unit, the Olympiad, it was undeniably representative of a new way of conceiving time, as it might be applied to historical narrative.

Diodorus too made clear his preference for the Olympiadic system in a programmatic statement at the start of his universal history. For the pre-Trojan period, he says that he can find no reliable chronological record; from the Trojan war he follows Artemidorus of Athens in calculating eighty years to the return of the Heracleidae; from then to the first Olympiad, he reckons 328 years according to the Spartan king-lists; and from then on he can use the Olympiadic system up to the end of his work (1. 5. 1). There is, in fact, far greater variety in Diodorus' methods for expressing time than simply employing the Olympiadic system. Sometimes he uses vague relative indicators, such as 'now', 'later', 'more recently' (18. 1; 32. 4); sometimes the generation is given as a unit of time-

[23] P. Pédech, La Méthode historique de Polybe (Paris, 1964), 448.

difference (4. 83);[24] sometimes, time is marked out in terms of the successive reigns of various rulers. The death of Gelon in 478 BC gives Diodorus the opportunity to comment that he had ruled for seven years, and that his heir, Hieron, ruled for eleven years and eight months (11. 38).[25] But the overriding temporal framework is provided by the system of Olympiads, in combination with the archon at Athens and the consul at Rome for each year. So, Xerxes' invasion of Europe took place 'when Calliadas was archon at Athens, and the Romans made Spurius Cassius and Proculus Verginius Tricostus consuls, and the Eleians celebrated the 75th Olympiad, in which Astylus of Syracuse won the stadion' (11. 1). This build-up of dating systems might, at first sight, appear to be an advance on the sole use of Olympiads; but this is, of course, not the case, since the magistracies did not change in different places at the same time in the year, thus requiring Diodorus to impose a seriously false synchronism every year.

In spite of the inadequacies of the Olympiadic system, its use in universal accounts was almost inevitable. While it is extremely difficult to conceive of a wholly abstract temporal or spatial system, this does not refute the existence of a wide variety in the degree of reference to human experience in the formulation of times and spaces, and we may place Olympiadic time towards the more abstract end of the spectrum, in so far as its continued counting was not dependent on the historical events to which it was applied. By contrast, Strabo used temporal indicators which were formulated through distance from named chronological markers and, very often, through reference to his own lifetime. We might say that he reveals a conception and system of time which was more clearly 'experienced'. So, just as with space, it is impossible simply to interchange 'history' and 'time', without being more careful to define what is meant by 'time'.

In any case, we cannot define history solely in terms of time and geography solely in terms of space, for two further reasons. Firstly, post-modernist social geographers have taken up the notion of history as 'the production of space'. Secondly, geo-

[24] Minos was honoured ἐπὶ γενεὰς πλείους ('for several generations', 4. 79).
[25] For more examples of this phenomenon, see 12. 71; 13. 108; 14. 37; 14. 83; 14. 93.

graphy itself has often been defined temporally, and this brings us to the second major model; namely, geography : present : : history : past.

The conceptual dominance of time may be partly attributed to the modern compression of space and time. According to Harvey, one of the most influential post-modern geographers, capitalism is primarily concerned with covering space as quickly as possible, a concern encapsulated in the expression 'time is money'.[26] Space must be compressed because time is precious, and we sacrifice the experience of space in a bid to get from 'a' to 'b' in as little time as possible. However, the use of time as a means of defining space was clearly to be found also in antiquity, where the privileging of time did not necessarily result from the need to speed it up. As I discuss later, time is frequently used in the ancient periplus texts as the unit of spatial measure, and often to a refined degree. Later in antiquity, instead of arranging his climatic zones by degrees like Hipparchus, Ptolemaeus defined them by differences in the length of the longest day.[27]

However, time has sometimes been used to define not only space, but also the academic subject of geography. The concern of geographers to appear useful and forward-looking has led easily to the association of history with the past, as opposed to geography's present and future. Many geographers applaud the qualification of a purely spatial definition of their subject.[28] However, both the association of history with the past, and that of geography with the present and future are open to attack. The geographer Darby formulated the analogy as follows: 'the

[26] D. Harvey, *The Condition of Postmodernity: An Enquiry into the Origins of Cultural Change* (Oxford, 1989), 265.

[27] Claudius Ptolemaeus *Geography* 1. 23 explains how the lines of longitude in his delineation are 20 minutes apart, and the lines of latitude 15 minutes apart. For example, the fourteenth parallel was 3 hours 30 minutes from the equator, as well as being 45° north. We may compare the use of light-years to measure distance in space.

[28] C. Harris, 'The Historical Mind and the Practice of Geography', in D. Ley and M. S. Samuels (eds.), *Humanistic Geography: Prospects and Problems* (London, 1978), 123–37, criticizes the dominance of what he calls the North American view of geography, exemplified by the work of Hartshorne, in which geography is chorological and history chronological (pp. 123–4).

geography of the present day is but a thin layer that even at this moment is becoming history'.[29] However, it is clear from his formulation that the margin is narrow, and prone to transgression in both directions.

Firstly, I deal with the association of history with the past. Opposition to the 'past : present' model has been formulated using the argument that 'the historian does not become a geographer when he studies the present', and clear counter-examples to the model exist in, for instance, Thucydides' contemporary history of the fifth century BC.[30] We would surely not choose to relabel the contemporary historian a geographer simply because of the temporal focus of his work. The identification of history with past time may be attacked also on the grounds that there is a distinction to be made between 'past events', which may simply be chronicled, and 'historical events', which can be drawn together to have greater significance.

A further blow to the notion that history belongs solely to the past can be adduced from certain ancient models for historical patterning. As Momigliano has pointed out, several alternative models were available, including Hesiod's succession of ages associated with different metals, and the 'biological' scheme which Seneca is said by Lactantius (*Inst.* 7. 15. 14) to have used in describing the whole of Roman history from Romulus to Augustus, following metaphorically the different stages of life.[31] However, the predominant pattern was the theory of the succession of empires. The associated and underlying view of history is revealed in Herodotus' promise to cover both great and small cities, 'since I know that man's good fortune never stays in the same place'.[32] This provided the basis for the

[29] H. C. Darby, 'On the Relations of Geography and History', *TIBG* 19 (1953), 6.

[30] J. B. Mitchell, *Historical Geography* (London, 1954), 12.

[31] A. Momigliano, *On Pagans, Jews, and Christians* (Connecticut, 1987), 31–57.

[32] Hdt. 1. 5. 4; also 1. 95 and 1. 130. On this see J. M. Alonso-Núñez, for whom the topic has become a specialism: 'Die Abfolge der Weltreiche bei Polybios und Dionysios von Halikarnassos', *Historia*, 32 (1983), 411–26; id., 'Die Weltreichsukzession bei Strabo', *Zeitschrift für Religions- und Geistesgeschichte*, 36 (1984), 53–4; id., 'Appian and the World Empires', *Athenaeum*, 62 (1984), 640–4; id., 'Die Weltgeschichte des Nikolaos von Damaskos', *Storia della Storiografia*, 27 (1995), 3–15.

structuring of his work. Because history brings to the fore one region after another, Herodotus' readers move around accordingly, as the Lydian and Persian histories appear in turn, and the Egyptians and Scythians are encountered *en route*. The theory that successive empires patterned history was, as Momigliano says, the scheme adopted by Jewish and later Christian apocalyptic writers, for the obvious reason that it was easily manipulated by groups opposed to Roman rule so as to forecast the imminent demise of that power.[33] One of its most prominent features is a sense of continuum through past, present, and even future, refuting the idea that we can dismiss history, and historical patterning, as exclusively consigned to the past.

Secondly, just as history is not entirely concerned with the past, so it is hard to envisage a geography that deals exclusively with the present. A clear historical dimension is brought to geography by the need to understand the causes for the earth's present state. The question 'what has given this landscape its present character?' means that geography must inevitably be in part backward-looking unless it is to ignore causation entirely.[34] It was this need to turn to the past to understand change in the physical world that underlay the historical interests of certain figures in the *Annales* school.[35]

However, the question of geography as a study of the present

---

[33] J. W. Swain, 'The Theory of the Four Monarchies: Opposition History under the Roman Empire', *Class. Phil.* 35 (1940), 1–21, shows how opponents of Rome subverted the theme to four transitory empires followed by one eternal empire. As B. Smalley, *Historians in the Middle Ages* (London, 1974) points out, the theory of the succession of empires was to prove problematic in the Middle Ages, when time was limited by Creation and Doomsday, since the end of the last (Roman) empire should signal the end of the world. Since the world was still in existence, the Roman empire had to be kept alive imaginatively in the form of the Byzantine and ecclesiastical empires (pp. 53–5).

[34] See Darby, 'On the Relations of Geography and History', 6.

[35] The concern of, for example, Vidal de la Blache with historical geography, in the sense of 'the history of travel and exploration', was overtaken by his wish to look at the forces of change and processes altering the organization of space. P. Claval, 'The Historical Dimension of French Geography', *Journal of Historical Geography*, 10 (1984), 229–45. The idea of the *longue durée* was particularly apt when geographical change was concerned.

not only springs from modern discussion, but was raised in antiquity. Strabo repeatedly asserts his interest, as author of a *Geography*, in the present over the past, and states 'I must speak of things as they are now' (12. 8. 7). An interesting parallel for this professed concentration of the geographer on the present, rather than the past, is seen in Defoe's *Tour through the Whole Island of Great Britain*. In the preface he states that 'the situation of things is given not as they have been, but as they are; . . .all respects the present time, not the time past.'[36] Like Strabo, Defoe seems to have abandoned this aim almost immediately. He colours his description of eighteenth-century Britain with pieces of historical information dating from the Roman period onwards. So the once overgrown countryside of Surrey is seen as a haven for native Britons, hiding from the Romans, and for Saxons, harassed by the Danes, although now, says Defoe, the place is mainly cultivated, and the detail he has just given 'is a piece of history, which I leave as I find it'.[37] When he reaches the prehistoric site of Stonehenge, Defoe again weakens in his resolution to steer away from the past. ''Tis indeed a reverend piece of antiquity, and 'tis a great loss that the true history of it is not known.'[38]

I discuss and exemplify Strabo's use of the past in his *Geography* in chapter V, but here offer a more theoretical response to why the association of geography with present and future, but not the past, must be seen as inadequate. The answer lies in the observation that, as I have discussed above (pp. 9–10), the space and time of geography and history exist not just as abstractions, but also as features of the world as it is experienced. The conceptual geographer, Tuan, has suggested that 'place' may be seen as 'lived-in space', space structured by human experience, as opposed to abstract, geometrical space.[39] Tuan has also asserted that a sense of

[36] D. Defoe, *A Tour through the Whole Island of Great Britain* (London, 1724–6; republished by Penguin 1971—all references are to the Penguin reprint of 1986), 45.

[37] Ibid. 164.

[38] Ibid. 201.

[39] See Y.-F. Tuan, 'Space, Time, Place: A Humanistic Frame', in *Making Sense of Time*, 7. See also A. Merrifield, 'Place and Space: A Lefebvrian Reconciliation', *TIBG* NS 18 (1993), 516–31; especially 522: 'place can be

place only develops over time, making passage of time essential for the transformation of abstract space into significant place. The same idea has been formulated as being that 'the realization of place lies in the temporal structuring of space'.[40] The point is that a place, as experienced by people, has a significant past, the stories which are told about the place and its inhabitants. This is what gives it a distinctive identity. So, the past of a place forms part of the description of its present state, and geography, in so far as it is concerned with places of human habitation, must necessarily concern itself with past time.

Just as geography is about both past and present, in so far as the present identity of a place is determined by the experiences of the past, so too can history be seen as concerned with the present, in so far as the past is viewed in the light of the author's own times, which provide the interpretative framework for any attempt to structure the past. It has been argued that the historian writes 'to help society understand better its collective story'.[41] Indeed we may see the process of structuring space into place through memory paralleled in the patterning of time through the memories evoked by particular days in the calendar. Collective stories, or social memory, are precisely what concern the geographer in his attempt to understand the present identity of a community, drawing the geographical and the historical projects close together.

The point is nicely illustrated by a conversation between the children in C. S. Lewis's *The Magician's Nephew*, on their discovering the land of Narnia:

'I wish we had someone to tell us what all those places are,' said Digory.

taken as practised space'; also, D. E. Cosgrove, 'Power and Place in the Venetian Territories', in J. A. Agnew and J. S. Duncan (eds.), *The Power of Place: Bringing together Geographical and Sociological Imaginations* (Boston, 1989), 104: 'places are physical locations imbued with human meaning'. Cosgrove argues that the North Pole is a place in a way that 76 °W, 43 °N is not.

[40] D. Parkes and N. Thrift, 'Putting Time in its Place', in *Making Sense of Time*, 119.

[41] G. Allan, reviewing E. E. Harris, *The Reality of Time* (Albany, 1988), in *History and Theory*, 28 (1989), 353.

'I don't suppose they're anywhere yet,' said Polly. 'I mean, there's no one there, and nothing happening. The world only began today.'
'No, but people *will* get there,' said Digory. 'And then they'll have histories, you know.'[42]

The arrival of the children at a new world requires the re-evaluation of the world they know, and the incorporation of what they have discovered. But the places cannot be defined or described, and remain without significance all the time that they are apparently uninhabited. Places are best described in terms of the activity that has occurred there, as we saw was the case with the Laestrygonians at Bonifacio. In the next section I discuss further the professed concern of both geographers and historians with the inhabited world, rather than with empty space. With no people, the places of Narnia are not 'anywhere yet'. However, the arrival of people in this landscape will immediately lead to the creation of history; and the people together with their history will, in turn, provide a way of defining the land.

These two major models for distinguishing between geography and history open up various ways of approaching ancient works in terms of time, space, and place; but caution is required. As I argued above (pp. 9–10), it is important not to confuse discussions of abstract time and space with those about the world as it is experienced. Attempts to derive arguments about the nature of historical time from the theories of Newton, for example, may be criticized on several grounds. Not only is there an objection to using notions of time as an abstract and separable entity in arguments about the experienced world, but Newton's interests in abstract time and in chronology were entirely different projects.[43] It is clear that no chronological system and no means of organizing historical time can be anything

[42] C. S. Lewis, *The Magician's Nephew* (London, 1955).
[43] C. G. Starr, 'Historical and Philosophical Time', *History and Theory*. *Beiheft*, 6 (1966), 24–35, also argues that historical time is different from that which is the subject of chronology. For him, however, the problem lies not in the distinction between absolute and relative time, but between time which can be marked off by mechanical celestial phenomena, and history, which is not just a relentless march through time, but forms an intelligible sequence (p. 24). See also S. Kracauer, 'Time and History', *History and Theory*. *Beiheft*, 6 (1966), 65–78, who argues that we cannot view 'history as a process in homogeneous chronological time' (p. 68).

other than relative. Absolute time may be useful as a concept in pure science, but it does not help directly in our understanding of history, although the associated ideas are at least thought-provoking, and may actually provide new insights into the conceptual framework of texts which deal most explicitly with time and space, namely historical and geographical works.[44]

Analysis of the 'space : time' model reveals that abstract and separable qualities of time and space provide useful ways of measuring and calibrating aspects of the world in the form of maps and time-systems, such as the one based on Olympiads. It has been argued in connection with the medieval world that our view that 'time and space are taken as objective, in the sense that their properties are not affected by the matter occupying them', is not universally shared, and was not a feature of the pre-Enlightenment world-view.[45] But this clearly overstates both the ancient and the modern viewpoint. Much greater complexity and variation needs to be built into the model, given the clear existence of time and space as abstract qualities in antiquity.

However, the 'space : time' model also reveals the importance of experienced time and space. This is confirmed by analysis of the 'present : past' model. It emerges that both the concern of geography with the past and that of history with the present may be partially understood in terms of the fact that geography and history describe the world as it is actually experienced. Human life takes place in or against the matrices of time and space simultaneously, making discussion of them as distinct entities strained. Anthropologists have pointed out that the separable concepts of time and space are not universally accepted. In particular, Skar has studied the inhabitants of Matapuquio in the Peruvian Andes, among whom the same word 'pacha' is used to refer to both time and space. The two are inseparable precisely because they have not been conceptualized as abstractions, but are entirely bound up with the world as a 'lived-in' entity, to which 'pacha' refers.[46]

[44] See P. Munz (review of D. J. Wilcox, *The Measure of Times Past: Pre-Newtonian Chronologies and the Rhetoric of Relative Time* (Chicago, 1987)), *History and Theory*, 28 (1989), 236–51.

[45] Gurevich, *Categories of Medieval Culture*, 26.

[46] S. L. Skar, 'Andean Women and the Concept of Space/Time', in S. Ardener (ed.), *Women and Space: Ground Rules and Social Maps*

The formulation that place, as experienced in the world and made distinctive by its collective memory, is 'space structured by time' shows how closely interrelated, even inseparable, are these matrices. It is interesting that the observations of anthropologists are here paralleled by scientific theory. As with Newtonian abstractions, the dangers in moving too far from the actual writing of history and geography are apparent. However, both Einstein's specific theory of relativity of 1905 and his general theory of 1915 may offer interesting insights into ways of conceptualizing the world.[47] It was the general theory which put forward the single notion of space-time, and made the radical proposition that space and time were not just the arena for the universe's events, but were affected by everything that happened within it. Einstein's earlier specific theory had importantly challenged the Newtonian idea of absolute time, and allowed time to vary according to the location of the observer. So time and space were not only inextricably linked, but also heterogeneous and subjective, rather than homogeneous and objective.

These theories at the time provided a stimulus for new ways of viewing the world. The development of GMT, the homogeneous time-system that replaced local time and so denied the importance of place, was challenged by the movement at the turn of the twentieth century 'to affirm the reality of private time against that of a single public time and to define its nature as heterogeneous, fluid, and reversible'.[48] Furthermore, the move in visual art away from the idea of perspective and a fixed viewpoint, to the multiple viewpoint of Cubist art, challenged the temporal limitation of perspective painting.

(Oxford, 1993), 31–45. Skar explains how, on the steep mountain slopes, time and space are inextricably bound through the difference between the quick-ripening of crops on the lower slopes and the longer time taken for crops to ripen higher up. The passage of time in so far as it affects the crops is linked to geographical location.

[47] See S. Hawking, *A Brief History of Time: From the Big Bang to Black Holes* (London, 1988), 38.

[48] For the importance of the Industrial Revolution and nationally co-ordinated transport systems in the move towards the imposition of GMT, see G. J. Whitrow, *Time in History: Views of Time from Prehistory to the Present Day* (Oxford, 1988), 158–65. For the affirmation of private heterogeneous time, see Kern, *The Culture of Time and Space*, 34.

Instead it represented a view across time rather than a momen-
tary snapshot, and thus opened up new possibilities for the
ordering of time and space.[49] It is not necessary to frame the
discussion in scientific terms in order to apply the idea that a
single event in time may occur differently for viewers at
different places, and to see its implications for notions of fixed
and multiple perspectives in textual deconstruction. The inextricable connection of time and space meant not only that
time was linked to the event, but also that the time of an event
was subject to its spatial relationship to the perceiver. This
leads us to notions of perspective, focus, and the relationship of
the author to text and reader, concerns of narratologists, which
may enhance a discussion of historical and geographical writings about the world, and to which I now turn.

ALL THE WORLD'S A STAGE: GEOGRAPHY, HISTORY, AND FOCALIZATION

The ideas of time and space as 'experienced' rather than
abstract entities, and as subject to 'perception' from one or
more viewpoints, immediately give importance to human
actors, viewers, and narrators. In some senses the argument
has gone full-circle. The replacement of individual mental
maps with a single map viewed from a single standpoint,
entailing the standardization of time across space, subsumed
spatial difference and privileged one authorized 'focalizer'.[50]
The move back towards the acknowledgement of many viewpoints can be seen in an extreme form in the work of Cubist
painters, but has been formally brought to the attention of
literary scholars more recently in the writings of narratologists,
and I think it has something to offer to a study of how the
world is, and was, perceived and constructed.

[49] See Kern, *The Culture of Time and Space*, 22. As Harvey, *The Condition
of Postmodernity*, 244, points out, the fixed viewpoint of perspective painting
in the Renaissance was important in giving a systematic view of space. It is
linked by D. E. Cosgrove, *Social Formation and Symbolic Landscape* (London
and Sydney, 1984), 21, to a claim to truth and objectivity.

[50] The attempt to depict a world with a single focalizer is in complete
antithesis to the multi-faceted nature of experienced space. For the view that
'the mental map of each person is unique', see P. Gould and R. White, *Mental
Maps* (Harmondsworth, 1974), 51.

The application of narratological techniques to non-fictional works has been slow to develop, and is problematic for those who stress the differences between fiction and non-fiction, on the grounds that 'time and space in a novel are not those of real life'.[51] However, the clear-cut distinction between history and the novel has been challenged from at least two angles: firstly by those who argue that the novel can refer indirectly to people in a particular real place and time, the space and time of history.[52] But a second and more controversial challenge was initiated by White, who exhorted historians to read their texts as 'narrative prose discourses' in which the form, rather than the content, was all-important.[53] The predictable objection was raised: namely that if the focus were to be solely on the literary form of the historical text, we should lose sight of the relationship between such texts and reality, which they purport to represent.[54] However, the literary analysis of such texts may help us better to decode the text and thus come closer to the reality being represented.[55] Or if we were to follow Fox's view, expressed with regard to the literary analysis of historical texts, such as Livy's *History*, we might argue that 'decoding' is not at issue. We must think Fox right if we agree with White's view of historical texts as 'opaque artefacts, rather than veils through which other veils, and ultimately *history* can be

[51] See R. Wellek and A. Warren, *Theory of Literature*, 3rd edn. (London, 1966), 25.

[52] See C. Strout, 'Border Crossings: History, Fiction and *Dead Certainties*', *History and Theory*, 31 (1992), 153–62.

[53] H. White, *Metahistory: The Historical Imagination in Nineteenth-Century Europe* (Baltimore, 1973). M. G. Morgan, 'Tacitus on Germany: Roman History or Latin Literature', in L. Schulze and W. Wetzels (eds.), *Literature and History* (Boston, 1983), 87–118, argues that the distinction between history and literature was blurred in antiquity partly because of the importance of rhetoric and rhetorical strategies in political life, the occupation of the expected readership. The acceptance of rhetoric disallowed a strict boundary between fact and fiction.

[54] A. Momigliano, 'The Rhetoric of History and the History of Rhetoric: On Hayden White's Tropes', in E. S. Shaffer (ed.), *Comparative Criticism. A Year Book*, iii (Cambridge, 1981), 259–68.

[55] I. N. Bulhof, 'Imagination and Interpretation in History', in L. Schulze and W. Wetzels (eds.), *Literature and History* (Boston, 1983), 17, complains that White never explains how the literary form of a historical narrative is relevant to revealing the past.

observed', and conclude rather that the literary analysis gives access to a different kind of reality, that of the representation.[56] What may usefully be gleaned from White's approach may have less to do with fact and fiction, and more with being aware of the literary style and rhetorical structure of non-fictional texts. Hornblower has shown how issues such as focalization, narrative displacement, and concealed authorial personae are of help in our appreciation of the subtleties of *all* texts.[57]

But, even if we do not dismiss the separable notions of fact and fiction, we cannot rule fiction out of apparently factual texts, and so justify the exclusion of a certain kind of literary analysis from historical and geographical works. It has, for example, been suggested that our text of the periplus of Hanno does not refer to a real journey, but is a Greek construction of different degrees of 'otherness'.[58] Further complicating the question of reality is the use of 'stock literary places' in geographical works. The islands of Cerne and Thule, for example, have been the subject of much debate over their precise identifications. It has been interestingly suggested, from the fact that the name 'Cerne' was applied to several *different* places, that the term 'represents not a geographical limit, but a fantastical boundary' ('non rappresenta una frontiera geografica, ma un confine fantastico').[59] The island of Thule has been found similarly elusive because in ancient literature the name Thule 'indicates the northern limit of the inhabited world' ('indica l'estremità settentrionale dell'ecu-

---

[56] M. Fox, *Roman Historical Myths: The Regal Period in Augustan Literature* (Oxford, 1996). Ch. 2 on theoretical considerations is particularly helpful. Fox sees the stress on rhetoric in history as a move away from the danger of claiming objectivity when talking about the past. See esp. p. 40.

[57] S. Hornblower, 'Narratology and Narrative Techniques in Thucydides', in S. Hornblower (ed.), *Greek Historiography* (Oxford, 1994), 131–66. A. Cameron (ed.), *History as Text. The Writing of Ancient History* (London, 1989), 1–10, adds weight to this view, arguing for the reading of 'historical' texts as literature.

[58] C. Jacob, *Géographie et ethnographie en Grèce ancienne* (Paris, 1991), 84.

[59] G. Amiotti, 'Cerne: "ultima terra"', *CISA* 13 (1987), 43–9. Other locations of Cerne were opposite the Persian Gulf according to Ephorus (Pliny *NH* 4. 35) and beyond the Pillars of Hercules, according to Eratosthenes (Strabo 1. 3. 2).

mene').[60] At the same time, we may choose to use these texts for insights into the conceptual world of their authors and of the time of writing in general. So the division between fictional and non-fictional writing is unclear.

Historians writing about the European discovery of the New World in the sixteenth century have commented on a similar blurring between fact and fiction which characterizes accounts of those explorations. According to Greenblatt, the European encounter with the New World 'brought close to the surface of non-literary texts imaginative operations that are normally buried deep below their surface'. This entitles the scholar to use 'the concerns of literary criticism to illuminate texts . . . and actions that register not the pleasures of the fictive but the compelling powers of the real'.[61] The literary nature of geographical texts, in particular the relationship between academic geography and the geography evoked in fictional literary works, has already been the subject of some scholarly discussion.[62] Later I shall employ these narratological tools to reveal different focalizations in Polybius' *History*, and especially in Strabo's geographical view of the world.

The opposition to regarding literary forms such as history and geography as suited to the critical theories applied to fiction stems partly from a belief that history and geography provide objective views of the world, as opposed to the authorially determined subjectivity of fiction. This is concordant with the comments of the conceptual geographer, Cosgrove, who suggests a difference between landscape, which 'denotes the external world mediated through subjective human experience', and the geographer's map, in which foreground is not distinguished from background by the author, giving no privileged view and forcing the process of interpretation on to the reader.[63] It has been argued that in this process of interpretation we, as land creatures, tend to 'see' land as

[60] F. Cordano, *La geografia degli antichi* (Rome, 1992), 107.

[61] S. Greenblatt, *Marvelous Possessions: The Wonder of the New World* (Oxford, 1991), 23.

[62] See Y.-F. Tuan, 'Literature and Geography: Implications for Geographical Research', in D. Ley and M. Samuels (eds.), *Humanistic Geography: Prospects and Problems* (London, 1978), 194–206.

[63] Cosgrove, *Social Formation and Symbolic Landscape*, 13 and 31.

foreground on a map, and sea as background.[64] This, however, does not alter the fact that the cartographer or literary geographer makes decisions of selection and presentation, which render objectivity an impossibility. So, both map-maker and map-reader must interpret, and the map itself is both subjective in this respect and objective in so far as it purports to represent reality.[65]

An important feature of medieval maps is that they did not attempt to present a view of space from one fixed, external position, but rather gave a sense of space as it was experienced by someone travelling around.[66] I have already mentioned the issue of experienced as opposed to abstract time and space, but these concepts can now be extended to incorporate notions of narration, and of single or multiple focus. 'Narrative time' has been seen as 'lived time' in so far as the authenticity of the story validates the temporal experience of the characters.[67] But the reverse is not necessarily true, making a precise equation of 'narrative time' and 'lived time' questionable. The premise of Carr's treatment of time and narrative reverses the argument in a way which reveals the problem.[68] It is one thing to argue that narrative time is 'temps vécu' rather than 'temps mésuré'; quite another to say, as Carr does, that narrative is a primary feature of lived time, and not an imposed structure. Similar questions have been discussed with regard to space; in particular, whether historians of the American West have forced 'stories on a world that doesn't fit them' by writing narratives of progress and decline concerning the development of that land-

[64] P. Janni, 'L'Italia di Strabone: descrizione e immagine', in *Italia Antica*, 147–59. Janni uses ideas formulated by scholars of perception theory to suggest that, in spite of our natural tendency to foreground land masses, this is reversed when a sea forms a simple, geometric figure, which is well defined and easy to recognize and classify. The Pontic sea, both in antiquity and now, formed a 'figure' rather than a background, being more distinctive in shape than the surrounding land mass (p. 153).

[65] See J. K. Wright, 'Map Makers are Human. Comments on the Subjective in Maps', in Wright, *Human Nature in Geography. Fourteen Papers 1925–1965* (Cambridge, MA, 1966), 33–52.

[66] As argued by Harvey, *The Condition of Postmodernity*, 241.

[67] See the interesting discussion by P. Ricoeur, 'Narrative Time', in W. J. T. Mitchell (ed.), *On Narrative* (Chicago, 1981), 171–2.

[68] See D. Carr, *Time, Narrative and History* (Bloomington, 1986); rev. N. Carroll in *History and Theory*, 27 (1988), 297–306.

scape; or whether narrative is so fundamental that it structures the changes in the landscape themselves.[69]

Two major and interrelated themes emerge from such debates: firstly, the active or passive nature of time and space in narratives involving them; and secondly, the discrete or continuous, local or universal views of the world associated with different types of focalization. Academic discussion of narratives concerning the past of the American plains has examined the role played in the story by the space whose transformation is the subject of the account. I treat in detail later the way in which Strabo reveals the two-way influence of time and historical powers on the shape of the world, and in turn of space and environment on the progress of history. The simple acceptance of environmental determinism, dominant in ancient medical, architectural, and geographical theory, has been left unchallenged in modern geography until recently.[70] The approach of Huntingdon, who introduced his book by stating that it would focus on 'the influence of heredity and geographic environment, especially climate, upon the cultural events which are described in a multitude of other books', is a prime example of the environmental determinism now opposed by many on ideological grounds, since it can be, and has been, used to advocate the innate superiority of certain races.[71]

The implications of environmental determinism extend to the narrative level. Although it has been said of Strabo that 'the earth he seems to regard somewhat as a stage, its relief being the background and setting in which historical events take place',[72] I hope to show that Strabo saw the earth as exerting a far greater influence on human affairs than this, even if geography could never be counted as the only factor in play.

[69] W. Cronon, 'A Place for Stories: Nature, History, and Narrative', *Journal of American History*, 78 (1992), 1368.

[70] For medicine, see *Airs, Waters, Places* and other works in the Hippocratic corpus; for architecture, see Vitruvius, *De architectura*.

[71] E. T. Huntingdon, *Mainsprings of Civilization* (New York and London, 1945), 35. The publication date of this work makes it remarkable that the explicit and implicit prejudices underlying its arguments were not opposed at the time.

[72] C. Glacken, *Traces on the Rhodian Shore: Nature and Culture in Western Thought from Ancient Times to the End of the Eighteenth Century* (Berkeley and Los Angeles, 1967), 103.

But the view that ancient authors used geography only as a setting for history is commonly held. Even of Herodotus' *Histories*, in which geography and history literally progress together, it has been said that 'geography provides the physical background, the stage setting, in relation to which historical events take on meaning'.[73] This is precisely symptomatic of the traditionally limited approach to the relationship between geography and history, in which the two are separable entities, one the setting for the other.

The notion of the earth as the setting for man's activities recalls the importance of experienced, as opposed to abstract, space and time, and is relevant to the scope of 'universal geography', to which I shall return. For geographers in the scientific tradition, the whole globe was included. The theories of Eudoxus of Cnidus, including the invention of a system of twenty-six concentric spheres around the earth and a calculation for the circumference of the earth, clearly show the interest of geographers in matters not only global, but universal, and I treat Polybius' application of such concepts in chapter II. However, Eratosthenes' division of the world into 'seals' (or vertical bands around the earth) was criticized by Strabo for its lack of relation to human affairs. Strabo likened Eratosthenes' 'unnatural' divisions to a surgeon cutting up a body haphazardly, rather than taking a person apart limb from limb, using an image which reinforces the importance of man in conceptions of the world and the notion of history and geography as biographical studies (2. 1. 30).[74] In particular, the concern with the human may explain Strabo's interest in places, transformed

---

[73] P. E. James and G. J. Martin, *All Possible Worlds: A History of Geographical Ideas* (New York, 1981), 21. A similar opinion is expressed by R. E. Dickinson and O. J. R. Howarth, *The Making of Geography* (Oxford, 1933), 13: that Herodotus 'was a historian primarily, but one with a full sense of the value of geographical setting'.

[74] P. M. Fraser, 'Eratosthenes of Cyrene', *Proceedings of the British Academy*, 56 (1970), 200, sees the non-subjective division of the world into 'seals' as precisely parallel to Eratosthenes' development of the Olympiadic system of time-reckoning. See also J.-P. Vernant, *The Origins of Greek Thought* (London, 1982), 121, who takes the attempt to gain an objective view of the earth back to the Ionian Greeks. Their geometrical model for the earth, unlike a mythical geography, did not privilege any one area. But Vernant seems to underplay the fact that no model can be totally objective.

from abstract space by human settlement over time and by the identities created by that past, an interest which, for Strabo, far outweighs that in the wider landscape. His statement that 'the geographer need not concern himself with what lies outside our inhabited world' can be interpreted at more than one level (2. 5. 34).[75] Not only was Strabo's interest confined to the portion of the globe inhabited by man, but also, within that portion, Strabo was not concerned with empty landscape.

The emphasis on human activity in, and relationship with, the world is prominent in many modern geographical works. It has been claimed that Kant was the first philosopher to see geography's concern as 'the study of man in relation to his physical environment' and that, in this, he was a true successor to Strabo, and possibly also to Ptolemaeus.[76] The same interest has been attributed to history as 'the study of the world humans have made for themselves'.[77] We could scarcely find a more explicit statement of the importance of human geography in history and, conversely, for a historical perspective in geography. Geography's concern with man's relationship with the earth, and not just with the earth itself, has clear points of contact with the Stoic notion that the earth is designed specifically for man, and Stoicism is a theme to which I return on several occasions.[78] But it is worth noting that human involvement has not always been considered essential to geography. Agathemerus' *Sketch of Geography*, probably written in the first or second century AD, attempted to set out the geographical tradition to date. It is interesting that Strabo finds no place in the list of geographers, presumably reflecting the fact that the text of the *Geography* was not in circulation by

[75] This view is further reinforced by the statement that a limit will be placed on the detail given for Laconia, 'a country which is now mostly deserted' (8. 4. 11). Without the human factor, Strabo was not interested in regions, reflecting the strongly ethnographical strand in ancient geography.

[76] May, *Kant's Concept of Geography*, 42. While this confirms the opinion that Strabo's prime concern is with human geography, it is unclear to me why a link with Ptolemaeus should be drawn in this respect.

[77] See L. Guelke, *Historical Understanding in Geography: An Idealist Approach* (Cambridge, 1982), 1.

[78] C. Glacken, 'Changing Ideas of the Habitable World', in W. L. Thomas (ed.), *Man's Rôle in Changing the Face of the Earth* (Chicago, 1956), 72, sees in Cicero's *De natura deorum* the idea of the earth as the fit and proper home for man.

this stage, but perhaps also or alternatively because Agathemerus conceived of geography as an entirely physical science.
He notes the shape of the world, the winds, the seas, distances
by land, and islands with their dimensions, but human habitation and activity go totally unmentioned.[79]

However, the commonly held view that geography should be
specifically devoted to understanding man's role in the environment, rather than the environment itself, has implications
for the relative importance we assign to man and nature in the
playing-out of history. The history of geographical ideas has
been defined as 'the record of man's effort to gain more and
more logical and useful knowledge of the human habitat and of
man's spread over the earth'.[80] But, taken to extremes by some
geographers, who argue that our concern should be *solely* with
man's role in the natural world, asserting that 'the physical
environment is passive and cannot actively influence human
activity', this approach begins to sound entirely incompatible
with ancient views on environmental determinism.[81]

Some partial answer may be drawn from discussions of the
history of the Plains Indians in America, which have explored
two appropriate structures for this kind of account. Either man
is pitted against stubborn nature, or man and nature change in
parallel and 'story and scene become entangled'. In either case,
nature is a protagonist in the story—either as ally of man or as
'worthy antagonist of civilisation'.[82] The problem is how we
can fit the natural world, with its often cyclical patterns, into a
humanly imposed narrative structure, with beginning, middle,

[79] For a text, translation, and notes, see A. Diller, 'Agathemerus, *Sketch of
Geography*', *GRBS* 16 (1975), 59–76.

[80] James and Martin, *All Possible Worlds*, 2.

[81] The view is that of J. A. Jakle, 'Time, Space, and the Geographic Past: A
Prospectus for Historical Geography', *American Historical Review*, 76 (1971),
1086. Given the polarity of his opinion, we may not be surprised by Jakle's
conclusion: 'I am hesitant to suggest how interaction between the disciplines
of academic history and geography might be cultivated' (p. 1103).

[82] Cronon, 'A Place for Stories', 1354 and 1356. The destruction of native
American peoples and their landscapes forms the subject for much modern
writing on the topic of the relationship between history and geography. See
also, for example, Meinig, 'The Continuous Shaping of America', 1186–205.
Meinig's belief in a close, even indelible, bond between the two disciplines of
geography and history means that his history of America would be no less a
history of the land than of the people.

and end. In the end human experience emerges dominant in our understanding of nature, even where we try to appreciate nature's agency. The issue has been to some extent explained, if not resolved, by drawing a distinction between the approaches of cultural geographers and environmental historians. Whilst cultural geographers describe landscapes as texts, with a symbolic language revealing culture, environmental historians see nature as a historical actor, existing outside our understanding of it.[83] So nature can be both a theatrical backdrop, manipulated by man, and an active agent in man's progress.

Examples of interest in the relationship between man and nature abound among authors in antiquity. In particular, the theme of the struggle against the natural world, which has been so important in discussions of narratives concerning the American West, has direct parallels in ancient texts. Herodotus' account of the Persian Wars against Greece involves battles and alliances between different peoples and the environment, and the natural world becomes not only a measure against which players in the narrative may be characterized, but also a player itself, strikingly personified as a potential subject for Xerxes (7. 35). The Persians cannot simply overcome a passive environment by drinking rivers dry, spoiling and diverting streams (7. 21; 9. 49; 7. 128). The battle between the Persians and the environment is far more evenly matched than this. Mardonius had previously lost 20,000 men in a storm off Athos (6. 44); the Persians retreating after Artimisium were struck by storms (8. 12); those approaching Delphi were hit by rocks falling from Parnassus and thunderbolts at the shrine of Athene Pronaos (8. 37). By contrast, nature could be a good ally to the potential victims of Persian imperialism. The Athenians, the

---

[83] D. Demeritt, 'The Nature of Metaphors in Cultural Geography and Environmental History', *Progress in Human Geography*, 18 (1994), 163–85. Environmental historians, says Demeritt, are committed to representing 'the agency of nature as autonomous from cultural ways of understanding it' (p. 164). The idea of landscape as text seems heavily influenced by C. Geertz, *The Interpretation of Cultures* (London, 1993), 452, where he asserts that 'the culture of a people is an ensemble of texts, themselves ensembles, which the anthropologist strains to read over the shoulders of those to whom they properly belong'.

people of Delphi, the Scythians were all allies of nature, and were positively assisted by it (7. 189; 7. 178; 4. 47).

In the Roman world, Julius Caesar takes on the role of opponent of nature in many accounts of his actions. Lucan describes how, at Pharsalia, Caesar created his own sombre landscape, looking on 'rivers driven on with gore and heaps of corpses equalling lofty hills' (*Bellum Civile* 7. 789–91). The battle between Caesar and nature mirrors that of the Persians in Herodotus in the meteorological opposition shown to him. As he made his way to Thessaly with his army, 'the whole sky set itself against their march' with thunderbolts and lightning sent by an environment that was far from being a passive backdrop (7. 154). And the act of crossing the Alps, the natural defence of Italy, is linked by Lucan in a single sentence with the aggressive act of instigating a civil war: 'Now Caesar had hastened across the frozen Alps and conceived in his heart the great rebellion and the coming war' (1. 183–5).[84]

The question of whether geographical features are active or passive in the literature that describes them may alter the way in which we view the literature itself. That is, we may choose to adopt the distinction between accounts which describe the natural world from a detached viewpoint as a static phenomenon and those which allow it a role in a historical narrative. Could this be a way of separating geography's treatment of the world from that of historical works? The model does not work well, as it requires history to give more active prominence to environment than does geography, which somehow goes against the sense in which geography, as reflected in its very name, should be primarily interested in the natural world. But the question of the viewpoint of geographical and historical accounts usefully brings us back to the issue of focalization and narratology.

I have already hinted at some of the problems associated with applying narratological techniques to non-fictional works, particularly those techniques concerning the relationship between text and reality. But the notion of narrativity can

---

[84] Note the language of victory: *iam gelidas Caesar cursu superaverat Alpes ingentesque animo motus bellumque futurum ceperat.*

helpfully be used to describe some of the features of geographical and historical texts: firstly, the location of the author
and his relationship to both text and reader; secondly, the
functions of space, place, and time in the creation of narrative,
perhaps giving us some new ways of distinguishing the 'geographical' from the 'historical'.

Firstly, the issue of single or multiple viewpoint, exemplified
by the difference between perspective painting and Cubism as
discussed above (pp. 21–2), and linked to the perception of
time according to location in space, has clear implications for
the well-worn narratological notion of focalization and the
location of the author in relation to events. I have already
mentioned the search for uniformity of time and space through
the introduction of, for example, fixed time zones and measures
of distance, and the development of standard maps and
calendars which are almost universally accepted. This does
not mean that we should see any of these as representing
absolute, abstract, objective time and space; they have still all
been constructed in relation to a viewpoint. But the point is
that they are attempts to conceptualize time and space from
just *one* uniform viewpoint. I have also mentioned the challenges to these constructions of the world and the reinstate-
ment of the multi-focused approach, accepting that time,
space, and the world are experienced differently by each
participant, viewer, and narrator.

In the case of both geographical and historical writings, some
attention has recently been paid to the fact that apparently
objective accounts, in which the author may hide his existence,
do not have only one viewpoint which we need to take into
account, namely the author's explicit persona, but are more
complicated in their focalization. It has often been asserted that
historical narrative is made credible by the absence of the
author from the text, in much the same way as an implicit
claim to truth could be made by painters using perspective
from a single external point articulated to the viewer. The
claim to realism in history allows the author no place in the
text, as the historian must be seen to relate the past rather than
comment on it. Such a view of history has been radically
challenged by White's call for fictionalizing history and the
realization that the author simply cannot be excluded from the

text.[85] Similar work has been done for geography by those who advocate the use of the imagination in geographical accounts.[86] The description of the resultant method of geographical enquiry is startlingly reminiscent of the way in which we may describe Herodotus' historical method, with the proposition that it is valid to borrow the imaginative response of others to a place, just as in history we would expect to use eyewitness accounts. Geographical study should include the stories of the people who live in each place, local newspapers, and folk-tales. In narratological terms, this proposition argues for geographical texts to encompass a multiplicity of spatially differentiated focalizations, all of which combine to make up the account.

The idea of the author as invisible and objective collator of information is unpopular in current scholarship. Work on Herodotus, in particular, has focused on the presence of the author, stressing the fractured nature of the Herodotean narrative, in which we need to be constantly redirected by the author, our guide.[87] Herodotus' view of the historian is, according to this reading, not as onlooker with no responsibility for the narrative, but as active participator in the recovery and ordering of information. A similar approach is adopted by those who emphasize Herodotus as a character in his own narrative, distinguishing, however, between the very strong authorial presence in the ethnographical/geographical first part of the work, and the relative absence of the author in the historical narrative in the last three books.[88] Are we to conclude that geographical description involves more of an authorial presence than does historical narrative?[89]

---

[85] See Bulhof, 'Imagination and Interpretation in History', 3–25. The issue of authorial self-presentation in ancient historiography has been excellently treated by J. Marincola, *Authority and Tradition in Ancient Historiography* (Cambridge, 1997).

[86] See, in particular, J. K. Wright, 'Terrae Incognitae: The Place of the Imagination in Geography', *Annals of the Association of American Geographers*, 37 (1947), 1–15.

[87] C. Dewald, 'Narrative Surface and Authorial Voice in Herodotus' *Histories*', *Arethusa*, 20 (1987), 147–70.

[88] J. Marincola, 'Herodotean Narrative and the Narrator's Presence', *Arethusa*, 20 (1987), 121–38.

[89] The opposite view of self-representation in historical texts is taken by J. J. Winkler, 'The Mendacity of Kalasiris and the Narrative Strategy of

Modern geographers have recently set out formally the problem of authorial presence or absence. It was long traditional for geographers to absent themselves from their texts in an attempt to appear to give the definitive account of a region, partly in reaction to preceding value-laden colonial accounts, in which the invariably superior cultural viewpoint of the conquerors was firmly written into the text.[90] The new, 'unbiased' geographical style has, however, been challenged in turn by those who have demanded an open acknowledgement of the author's standpoint. We have been reminded that, although it was traditional for the ethnographer 'to erase himself or herself from the text to report with omniscient authority—there, of course, could be no ethnography without the ethnographer'.[91] The same could be said of the human geographer. In particular, modern feminist geographers have complained that the pretence of an objective, anonymous geography implicitly and without justification makes a claim to omniscience and the incorporation of *all* viewpoints.[92] Their demand for authors of geographical texts to state their social and intellectual background, in other words to give a thorough representation of themselves in the text, is seen as the only honest way for the

Heliodoros' *Aithiopika*', *Yale Classical Studies*, 27 (1982), 93–158. He stresses the absence of the author in this work as setting it apart from the 'historiographic verisimilitude' created by the use of the first person by historians such as Polybius and Herodotus.

[90] For nineteenth-century depictions of subject peoples in artistic representations designed to make them conform to the ideals of their conquerors, see L. Bell, 'Artists and Empire: Victorian Representations of Subject People', *Art History*, 5 (1982), 73–86. A. Godlewska, 'Map, Text and Image. The Mentality of Enlightened Conquerors: A New Look at the *Description de l'Egypte*', *TIBG* NS 20 (1995), 5–28, has studied the way in which written text and cartographic representations, collated in the course of Napoleon's conquest of Egypt, were designed to justify the conquest and confirm France's cultural superiority.

[91] See C. Katz, 'All the World is Staged: Intellectuals and the Projects of Ethnography', *Environment and Planning D: Society and Space*, 10 (1992), 496. Geertz is clearly influential in the formation of such views, leading to a greater focus on the autobiography of the author.

[92] S. Christopherson, 'On Being Outside "the Project"', *Antipode*, 21 (1989), 83–9, argues for the acceptance of different authorial perspectives in geography; see also A. Merrifield, 'Situated Knowledge through Exploration: Reflections on Bunge's "Geographical Expeditions"', *Antipode*, 27 (1995), 49–70.

subject to proceed. It should, they argue, be to the benefit of the subject to embrace the variety of these 'situated knowledges'.[93] So, at least one present trend would support the view that geography has the author and the author's focalization very much in the foreground.

I argue in chapter IV that Strabo himself is relatively absent from his *Geography*, by contrast with the normal practice of Greek historians to present themselves to the reader at the start of the work.[94] But, as we shall see, Strabo asserts his presence in the *Geography* indirectly, through implicitly self-referential phrases, and it is possible to identify not just one, but several, authorial focalizations within the work. As with other approaches, the straight opposition between authorial presence or absence from the text is unsatisfactory as a means of defining history and geography.

Secondly, space, place, and time can be usefully linked to notions of narrativity. As I discussed in the previous section, Tuan has made some suggestive assertions about the relationship between these. He contends that 'place is pause in movement. That is one relation between time and place.'[95] I have already noted his view that a sense of place is developed only over time, making time necessary for the transformation of space into place. Another relationship between space, place, and time, which he identifies, is reminiscent of specific relativity theory, namely that other places appear in our minds associated with the past because we always hear of events in them after a time gap. In other words, contemporaneous events are perceived as happening at different times by people in different places.[96] In narratological terms, these refer to differ-

---

[93] D. Haraway, 'Situated Knowledges: The Science Question in Feminism and the Privilege of Partial Perspective', in D. Haraway (ed.), *Simians, Cyborgs and Women* (London, 1991), 183–201, coined the phrase for geographers.

[94] I have set out this argument more fully in, 'In Search of the Author of Strabo's *Geography*', *JRS* 87 (1997), 92–110.

[95] Tuan, 'Space, Time, Place', 14. I shall discuss this statement in chapter IV in relation to ancient geographical texts.

[96] Ibid. 12. This relationship between space and time has not been universally held. Smalley, *Historians in the Middle Ages*, 63, points out that in the Middle Ages past and present were not fully distinct; without an interest in the progress of time, contemporaneous events, and even those

ent focalizations of the same moment in time. But we can go further. Place and space have been seen as linked by 'emplotment' or narrative.[97] Thus narratives encompass different viewpoints with their varying levels of involvement and their different types of location—'place', experienced internally, and 'space', viewed from an external point. Since narrative inevitably takes place through time, this formulation neatly relates time, space, and place. The role of narrative has also been, slightly differently, defined as a link between events which occur in time and space: 'Spacing and timing define the positions and occasions of singular occurrences, and narration connects them together.'[98]

I shall come back to the questions of space and place, of their relationship to discrete and continuous notions of space and time, and of the implications for universal accounts. For the moment, however, I wish to explore yet another formulation of the relationship between narrative, time, and space. In exact parallel to Tuan's 'place is pause in movement', Fowler defines ekphrasis as the suspension of a story, a narrative pause.[99] The parallel fits the periplus model, in which the narrative is the link between places on the journey, and the description occurs when a 'lived-in' space or a 'place' is reached. The notion of narrative *pause* suggests that description is not part of the story and is thus not totally necessary, but as Fowler himself goes on to explain, the divide between narrative and description is far from clear-cut. Being a verbal series, the description cannot itself avoid having a chronological order, but does this mean that it also has a narrative?

We might say that description through time is precisely what constitutes narrative, but many narratologists also see as being necessary a 'plot' or 'story-line', which leads us to expect a

belonging to different times, could be conceived of and represented artistically as belonging to the same moment in time.

[97] Merrifield, 'Place and Space', 518. All of Merrifield's types of space are to be found in the periplus texts: (a) representations of space (conceived as an abstraction); (b) representational space (directly lived in and experienced); (c) spatial practices (routes through space) (p. 524).

[98] H. Prince, 'Time and Historical Geography', in *Making Sense of Time*, 18.

[99] D. P. Fowler, 'Narrate and Describe: The Problem of Ekphrasis', *JRS* 81 (1991), 25.

certain structure with beginning, middle, and satisfactory end.[100] To take a simple example, a description of the rooms in a house *could* be written in such a way that we would know when to expect the end, but would it not also be possible to write such a description so as to give no clue as to the logical conclusion (other than that the house *must* end at some point)? Thus it seems fair to make some distinction between 'description through time' and 'narrative'. Is this, then, one of the factors which separate geography from history, making history a narrative, with a plot, and geography a description which could end at any point?[101]

If we test this against even the simplest form of geographical work, the linear progression along a journey, the model loses credibility. The apparently shapeless list of places that comprises some periplus literature may seem to fulfil the criterion for a non-narrative text, namely that it would be comprehensible if we stopped at any point. But the very name periplus should perhaps warn against this conclusion. A voyage round in a circle must expect an end, when the voyager reaches the starting-point again. Indeed the fact that the earth is finite and spherical, and not simply a line of places stretching out into eternity, should make it an impossibility for geographical accounts *not* to expect an end, although it could be argued that the expectation of *some* end, as opposed to a restricted range of endings, does not constitute narrative.

An example of how the model of geography as a pure description, with no narrative expectations, may be challenged is the mid-fourth-century BC periplus attributed to Scylax of Caryanda. The structure is simple to the point of monotony, but right from the start we have an idea of where the account is going and where it will end.[102] The author announces that he will start at the Pillar of Hercules on the European side and

---

[100] The idea of narratives being 'emplotted' so as to lead to certain expectations and 'the sense of an ending' is discussed in detail by Ricoeur, 'Narrative Time'. Plot, according to Ricoeur, imposes on mere succession an episodic dimension and pattern, which lead to the sense of ending. I recall Starr, 'Historical and Philosophical Time', on the patterned nature of history, as opposed to a strict chronological succession (See above, p. 19 n. 43).

[101] Kant explicitly associated geography with description and history with narrative in *Physische Geographie*, §3.

[102] For the text, see *GGM I*.

work round to the Pillar on the Libyan side. Having been given this explicit statement of what to expect, the reader would feel dissatisfied if the account were cut short. What is particularly interesting about this text from the narratological point of view is the hint that the author may take us even further than the Pillars of Hercules. He enigmatically promises at the start to go not only back to the Pillars, but 'as far the great Aethiopians', although it is not made clear what kind of a journey this will involve. On reaching the Libyan side of the Pillars of Hercules, the account indeed continues out into the Ocean, towards the landmarks of Thymaterion, Cape Soleis, and the island of Cerne. We could hardly argue that this geographical writer had no sense of narrative ending. But it is more complex than a simple itinerary-plan. Before going beyond the Pillars, the author stresses their linking role between Europe and Libya. The Mediterranean narrative is over; he has reached the start again. The world beyond the Pillars is quite literally a different story from what lies within the Mediterranean basin, and the whole structure shows a quite self-conscious manipulation of narrative expectations. If geography has its own narrative, then the dichotomy between history as narrative and geography as description will not stand. In particular, as I discuss in chapter V, Strabo's *Geography* confirms the weakness of this model. It is precisely at the places in between the geographical description, or the 'narrative covering space', where narrative as 'description through time' takes over, in his relation of the history of cities and peoples encountered along the way.

UNITY, DISJUNCTION, AND MODELS OF UNIVERSALISM

So, narratological approaches alert us to different types of focalization, and to new ways of formulating the relationship between space, place, and time. One aspect of this approach is the distinction between discrete and local, or continuous and universal views of the world. The multi-focused nature of the world as it is actually experienced has been associated with disjointed notions of space and time; the single, external viewpoint has been linked with homogeneous time and space.

Furthermore, the distinction between the discrete and the

continuous may be linked, although not straightforwardly, to notions of abstract and experienced time and space. One feature of abstract time is that it can be calibrated into discrete, consistent, and countable units. But the development of calibrated time, in the form of the calendar, has equally been seen as representative of non-discrete temporal concepts: 'Just as the map replaces the discontinuous patchy space of practical paths by the homogeneous, continuous space of geometry, so the calendar substitutes a linear, homogeneous, continuous time for practical time, which is made up of incommensurable islands of duration each with its own rhythm.'[103] So, it is the 'lived-in' experienced space of individual places which is more easily described in terms of discrete units. The issue of continuity and fragmentation will be important when considering the nature of different attempts to describe and configurate the world. The periplus texts would clearly give a quite different analysis in these terms from, say, a universal history. As Greenblatt has noted in his discussion of sixteenth-century voyages of discovery, by comparison with universal histories, 'the chronicles of exploration seem uncertain of their bearings, disorganised, fragmentary'.[104]

In this section I examine first of all the consequences of the idea that man is a microcosm of the world, before moving on to the conflict between discrete and continuous space and time in relation to the question of universalism. I have mentioned several times Gurevich's study of medieval culture. Gurevich identifies in medieval literature the notion that man, the world, and all things in the world are made up of the same elements, and so are analogous creations. This led to the idea that the whole of the universe could be viewed through examination of a single part of it. The implication for accounts of the world was that a local history was an adequate substitute for a universal history.[105] Thus 'they set out to write universal

---

[103] Harvey, *The Condition of Postmodernity*, 253.

[104] Greenblatt, *Marvelous Possessions*, 2.

[105] Smalley, *Historians in the Middle Ages*, discusses the same period of history in terms of the dominance of Christianity, coming to similar conclusions to those of Gurevich. The universal empire of the Church meant that *all* history was, in effect, universal. 'What was history (in the twelfth century) if not universal? To deny its universality would have amounted to denying the

histories, but, paradoxically, produced provincial chronicles with very limited horizons.'[106] Glaber promised to write the events that had taken place in the four corners of the earth, but ended up writing the history of Cluny in Burgundy.

The concept of man and the world being complete telescopic versions of each other brings us back to the point that geography and history may both be seen as forms of biography, a notion which allows us to dispense with the matrices of time and space in defining the subjects. In the wake of Theopompus' *Philippica* and accounts of Alexander the Great, biographical histories became a common form of writing in the Hellenistic period.[107] The parallel use of the form -ικα/ιακα to refer to Hellenistic regional histories emphasizes the way in which these could be seen as accounts of the whole life of a place. The same notion of biographical history was taken up by the Christians, as can be seen in Augustine's scheme, by which the history of the world was to be divided into six ages, representing the six stages of a human life.[108] It is interesting that when the ancient rhetoricians set out the criteria by which to construct a speech in praise of a city, they used the same categories as those which were applied to the lives of individuals. Menander says that the basis for an encomium of a city should be not only its position (θέσις), but also the ancestry (τὸ γένος), the deeds (αἱ πράξεις), and habits (αἱ ἐπιτηδεύσεις) associated with the place. So, writing the life of a city was parallel to writing a human biography.[109] In the Hellenistic

truth of Christianity' (p. 95). For a different view of medieval notions of space, see Kimble, *Geography in the Middle Ages*, 3–4, on the preponderance of itinerary descriptions, such as the *Bordeaux Itinerary*, the first extant pilgrim record, providing an account of the journey from Bordeaux to Jerusalem, and in which linear space was dominant.

[106] See Gurevich, *Categories of Medieval Culture*, 68, for local 'universal' histories. D. S. Levene, 'Sallust's *Jugurtha*: An "Historical Fragment"', *JRS* 82 (1992), 53–70, explores the similar notion that a monograph of apparently restricted chronological scope could be written as a conscious part of a larger whole.

[107] See C. W. Fornara, *The Nature of History in Ancient Greece and Rome* (Berkeley, 1983), 35.

[108] Smalley, *Historians in the Middle Ages*, 30.

[109] See D. A. Russell and N. G. Wilson (eds.), *Menander Rhetor* (Oxford, 1981), 346.

world, the idea of the life or βίος of a whole nation was
exemplified by Dicaearchus' *Life of Greece* (Βίος Ἑλλάδος),
but was symptomatic of a wider sense in the Greek world
that man and the universe were inseparable.[110] Philosophical
theories to back up the parallel are easily identifiable. Empe-
docles' four elements making up the world were parallel to the
four humours of man; and Stoicism, as I shall discuss later, was
based largely on the idea that man and the universe were
linked.[111]

I shall return to the notions of biographical history and
geography, and the underlying premise that man is a microcosm of the world, in relation to Polybius, Posidonius, and
Strabo. This provides a way of conceptualizing the whole
world through one of its parts. One could argue for an
association of this kind of universalism with notions of time
and space which are continuous and abstract—the geometrical
model. To use a term from mathematics, the world and all its
parts are, in the strictest sense, 'similar shapes'.

But it is important to note also the very earliest philosophical
moves to understand the world as a coherent whole, especially
since these offer ways of combining the universal with the
fragmentary. Later in this chapter I discuss the influence of
Hecataeus of Miletus on the development of Greek prose
writing. But his sixth-century compatriots had already overthrown previous world-views, going far beyond Hesiod's
attempt to create in the *Theogony* a 'unified and reasonable
picture of the workings and history of the universe'.[112] Hussey
has pointed out the difficulty in identifying precise trains of
thought among the Milesians—Thales, who left no writings at
all, Anaximander, and Anaximenes—but he discerns a
common belief in a 'single boundless all-powerful and immor-
tal divinity which encompassed and controlled the universe',
replacing the disparate polytheism of Hesiod.[113] The cosmos
(κόσμος) or possibly cosmoi (κόσμοι) in the plural, limited in

---

[110] On this see A. Momigliano, *The Classical Foundations of Modern
Historiography* (Berkeley, 1990), 65–6.

[111] See Glacken, *Traces on the Rhodian Shore*, 6, 10, 51.

[112] See E. Hussey, *The Presocratics* (London, 1972), 11–13. My view of the
Presocratics is largely indebted to Hussey's work.

[113] Ibid. 16.

space and time, were bounded and controlled by the limitless divinity (τὸ ἄπειρον).

Further coherence was given to this world-view by Thales with his suggestion that the κόσμος was made up entirely of one element, water. Anaximander posited instead forces of opposites at work in the world (hot, cold, wet, and dry), which were constantly jostling for dominance, but which were balanced overall by the guiding principle of τὸ ἄπειρον. Within this framework, the fragments of Anaximander's work reveal an interest in the earth's shape, the causes of natural phenomena, and the mapping of the earth's surface. However, the problem of precisely how the opposite forces in the world related to τὸ ἄπειρον seems to have waited for treatment by Anaximenes. He argued that the constituent parts of the κόσμοι actually came from τὸ ἄπειρον itself, that they were interconvertible with it and with each other. Everything could be made up of fire, air, wind, cloud, earth, and rock in various states of compression and rarefaction.

This theory gave great coherence both to the world itself and to its relationship with the single controlling divine force. The possibilities for man as a microcosm of the world and of the whole universe, made up of the same elements, are obvious. It is no surprise to find further foreshadowing of Stoic thought in the explicit analogy drawn by the Milesians between the role of the soul (ψυχή) in the body and of the divine air in the cosmos.

In the terminology of modern geographical thought, continuous time and space, inextricably bound with each other and the world, are not the only models available. Alongside these, we have the notion of discrete units of time and space, which raises other possibilities for the construction of universal accounts. But we may add to this expression of duality the work of the early philosophers in the Greek cities of Asia Minor, who were already in the sixth century BC wrestling with the problem of creating an understanding of the world which would take into account both the coherence of the universe and the diverse phenomena found within it.

It has often been said that geography is concerned with uniqueness, that is, with understanding areas in terms of their difference from others.[114] The view has been summed up: 'Geography is about describing how and accounting for why the world, as the home of humankind, differs from place to place.'[115] So, a major concern of geography is with discrete place as opposed to geometrical, or abstract, space. I have already discussed the parallel notions of discrete and continuous time, and the tension in historiography between, on the one hand, the use of standard, discrete units of temporal calibration, sometimes considered the result of the imposition of a single, almost external, viewpoint on the world, and on the other hand the fact that our temporal experience of the world is continuous, heterogeneous, and relative to our position in space, that is, it varies depending on the focalizer.[116] The fact that our predominant spatial conception is of discrete places, but our temporal experience is of continuity, suggests that accounts of the world could not be constructed from either exclusively discrete or exclusively continuous notions of time and space.

Langton has formulated for the geographers what I think is a satisfactory response to such divisions, calling for a coexistence of two types of geography, both still concerned to study and explain the uniqueness of a place: the first explains the nature of an aspect of life in a particular place by reason of its location in a pattern produced by large-scale organization of that aspect of life across space; the other explains that feature in terms of other aspects of life in that one place. Thus, one is primarily concerned with space and the other with place.[117] So, besides

---

[114] See Guelke, *Historical Understanding in Geography*, 101: 'Uniqueness is at the heart of geography.'

[115] J. Langton, 'The Two Traditions of Geography. Historical Geography and the Study of Landscapes', *Geografiska Annaler*, 70B (1988), 21.

[116] On discrete and continuous time and space, see Kern, *The Culture of Time and Space*. The coexistence of continuous and discrete time led to confusion for Whitrow, *Time in History*, over the ancient world. He both asserts that in antiquity there was an 'absence of a continuous sense of time' (p. 25) and points out that the clepsydra provided a measure of continuous time, as opposed to the discrete units measured by the mechanical clock (p. 99).

[117] Langton, 'The Two Traditions of Geography', 21. Mitchell, *Historical Geography*, 6, too argues for both patterns and individuality as concerns of historical geography.

the idea of place as experienced space, we may also define it as discrete, as opposed to continuous, space. As has been pointed out in many books on the geographical tradition, these two types of geography had a long history. Varenius in the seventeenth century formally set out this relationship between place and space, stressing in his *Geographia Generalis* (1650) the importance of relating the specific (proved by experience) to general laws (explained in terms of mathematical and astronomical laws). But we can trace the distinction between *geographia generalis* and *geographia specialis* further back to Keckermann (1572–1609), and set this in the context of sixteenth-century interest in far-away places and a broader picture of the world, resulting in topographical compendia such as Heylyn's *Microcosmus* (1621) and Abbot's *A Briefe Description of the Whole World* (1599).[118] The parallels between sixteenth-century responses to the newly expanded world and the reactions to similar phases of conquest in antiquity are strong, and as I shall show in the following chapters, both *geographia specialis* and *geographia generalis* can be seen in ancient accounts of the world, the former predominant in Strabo's *Geography*, the latter in Polybius' *History*.[119] But I shall also argue that Strabo's concentration on discrete units of place, and his lesser interest in the continuous space between, does not make his account any less universal. Rather, his universalism lay in a spatial conception of the world in which all individual places were united through their relationships to Rome.

GEOGRAPHICAL HISTORIANS: FROM GRUNDY
TO THE *ANNALES*

Practitioners of academic geography now seem to be leading the field in constructing theories concerning the relationship of

[118] For Varenius, see James and Martin, *All Possible Worlds*, 96–8; on Keckermann, see D. N. Livingstone, *The Geographical Tradition: Episodes in the History of a Contested Enterprise* (Oxford, 1992), 85; 94.

[119] It is interesting that, according to May, Kant himself defined two strands of geography—the single, universal conception of Eratosthenes and Ptolemaeus, in which geometrical, continuous space was prime, and the heterogeneous description of Strabo's *Geography*. See May, *Kant's Concept of Geography*, 53.

their subject with history. Geographers seem to have far
surpassed historians in developing sophisticated arguments
about time, space, history, and geography, and I would claim
that many of their arguments can be successfully applied to the
texts in which ancient historians are primarily interested. I
shall demonstrate throughout this book that an approach
influenced by the ideas discussed by modern geographers can
suggest new questions to ask of our ancient texts, and thus
greatly enhance our understanding of the conceptual world of
the society which produced them.

It is, however, important to acknowledge that within the
discipline of history itself geography has not been ignored.
Indeed the School of Geography in Oxford was originally an
adjunct of the Faculty of Modern History. In 1887, H. J.
Mackinder was appointed the first Reader in Geography at
Oxford since Hakluyt in the sixteenth century, but his lecture
audiences were made up of historians and he was himself an *ex
officio* member of the Board of the Faculty of Modern History.[120] Indeed the prospect of a separate geography school
seemed so remote that Mackinder himself conceded that if he
was to succeed at all in the scheme for the introduction of
geography, it was absolutely essential that he should subordinate it to the history faculty, a comment which makes the
eventual establishment of a School of Geography in 1899 all
the greater an achievement.[121]

The nature of the relationship between the concerns and
approaches of historians and geographers has rarely been
discussed explicitly and at a theoretical level by ancient
historians, but I propose in this section to trace just some of
the trends in the discipline of ancient history which have, in
different ways, worked towards the creation of a 'geographical
history' either consciously or subconsciously.

[120] For the development of the School of Geography under Mackinder, see
W. H. Parker, *Mackinder: Geography as an Aid to Statescraft* (Oxford, 1982),
1–27. Richard Hakluyt (1552–1616) was a Student of Christ Church, Oxford.
It is interesting that a post in geography was considered worth filling at this
period of discovery and expansion (one of Hakluyt's works was *Divers
Voyages touching the Discovery of America* (1582)), only to fall vacant after
Hakluyt's tenure. I shall discuss further the link between conquest and
geographical writings in the final section of this chapter.
[121] Parker, *Mackinder*, 17.

G. B. Grundy, Fellow and Tutor in Ancient History at Corpus Christi College (1903–31) and Tutor in Ancient History at Brasenose College (1904–17), provides a perfect example of the interest taken in geography by Oxford ancient historians during the early part of the twentieth century. A career as an academic could hardly have seemed likely for one who left school at the age of fourteen, but, after teaching in various schools, Grundy joined Brasenose as an undergraduate in 1887 in his mid-twenties. His autobiography paints a fascinating picture of life in Oxford during the following five decades, an association with the University which would span two world wars.[122] It is very clear from his views on various ancient historical debates that the history through which he lived had exerted a strong influence over him.[123]

Of particular relevance to this chapter is the further biographical fact revealed by Grundy's memoirs, that he was one of a number of historians around this time to be quite at home in the field of geography. In 1892 he was awarded the University Geography Scholarship, which Mackinder had persuaded the University and the Royal Geographical Society to join in establishing the previous year. This enabled Grundy to finance surveys of the battle-sites at Plataea and Leuctra (winter 1892–3) and Trebbia and Lake Trasimene (1893–4).[124] It was Grundy's topographical work in Greece in particular, including a survey of Pylos and Sphacteria in 1895, which impressed Pelham, then Professor of Ancient History in Oxford, and led to Grundy's appointment as lecturer for the professor, Grundy's first official post after years as a private tutor. His particular expertise was to lead to a further

---

[122] G. B. Grundy, *Fifty-five Years at Oxford: An Unconventional Autobiography* (London, 1945).

[123] See, for example, his comments on the dangers of uncritically appropriating the superiority of a civilization. He put firmly in its place the possibility of reading Pericles' funeral oration as the representation of a perfect culture. 'Thucydides wrote the speech as either his own or Pericles' conception of the highest form of democracy. He could not have supposed that any reader of his history who read the Mytilenian Debate or the Melian Dialogue would regard the Funeral Oration as being a picture of a political and social life which was ever realised at Athens', Grundy, *Fifty-five Years at Oxford*, 221.

[124] Ibid. 73 and 81.

lecturing appointment in 1899, this time in the newly established School of Geography, a potent reminder of the link
between the now separate subjects. Grundy was to follow up
this geographical interest throughout his career, with work in
Greece, Macedonia, and Romania financed by the Craven
Fund and grants from his two colleges, Corpus Christi and
Brasenose. His accounts of extensive travel in the remote areas
of north-east Greece during the period 1880–1913 paint a
hair-raising though sympathetic picture of the continuing
brigandage, and testify to the considerable hazards which
faced the geographical historian.

But at the same time as pursuing his interest in travel and in
gaining an understanding of the physical environment within
which episodes of ancient history had taken place, Grundy was
working on a project which would secure the benefits of his
approach for later students of ancient history. In 1900, he was
asked by the publisher Murray to produce a new edition of the
classical atlas. Grundy agreed on condition that he be allowed
to use the coloured contour system to represent the lie of the
land. Although this request was at first turned down on
grounds of expense, Murray finally conceded, and the atlas
was published in 1904.[125] In his preface, Grundy remarked that
'the configuration of a country must necessarily be the most
important factor in its history, since it exercises an influence
not only on events but also on the character of its population'.[126] The result stands as a testimony to Grundy's conviction that ancient history could not be understood
independently of its geographical aspect.

The influence of Grundy's stress on geographical factors in
history continued through the Second World War. Chilver's
study of Cisalpine Gaul, which had been the subject of his
doctoral thesis, was prefaced with the acknowledgement that
the reasons for the late development of the region may 'lie as
much in geography which gives the Po valley a close connexion
with the transalpine lands, as in the purely historical fact,
which in itself needs further explanation, that the Romans

[125] The atlas incidentally incorporated topographical plans of the various
battle-sites which Grundy had visited using his Geographical Scholarship, in
addition to maps of larger areas.
[126] G. B. Grundy (ed.), *Murray's Classical Atlas* (London, 1904).

were so late in penetrating to this fertile plain'.[127] His book started with a section on the physical geography of the area, and chapters throughout the work revealed an interest in communications and various aspects of agriculture and natural resources.

A similar emphasis on physical geography underlay Cary's work on *The Geographic Background of Greek and Roman History*, published a few years after Chilver's study of Gaul. Cary set out his aim in the preface: 'In this book I have endeavoured to make a fresh contribution to a subject whose importance is now generally recognized, the influence of geographic environment on human history, in a study of this influence on the world of ancient Greece and Rome.'[128] There then followed a detailed description of the physical conditions of the Graeco-Roman world, in which climate-change, geology, flora, fauna, and communications led on to a discussion of the implications for social and political life. The link between geography and history was clearly stated as being one of environmental determinism. 'Above all, the clear, crisp, and luminous air of the Mediterranean region provides a stimulus such as few other parts of the world can offer.'[129] So Cary's 'geographic background' turns out to have been more integral to Greek and Roman history than the title suggests. However, like Chilver, Cary ran the risk of compartmentalizing the geographical side of history, not in an introductory chapter in this case, but in a separate book. He did not write geographical history in the integrated manner of, for example, the writers of the *Annales* school, discussed below (pp. 52–4). Thus he covered only one of the ways in which geography and history are connected; namely, the impact of the physical environment on historical events and processes. For historians such as Grundy, Chilver, and Cary, the question of how the academic subjects might be defined, and the philosophical and literary issues of conceptualizing and describing the world according to time and space, were not the prime concerns.

[127] G. E. F. Chilver, *Cisalpine Gaul: Social and Economic History from 49 B.C. to the Death of Trajan* (Oxford, 1941), Preface, p. v.

[128] M. Cary, *The Geographic Background of Greek and Roman History* (Oxford, 1949), Preface, p. v.

[129] Ibid. 6.

The place of geography in the study of ancient history in Oxford, as witnessed in the work of Grundy, had meanwhile been confirmed and developed in a new direction with the appointment of J. L. Myres as the first Wykeham Professor of Greek History in 1910. In his inaugural address on 'The value of ancient history' he called for breadth of approach, and stressed not only the role of geography in the subject, but the near inseparability of the two fields.

All history, therefore, has a geographical aspect. It asks, of course, primarily, 'What was it that happened, and how?' But just as it necessarily asks 'when?', so also must it ask 'where?' The converse is, of course, true also. All geographical facts occur 'somewhen' as well as 'somewhere'; all geography takes account of processes in time as well as distributions in space, and consequently needs must have an historical aspect. At first sight, therefore, there is complete overlap between the history and geography of Man.[130]

In various addresses, many of them to geographical societies and collected in his essays on geographical history, Myres went on to modify and refine this striking claim. The resistance to any notion of geography as being subordinate to history took Myres further than Grundy, whose interests lay in topography, the location of episodes in history, and the backdrop of events. Myres saw geography not as a secondary ornament to a historical account, nor only as the explanation for particular events, but as integral to the whole historical enterprise. 'In this general sense, geography is the *coequal* sister-science of history, which studies and interprets the relations of events in time' (my italics). In the same address Myres linked the philosophical relationship between time and space to the parallel relationship between history and geography. 'Every relation between objects in space is bound up with a relation between events in time. Consequently every geographical fact has its historical aspect, and every historical fact its geographical aspect.'[131] These reflections clearly foreshadowed many of the theoretical discussions which would be put forward later by

[130] J. L. Myres, 'The Value of Ancient History', delivered 13 May 1910, in *Geographical History in Greek Lands* (Oxford, 1953), 59.
[131] J. L. Myres, 'Ancient Geography in Modern Education' = Presidential Address to the Geography Section of the British Association, Glasgow, 1928, in Myres, *Geographical History*, 74, 75.

geographers, and which I have mentioned earlier in this chapter. Myres was careful to make plain in his inaugural address as Professor of Ancient History his conviction that 'geography is not history, and cannot be confused with it', but his concern with geography as an academic subject intimately related to his own is apparent from his various papers. He was unusual among ancient historians in that he, like many modern geographers, was interested in formulating some notion of exactly how the fields could and should be related, philosophically, in practice, and particularly in education. He regularly rounded off an address with the exhortation that in both schools and universities geography and history should be taught alongside each other; a process which he called 'teamwork in the pursuit of knowledge'.[132]

One of the recurrent themes in Myres's essays on geographical history is the importance of regional history. It was the need for historians to understand the events, culture, and interactions within a given area that, for Myres, brought them closest to the concerns of geographers. 'All human history, then, is regional history, and loses its value and meaning when its geographical aspect is overlooked.'[133] Myres argued that his discussions of geography and history were concerned with setting up a method and an approach rather than providing any particular set of answers, but he then went on to put his methodology into practice, with essays on 'The geographical aspect of Greek colonization', 'The geographical distribution of the Greek city-states', and regional studies on,

---

[132] J. L. Myres, 'Geography in Relation to History and Literature' = Address to the British Association, Johannesburg, 1929, in Myres, *Geographical History*, 107.

[133] J. L. Myres, 'Ancient Geography in Modern Education', in Myres, *Geographical History*, 75. The regional nature of many works of the Hellenistic period is apparent, and is reinforced by the fact that many were accounts of the author's *native* land. Paion of Amathus wrote a work called Περὶ Ἀμαθοῦντος (*FGrH* 757), Asclepiades of Cyprus wrote Περὶ Κύπρου (*FGrH* 752), and Athenodorus of Tarsus wrote Περὶ τῆς πατρίδος (*FGrH* 746). Note also Dionysius of Halicarnassus' reference (7. 70–3) to 'the early histories of particular lands'; at 2. 49. 1–5 to local historical traditions in his account of the ethnography of the Sabines and their possible Spartan origins: ἔστι δέ τις . . . ἐν ἱστορίαις ἐπιχωρίοις . . . λόγος ('there is a story . . . among the local accounts'); and Diodorus Siculus' use of the local accounts of the burial of Dionysus (3. 67. 5).

for example, the Dodecanese and the Marmara region. The region which formed a coherent area of study might, however, be more extensive than these; as broad as the Mediterranean world itself. Myres, along with many other historians, saw the environment of the Mediterranean basin overall as having strongly influenced the history of its inhabitants. Indeed, he saw the Greek and Roman civilizations as marked by the 'supreme effort to live well under Mediterranean conditions'.[134] But for Myres, the notion of environmental determinism was only part of a much broader understanding of the relationship between geography and history.

Some aspects of this approach were meanwhile being mirrored in continental Europe with the development of the *Annales* school. The move away from history in the form of political or military narrative towards a study of human society in its entirety was bringing academic history into closer contact with the social sciences. It is, however, all too easy to generalize about the motives and methods of the *Annales* historians, and it is important to recognize the differences that existed among its founders, and the developments that took place over time.

The stress placed by Henri Pirenne, Bloch's mentor and the inspiration for the *Annales*, on comparative history, and his readiness to place past and present alongside each other would be reflected both in the conviction of the *Annales* editors that the interdependence of past and present formed the main justification for the existence of history as a field of study, and in the predominance of contemporary issues in the articles published.[135] Bloch, however, who together with Febvre actually set up the *Annales d'histoire économique et sociale*, although being heavily influenced by sociological approaches, continued to insist on the dimension of change through time, and feared

[134] J. L. Myres, 'The Geographical Study of Greek and Roman Culture' = Address to the Scottish Geographical Society, 1910, in Myres, *Geographical History*, 130.

[135] The idea that history concerned the past and geography the present (see Darby, 'On the Relations of Geography and History', 6) might appear at first to be in strict opposition to the concept of comparative history. If, however, the division between geography and history is ignored and the two are seen as part of a comprehensive account of society, then a comparative 'history' concerning both past and present becomes perfectly possible.

that comparative history, if applied indiscriminately, might obscure the 'unique characteristics of time and place'.[136] But this reservation strengthened rather than weakened his aim to study society in a comprehensive manner. Bloch's *Les Caractères originaux de l'histoire rurale française* (1931), drawing on regional and local histories, geography, law, linguistics, archaeology, and economy, exemplified the interdisciplinary approach necessary for the new *histoire humaine*, and incidentally recalled Myres' claim of only three years earlier that 'all human history is regional history'.

This strongly geographical approach was reflected in the *Annales* themselves, established in 1929. The journal was published by Colin, who also produced the *Annales de géographie*; Bloch's co-editor, Febvre, had passed the *agrégation* in geography as well as in history in 1902. Febvre's doctoral thesis was a study in the history, geography, economy, and society of Franche-Comté in the age of Philip II, a field which foreshadowed the work of his pupil, Braudel. Some tensions and disagreements clearly existed. Bloch remained firmly tied to the evidence; Febvre was more committed to a journal of ideas. But neither was interested in narrative history, and both agreed in focusing the *Annales* instead on economic and social issues. The mission to heal the rift between history and the social sciences developed a school of thought which was only rarely glimpsed in ancient history as it was studied in Britain.

The *Annales* were to take a slightly new direction after the Second World War. Bloch had been shot dead in a field near St.-Didier-de-Formans in 1944, and Febvre refounded the journal, this time with the adjusted title *Annales: Economies, Sociétés, Civilisations*, and with the addition of Friedmann, Morazé, and his own student, Braudel, on the board of directors. When Febvre died in 1956, Braudel took over the journal. His doctoral thesis on *La Méditerranée et le monde méditerranéen à l'époque de Philippe II* was heavily influenced by Febvre, and was written largely without notes during his five years in a prisoner-of-war camp. With Braudel the emphasis of the journal shifted not only from chronological and fact-based history, but also from the problem-orientated

[136] C. Fink, *Marc Bloch: A Life in History* (Cambridge, 1989), 110.

history of Bloch and Febvre, towards the understanding of the *longue durée*, a comprehensive history of vast scope.

In spite of variations in approach among those involved in the development of the *Annales*, all agreed on the interdisciplinary nature of the subject. This was true for these historians not only in so far as history itself was seen as being influenced by factors such as environment, but also because studying and writing history as a chronological narrative in isolation from synchronic considerations was deemed impossible. Meanwhile, British scholars were advocating the interdisciplinary approach for history and the social sciences from the other side of the subject divide. Evans-Pritchard, Professor of Social Anthropology at Oxford from 1946, repeatedly addressed the issue of the relationship between anthropology and history.[137] In opposition to the functionalist approach to anthropology, which allied the subject to the human sciences, and reduced society to a series of natural laws, which were constant through time, Evans-Pritchard argued that society could only be fully understood through a study of its diachronic development. The fact that the anthropologist studied societies directly through contact with them, and the historian indirectly through documents, was for Evans-Pritchard an evidential rather than a methodological difference. His assertion that 'the fundamental characteristic of historical method is not the chronological relation of events but the descriptive integration of them; and this characteristic historiography shares with social anthropology', made clear that it would be difficult to define precise theoretical boundaries for history and the social sciences, including geography.[138]

Evans-Pritchard highlighted the work of sociological historians, such as Bloch and Febvre, who were interested not in political or military narratives, but in social institutions and cultural change, as being virtually indistinguishable from that of anthropologists. In terms of subject matter, he posited a slightly different emphasis for historians, who might focus more on politics, while the anthropologists concentrated on

[137] See E. E. Evans-Pritchard, *Essays in Social Anthropology* (London, 1962).

[138] E. E. Evans-Pritchard, 'Social Anthropology: Past and Present' = The Marett Lecture, 1950, in Evans-Pritchard, *Essays in Social Anthropology*, 24.

domestic or community relations. 'Is there any history of marriage and the family, or of kinship in England?'[139] But it is easy to think of recent studies by ancient historians in all of Evans-Pritchard's subjects—marriage, family, and kinship— making even this reservation obsolete.[140] He saw anthropology and history as differing only slightly in approach: 'The fact that the anthropologist's problems are generally synchronic while the historian's problems are generally diachronic is a difference of emphasis in the rather peculiar conditions prevailing and not a real divergence of interest.'[141] So, even the most commonly acceptable distinction between history and social sciences, such as geography or anthropology, namely, that the former more than the latter is organized through time, seemed contentious to Evans-Pritchard. Indeed he revealed the unthinking embeddedness of the distinctions and the arbitrariness of our appellations by observing that if a historian fixes on one culture for a restricted temporal period, we relabel the work as an ethnographic monograph (one might cite as an ancient example Tacitus' *Germania*), whereas the work of a social anthropologist, if he writes about the development of a society through time, is termed a social history.

Much of what Evans-Pritchard has argued for anthropology is, of course, applicable also to geography. In many ways, like the modern geographers, he surpassed historians themselves in working out a methodological, theoretical approach to history and its relationship to other subjects, although in both cases

---

[139] E. E. Evans-Pritchard, 'Anthropology and History' = Manchester, 1961, in Evans-Pritchard, *Essays in Social Anthropology*, 59.

[140] See, for example, on marriage: S. Treggiari, *Roman Marriage: Iusti Coniuges from the Time of Cicero to the Time of Ulpian* (Oxford, 1991); on family: T. Wiedemann and J. F. Gardner, *The Roman Household: A Sourcebook* (London, 1991) and T. Wiedemann, *Adults and Children in the Roman Empire* (London, 1989); on kinship and friendship: L. G. Mitchell, *Greeks Bearing Gifts: The Public Use of Private Relationships in the Greek World, 435–323 B. C.* (Cambridge, 1997). The essays in B. Rawson and P. Weaver (eds.), *The Roman Family in Italy. Status, Sentiment, Space* (Oxford, 1997), cover all of these themes: family, childhood, social structure, and kinship.

[141] E. E. Evans-Pritchard, 'Social Anthropology: Past and Present', in Evans-Pritchard, *Essays in Social Anthropology*, 24. Note the strong echo of Meinig, 'The Continuous Shaping of America', 1187, on geography and history which are 'not the study of any particular set of things, but are a particular way of studying anything'.

this may have been due to their emergence as new academic subjects, forced to define themselves against the older university discipline of history. Like the historians of the *Annales* school, or Myres himself, Evans-Pritchard saw a much more profound relationship between history and the social sciences, which not only involved questions of environmental influence on the course of history, but also raised philosophical issues about time and space, and literary issues about how historical, anthropological, ethnographical, or geographical accounts might be written.

But we need to go right back to the start of the twentieth century, even before the appointment of Myres to the Wykeham chair, to find the most thorough and significant treatment of the nature of history and historiography in relation to what have been seen as other types of academic prose. Jacoby's explanation for the organization of his collection of historical fragments set out at length why history, geography, and ethnography, for example, must be viewed as virtually inseparable. His article was not concerned with the relationship between specific historical and geographical issues such as those which Grundy had treated, and Chilver and Cary would go on to develop, to wit the influence of environment on history, or the importance of battle topography. Instead, Jacoby's was, and still is, the most comprehensive discussion of why we should not draw sharp distinctions between the *writing* of history and geography in antiquity, his reason being that these, along with all prose genres, derived from a common source, and were indeed never fully distinguished in the ancient world.

Before setting out Jacoby's important ideas, it seems worth taking a brief glance at what his collection of *Fragmente der griechischen Historiker* was intended to supersede.[142] C. Müller, with the help of his brother, had compiled two collections in the mid-nineteenth century, one of geographical and one of historical fragments. The principles underlying these works were not set out explicitly at any great length. Müller provided

---

[142] A. Grafton, 'Fragmenta Historicorum Graecorum: Fragments of Some Lost Enterprises', in G. W. Most (ed.), *Collecting Fragments* (Göttingen, 1997), 124–43, conveniently sets out the history of the attempt to make such collections.

in his prefaces some discussion of the ordering of fragments, but not a justification for the selection of passages included in each work. He never really explained what was geographical about his *Geographici Graeci Minores*, nor historical about the *Fragmenta Historicorum Graecorum*. However, a summary of his Latin prefaces gives some idea of his approach and purposes.

The first volume of *Geographici Graeci Minores* was published in 1855. Müller started by privileging the Greek over the Latin geographical tradition for its greater breadth, and by acknowledging the influence of Hecataeus. Hecataeus' exposition of the world at the start of the prose tradition incorporated philosophy, history, natural science, and astronomy in its enormous scope, a description which would be repeated by Jacoby. The foundations of the geographical tradition had been laid, and would develop until Ptolemaeus, at which point originality ceased, and only collations of old geographies were produced. Müller lamented the fact that so little had survived intact from so long a tradition. For this reason, it was important to glean as much as possible from fragmentary geographical texts. He then surveyed the history of attempts to produce collections of geographical fragments, most of which were thwarted either by lack of time, loss of interest, or, in the case of Hudson's four volumes of 1698–1712, scarcity, since many copies were lost in a fire at the Sheldonian Theatre.

This was the background against which Müller and Letronne were asked by Didot to produce a new collection. Letronne died shortly after the work had been defined, so Müller carried out the project alone. He set out in the preface to the first volume of *Geographici Graeci Minores* his plan for the extant geographical texts. Strabo, Ptolemaeus, and Stephanus would each require separate treatment, with the anonymous geographical fragments from the grammarians, scholia, and inscriptions included in the volume devoted to Stephanus. The collection of minor geographers was to be organized as follows: periplus texts, periegeses, systematic accounts of the world, and various geographical excerpts would be followed by the geography of the Byzantine empire, including sacred and ecclesiastical geography, and also by the Latin geographers, itineraries, and the Peutinger table. All of this would fill three volumes. A fourth volume of minor Arab geographers was also to be compiled. This plan appears to have been only partially fulfilled. A single volume on Ptolemaeus was published and one on Strabo, although nothing on Stephanus. Three volumes of *Geographici Graeci Minores* also appeared, two of texts and one of maps, although neither the Byzantine and ecclesiastical geography, nor the Latin texts were incorporated.

Müller's organization of fragments within each volume was to be chronological. Any fragment of uncertain date would be juxtaposed with a fragment of similar nature. So, for example, the anonymous periplus of the Euxine was placed after Arrian's periplus of the same sea. Müller's collection was useful as a reference work, but crudely conceived. His view of geographical texts was clearly limited to a very particular type of work which mapped out space, and theoretically allowed no room for the type of human geography which overlaps with the ethnographic, and edges towards the historical.

Müller's *Fragmenta Historicorum Graecorum* were similarly arranged according to a principle, but one of questionable value.[143] The first volume contained an apparently random selection of fragmentary authors. The idea was that the volume should be so shaped as to rise and fall with the quality of the tradition.[144] However, the second volume of Müller's *Fragmenta* was prefaced with a programme setting out a new, and much more comprehensive, collection of historical fragments. Müller would arrange the authors into eight *saecula* in chronological order, from the beginning to the age of Constantine; these would be followed by a book of fragments from authors whose dates were uncertain. The outline of the books was as follows: Book 1 from the start of historiography to the end of the Peloponnesian war (520 BC–404 BC); Book 2 from the end of the Peloponnesian war to the time of Alexander the Great; Book 3 Aristotle and his successors; Book 4 from Alexander to the death of Ptolemy Philadelphus (336 BC–247 BC); Book 5 from Ptolemy III Euergetes to the death of Ptolemy Philo-

---

[143] C. Müller (ed.), *Fragmenta Historicorum Graecorum* (Paris, 1853).

[144] The authors included were Hecataeus, Charon, Xanthus, Hellanicus, Pherecydes, Acusilaos, Antiochus, Philistus, Timaeus, Ephorus, Theopompus, Phylarchus, Clitodemus, Phanodemus, Androtion, Demon, Philochorus, and Istrus.

metor or the sack of Corinth (247 BC–146 BC); Book 6 from the sack of Corinth to the time of Augustus (146 BC–27 BC); Book 7 from Augustus to Trajan (27 BC–AD 98); Book 8 from Trajan to Constantine (AD 98–306). The expected end was passed, however, with a Book 9 dealing with the period from Constantine to Phocas, and it was actually Book 10 which contained the undated authors in alphabetical order. In spite of what Jacoby would see as the sketchy coverage and the apparently arbitrary arrangement, in addition to the absence from the main corpus of those authors who had been arbitrarily selected for volume I, there were clearly merits in having a collection which provided a view of the historical literature of a particular period.

These collections of geographers and historians were, however, to be superseded by the work of Jacoby. His replacement project has never yet been completed, but his explicit justification for its scope and organization was set out in 1909, and revealed a quite revolutionary notion of the nature of Greek historiography.[145] Jacoby examined various possible methods for arranging a collection of historical fragments: alphabetical ordering was rejected as coarse, and unrevealing about the relationship between authors or traditions; chronological order was rejected since it too ignored the question of genre and contents, and would be useless for the many undatable works (as Müller had found); spatial organization seemed to Jacoby more promising. He postulated a collection which began with works dealing with the whole world, followed by *Hellenica*, histories of individual non-Greek peoples, and specialized city-histories, but found it unacceptable that the *Descriptions of the Earth* (Περίοδοι γῆς) would be followed by late excerptive histories, such as that of Diodorus. With all of these alternatives rejected, an arrangement according to the development of historiography in terms of literary genres was the method favoured by Jacoby.

He then justified this scheme. Jacoby argued that all prose genres were originally indistinguishable, and only gradually

---

[145] F. Jacoby, 'Über die Entwicklung der griechischen Historiographie und den Plan einer neuen Sammlung der griechischen Historikerfragmente', *Klio*, 9 (1909), 80–123.

evolved into different styles.[146] For Jacoby, Hecataeus and Herodotus together laid the foundations for Greek prose writing. I return to Herodotus in the next section, but first discuss Hecataeus of Miletus. Hecataeus gave the earliest glimpse of the Greek prose tradition, and Jacoby argued that in his *Genealogies* (Γενεαλογίαι) and *Description of the Earth* (Περίοδος γῆς) could be traced the origins of the major prose genres: genealogy, ethnography, and the history of Greek peoples.[147] There are certainly indications in the extant fragments to support this picture of diversity of interests in these works. Mythological accounts of the three children of Deucalion (F 13–16), of Hercules and the Heracleidae (F 23–30); ethnographical details, such as the eating habits of the Paeonians (F 154); attempts to map out the peoples of Asia (in F 204 the Mossynoeci are said to share a border with the Tibareni); the detail that the Gulf of Psyllus in Libya was three days' voyage around (F 332)—all foreshadow the interests of later prose authors.[148]

But Hecataeus must be treated with care. It seems at first clear-cut that the existence of two separate works, the Περίοδος γῆς and Ἱστορίαι or Γενεαλογίαι, indicates a pre-Herodotean distinction between the geographical and historical traditions

---

[146] O. Murray, 'History', in J. Brunschwig and G. Lloyd (eds.), *Le Savoir grec* (Paris, 1996), clearly sets out Jacoby's argument, and summarizes the heart of the matter as being that 'the origins of Greek history lie in the undifferentiated sphere of early Greek prose writing which was as much about myth, about the geography of the world and the customs of other peoples, as about the unfolding of events' (this and subsequent quotations from Murray, 'History' are taken from a print-out of the version of his chapter which is to appear in the English edn. of Brunschwig and Lloyd).

[147] The question of whether the field of ethnography can be traced further back to the Homeric epics, and even beyond them to early periegetic accounts, is a vexed one. E. Norden, *Germanische Urgeschichte in Tacitus* Germania (Leipzig, 1922), argues for a strong correlation between Homer and the later tradition; O. Murray, 'Omero e l'etnografia', *Κώκαλος: Studi pubblicati dall'Istituto di Storia Antica dell'Università di Palermo* (1988–9), 1–13, argues for greater differentiation between the ethnography of the *Odyssey*, for example, in which any people who cannot be framed in Greek terms are consigned to the realm of the fabulous, and the much more sophisticated view of 'the other' found in Herodotus.

[148] All fragment numbers given for Hecataeus are those used by Jacoby in *FGrH*.

which would be fused by Herodotus himself, qualifying the idea of an undifferentiated early prose style. However, it is not always clear from the sources which work of Hecataeus a particular fragment may have come from, and it appears that many of the fragments could belong equally well to either work. It is not obvious that the fragment (F 18) on the voyage of the Argonauts should belong to the Γενεαλογίαι rather than to the Περίοδος; by contrast, the passage on the ousting of the Pelasgians from Attica by the Athenians (F 127) could have come from the Γενεαλογίαι just as well as from the Περίοδος; in yet another fragment (F 119), it is only the detail that Greece was seen as a settlement of barbarians that is attributed by Strabo to Hecataeus, but the following discussion concerning the various migrations of the Pelopides and Danaids suggests that the initial comment could well have been stimulated not by the Περίοδος, to which the fragment is commonly assigned, but by a passage from the Γενεαλογίαι, which seems to have dealt with exactly such ethnic histories;[149] and it is hard to understand why Hecataeus' attempt (F 300) to trace his own genealogy with the help of the priests at Thebes in Egypt should have been attached to the Περίοδος rather than to the work specifically devoted to genealogy.

The fragments assigned by the sources to either of these works are extremely similar in nature, often a mere note to the effect that Hecataeus mentioned a particular place, city, or people. The fact that this interest in place is true of fragments said to be from the Γενεαλογίαι as well as those from the Περίοδος indicates that it is a function of the major source for Hecataeus, namely Stephanus of Byzantium, rather than any accurate guide as to the nature of either work. Stephanus' compilatory style confuses the issue both ways round. While fragments said by him to come from the Γενεαλογίαι seem remarkably geographical, many of those apparently taken from the Περίοδος might seem more at home in the other work. A note on Mytilene (F 140), for example, indicates that Hecataeus mentioned the place in his account of Europe, that is, in the Περίοδος, but the following details on the etymology of the place-name, in which it is derived from

[149] T 3 = Strabo 14. 1. 7 indicates that Strabo was certainly aware of Hecataeus' Ἱστορίαι in addition to the more obviously geographical work.

Mytilene, the daughter of Makar or Pelops, take us back to matters genealogical.

The picture gained from the fragments is thus one in which those securely assigned to one work or another do not allow us to characterize either accurately, and those not assigned in the sources often seem to have been rather randomly allocated in modern collections. It seems likely that Hecataeus was in both works engaged in ἱστορία in its broad sense, and we should not be surprised to find accounts of Herodotus' debt to Hecataeus—one of the testimonia (T 18) refers to Hecataeus 'by whom Herodotus was greatly helped' (παρ'οὖ δὴ μάλιστα ὠφέλη-ται ὁ Ἡρόδοτος). We have too little on which to base any judgement of the quality and sophistication of Hecataeus' works, and it is likely in any case that Herodotus developed the prose tradition, but that the ground seems to have been cleared for him by his predecessor. In Jacoby's view, the scope of Hecataeus' two works covered genealogy, ethnography, and the history of Greek peoples, just as Herodotus' all-encompassing *History* would do. The fact that Hecataeus' material was divided between two separate works perhaps foreshadows the later evolution of interrelated genres, but, as I have argued, the division was certainly not clear-cut.

Müller had acknowledged the difficulty involved in distinguishing 'whether authors have dealt with the affairs of city-states in the manner of historians or that of periegetes, or whether they have carried out the task jointly'.[150] His stated solution was to err on the side of inclusivity. However, his separation of geographers and historians revealed a deep-seated belief that the two groups could and should be viewed as distinct fields of study. By contrast, Jacoby's integrated view of historiography as being inseparably bound up with geographical, ethnographical, and mythological accounts of the world meant that his *Fragmente der griechischen Historiker* would naturally incorporate material deemed by other editors to belong to 'non-historical' genres. The second-century BC works of Agatharchides of Cnidus neatly illustrate the difference in approach. *On the Erythraean Sea* was part of Müller's

---

[150] Müller, *Fragmenta Historicorum Graecorum* II, ii: *num historicorum an periegetarum more auctores res civitatum tractaverint, an utrumque munus coniunctim praestiterint.*

geographical collection; *Affairs in Europe* and *Affairs in Asia*, being 'historical', fell within the collection of historical fragments.[151] However, all three works would fall within the scope of Jacoby's collection of Greek historians. Jacoby's approach was certainly not undiscerning. The work on the Arabian Gulf would appear in a different volume from the other two; but the principle was that all were interrelated and fell under the umbrella of Greek historiography.

Another second-century author, pseudo-Scymnus of Chios, who wrote a periplus in iambic verses for Nicomedes II of Bithynia, lends further support to the abandonment of Müller's segregation of geographical from historical fragments. Müller had predictably included this periplus in his *Geographici Graeci Minores*. Indeed, most of what survives would support this characterization. But much is missing, and the author himself complicates the generic classification of his work at the end of the introduction:

Now I progress to the start of my work, setting out the writers on whom I have drawn so as to imbue my historical work (ὁ ἱστορικὸς . . . λόγος) with authority. For I have put most trust in the one who wrote geography (ἡ γεωγραφία) with the greatest care, with climatic zones and geometrical figures, Eratosthenes; and I have also used Ephorus, who has spoken in five books about foundations; and Dionysius of Chalcis; and the historian (συγγραφεύς) Demetrius of Callatis; and Cleon of Sicily; and Timosthenes . . . and Timaeus of Tauromenium in Sicily.[152]

Whatever the outward appearance of the text, the narrow confines of Müller's divisions hardly seem appropriate for an account that claims such a broad scope. Here geography, the mythology of foundations, the history of Greek peoples, and the ethnography of others will be combined. Although this text is in verse, it conforms beautifully to Jacoby's model of Greek prose writing. The only point on which this author and Jacoby might disagree is the process which led to this interdisciplinary medley. For Jacoby, the different genres were always interrelated; for Scymnus, part of the author's

---

[151] Both works came within the scope of Book 6 in vol. III of the collection.
[152] *GGM I*, Scymnus ll. 109–26. It is of course possible that Scymnus' reference to his use of a whole panoply of sources is intended to be humorous.

task lay in gathering the threads together and weaving them into a coherent and unified account: 'From several scattered histories, I have written in summary for you of the colonies and city-foundations.'[153]

Jacoby's thesis of the gradual evolution of different genres, which would never be truly distinct, has, of course, not gone unchallenged. There are, for example, clear problems with Hecataeus' two works, rather than one all-encompassing account, making it hard to argue for the development of genres from one single undifferentiated origin. Furthermore, Fowler has opposed Jacoby's stress on Herodotus at the expense of other writers of the period. Determining a history of historiography in terms of individual influential authors runs the risk of overlooking the intellectual context within which Herodotus, for example, operated.[154] In addition, the writing of 'contemporary' history, which Jacoby saw as a fourth-century development from the work of Thucydides, had no major precedent in Hecataeus or Herodotus; nor did 'horography', the study of individual Greek cities. Fornara argued against the idea of interconnected genres, and identified five historical genres of genealogy, ethnography, history or accounts of man's deeds, horography, and chronography which had 'come into existence by the end of the fifth century BC and generally retained their formal integrity thereafter'.[155] Fornara further contested Jacoby's historical categories. He objected to Jacoby's replacement of 'history' with 'contemporary history', on the grounds that all the genres mentioned could be termed 'history'. So Fornara argued for a category of historical writing in antiquity which might correspond to a modern definition of history, namely 'the description of res gestae, man's place in politics, diplomacy and war, in the near and far past'.[156]

Furthermore, he stressed the digressive rather than integral nature of ethnography in historical works, such as the Histories of Herodotus. Fornara's assessment of 'historical' works which

---

[153] GGM I, Scymnus ll. 65–7: ἐκ τῶν σποράδην γὰρ ἱστορουμένων τισίν | ἐν ἐπιτομῇ σοι γέγραφα τὰς ἀποικίας | κτίσεις τε πόλεων . . .

[154] See R. L. Fowler, 'Herodotus and his Contemporaries', JHS 116 (1996), 62–87.

[155] Fornara, The Nature of History in Ancient Greece and Rome, 2.

[156] Ibid. 3.

contain ethnographic digressions, namely that 'the writer was
guided by the conventions of ethnography (as if he were, in
fact, an ethnographer); once finished with the ethnographical
digression, he resumes his allegiance to the rules of history',
seems to require an excessively disjointed reading of the
texts.[157] But the question of ethnography as digressive is
important, since the answer will have a bearing on our view
of the limits of historiography. Fornara's attempt to differenti-
ate more clearly between his five historical genres does offer a
useful corrective to the undifferentiated view of Greek prose
writing, which had been put forward by Jacoby and which did
not fully account for why an author such as Strabo might have
chosen to write both a 'historical' and a 'geographical' work.

Besides these objections to Jacoby's main thesis, more
specific attacks have been made on his methods. Schepens
has noted some of the practical difficulties facing those who
attempt to complete Jacoby's project; in particular, the issue of
how to define a fragment.[158] Bowersock has identified the
further problem that Jacoby's fragments are read in isolation
from the context in which they were preserved.[159] However, in
spite of such criticisms, Jacoby's view has been highly influential, accounts for many features of the Greek historiography
which is extant, and provides a justification for why it makes
sense to re-examine the way in which we read, for instance,
historical and geographical texts from antiquity. It is not only
that modern theories of the relation between the academic
subjects and the inseparability of time and space suggest
interesting questions that may be applied to ancient texts; it
is not even that certain ancient historians have seen the
importance of the physical world in the understanding of
past events; but Jacoby set out a third reason why ancient
historiography should be studied in conjunction with ancient
geography, and other genres, namely that they were originally
conceived of as indistinct, or at least problematic to distinguish, in literary terms.

[157] Ibid. 15.
[158] See G. Schepens, 'Jacoby's *FGrHist*: Problems, Methods, Prospects', in
Most (ed.), *Collecting Fragments*, 144–72.
[159] See G. W. Bowersock, 'Jacoby's Fragments and Two Greek Historians
of Pre-Islamic Arabia', in Most (ed.), *Collecting Fragments*, 173–85.

THE DEBT TO HERODOTUS; THE
CONSEQUENCES OF CONQUEST

In Jacoby's view, the first true historian was Herodotus, who had combined the ethnographic interests of Hecataeus with the narrative of a war between East and West, although, as I have argued, this picture may depend on an oversimplified vision of Hecataeus. Herodotus' form of history was, as Murray has argued, 'not bound by concepts of political narrative, but attempted to view societies as a whole, through the interrelationship of religious, social and geographical factors', a description which would closely fit the ideal of interdisciplinary, comprehensive *histoire humaine* aspired to by the *Annales* historians.[160] It is, however, Thucydides who has traditionally been seen as the founder of the dominant strand of ancient historiography. Because this view has been extremely influential in determining the interpretation of Hellenistic historiography, I shall set out briefly some of the discussions which have focused on the nature of Herodotean and Thucydidean history, with the initial caveat that no polarity between the two authors as representatives of opposing styles will accommodate the evidence. Whether a work is 'Herodotean' or 'Thucydidean' must be a matter more of emphasis than of mutual exclusivity.

Jacoby saw Thucydides, not Herodotus, as the predecessor of the many *Hellenica* which provided a view of Greek history, either contemporary or with an earlier start-point, which was Panhellenic rather than local, and always conceived from a Greek perspective, possibly under the influence of the Persian Wars. But the important point for Jacoby was that the development of Thucydidean contemporary Greek history was not

---

[160] Murray, 'History'. On the nature and generic affiliations of Herodotus' *Histories*, see E. Lanzillotta, 'Geografia e storia da Ecateo a Tucidide', *CISA* 14 (1988), 19–31, who views Herodotus' work as a balance between geography, ethnography, and history, with no single approach dominant (p. 25). For a different idea of how geography and history fit together in Herodotus' account, see Prontera, 'Prima di Strabone', who argues that the two do not run parallel to each other, but that geographical information dominates the descriptions of the non-Greek world, and history the treatment of the Greek world. Thus, for Prontera 'Greek geography is primarily a geography of the other' ('la geografia greca è anzitutto una *geografia degli altri*') (p. 194).

simply to provide a successor to Hecataeus' Γενεαλογίαι, but to complement the ethnographic history that underpinned Herodotus' work. Thucydides would provide the model for works of unified scope and limited theme, such as the accounts of Alexander, those of his successors, and the monographs on the rise of Rome. But the fact that his history was to turn into an 'ongoing history' or *historia perpetua*, made it in a sense universal. In the Hellenistic period it seems that the universality of Herodotean history and that of Thucydidean *historia perpetua* might on occasion be blurred, bringing us back round to the earliest undifferentiated historiographical model.

Strasburger has examined how the two traditions of Herodotean and Thucydidean historiography were at the same time distinct and yet often combined in the Hellenistic period. He traced the simultaneous development of 'the restrictive impulse of the Thucydidean model alongside the integrating impulse of the Herodotean model', and specifically characterized the comprehensive and synthetic Herodotean model as static, and the Thucydidean model as kinetic or dynamic.[161] Strasburger's analysis supported the generally held view that Hellenistic historiography tended to follow Thucydides' model for dynamic history. He was, however, also keen to stress the continued importance of Herodotus in historiography. He argued firstly for a broad conception of Hellenistic historiography which would encompass, for example, Agatharchides' *On the Erythraean Sea*. In accord with Jacoby's principles and in contradiction to the practice of Müller, Strasburger saw the work as having been misplaced among the *Geographici Graeci Minores* because of its title and outward appearance. In Agatharchides, Strasburger saw the combination of static Herodotean ethnography, a Thucydidean interest in historical dynamics, and a Hellenistic concern for social issues.

If Herodotus was so important in influencing the type of late

[161] H. Strasburger, *Die Wesensbestimmung der Geschichte durch die antike Geschichtsschreibung* 2 (Wiesbaden, 1966), 57–8. Strasburger pointed to Thucydides' claim that 'this [sc. the Peloponnesian war] was the greatest upheaval' (ἡ κίνησις γὰρ αὕτη μεγίστη) (1. 1), and cited the description of the plague, *stasis* in Corcyra, the Sicilian expedition, the events concerning Mytilene, Plataea, and Melos as further confirmation of this characterization, and evidence that Thucydides was primarily interested in social change.

Hellenistic historiography which I shall examine, it may seem paradoxical not to include a chapter on Herodotus himself. Much Hellenistic historiography was deeply indebted to the Herodotean model, in so far as it was an *histoire humaine*, in which mythology, ethnography, geography, and economics would be just as important as history in the sense of political narrative. Murray has summed up the situation very effectively in his explanation of why he believes Jacoby's view of history to be right: 'it is impossible to consider Greek historiography as an entity, unless ethnography, mythography, local history, geography, etc., are included; and the reason is that the tradition of Ionian historiography which was taken over by the Hellenistic world did not recognize such distinctions as absolute.'[162] What I shall be arguing throughout is that a renewed awareness of this element in Hellenistic histori-ography casts new light on well-known authors, and helps us to contextualize and evaluate more accurately those authors whose work has survived only in fragments.

Jacoby's project at the start of this century was extremely important in so far as he tackled at a literary level the issues that were being addressed more concretely by scholars such as Grundy. I shall explore the relationship between geography and history in the writings from the late Hellenistic period from the philosophical perspective adopted by modern geo-graphers who discuss the issues in terms of time and space, in terms of the more tangible influences of geography and history on each other, discussed by scholars such as Grundy and Chilver, and from the point of view taken by Jacoby, namely an interest in the literary questions of genre and tradition.

Jacoby's treatment of the Herodotean influence may be convincing in literary terms, but we need to return to the real world for the full implications to be understood. The link between the conceptual world and historical reality is not only crucial in explaining why the expansive Herodotean model for historiography would continue to be relevant and influential through the Hellenistic period, but it also paradoxically jus-tifies the omission of Herodotus from the main body of this book.

[162] O. Murray reviewing Strasburger, *Die Wesensbestimmung der Geschichte*, in *Classical Review*, NS 18 (1968), 218–21, at 220–1.

The point was made succinctly by Murray in his review of Strasburger's book. He states, in complaint at what he sees as the overestimation of Thucydides' influence even by Strasburger, that 'the most important single influence on Hellenistic historiography was not Thucydides, but Herodotus; it was he who enabled the prose writers of the Hellenistic period to face and overcome the problems created by Alexander's conquests.'[163] The vital factor is that of conquest, to which both real and conceptual geography and history are intimately bound. Conquest leads not only to the physical alteration of the political world and to the real historical changes entailed, but also to new ways of looking at the world, and consequently to new ways of writing about it. Herodotus' *Histories* were so important because they provided not only a model for an all-encompassing *histoire humaine*, but specifically one for how to rewrite the world once horizons had changed.

As Murray has argued, periods of conquest result in 'a re-evaluation of the external world, both that which was already known and that which was previously unknown'.[164] The phenomenon can be illustrated from various historical periods: the works of geography, ethnography, and history which followed the great Arab expansion in the ninth to eleventh centuries; the accounts by European discoverers of the New World in the sixteenth century; the writings following in the wake of Alexander's conquests; the responses to Rome's expansion in the late Hellenistic period; and Herodotus himself. Murray argued that Herodotus was widely read in the Hellenistic period, and was certainly no less well known than Thucydides. He examined the writings of prose authors in the early Hellenistic period, 'who interpreted for the new rulers of the world the alien cultures which now belonged to them',[165] and showed that writers such as Nearchus, Hecataeus of Abdera, Megasthenes, Berosus, and Manetho were working in the Herodotean tradition, even when trying to correct or improve it.

Scholars studying the conquests of the sixteenth century

[163] Ibid. 220.
[164] O. Murray, 'Herodotus and Hellenistic Culture', *CQ* NS 22 (1972), 200–13, at 200.
[165] Ibid. 204.

have similarly remarked upon the consequent broadening of
horizons and the rewriting of the world. Elliott has examined
the impact of the discovery of America not just on the
inhabitants, but on the Europeans whose world would need
to be reconceptualized. I can find no more striking expression
of the way in which the entire world-view of the Europeans was
forced to change than the passage from Pedro Nunes' *Treatise
of the Sphere* (1537) cited in translation by Elliott: 'New
islands, new lands, new seas, new peoples; and, what is more,
a new sky and new stars'.[166]

It is interesting that periods following conquest and discovery seem to have been particularly rich in works of history
in the all-encompassing style of *histoire humaine*. Las Casas'
Apologética Historia of the 1550s has been described by Elliott
as 'a great essay in cultural anthropology in which the social
and religious habits of the Greeks, Romans, and Egyptians,
ancient Gauls and ancient Britons, are examined alongside
those of the Aztecs and the Incas'.[167] This would hardly be
out of place among the works of the *Annales* school. Murray
points to the work of the Arab writer al-Mas'udi, 'traveller,
geographer, historian, who believed that geography was a part
of history, and wrote his geographical account as an introduction to and integral part of his history'.[168] One could hardly
argue that these periods were not ones of great change, times of
upheaval perhaps more suited to the Thucydidean model of
kinetic history. But the writings under discussion were concerned not so much with describing the upheaval as setting up
a new world order in its wake, and so were perfectly fitted to
the synthetic history of cultures and civilizations. This was
clearly true not only of the Arab and Renaissance writers, but
also of authors describing the new world after Alexander and
those, who will be the focus of this book, who rewrote the
world of the Romans.

A perfect example emerges from the world of fiction: the
children's conversation on arriving at the new world of Narnia
(see pp. 18–19 above) illustrates the re-evaluation necessitated
by the expansion of one's horizons. They must both reassess

---

[166] See J. H. Elliott, *The Old World and the New* (Cambridge, 1970), 39–40.
[167] Ibid. 48.
[168] Murray, 'Herodotus and Hellenistic Culture', 201.

the world they knew and incorporate the one which they have discovered. We can foresee that the appropriate account to give of the new world of Narnia will be one that combines the inhabitants, their histories, their habits, and habitat, in other words a Herodotean synthesis, neither historical, geographical, nor ethnographical, but all of these things at once.

The Herodotean influence on accounts of the New World of America has been openly acknowledged as having instituted certain key discursive principles, such as the importance of travel for an understanding of the world.[169] But Greenblatt's comment that 'Herodotus is at once a decisive shaping force and a very marginal figure in our inquiry' concisely expresses the ambiguity of his importance for the sixteenth-century attempt to represent new horizons.[170] A similar point could be argued for the reconfigurations of the world which took place in both the early and the late Hellenistic periods, although seeing Herodotus as being 'very marginal' here would be a little strong. The Herodotean style of historiography was the natural response to conquest, and Herodotus provided an example of how to see a world that had been recently expanded; so Herodotus would continue to be a crucial model. But each phase of conquest and each subsequent reevaluation of the world would be different. The expansionist ambitions of Persia, Alexander, Rome, Islam, and sixteenth-century Europe would all yield a distinctively different rewriting of the world. Within each phase, there would of course be variation. Greenblatt has argued: 'I am not identifying an overarching Renaissance ideology, a single way of making and remaking the world . . . But the variety is not infinite, and in the face of the New World . . . the differing responses disclose shared assumptions and techniques'.[171] We shall see

---

[169] The importance of conceptual frameworks within which to set discoveries has been discussed by A. Pagden, *European Encounters with the New World: From Renaissance to Romanticism* (New Haven, 1993). He argues that the Europeans who discovered America needed a pre-existing model into which to fit their new discoveries (p. 10). Anything which could not be accommodated by the conceptual grid was relegated to the realm of the marvellous.

[170] Greenblatt, *Marvelous Possessions*, 122–3.

[171] Ibid. 23.

that the rise of Rome in the late Hellenistic period evoked
varying responses among different authors. But, just as it made
sense for Murray to consider as a whole the writings produced
in the wake of Alexander, and just as the accounts of the New
World of America have been treated together, so too does it
make sense to look at late Hellenistic responses to Rome as a
coherent, though of course not uniform, group.

I finished my survey of some approaches which may usefully
be taken from the discussions of modern geographers with the
issue of fragmentation and universalism. It is clear that the
notion of universal historiography may be considered not only
in terms of discrete and continuous time and space, but also in
the context of all-encompassing, comprehensive *histoire
humaine*, as developed by the *Annales* school, but already
evidenced in Herodotus' *Histories*. The phase of rewriting on
which this book will focus is particularly suited to the question
of universalism in its many senses, since it concerned the
period when, for the first time, almost the entire known
world was brought by conquest under the rule of a single
power—that of Rome.

I have argued that the tradition which has neatly defined
geography and history in terms of time and space does not take
full account of our experience of the world in which time and
space are inseparable, and also sweeps aside the variety of
different types of time and space. Modern geographical debates
on the unsatisfactory nature of subject distinctions in terms of
time and space, on the grounds of past or present focus, and in
terms of the difference in the relationship of the author to the
text, can suggest helpful questions, and can in turn be enriched
by answers given by the ancient evidence. Another, and
complementary, way forward is to take up the interests of
certain historians from the start of the twentieth century, set
out in terms of ancient literary genre by Jacoby, and developed
by the *Annales* historians as *histoire humaine*, a comprehensive
history in the Herodotean manner, which is constantly in
danger of being overlooked in favour of the Thucydidean
type. It will not be possible to say that geography and history
were inseparable in the late Hellenistic period, subsumed in a
single undifferentiated prose genre, the perfect and all-encom-

passing response to the new world of Roman power. Strabo's two works, one geographical and one historical, cannot be accommodated by such a picture. However, I propose at least to explore some of the parameters within which late Hellenistic prose accounts were written, and to show that narrow definitions of history and geography are unsuited to these writings.

One reason for choosing to investigate these issues through a study of Polybius, Posidonius, and primarily Strabo is that they were all engaged in writing about the world in ways which highlight the problems of time and space, having taken on projects that covered a large scope both temporally and spatially. In addition, they all wrote during the protracted period through which a single power, Rome, was gradually transforming the world—changing space through time, and necessitating a re-evaluation of the world, in a way which lent itself to comprehensive historiography. Adapting Greenblatt's words, I am not identifying an overarching late Hellenistic ideology, a single way of making and remaking the world. As will become apparent, it is not possible to apply exactly the same approaches and questions to all three authors. In particular, the fragmentary nature of Posidonius' texts imposes severe restrictions on the possibility of making positive assertions about the works, rather than simply challenging previous approaches. And, of course, the three authors whose works I shall study wrote over the span of nearly two centuries. The world of Polybius was not identical to that of Strabo.

My main task in dealing with each author will be different. Polybius has most often been seen as the true successor to Thucydides, even by those who are strong proponents of the influence of Herodotus in this period. Murray stated that 'Thucydides certainly provided the model for the main tradition of western historiography, with its interests in political and military history, factual accuracy and causation. Polybius is his worthy successor in these respects.'[172] Murray's picture of Polybius, in whom, as he notes, there is no reference at all to Herodotus, sets this author outside the dominant model of Hellenistic historiography, namely the Herodotean one. 'For Polybius was a political historian, in

---

[172] Murray, 'History'.

the tradition of Thucydides: he is not particularly interested in other types of history, though he could of course achieve remarkable standards of cultural history with his description of the Roman constitution or his geographical sections.'[173] This view was formulated in opposition to those who would characterize Hellenistic historiography as predominantly political and military, in the Thucydidean mould. The point was that, even though Polybius may have been Thucydidean, he was not necessarily representative of the majority of Hellenistic historians, and that other authors were at this time writing broad cultural histories.

It is clear that Polybius fits well into a dynamic model of historiography, as I shall argue in chapter II, and that in this sense, as well as many others, he could be seen as a worthy successor to Thucydides. However, my discussion of Polybius will have a different emphasis. I shall argue not that Polybius was Thucydidean and so outside the mainstream of Hellenistic historiography; but rather that the geographical, ethnographical, cultural, Herodotean aspects of Polybius' *Histories* have been underplayed, that modern geographical debates on the complex relationship between time and space and the location of the author are highly relevant to his work, that sophisticated geographical concepts were central to his theme of Roman expansionism, and that therefore Polybius could and should be given his proper place in the history of mainstream Hellenistic cultural historiography.

Posidonius clearly poses quite different problems. But here again, the major difficulties arise from an assumption that 'historical' works must necessarily be in the Thucydidean narrative mould, and that discursive prose, in which geography, history, ethnography, mythology all contribute towards the creation of an *histoire humaine*, is somehow alien to the Hellenistic historiographical tradition. Strasburger saw the *Histories* of Posidonius as consciously drawing together the broad scope of Herodotus with the sharpness of the Thucydidean treatment of causal relations.[174] While taking a much more cautious line than some commentators on what we can

---

[173] Murray, 'Herodotus and Hellenistic Culture', 211.
[174] Strasburger, *Die Wesensbestimmung der Geschichte*, 93.

say positively about the nature of works of which so little has survived, I too shall argue for a more broadly based characterization of Posidonius' *Histories*, and suggest that the generic differences between them and the 'geographical' work, *On Ocean*, may be slighter than has often been assumed.

Strabo's *Geography* is one of several extensive texts which have survived from antiquity largely intact, but which have since received minimal attention, particularly in English. However, it provides an excellent *exemplum* for many of the points which I have discussed in this introductory chapter. As a work of geography written by the author of a separate history, it leads to the expectation that it will conform to the crude notion of geography as the static spatial description of a physical landscape, while the history fulfilled the Thucydidean model of kinetic, chronologically ordered, political narrative. It is impossible to say what Strabo's *History* was like, but I shall be exploring his *Geography* in some detail in order to formulate a more sophisticated view of that particular project. This broad work of ethnography, mythology, religion, economy, past events, and the evolution of settlements perfectly illustrates the importance of the synthetic cultural history in the late Hellenistic period. The debt to Herodotus is made explicit on only a few occasions in Strabo's work; but the suitability of this style of historiography in the re-evaluation of the world under Roman rule is clear.

It is revealing to consider a 'historian', an author whose geographical and historical works survive in part, and a 'geographer' in the light of these debates, precisely because they all so obviously defy neat definitions. The rewriting of the world in the face of Roman imperialism led to the creation of works which would cover a vast temporal and spatial scope in an integrated way, making generic distinctions inappropriate. A further complication is that, although the Herodotean model clearly has much to offer in illuminating these works, and although the ethnography of Herodotus had advanced and evolved greatly from that of Homer, nevertheless Strabo, repeatedly and explicitly, and Polybius, less insistently but still clearly, set Homer at the head of the tradition, as the key precedent for what they were doing.[175] Not only the political situation of the time of writing, but also the complexities of the literary tradition are relevant to our understanding of late Hellenistic historiography.

In a recent book on the culture, geography, history, mythology, and people of Yemen, Mackintosh-Smith set out a figurative methodology which strongly evokes the intricately intertwined prose styles of genealogy, ethnography, and the history of Greek peoples, seen by Jacoby as the foundations of Greek historiography.

Early Yemeni historians, though, produced their own interpretation using genealogy . . . In the process, the names of people and places have become inextricably intertwined: the family tree has grown luxuriantly, fed by the genealogists on a rich mulch of eponyms and toponyms. To get to know Yemen as the Yemenis see it means clambering around this tree, one which spreads vertically through time and horizontally through space. History and geography, people and land, are inseparable.[176]

It is the tree of the late Hellenistic world, created in response to Rome, around which I now propose to clamber.

---

[175] It must surely be significant that Hecataeus himself was described in Agathemerus' *Sketch of Geography* as an Odyssean 'man of many wanderings' (ἀνὴρ πολυπλανής) (T 12a).

[176] T. Mackintosh-Smith, *Yemen: Travels in Dictionary Land* (London, 1997), 8–9.

II

Polybius and the 'Geographical' *History*

INTRODUCTION

Polybius' *History*, composed explicitly in order to explain the rise of Rome over almost the entire known world, is an obvious example of a work written in response to conquest. It also provides a good starting-point for the discussions of Posidonius and Strabo which will follow. Not only does Strabo list Polybius as one of the major influences at the start of his *Geography* and devote a section of his treatment of the geographical tradition to Polybius' contribution (1. 1. 1);[1] not only did both Strabo and Posidonius write historical works which were described as continuations of Polybius' *History*, and called *Events after Polybius* (τὰ μετὰ Πολύβιον);[2] but, most importantly, we can see in Polybius a crucial predecessor in the attempt to encompass the new world of Rome in a unified and coherent account. In this chapter I argue in particular against the view that Polybius relegated all geographical information to a digressive thirty-fourth book in his attempt to write a political narrative. I shall show that geography of different types was integral to the work, in terms both of its conception, and of its execution, in Polybius' construction of the new world-view.

Polybius' *History* is relatively well known, but since my approach is historiographical rather than purely historical, as I attempt to set Polybius against some of the important intellectuals of the Hellenistic period, it is worth giving the briefest outline of the scope of Polybius' work and of his own background. Polybius was born around the end of the third century BC in Megalopolis into a family deeply involved in politics. His father, Lycortas, was a follower of Philopoimen;

---

[1] See also 8. 1. 1. At 2. 4. 1–8 Strabo discusses Polybius' geography.
[2] *FGrH* 91 T 2 for Strabo; *FGrH* 87 T 1 for Posidonius.

and, following the death of Perseus, Polybius himself was summoned along with other prominent Achaeans to Rome. The ensuing period of internment led to Polybius' close friendship with Scipio Aemilianus, and involvement in Scipionic circles. The connection was crucial in the complexity it gave to Polybius' world-view. Not only was his Greek perspective given a new angle through Roman affiliations, but it seems likely that it was with Scipio that Polybius visited, for example, Spain, Africa, Gaul, and the Alps.

Polybius is, of course, known to us as a historian, but it is worth recalling the fact that Geminus attributed to him a further work entitled 'On the inhabiting of the equatorial region' (Περὶ τῆς περὶ τὸν ἰσημερινὸν οἰκήσεως) (Polybius 34. 1. 7). Just as we tend to think that Strabo could write only 'geography' and look for that alone in his *Geography*, partly because we forget that he was also a historian, so too with Polybius is it too easy to ignore all but his writing of 'history', and so to overlook the possibility that his other interests, such as geography, are unlikely to have been entirely confined to separate works. I shall be arguing in this chapter for a reading of the *History* which is alert to 'geographical' aspects.

It remains to outline the scope of the work. The main narrative runs from the 140th Olympiad (220–216 BC) to the fall of Carthage and Corinth in 146 BC, although the original plan had been to end the work with the year 168 BC. It was thus a contemporary history, and was devoted to describing to the Greeks not only the rise of Roman domination over most of the known world, but also, with the scope of the work extended, the way in which this Roman power was subsequently exercised. The huge spatial scope immediately indicates that geography must be an important factor in this work, and it is, as I shall argue, significant that this was a period of Roman expansion, resulting in a very different kind of spatial conception from that of Strabo's *Geography*, which describes a relatively stable world. From the start the aim was to analyse the gradual and dynamic interweaving of different areas. In the words of Dubois: 'Il [sc. Polybius] est le fondateur d'un genre historique fort voisin de la géographie.'[3]

---

[3] M. Dubois, 'Strabon et Polybe', *Revue des Études Grecques*, 4 (1891), 343:

It is Polybius' own brand of 'geographical' history to which I now turn.

GEOGRAPHY AS A COMPONENT ($\mu\acute{\epsilon}\rho os$) OF HISTORY

In the twelfth book of his work Polybius defined serious political history ($\pi\rho\alpha\gamma\mu\alpha\tau\iota\kappa\grave{\eta}$ $\iota\sigma\tau o\rho\acute{\iota}\alpha$) as being tripartite ($\tau\rho\iota\mu\epsilon\rho\acute{\eta}s$). The three components or $\mu\acute{\epsilon}\rho\eta$ were the study of memoirs and documents, a consideration of political events, and the 'survey of cities, places, rivers, harbours and, in general, all peculiar features of land and sea and distances of one place from another'.[4] So, the study of the physical landscape, which forms a major part of the modern discipline of geography, was given a place in the composition of $\pi\rho\alpha\gamma\mu\alpha\tau\iota\kappa\grave{\eta}$ $\iota\sigma\tau o\rho\acute{\iota}\alpha$, but it could be argued that this refers simply to the existence of a 'geographical' book in Polybius' work, and has no implications for the way in which the whole project was conceived or executed. Modern scholars have often, either implicitly or explicitly, indicated the digressive nature of geographical material in Polybius. In a section on digressions, Walbank notes the 'frequent geographical excursuses, with a didactic purpose, which do not always seem particularly at home at the points where they now stand'.[5] Walbank has a great deal to contribute more positively to the debate over the place of geography in Polybius' work, to which I shall return, but it is worth noting his reservations over whether geographical considerations

'He [sc. Polybius] is the founder of a historical genre which is a close neighbour of geography.'

---

[4] Polybius 12. 25^{e}: τὴν θέαν τῶν πόλεων καὶ τῶν τόπων περί τε ποταμῶν καὶ λιμένων καὶ καθόλου τῶν κατὰ γῆν καὶ κατὰ θάλατταν ἰδιωμάτων καὶ διαστημάτων. Cf. 3. 58. 1, where geography is described again as a μέρος of history. The translation of πραγματικὴ ἱστορία is highly problematic. F. W. Walbank, *A Historical Commentary on Polybius* (Oxford, 1957–69), i. 8 n. 6, discusses the options.

[5] F. W. Walbank, *Polybius* (Berkeley, 1972), 47. By contrast, M. Vercruysse, 'À la recherche du mensonge et de la vérité. La fonction des passages méthodologiques chez Polybe', in *Purposes of History*, 17–38, distinguishes between programmatic statements, which disrupt the narrative, and descriptive passages, geographical or biographical, which are integral to it (p. 18).

played a fundamental part in the conception of the *History*. He is more inclined to see geography as creeping into the account in the form of later additions.

It is my purpose in this chapter to explore the ways in which geography and spatial considerations came into Polybius' *History*, and to assess in what sense they formed a component (μέρος) of that undertaking. The formulation used by Polybius suggests that he conceived of space as a category distinct from that of time, which is in itself striking in the light of the belief of some modern geographers that such a conceptual separation was the result of Kantian philosophy, reinforced by the preoccupations of the Enlightenment project. If there were no sign of such a conceptualization in the ancient world, there would be no point in taking the discussion any further. We could simply conclude that it would be anachronistic to apply the modern notions of separate disciplines of geography and history, related to the discrete categories of time and space, to ancient texts. But, as I shall argue, there is evidence that the discrete categories of time and space, with which the two subjects of history and geography were associated, were part of the ancient mind-set.

Augustine discussed the nature of time at length in his *Confessions*. He makes clear the extreme difficulty encountered when we try to formulate what we mean by time, and provides evidence that time as an abstraction was not alien to thinkers in antiquity: 'For what is time? . . . If no one asks me, I know; but if I should wish to explain it to an enquirer, I don't know the answer.'[6] For Diodorus, the task of the universal historian was 'to draw all men, joined to each other by kinship, but separated by space and time (τόποις δὲ καὶ χρόνοις διεστηκότας) into one single order' (1. 1. 3). Polybius' apparent subordination of geography to history, of which it forms a component, provides some evidence of his separation of the temporal and the spatial. In his striking formulation of how the affairs of Greece, Italy, and Africa were first brought together in 218 BC, a moment in time and a spatial union are not only separately denoted, but also turned into the joint subject of an active verb: τὰς μὲν οὖν

---

[6] Augustine *Confessions* 11. 14: *quid enim est tempus?* . . . *si nemo ex me quaerat, scio; si quaerenti explicare velim, nescio.*

Ἑλληνικὰς καὶ τὰς Ἰταλικάς, ἔτι δὲ τὰς Λιβυκὰς πράξεις οὗτος ὁ καιρὸς καὶ τοῦτο τὸ διαβούλιον συνέπλεξε πρῶτον.[7] The temporal and spatial elements act in conjunction, bringing about in turn a union of history (reinforced by the συν-prefix), but they can be conceptualized individually. So, geography (in the sense of space) and history (in the sense of time) may be separated, as long as they are reunited, each being unable to operate without the other.

I shall argue that Polybius shows the interdependence of the temporal and the spatial on all levels. He expresses the fact that human experience occurs in an inextricable mesh of time and space, when he laments that no one can experience everything at once (12. 4c. 4). Events take place against a particular and unique temporal and spatial background. If one or other of these matrices could be suspended, Polybius' complaint would be redundant. However, in the final section of this chapter I argue that, while Polybius in some ways tries to fuse geography and history intellectually in his work to reflect their inseparability in reality, there are also features of his universal approach which allow for the world to be conceived independently of these categories, so answering the problem faced by modern geographers of how to engage in a discourse about the world which is *not* formulated in terms of time and space.

But firstly I discuss the various ways in which Polybius' text shows the mutual dependence of geography, history, and historiography. Secondly, I consider Polybius' conceptions of space, his methods for bringing his own geographical visions to his readers, his various geographical foci, and his grasp of spatial networks and relative position. Finally, I look at the scope of the work and its spatial implications, ideas of universalism, and the general problem of how to write about a world that was taking on immense proportions.

GEOGRAPHY IN THE *HISTORY*

Why should Polybius need to include geography in his *History* at all? According to the 'digressive' view, only *variatio* might

---

[7] Pol. 5. 105. 4: 'This moment and this conference for the first time wove together the affairs of Greece, Italy, and Libya.' Note the first of many examples of weaving imagery.

encourage its inclusion.[8] It is, however, clear from the text that Polybius' belief in the interdependence of geography and history, both in reality, and in a literary and philosophical sense, dictated that geography be integral to the work. In this section I shall discuss four ways in which this may be seen in Polybius' *History*. Firstly, the ideas of process, causation, and explanation created a parallelism between geography and history; secondly, geography affected 'real' history, influencing the course of events; thirdly, geography was a necessary component of historiography; and finally, the writing of Polybius' geography was dependent on a knowledge of historical narratives, which his readership presumably shared.

Firstly, I turn to causation and process. In the key passage dealing with physical change Polybius investigates the reasons for the constant flow of water from the Palus Maeotis and the Pontus (4. 39. 7–42. 8).[9] The reasons given, namely that the influx of water into the basins from rivers must have some outlet, and that silting by alluvial deposits further displaces the water, are summed up as 'the true causes' (αἱ ἀληθεῖς αἰτίαι) (4. 39. 11). But αἰτία is also the term used to denote the cause of 'historical' processes, and Polybius devotes a great deal of attention to defining the term. At 3. 6. 1– 9. 5, on the causes of the war between Hannibal and Rome, he contends that previous authors have confused beginnings (ἀρχαί) with causes (αἰτίαι). The cause of an event, he claims, predates the beginning, which is the point at which the notion is first realized. It

---

[8] Polybius himself hints at the idea of shifting location for the purpose of variety (ποικιλία) and change of scene (μεταβολὴ τῶν ὁρωμένων) (38. 5. 8–6. 1). His parallel with the inability of the eyes to focus on one object for long suggests the strongly visual effect Polybius wants his narrative to evoke in the reader. Lucian urges historians to be as brief as possible in their descriptions of mountains, fortifications, and rivers, reinforcing their digressive nature (*On How to Write History* 57).

[9] Theories on the current through the Dardanelles were the main contribution of Strato of Lampsacus to ancient geography. Head of the Peripatetic school from 287 BC, he formulated the theory that the Pontus had once been a lake, unconnected to the Mediterranean until silting raised its level so that it broke through the Hellespont. The same process made the Mediterranean break through the Pillars of Hercules. It is interesting that, although Polybius and Strato envisaged the opposite process, respectively the isolation or connection of these waters with each other, both expected the same end-result: that the Pontus would one day dry up.

is the cause, rather than the beginning, for which the historian should search, 'since matters of the greatest significance often arise from mere trifles, and the initial impulses and notions of all things are most easily remedied' (3. 7. 7). In the case of the Palus Maeotis and Pontus, it is clear that no human remedy can be easily applied to the problems of overflow. Why, then, do we need to understand the process at all?

One reason is that Polybius uses the passage to reinforce his credibility as an investigative historian. Elsewhere, his choice of sources is determined by their reliability and clarity; the memoirs of Aratus of Sicyon are used because they are 'true and clear' (ἀληθινοί καὶ σαφεῖς) (2. 40. 4).[10] He set his true causes (ἀληθεῖς αἰτίαι) for the flow of water through the Dardanelles against the reports of traders, preferring reasoning from the facts of nature, 'a more accurate method than which it is not easy to find' (ἧς ἀκριβεστέραν εὑρεῖν οὐ ῥᾴδιον, 4. 39. 11).[11] The aim is to present the reader with a proof which rests securely on its own narrative (δι' αὐτῆς τῆς ἱστορίας ἱκανὴν...πίστιν) (4. 40. 3). The use of the term ἱστορία does not provide grounds to argue that this piece of geographical explanation is to be seen as a 'history'. The term does, however, indicate the intention to set out a coherent account of causation and process, of the kind which Polybius undertook for historical events. The 'historical' aspect of the geographical process, in the sense of its being considered over time, is brought out strongly by Polybius. He says that the silting has occurred 'both in the past and now' (καὶ πάλαι καὶ νῦν), and that if the same conditions remain in place and the same causes (αἰτίαι) continue to function, both the Palus Maeotis and the Pontus will one day be entirely silted up (4. 40. 4).

Polybius' conceptions of time as expressed in this passage are worthy of mention. The silting of these basins is a process which, given the continued presence of certain conditions, will one day be completed, since 'it is in accord with nature (κατὰ

---

[10] As is noted by Vercruysse, 'À la recherche du mensonge et de la vérité', 37, such passages are designed to build up a picture of Polybius and his historical method, rather than as serious source-criticism.

[11] I shall return to the question of Polybius' view of phenomena which are 'in accord with nature' (κατὰ φύσιν). For the moment, note the possible Thucydidean echo of the call for accuracy (ἀκρίβεια) (Thuc. 1. 22. 2).

φύσιν) that if a finite quantity (the basins) continually grows or decreases in infinite time . . . it is a matter of necessity that the process finally be completed' (4. 40. 6).[12] The methodology of using theories of causation and the identification of physical process in order to predict future events brings Polybius (and Strato of Lampsacus) into line with the aims of modern geographers, in a way which was not extended by Strabo beyond the same topic of silting and sea-levels. Strabo acknowledged his debt to geographical predecessors for his information on such theories, and it is clear that his own interests lay in the geographic past rather than in the future. Polybius seems to mean that his investigation will enable us at least to see into the future, even if not to change what we see there.[13] Polybius' interests and theories in physical geography are thus expressed in a similar format to his discussion of historical processes, bridging an apparent gap between the scientific and the human spheres. The hint at the wider implications of αἰτίαι ('matters of great significance often arise from mere trifles') raises the important issue of how a chain of natural processes links small-scale phenomena, such as the overflow from the Palus Maeotis, with much greater ones. The water which is displaced out of the Palus Maeotis will one day flow out into the great Ocean.

In all of this there are clear echoes of Herodotus. Both authors use physical explanations, perhaps even more than historical events, as the *locus* for debate about causation. In particular, Polybius' account of the chain of natural processes which leads the waters of the Palus Maeotis out to the Ocean is strongly reminiscent of Herodotus' discussion of the nature of the Nile and its floods. The stress on different causes (αἰτίαι) and their relative merits structures Herodotus' account. One explanation for the Nile floods is that the Etesian winds are

[12] At 9. 43. 3 Polybius notes that the Euphrates, which loses, rather than gains, water along its course, has the opposite nature (ὑπεναντία φύσις) to other rivers.

[13] Perhaps again reminiscent of Thucydides. At 2. 48, Thucydides says that, although he must leave discussion of the αἰτίαι of the plague to the doctors, he can himself describe the symptoms, so that his readers will recognize the disease in the future, although still unable to alter its course. Polybius goes one stage further by taking on the discussion of αἰτίαι himself.

responsible (αἴτιοι), one that the river causes the floods itself because it is derived from the Ocean; the third explanation is that the floods are brought on by melted snow (Hdt. 2. 20–2). The refutation of the third explanation itself falls into three proofs, and Herodotus finally gives his own preferred explanation of the floods, concluding that 'the sun is the cause of these matters'.[14] The language of aetiology, as in Polybius' discussions of physical geography, is all-pervasive.

Secondly, a knowledge of topography as a prerequisite for military success is perhaps the most obvious effect of geography on 'real' history, and, although limited in its scope as an approach, has dominated the way in which ancient historians have thought of the link between the much broader realms of geography and history. Polybius fully acknowledges the need for commanders to be aware of the lie of the land. Hannibal, he says, would not take a large army into regions about which he had not thought in advance (ἀπρονοήτους . . . τόπους) (3. 48. 4).[15] In his description of the battle between Sparta and Philip in 218 BC at Sparta, Polybius shows how exploitation of the topography was crucial to the Spartans' success. Their greater topographical knowledge enabled them to trap Philip's men between the river and mountains before damming the river and flooding the plain (5. 22. 5–7). It was because the outcome of most battles was due to differences of position (αἱ τῶν τόπων διαφοραί) that Polybius included topographical descriptions before battles. Although Polybius does not make an explicit connection here with the desire to uncover the 'true causes' of events, he does state the need to know not so much what happened (τὸ γεγονός), as *how* it happened (τὸ πῶς ἐγένετο) (5. 21. 6).

One of the limitations, however, of looking at the influence of geography on history simply in terms of battle topography is that this approach tends to make nature appear as little more than a theatre for events; a theatre whose shape may affect the way in which the action is played out and which can itself be manipulated by the actors, but still, nevertheless, a largely

---

[14] Hdt. 2. 25. 5: οὕτω τὸν ἥλιον νενόμικα τούτων αἴτιον εἶναι.

[15] Although the ideal is for the general to have had first-hand experience of 'the roads, his destination, and the nature of the place' (9. 14. 2), second-hand reports are preferable to no knowledge at all.

passive backdrop for man's activities. The question of nature as
theatre or actor, the subject of much modern geographical
debate which I discussed in chapter I, is highly pertinent to
Polybius, not least because he himself applied theatrical
imagery to the natural world. The Capuan plain is said to be
surrounded by sea and the mountains so that, by stationing
themselves there, the Carthaginians with Hannibal turned it
'into a kind of theatre' (ὥσπερ εἰς θέατρον) (3. 91. 8–10). The
landscape forms a backdrop for events. The use of theatrical
imagery reinforces the idea of history as a spectacle, viewed by
contemporary onlookers, the historian and the reader.[16] Theories on the silting of the Pontus were all the more convincing
because the process was visible.[17] Polybius agrees with Her-
aclitus that, of the two aids to enquiry given by nature, 'the
eyes are more accurate witnesses than the ears' (12. 27. 1). His
own authority is increased by his claim to autopsy. He not only
witnessed most of the events which are related in the work, but
also participated in and directed some (τῶν πλείστων μὴ μόνον
αὐτόπτης, ἀλλ' ὧν μὲν συνεργός, ὧν δὲ καὶ χειριστής) (3. 4. 13).[18]
His authority to describe Hannibal's passage across the Alps
was strengthened by the fact that he himself undertook the
journey (3. 48. 12); he claims to be able to refute Timaeus on
Locri, having been there himself (12. 5. 1); and he can correct
the estimations of authors for the circumference of New
Carthage 'not from hearsay (ἐξ ἀκοῆς), but because I have
been there (αὐτόπται γεγονότες) (10. 11. 4)'.[19]

---

[16] On the whole question of the visual, see J. Davidson, 'The Gaze in
Polybius' *Histories*', *JRS* 81 (1991), 10–24. Davidson argues for a layered
narrative in which the different perspectives of the participants, spectators
within the text, and Polybius himself are all to be found. For Davidson,
Polybius' apparent objectivity is enhanced by his use of spectators within the
text as filters of information.

[17] See 4. 40. 8: ὃ δὴ καὶ φαίνεται γινόμενον.

[18] At 4. 2. 2, Polybius' ability to provide eyewitness accounts of events of
the late 3rd and early 2nd cents. BC is seen as a cogent reason for focusing his
History on those years.

[19] Polybius' most strongly expressed views on the subject come at the end
of Book 12, his attack on Timaeus. Here he explicitly contrasts the account
founded on participation, active or passive (τὴν ἐξ αὐτουργίας καὶ τὴν ἐξ
αὐτοπαθείας ἀπόφασιν), and that written from reports and narratives (ἐξ ἀκοῆς
καὶ διηγήματος) (12. 28a. 6). G. Schepens, 'Polemic and Methodology in
Polybius' Book XII', in *Purposes of History*, 39–61, argues wrongly, I think,

The ideal must be autopsy and personal involvement, incidentally providing a cogent counter-example to the schema that history deals with the past as opposed to geography's present, but the ideal could not always be realized.[20] Polybius simply dismisses the claim of Pytheas to have seen the whole northern coast of Europe as far as the ends of the earth, and concedes elsewhere that no one can see everywhere in the world (34. 5. 9; 12. 4c. 4). The issues of autopsy and of theatrical imagery are, of course, not straightforward. To what extent could the autoptic participant in events be considered a spectator at the theatre? I shall return to the question of Polybius' self-representation and his triple role as actor, spectator, and relater of events. For the moment, I wish simply to stress the importance of the visual in Polybius, and the implications of this emphasis for the idea of history as a play acted out against the backdrop of nature.[21]

Geography affects history in so far as it provides the scenery for history, and this topography may be such as to determine or restrict the possible course of events. However, the more active role played by geography in Polybius' account is manifested in various ways.[22] Capua not only had theatre-like scenery, but this landscape joined in determining the history played out there. The fertility of the land led to the acquisition of great wealth, which drew the Capuans towards a life of luxury and extravagance (εἰς τρυφὴν καὶ πολυτέλειαν) (7. 1. 1). Unable to support their prosperity, they called in Hannibal, and were ruinously punished by the Romans. Or take the example of the flow of water down the Hellespont, which was such as to make

that Polybius' attacks were against the personal reputation of Timaeus, rather than methodologically motivated.

[20] There was, however, a sense in which seeing the site of an event from the past counted as a substitute for seeing the event itself.

[21] J. N. L. Baker, *The History of Geography* (Oxford, 1963), 98, cites Hakluyt, who in 1587 called geography 'the eye of history', nicely formulating the visual sense that we find in Polybius.

[22] On the rehabilitation of nature as actor rather than just theatrical backdrop, see W. Cronon, 'A Place for Stories: Nature, History and Narrative', *Journal of American History*, 78 (1992), 1347–76, and D. Demeritt, 'The Nature of Metaphors in Cultural Geography and Environmental History', *Progress in Human Geography*, 18 (1994), 163–85, both discussed in chapter I. See above, p. 27 and 31.

Byzantium rich and Chalcedon poor (4. 44. 1–10). Polybius'
belief in the potential for environmental determinism is
nowhere more clearly stated than with regard to the people
of Arcadia. The forced improvisation of music and dancing in
Arcadia was a direct result of the difficulties of life in a cold and
gloomy environment. The practices were introduced with the
purpose of softening the effects of the harshness of nature. The
people of Cynaethea, although they inhabited the most incle-
ment part of Arcadia, failed to take these palliatory measures
and so, totally conditioned by their environment, theirs became
the most savage and violent city in Greece (4. 21. 1–6). In
Polybius' view, there was no reason other than the powerful
effect of the environment upon man, 'why separate nations and
peoples living far apart differ so much from each other in
character, feature, and colour as well as in most of their
pursuits' (4. 21. 2).[23]

Man's vulnerability to the influence of nature is brought out
in the description of the battle between the invading Carthaginians and the troops of Tiberius Sempronius near Placentia.
Tiberius' troops were hindered by the river Trebia and by the
heaviness of the rain; but the Carthaginians were unable to
carry out their pursuit fully, also held back by the storm.
Although the Carthaginians saw the battle as a success, the
natural world took its toll, killing all but one of the elephants
and many men and horses with the cold (3. 74. 5–11). One
reason given by Polybius for commanders to make careful
meteorological observations is that since so many of the
phenomena which can hinder expeditions, such as rains,
floods, frosts, snowfalls, and fog, are unpredictable, it is crucial
to avert disasters which *can* be foreseen (9. 16. 1–4).

A quite different way in which geography affects historical
events, as told by Polybius, is that the nature of a place makes it

---

[23] For a near-contemporary's similar wonder at cultural diversity, see
Agatharchides, *On the Erythraean Sea*, §66 (*GGM I*, 157). Agatharchides
comments on the remarkable cultural differences between peoples who lived
only small distances apart. A ship, he says, could sail from the Palus Maeotis
to Aethiopia in 24 days, but move from the most extreme cold to the most
extreme heat in this time and, due to the change in climate, it is not surprising
if 'the habit and lifestyles, and even the physiques are very different from
ours' (τὴν δίαιταν καὶ τοὺς βίους, ἔτι δὲ τὰ σώματα πολὺ διαλλάττειν τῶν παρ' ἡμῖν).

either attractive or repellent as a potential conquest. This may seem too obvious to deserve mention, but it is explicitly brought out by Polybius as a motive for certain historical decisions. In the 310s BC the Campanians under Agathocles saw and coveted the beauty and general prosperity of Messene.[24] Similarly, the Celts were led to attack neighbouring Etruria when they saw the beauty of the land.[25] These passages echo one of the incentives for Xerxes' invasion of Europe according to Herodotus, namely Mardonius' goad that Europe was a very beautiful land (ὡς ἡ Εὐρώπη περικαλλὴς [εἴη] χώρη) (Hdt. 7. 5. 3). The fear of invasion for those who inhabit or possess prosperous lands was exemplified by the Carthaginians, who, according to Polybius, refused to allow the Romans to sail to the south of the 'Fair Promontory' on its western side because they did not want the Romans to find out about the areas around Byssatis or the Lesser Syrtis because of the quality of the land (διὰ τὴν ἀρετὴν τῆς χώρας) (3. 23. 2). Polybius saw the effects of beautiful places on both the inhabitants themselves, who, like the Capuans, might become degenerate; and on other peoples, who might launch an invasion, perhaps unaware of their folly, since their conquests might, paradoxically, result in their own decline.

The fact that Polybius saw the environment as a motivating factor in history may seem to contradict the agenda set out in his preface, namely that history, particularly that of Rome's expansion, could be explained in constitutional terms (through πολιτεία). 'Who would not want to find out . . . what sort of πολιτεία had enabled the Romans to achieve domination of almost the whole inhabited world?' (1. 1. 5). This constitutional approach to explaining the way the world had come to look contrasts with the geographical explanations of Vitruvius and Strabo, both of whom took Rome's success to be a direct result of the city's location at the privileged centre of the world.[26]

---

[24] 1. 7. 2: περὶ τὸ κάλλος καὶ τὴν λοιπὴν εὐδαιμονίαν τῆς πόλεως ὀφθαλμιῶντες.

[25] 2. 17. 3: περὶ τὸ κάλλος τῆς χώρας ὀφθαλμιάσαντες. The verbal similarities with 1. 7. 2 are striking. Note again the stress on Davidson's visual.

[26] Vitruvius, *De architectura*, 6. 1. 11; Strabo 6. 4. 1: ἐν μέσῳ δὲ...οὖσα...τῷ μὲν κρατιστεύειν ἐν ἀρετῇ τε καὶ μεγέθει...πρὸς ἡγεμονίαν εὐφυῶς ἔχει ('being *in the middle* . . . and through its superiority *in courage and size . . . it is naturally suited to hegemony*').

Walbank's observation that Hellenistic historiography
tended to accept a range of causative factors in history, including political institutions, fate, *and* geography, sets the scene for
a variety of academic propositions as to which factors were
important to Polybius.[27] Millar argues for a shift in Polybius'
focus away from the promised study of the Roman constitution
to a decidedly Greek view of Roman history and expansion.[28]
One could argue that an explanation of Rome's expansion in
purely constitutional terms is compromised also by Polybius'
interest in the influence of climate. In spite of Walbank's
acceptance of many explanatory factors, he places them in a
hierarchical system by privileging Polybius' account of the
Roman constitution over his books devoted to historiography
and geography (130).

However, there is a case for seeing the constitution (πολιτεία)
and environmental factors as complementary, and indeed inextricably linked.[29] Taking the example of the Cretans, in
connection with whom Polybius says explicitly that customs
and laws (ἔθη καὶ νόμοι) make or break the constitution, it is
possible to see customs as both a geographical consequence and
a constitutional component, thus forming the link between
explanations involving environmental determinism and
Polybius' overt claim to be studying the Roman πολιτεία
(6. 47. 1–6).

As so often, Herodotus may provide a clue to interpretation.
While the Hippocratic author of *Airs, Waters, Places* concludes
with the connection between environment and behaviour: 'For
the most part you will find assimilated to the nature of the land
both the physique and the ways of the people,'[30] Herodotus'
Histories takes this idea a stage further, famously ending with
the striking comment of Cyrus, that soft environments produce
soft men, who are not fit to be rulers themselves, but only to be
ruled by others. Here the political state of the entire people is

---

[27] Walbank, *Polybius*, 157.

[28] F. G. B. Millar, 'Polybius between Greece and Rome', in J. T.
A. Koumoulides and J. Brademas (eds.), *Greek Connections: Essays on Culture
and Diplomacy* (Notre Dame, 1987), 1–18.

[29] As made by J. R. F. Martinez Lacy, 'ἔθη καὶ νόμιμα. Polybius and his
Concept of Culture', *Klio*, 73 (1991), 83–92.

[30] *Airs, Waters, Places* 24: εὑρήσεις γὰρ ἐπὶ τὸ πλῆθος τῆς χώρης τῇ φύσει
ἀκολουθέοντα καὶ τὰ εἴδεα τῶν ἀνθρώπων καὶ τοὺς τρόπους.

seen as a direct consequence of their customs and behaviour, which are in turn the result of the physical environment. The final sentence of the work comprises the Persians' considered conclusion that they would rather 'rule, living in a harsh land, than sow level ground and be slaves to others'.[31] If we return to Polybius, we would no longer need to think in terms of a hierarchy, but of factors that were inseparable and so impossible to rank.

Geography and environment had a profound impact on historical processes and events.[32] They not only formed a backdrop for history but also took on an active role in its production, suggesting an integrated interpretation of the term μέρος. But, to turn to my third point, geography and conceptions of space were fundamental to history also in its literary form, as Polybius discusses in several programmatic passages. It was not only commanders who needed a good geographical knowledge, but also the writers of history. An example of bad practice in this regard was Zeno of Rhodes, whom Polybius reproaches for his errors on the topography of Sparta and Messene (16. 16. 1–9). The errors are the cause of a fascinating vignette concerning ancient literary criticism and book production. Polybius wrote to point out the mistakes in Zeno's Laconian topography, but not soon enough for correction before the work was published (16. 20. 5–8).[33]

Part of the historian's task is to recreate landscapes which the reader has not seen. Here the author acts as intermediary between the experience of the reader and the experience of the narrative, in which he himself may or may not have played a part. Whether or not Polybius had seen the places he describes any more than had his readers, it was his job to become sufficiently informed to carry out this role. He specifically

---

[31] Hdt. 9. 122: ἄρχειν τε εἵλοντο λυπρὴν οἰκέοντες μᾶλλον ἢ πεδιάδα σπείροντες ἄλλοισι δουλεύειν.

[32] At the same time, Polybius was fully aware of man's manipulation of the environment. As P. Pédech, *La Méthode historique de Polybe* (Paris, 1964), 537, notes: 'la terre s'impose à l'homme, mais l'homme l'utilise et la transforme; l'espace participe au déterminisme' ('the earth imposes itself on man, but man uses and transforms it; space has a role in determinism').

[33] Polybius assures the reader that Zeno was grateful to have his now irreparable errors pointed out.

notes the importance of his description of the Pontic region and particularly of Byzantium as lying in the fact that

most people are unacquainted with the peculiar advantages of this site, since it lies somewhat outside the parts of the world which are generally visited. We all wish to know about such things, and especially to see for ourselves places which are so peculiar and interesting, but if this is not possible, to gain impressions and ideas of them as near to the truth as possible. (4. 38. 11–12)[34]

The practical purpose to which such descriptions were directed may be seen in Polybius' treatment of the siege of Abydus. Before the narrative, he dismisses the need for a detailed topography of Abydus and Sestus since all intelligent readers would already know about the cities because of their unique positions (16. 29. 3–4). Instead, he draws a striking geographical parallel to which I shall return. However, on many occasions Polybius does need to describe unfamiliar places. In his account of the war over Sicily, Polybius promises to give an idea of the natural advantages and position of the places referred to, so as to prevent the narrative from becoming obscure (ἀσαφής) to those ignorant of the localities (1. 41. 6). Similarly, the fighting between the Spartans and Philip's troops at Sparta, mentioned above, required a geographical preface, not only because the topography affected the battle, but also because, otherwise, the narrative might become vague and meaningless through ignorance of the localities (5. 21. 4). The war between the Romans and Celts could not be narrated before Polybius had described the nature of northern Italy, both in detail and as a whole (2. 14. 3).[35] Among the fragments

---

[34] παρὰ τοῖς πλείστοις, ἀγνοεῖσθαι συνέβαινε τὴν ἰδιότητα καὶ τὴν εὐφυΐαν τοῦ τόπου διὰ τὸ μικρὸν ἔξω κεῖσθαι τῶν ἐπισκοπουμένων μερῶν τῆς οἰκουμένης, βουλόμεθα δὲ πάντες εἰδέναι τὰ τοιαῦτα, καὶ μάλιστα μὲν αὐτόπται γίνεσθαι τῶν ἐχόντων παρηλλαγμένον τι καὶ διαφέρον τόπων, εἰ δὲ μὴ τοῦτο δυνατόν, ἐννοίας γε καὶ τύπους ἔχειν ἐν αὐτοῖς ὡς ἔγγιστα τῆς ἀληθείας. Note the stress on the visual in τῶν ἐπισκοπουμένων μερῶν ('the parts which are viewed') and αὐτόπται γίνεσθαι ('to be eyewitnesses'). The phenomenon to which Polybius alludes is exemplified in the popularity of modern travel books, which provide the chance vicariously to experience unknown lands.

[35] The nature of the account which follows will be discussed later. The parallel with Diodorus is very strong. Diodorus prefaces his account of the struggle between the successors of Alexander in the following way. 'Because of the nature of the events about to be narrated, I think it appropriate to set

assigned to Book 34 is one from Strabo in which Polybius is cited as having written 'I will describe the present situation concerning locations and distances; for this is most pertinent to chorography' (ἡμεῖς δέ . . . τὰ νῦν ὄντα δηλώσομεν καὶ περὶ θέσεως τόπων καὶ διαστημάτων· τοῦτο γάρ ἐστιν οἰκειότατον χωρογραφίᾳ, 34. 1. 3–6).[36] The Loeb inaccurately translates χωρογραφία as 'geography', an important mistake, since one could argue that the Loeb translation thus severely limits Polybius' approach to geography as a whole. As I shall contend, Polybius' geographical conceptions extended far beyond the confines of chorography.[37]

The idea of topography as a prefatory aid to the reader in picturing a battle-scene or some other part of the narrative is tending back towards the view of geography as a stage for history, rather than as an active player in the narrative. Clearly this 'scene-setting' was an important part of geographical description. But even here, interesting points arise concerning the relationship between landscape, history, and historiography. Polybius suspends Hannibal's progress over the Alps into Italy in order to give the topography of the journey, its start and finish, 'so that the narrative may not be totally obscure (ἀσαφής) to those ignorant of the localities', using exactly the same formulation as above (3. 36. 1). Rather than give a description of this region, he sketches a picture of the

out beforehand the causes of revolt, and the situation of Asia as a whole (τῆς ὅλης Ἀσίας τὴν θέσιν), and the size and peculiarities of its satrapies. For thus the narrative will be very easy for the readers to follow, with the overall topography and the distances (ἡ ὅλη τοποθεσία and τὰ διαστήματα) set out in front of their eyes' (18. 5. 1).

[36] The stress on 'the present situation' (τὰ νῦν ὄντα) is interesting in relation to Strabo, since it is what he claims as the realm of geography. Here it is contrasted with accounts of foundations, genealogies, and migrations, precisely the kind of material about the past which is actually so prominent in Strabo.

[37] Claudius Ptolemaeus interestingly defined the difference between geography and chorography in terms of the image of the body. 'Chorography has as its aim the treatment of the subject piece by piece, as if one were to depict an ear or an eye by itself; but geography aims at the general survey, in the same way as one would depict the entire head' (*Geog.* 1. 1). Given Polybius' use of precisely the image of the whole body to refer to his work and to world history (1. 3. 3–4; 1. 4. 7), it is clear which of the terms 'geography' and 'chorography' would be better applied to his *History*.

entire known world, according to a logic which I shall discuss below, and then returns to his explicit methodology. 'I have said this so that my narrative might be ordered in the minds of those who do not know the localities, and that they should have some idea of the main geographical distinctions . . .to which they can refer my statements' (ταῦτα μέν οὖν εἰρήαθω μοι χάριν τοῦ μὴ τελέως ἀνυπότακτον εἶναι τοῖς ἀπείροις τῶν τόπων τὴν διήγησιν, ἀλλὰ κατά γε τὰς ὁλοσχερεῖς διαφορὰς συνεπιβάλλειν . . . τὸ λεγόμενον, 3. 38. 4). This process suggests a closer, more active, interrelationship between the text, its readers, the narrative, and the location than one in which the geographical description is a discrete unit, simply setting the scene. The interlocking elements of history, its narration, the leaders of both sides, and its location, are most clearly bound together at the point when all three are used as joint objects of the same verb and move through the same landscape: καὶ τὴν διήγησιν καὶ τοὺς ἡγεμόνας ἀμφοτέρων καὶ τὸν πόλεμον εἰς Ἰταλίαν ἠγάγο-μεν.[38]

In addition, we should add to the practical purpose of informing the reader about unknown places the element of literary competition. The author is not just setting the scene for the next stage of the narrative, but participating in a tradition of geographical ekphrasis. Polybius presumably hopes to enhance his literary credentials by assisting his reader's under-standing of the setting, by allowing his reader the pleasure of reading about new places (4. 38. 11–12), and by improving upon the accuracy of his rivals, such as Zeno on Laconia. Thus passages of pure description may play an active role in promot-ing the historian himself.

I turn finally in this section to my proposition that the writing of Polybius' geography depended upon a shared know-ledge of the past, both mythical and historical, making history the active foil to geographical exposition. He states that the Thracian Bosporus at the Pontic end starts at the so-called Holy Place where Jason, on his journey back from Colchis, sacrificed to the twelve gods (4. 39. 6). Half-way along this stretch of water was the Hermaion, defined not only by its

---

[38] 3. 57. 1: 'I have brought the narrative, the leaders of both sides, and the war into Italy'.

equidistance from the ends and by its position at the narrowest part on the strait, but also as the place where Darius built his bridge when he crossed to attack the Scythians (4. 43. 2).[39] Further down still, the current reaches a place called the Cow, where, according to myth, Io first stepped down after crossing the Hellespont (4. 43. 6). Hercules appears in various contexts of geographical definition. The Dymaean fort called the Wall, taken by Euripidas, who had been sent by the Aetolians to command the Eleans, is described as being near the Araxus and, according to myth, was built long ago by Hercules when he was making war on the Eleans (4. 59. 4–5). The African realm of the Carthaginians was demarcated by the Altars of Philaenus and the Pillars of Hercules, and this formulation is later repeated to describe Scipio's African conquest (3. 39. 2; 10. 40. 7).[40]

All of this may seem to be at odds with Polybius' assertion that 'in the present day, now that all places have become accessible by land or sea, it is no longer appropriate to use poets and writers of myth as witnesses of the unknown' (4. 40. 2). When he mentions the myth of Phaëthon associated with the river Po, he says that detailed treatment of such things does not suit the plan of the work, although he will set aside space later for them (2. 16. 13–15). As we shall see, Polybius employed many methods to express geographical information, and references to well-known narratives of the past form only part of his definitions, as in the case of the Hermaion.

[39] Cf. Hdt. 4. 83. 1.

[40] For the Altars of Philaenus in ancient geographical writings, see the periplus attributed to Scylax of Caryanda §109 in *GGM I*, 85, in which the innermost recess of the Bay of Syrtis is given as the location of the Φιλαίνου βωμοί. Cf. also Sallust, *Jugurtha* 79 for Sallust's aetiological account of the landmark. The Pillars of Hercules need no elaboration as a key marker in the attempt to map out the world. They form the start- and end-points in many ancient periplus texts, such as those attributed to Scylax and Scymnus of Chios. For one narrative surrounding them, see Diodorus 4. 18. 5. His account of how Hercules 'unyoked' the continents of Europe and Libya here (τῶν ἠπείρων ἀμφοτέρων συνεζευγμένων διασκάψαι ταύτας) links the area conceptually with the Hellespont, 'yoked' by Xerxes' bridge of boats (ζεύξας τὸν Ἑλλήσποντον) (Hdt. 7. 8b. 1) and the Thracian Bosporus, 'yoked' by Darius (Hdt. 4. 83. 1). These key points in the geography of the Mediterranean world, linked through this image, were in turn linked scientifically by Polybius as we have seen on pp. 82–4; see also pp. 110–11.

But the practice of using the geographical associations of historical narrative to define place and space may be paralleled elsewhere in ancient literature. Thucydides, to name one example, recalls that the strait between Rhegium and Messina was the Charybdis of the Odysseus legend (Thuc. 4. 24. 5). One of the most striking examples of the interaction of geography and history comes from Justin's epitome of Pompeius Trogus' *Historiae Philippicae*. Trogus' description of Armenia prefaces the account of the war between Mithridates and Artoadistes, the Armenian king. 'We should not pass over in silence a great kingdom, which is bigger than all except Parthia.'[41] The following description includes the dimensions of the area and geographical details of the underground route taken by the Tigris to emerge after 25 miles, near Sophene: 'From the mountains of Armenia the river Tigris takes its beginning, at first growing only gradually. Then after some distance, it goes underground and then emerges 25 miles later in the area of Sophene, now a large river, and so is incorporated into the marshes of the Euphrates' (Justin 42. 3. 9). However, the mythological early history of the area is also of great importance. The founder of the nation is named as Armenus, and clearly fits into the tradition of foundation stories found in works like that of Herodotus.[42] The identification of Armenus as a companion of Jason (which leads to a digression on the story of Jason and Medea) links the foundation of Armenia with one of the most prominent Greek myths in literature surrounding the Pontic region. The city of Media was, by the same account, founded by Medus, after the death of his father, Jason, in honour of his mother.

[41] *FGrH* 679 F 2b = Justin 42. 2. 6– 3. 9. For the dimensions of the region, given in miles (42. 2. 9): *siquidem Armenia a Cappadocia usque mare Caspium undecies centum milia patet, sed in latitudinem milia passuum septingenta porrigitur* ('Indeed, Armenia extends 1,100 miles from Cappadocia all the way to the Caspian sea, and in breadth it stretches 700 miles'). The combination of the concrete (from *x* to *y*) with the more abstract conception of magnitude (*in latitudinem*) is indicative of the complex way in which space was envisaged in the ancient world.

[42] For example, the story of the foundation of Cyrene by Battus (Hdt. 4. 153–9). These foundation stories seem to be more common for some regions than others. One area to abound in them is Etruria, presumably because of the wish to discover the origins of the Romans.

It is worth noting that, although this description of Armenia contains some strictly geographical information, most of it is concerned with early history and mythology. It is perhaps still more striking that the predominant result of the introduction of this historical/mythological material in the digression is paradoxically a spatial, rather than a temporal, definition. It is with reference to the earliest period in Armenian history that the region is defined geographically in the mind of the reader through the Greek mythological figures and their own geographical associations. Thus we find a very complicated interaction of 'history' and 'geography', or rather of time and space. The main narrative is historically motivated, and requires a geographical setting at this point. However, the author achieves this, not through a spatial description, but through another almost historical narrative, greatly distanced in time from the main narrative. It is the associations of this inserted narrative which result in the location of the main account, illustrating on a larger scale the technique used by Polybius himself. As I discussed in chapter I, memories and traditions of all kinds are what give a place its present identity.

POLYBIUS' CONCEPTIONS OF SPACE

In the last section I considered various ways in which geography, history, and historiography were bound together by Polybius. I now turn more specifically to Polybius' conceptions of space, and to his methods for expressing the spatial or geographical aspects of the work. Since geography was integral to the writing of a historical work, and locations must be brought to the reader's mind, how successful was Polybius in dealing with this, and what kind of geography emerged? In this section, I move in general from the small- to the large-scale. Firstly, I consider to what extent we may detect one or more geographical focal points for the work. Secondly, I look at the use of geographical similes and parallels in the creation of spatial images. Thirdly, I consider Polybius' use of geometrical figures to indicate two-dimensional space, and finally the creation of large-scale geographical images and spatial networks at both a local and a global level.

The question of geographical focus is related to the wider

debate over Polybius' attitudes to Rome and to the subjugation of Greece.[43] A discussion of Polybius' role in the Achaean league and his eventual complicity with Rome and friendship with leading Romans of the time, such as Scipio Aemilianus, does not fall within the scope of this chapter, but the geographical implications should be noted; namely, that we have at least two possible candidates as foci for the authorial viewpoint. Proponents of the view that Polybius wrote from a Roman perspective, or at least in a manner that was sympathetic to Rome, include Walbank and Dubuisson. For Walbank, the degree of Romanness increases towards the end of the work and is manifested particularly in the scene at the fall of Carthage, although the whole project is introduced in a Romanocentric way as a study of the rise of that state.[44] For Dubuisson also, Polybius' spatial standpoint changed as he worked on the project. An outsider at the start, Polybius, in Dubuisson's view, came to admire Rome and its achievements: 'Polybe est lui-même sorti du cadre de la question précise qu'il s'était posée (les causes de la rapide conquête du monde grec) pour succomber à une certaine fascination pour le vainqueur.'[45] Admiration for the conqueror is not in itself evidence for adoption of a Roman viewpoint. In fact, it shows precisely the opposite, that Polybius was located at a point from which he could look upon Rome as *le vainqueur*. Dubuisson's suggestion that Polybius underwent Latinization in terms of language and *mentalité*—a subconscious Romanization, which rendered him unable to pass judgement on Roman rule as he had promised, because he was no longer an external observer—is

---

[43] Although some caution should be observed in blurring too casually the distinction between geographical and ideological/political focus, the connection seems to me undeniable. The adoption of a Greek persona, or alternatively the appropriation of a Roman perspective, or even a combination of both, inevitably carries with it a spatial counterpart in our placing, or placings, of Polybius on the mental map of the Mediterranean world. The same issue will arise, with even more complexity, when dealing with Strabo's location of himself, and with his adoption of multiple viewpoints.

[44] Walbank, *Polybius*, 30.

[45] M. Dubuisson, 'La Vision polybienne de Rome', in *Purposes of History*, 241: 'Polybius himself left the framework of the exact question which he had set himself (the causes of the rapid conquest of the Greek world) to succumb to a certain fascination with the conqueror'.

interesting for its spatial consequences, but is a rather strained interpretation of the text as it stands.

Against the picture of a 'Romanized' Polybius we have Millar's strong assertion that the historian remained utterly Greek in his outlook and historiographical approach, and 'though he expresses himself obliquely, took an increasingly distant and hostile view of Roman domination'.[46] So, Dubuisson's intellectual move for Polybius towards Rome would be reversed.[47] The non-Roman nature of Polybius' viewpoint is manifested in both his historical and geographical conceptions.[48]

Historically, the account is bound to Greek chronological markers such as the crossing of Xerxes to Europe. It was twenty-eight years before this event that the first treaty between Rome and Carthage was forged; and in the year of the crossing itself that Rome's constitution became worthy of study (3. 22. 2).[49] The Xerxes episode in Greek history is a recurrent theme through Polybius' work, and as various characters play out or threaten similar invasions, Herodotus' work is repeatedly evoked. The motif has clear geographical associations in addition to its use as a temporal marker. The crossing of natural boundaries, such as rivers, is often accompanied by attempts to subject peoples and rewrite the map of world powers. By crossing the river Iberos, the Carthaginians broke the treaty of 226 BC, thus precipitating war with Rome (3. 6. 2). The theme of man pitted against an active natural world, which I discussed in chapter I with regard to the history of the American West as well as to some ancient texts, is highly relevant here. Polybius relates how Hannibal's crossing of the Rhône was accompanied by conquest over his enemies; his two victims are linked as the joint object of one verb.[50] Hannibal's

---

[46] Millar, 'Polybius between Greece and Rome', 4.

[47] In support of this reading, Lacy, 'ἔθη καὶ νόμιμα', 83, argues that the purpose of Polybius' work was to explain to his compatriots the causes and mechanisms of Roman rule so that they could react politically to the new power.

[48] Also in the purpose of the work, for one of Polybius' express aims was to make known to the *Greeks* the parts of the inhabited world as yet unknown to them (3. 59. 8).

[49] See Millar, 'Polybius between Greece and Rome', 12, on this point.

[50] 3. 44. 1: τῆς τε διαβάσεως καὶ τῶν ὑπεραντίων κεκρατηκώς. Cf. Hdt. 7. 8c. 3,

crossing of the Po using a bridge of boats further reinforces the parallel with Xerxes.[51] It is easy to see why Rome should be worried by Hannibal's Xerxes-like actions, and why Greece in turn should fear similar moves from the West. At the Spartan conference in the spring of 210 BC the Acarnanian, Lyciscus, begged the Spartans to see the parallels between the storm approaching from Rome and Xerxes' demands for submission (9. 38. 1–2). The struggle for Greek liberty is seen to have been helped by writers recording the Persian and Gallic invasions; perhaps Polybius saw himself as continuing this tradition (2. 35. 7). All this supports Millar's assertion that the real issue was 'the preservation of the freedom of the Greek cities in the face of the threats posed by successive kings and dynasties'.[52]

From a geographical point of view, in opposition to the idea of a Roman focus, Millar stresses the vast spatial scope of the work.[53] Whereas, in historical conception and ideological outlook, there are two plausible focal points for the author, Rome or Greece, this restricted choice is not reflected geographically. The ideal of autopsy and the reality of Polybius' own travels make the spatial focus indefinable. Polybius appears as an Odyssean figure in the work. As Walbank points out, Polybius' pride in his travels evokes quotations from the *Odyssey*.[54] The wandering Odysseus found a second-century counterpart in Polybius, as celebrated in an inscription set up by the Greeks of Polybius' native city of Megalopolis, and recorded by Pausa-

---

where Xerxes is described as yoking both the Hellespont and the people of Europe.

[51]   3. 66. 6: γεφυρώσας τοῖς ποταμίοις πλοίοις.

[52]   Millar, 'Polybius between Greece and Rome', 16. See also Walbank, *Polybius*, 2, on Polybius' interest in the mutual impact of Greek and non-Greek peoples on each other. This formulation of Greek or non-Greek decisively locates the focus away from Rome. Ephorus' treatment of world history in terms of the Greek and non-Greek worlds has been traced by Alonso-Núñez, 'The Emergence of Universal Historiography from the 4th to the 2nd Centuries B. C.', in *Purposes of History*, 173–92, to the 4th-cent. Panhellenic ideals of his tutor, Isocrates (p. 177). From Ephorus onwards, the notion that universal history should include both Greeks and barbarians was fixed, but only with Polybius did 'universal' take on the sense of 'global'.

[53]   Millar, 'Polybius between Greece and Rome', 6.

[54]   Walbank, *Polybius*, 51. Cf. Pol. 12. 27. 10–11.

nias. The inscription noted that Polybius 'wandered over land and all the sea' (ὡς ἐπὶ γῆν καὶ θάλασσαν πᾶσαν πλανηθείη) (Paus. 8. 30. 8).[55]

Having considered briefly various focalizations of Polybius' own viewpoint, and also his resistance to being fixed to a single point in space, I turn now to the use of geographical similes in creating the pictures of space that he considered integral to the work. By far the most common similes are those likening parts of the broader landscape to parts of the city. The layout of the military camp as described in Book 6 made it resemble a city.[56] I have already mentioned the way in which the Capuan landscape took on the appearance of a theatre. But the image which recurs with greatest frequency is that of the acropolis. Hannibal encouraged his troops with a view of their goal, Italy, from their position in the Alps. To enhance the reader's imagined view of the scene, Polybius elaborates the idea that Italy lies so close under the Alps that 'when both are viewed together, the Alps appear to take on the position of an acropolis to the whole of Italy' (3. 54. 2).[57] Philip's troops looted the stores of Thermus in Aetolia, which had been the treasury of Aetolia's most precious goods, since it had never been invaded and 'naturally held the position of being the acropolis of all Aetolia' (5. 8. 6). Antiochus III was anxious to gain control of Ephesus for its location, since it 'held the position of an acropolis both by land and sea for anyone with designs on Ionia and the Hellespontine cities' (18. 40a).

Polybius uses a telescoping effect, comparing the larger landscape with the individual features of the well-known city layout. He explicitly states his practice as being that 'throughout the whole undertaking, I attempt to link together and harmonize those places which are unknown with things that are familiar from personal experience or hearsay' (5. 21. 5). It is

---

[55] Cf. Hecataeus as ἀνὴρ πολυπλανής (p. 76). J. L. Moles, 'Truth and Untruth in Herodotus and Thucydides', in C. Gill and T. P. Wiseman (eds.), *Lies and Fiction in the Ancient World* (Exeter, 1993), 88–121, at 96 makes the same point about the Odyssean nature of Herodotus, advancing together with his text through the 'cities of men' (1. 5. 3). The claim to experience of travel may be yet another competitive element.

[56] 6. 31. 10: πόλει παραπλησίαν ἔχει τὴν διάθεσιν.

[57] Note yet again how Polybius' geographical information seems to be directed towards creating a visual image in words.

noteworthy that features such as the acropolis reflecting Polybius' roots in the culture of the Greek city are evoked as the
'known' part of the comparison; the Roman camp is not used to
illuminate anything, but is itself brought into focus by comparison with the shape of the city (πόλις). Polybius writes so as
to help a *Greek* reader to picture the scene.

Rather than liken a geographical site to a piece of architecture or part of a city's topography, Polybius sometimes relies
on drawing parallels between two similar geographical features.
Sicily, he says, lies in a position relative to Italy as the
Peloponnese does to Greece, with the difference that Sicily is
an island rather than a peninsula (1. 42. 1–2). The implication
must be that knowing one of these areas immediately gives one
a picture of the other. Similarly, the confluence of the Rhône
and the Isaras has a size and shape like those of the Nile Delta,
except that, in the latter case, the base line (presumably
Polybius wants the reader to imagine a triangular effect) is
made up of the coast, whereas in the former it is formed by a
mountain range (3. 49. 6–7). The prime example of this
comparative technique is the description of Abydus and
Sestus on the Hellespont. Polybius remarkably says that the
best way to gain an impression of these cities is not by a study
of their actual topography, but by a comparison (16. 29. 5). Just
as it is impossible to sail from the Ocean into the Mediterranean without passing through the Pillars of Hercules, so it is
impossible to sail from the Mediterranean to the Propontis or
Pontic sea except by passing through the passage between
Sestus and Abydus.

Again, there is a clear echo of Herodotean techniques here,
in particular of his comparison between the Nile and the
Istros which forms part of his discussion of Scythian rivers,
itself set in the context of a wider global description.[58] The
symmetry of the great northern and southern rivers of the
world performs a similar function in Herodotus' account to
that of the eastern and western straits in that of Polybius,

---

[58] Hdt. 4. 50 on the Nile and Istros. The global description is at 4. 36–45,
and is elicited by the Scythian claim that there are Hyperboreans living
further north even than Scythia, a claim which forces Herodotus to set his
reader straight on the confused issue of world geography; 4. 47–58 deals with
Scythian rivers.

namely to add coherence, through natural logic, to the attempt to encompass the world in the mind's eye. One wonders here, as elsewhere, whether Polybius is merely employing similar techniques to those of a generic predecessor because they represent an approach which is appropriate to the task, or whether a more self-conscious intertextuality is in play, and Polybius is critically engaging with particular passages of Herodotus' *Histories*.

Thirdly, Polybius evokes larger areas through their similarity to geometrical figures, giving a sense of space rather than of place.[59] This practice is mirrored in Eratosthenes and Hipparchus.[60] For Polybius, Sicily was triangular in shape, with the corners being formed by capes, which Polybius then went on to orientate (1. 42. 3). Italy too was triangular, and located with reference to the seas which surround it on two sides, the Alps on the other and the southern apex (Cape Cocynthus). Polybius describes the entire geographical layout of the country using the triangle for points of reference. The Alps, stretching from Massilia almost to the head of the Adriatic, are said to form the base of the triangle (βάσις τοῦ τριγώνου). The use of geometry to convey geographical images does not stop here. The most northerly plain in Italy, lying immediately to the south of the base of the 'Italian' triangle, is also triangular in shape. This geographical area too is defined with reference to its sides and corners. One side is formed by the Alps, one by the Apennines, the third by the Adriatic coast, and the apex is the meeting point for the Apennines and Alps, near Massilia. The scientific aspect of the description is reinforced by the inclusion of distances for all the sides of the triangle (2. 14. 4–12).

Other geometrical images are more fleeting. The overall

[59] On the modern debate over the question of place and space, see above, pp. 17–18. Polybius totally confounds generalizations about ancient concepts of space, exemplified by E. Rawson, *Intellectual Life in the Late Roman Republic* (London, 1985), 259, where she asserts that people in antiquity thought in predominantly linear terms, through itineraries and periplus journeys.

[60] For an excellent edition of the fragments of Hipparchus, see D. R. Dicks, *The Geographical Fragments of Hipparchus* (London, 1960). Hipparchus is reported as saying that Eratosthenes stated the shape of India to be a rhombus (Strabo 2. 1. 34). Hipparchus himself seems to have used triangles almost exclusively, particularly for measuring distances, as at Str. 2. 1. 29.

shape of Sparta was a circle (5. 22. 1); the Roman camp was
square (6. 31. 10). Polybius stresses the importance of a good
knowledge of geometry for those involved in military affairs, at
least to the extent of understanding proportion. He laments the
way in which people have forgotten the basic geometry which
they had learned at school, with the result that they misunderstand the relationship between the perimeter of a place and its
area (9. 20. 1; 9. 26a. 1–4). The fragments which have been
assigned to the 'geographical' book are predominantly concerned with geometry and measurements, comprising what we
might call 'mathematical geography' of the kind that Strabo
deals with in the first two books, before largely abandoning the
approach. There is nothing to indicate that these fragments
were part of a separate geographical book in Polybius, and I
feel sure that their having been grouped in this way is largely a
reflection of modern ideas on what comprises geography,
rather than an accurate representation of how they fitted into
the original text. The fragments in which the actual book
number is given as 34 are rather orientated towards questions
of produce, flora, and fauna.[61] It is on the basis of a book
created according to modern assumptions that Polybius' 'geographical' approach is characterized as scientific, and distinct
from the rest of the work.

It is certainly reasonable to argue that Polybius' geography
was scientific in some of its methods of conceiving space, but,
as I have already mentioned, this way of bringing the picture to
the reader was used throughout the work and gives no reason
for assigning such passages to a separate book. It is interesting
that Polybius calculated the length of the river Tagus without
taking into account the windings, but in a straight line: 'this is
not geographical' (οὐ γεωγραφικὸν τοῦτο) according to Strabo
(Pol. 34. 7. 5). Strabo's assertion of the incompatibility of
mathematical approaches with geography is raised also in
connection with Hipparchus' criticisms of Eratosthenes on
the western Mediterranean, in which Strabo says that Hipparchus tests each statement 'geometrically rather than geographically' (γεωμετρικῶς μᾶλλον ἢ γεωγραφικῶς), implying that

---

[61] 34. 8. 1–2 on oak-trees planted in the sea off Lusitania; 34. 8. 4–10 on the
extreme fertility of Lusitania.

the two approaches are in some way contradictory (Str. 2. 1. 40).[62]

But by contrast with Polybius' approach to the Tagus, we have the intriguing note that his figure for the distance from Cape Malea to the Istros was at odds with that given by Artemidorus because Polybius did *not* reckon the distance in a straight line, but according to the route taken by some general (34. 12. 12).[63] Here, he chose the eyewitness approach to geography, rather than the theoretical one. Presumably Polybius had the chance in Rome to consult either the general or his notes. It is a side issue, but I can see no reason why Polybius might not have given this distance as part of his main narrative, rather than in Book 34, maybe in one of the descriptive passages like that preceding Hannibal's descent into Italy. However, the main point is that, alongside his stress on autopsy, Polybius also used geometrical figures and distances as a method of helping his reader to visualize the world. The combination of geometrical abstraction and eyewitness accounts adds a further twist to the focalization of the work. Not only is it unclear precisely where we should locate Polybius with regard to his possible ideological perspectives—Greece and Rome—but there is an additional tension between the external perspective which enables him to describe the world in terms of geometrical shapes, and the internal viewpoint of the Odyssean eyewitness guide, familiar from the *Histories* of Herodotus.

The use of shapes to convey a spatial, rather than a place-orientated, picture brings us fourthly to the question of Polybius' wider geographical conceptions. The writing of political history may lead us to expect that Polybius would have concentrated on significant places, such as the cities, and to some extent he did. But we have already seen his concern to give a sense of wider space and also his interest in the customs

---

[62] This problem of the distinction between geography and geometry applies also to Eratosthenes himself, who was caught between the two disciplines and criticized by both parties. 'Being a mathematician among geographers, but a geographer among mathematicians, on both sides he gives his opponents occasions for contradiction' (Str. 2. 1. 41).

[63] This raises the problem of which general was meant. Walbank confesses ignorance on this point.

and lifestyle of non-city dwellers, such as the Arcadians.[64] This persistent sense of space is unlike anything which appears consistently in Strabo's *Geography* beyond the first two books, and is developed far beyond the use of two-dimensional geometrical images. On all scales, Polybius builds up a complex picture of the relationship between places and the space surrounding them, enabling us to imagine a fairly coherent mental map for much of the Mediterranean world. This is, of course, fully in accord with his professed aim to write a unified world history, but it is nonetheless striking that this aim so greatly affected his geographical conceptions and the view of the world which he created for the reader, showing once again how closely integrated geography and history were in his account.

It is possible to identify various ways in which Polybius creates a broader spatial picture than that of individual sites. Often he includes as part of the description information on how the site relates to its immediate surroundings. Carthage, for example, lay in a gulf, on a promontory surrounded mostly by sea, and partly by a lake. It was joined to Libya by an isthmus, which was around $2\frac{1}{2}$ stades wide. On the sea side of the isthmus was Utica; on the land side, Tunis (1. 73. 4–5).[65] So, we are told the nature of the position of Carthage, as well as how it fits into the wider landscape on all sides. The district of Ariminum, under the command of the consul, Cn. Servilius, is described as being on the coast of the Adriatic, where the plain of Cisalpine Gaul joins the rest of Italy, not far from the mouth of the Po (3. 86. 2). Here the site is linked in to a geographical network of mountains, rivers, and seas, which Polybius has already elaborated on at length in his description of Italy. The

---

[64] See Lacy, '*ἔθη καὶ νόμιμα*', who argues that Polybius was interested in both *πόλεις* ('cities') and *ἔθνη* ('peoples'). There is, however, a tendency in Lacy's argument to confuse an interest in *ἔθνη* ('peoples') with one in *ἔθη* ('customs'). Polybius' concern with peoples such as the Arcadians was not necessarily linked with his interest in the relationship between constitution and customs.

[65] M. Sordi, 'Gli interessi geografici e topografici nella "Elleniche" di Senofonte', *CISA* 14 (1988), 32–40, argues that Xenophon too displays this kind of broad spatial awareness, but it seems to me that there is nothing on the scale of what we find in Polybius. Most of Xenophon's descriptions are of individual cities, rather than whole landscapes or regions.

account of Sparta, mentioned above, is introduced by the comment that one of Polybius' aims in site descriptions is to give the relative positions or arrangement (τάξις) of places (5. 21. 4). This is made explicit when Polybius comes to talk about Seleuceia, and prefaces a long account by promising to give the position of Seleuceia and to tell of the peculiarity of the surrounding area (τὴν δὲ τῆς Σελευκείας θέσιν καὶ τὴν τῶν πέριξ τόπων ἰδιότητα) (5. 59. 3).[66] The siege of New Carthage is introduced in exactly the same way, with a promise to give the reader a description of the surroundings and the site of the city itself (τοὺς παρακειμένους τόπους καὶ τὴν θέσιν αὐτῆς) (10. 9. 8). What follows is an account relating the position of the city both to the whole of Spain (it lay half-way down the coast), and to the immediate area, in a gulf whose orientation and dimensions are given, and surrounded on the land side by mountains and lagoons.

This method of relating places to surrounding regions is used not only of cities. The struggle between the Celts and Romans required an account not only of the region concerned, but also of its relationship to the rest of Italy.[67] On the basis of the geometrical analysis of the land, and the information on the various sides of the triangle of Italy, Polybius fills out this picture with mountain ranges and rivers. The Apennines join the Alps at Massilia, that is, at the apex of the 'inner' triangle of Polybius' earlier description. The river Po rises in the Alps near the apex of the triangle before descending southwards to the plain and turning to the east and the Adriatic (2. 16. 1–7).

The tracing of river courses, mountain ranges, and roads is one of the ways in which Polybius reveals his sense of wider geographical space. I have already mentioned his orientation and location of the Alps and Apennines, but sometimes the river network too is incorporated into his description of mountains. The course of the Rhône runs from beyond the

---

[66] An interesting example of the same phenomenon is the city of Hecatompylus, which Polybius (10. 28. 7) says took its name from the fact that it lay at the nexus of all the roads leading to the surrounding districts (ἐπὶ πάντας τοὺς πέριξ τόπους). Here the significant naming of the place reflects its relationship to the surrounding area. Tarentum (10. 1. 5) also lay at the centre of a network, not of monumentalized roads, but of trade routes.

[67] 2. 14. 3: πῶς κεῖται πρὸς τὴν ἄλλην Ἰταλίαν.

north-west recess of the Adriatic, along the northern slope of
the Alps, to the Sardinian sea in a south-westerly direction. For
its whole length it is bounded to the south by the northern
Alps, which separate the valley of the Rhône from that of the
Po (3. 47. 2–4).[68] The river Aufidus is described as the only one
to traverse the Apennines, the chain of mountains which
separates all the Italian streams into those which flow into
the Adriatic and those flowing into the Tyrrhenian sea
(3. 110. 9). In this passage not only mountains and seas, but
the whole Italian river network is called into play to define the
character of the Aufidus.

As far as land routes are concerned, Polybius displays the
kind of knowledge that might have come from generals' reports
or itinerary maps. In relating Hannibal's invasion of Europe,
Polybius maps out the route from the Pillars of Hercules to the
Po valley, giving the distance along each section of the journey.
The road from Narbo to the crossing of the Rhône had been
'measured out and marked with milestones at every eighth
stade by the Romans with care' (3. 39. 8).[69] An interesting
example of how the itinerary might be deliberately concealed
for strategic purposes occurs in Philopoimen's mustering at
Tegea of an army against Nabis, and reveals precisely the kind
of disjointed geographical picture that Polybius himself needed
to avoid (16. 36. 1–9). Philopoimen sent out letters to each
town with instructions to march to one named city. The idea
was that the troops would advance to Tegea, gathering

[68] Polybius' schematic geographical picture is somewhat misleading. The
confusion over the source of the Rhône stems from his belief that the Alps ran
directly from west to east.

[69] See also 34. 11. 8 for the use of milestones. The whole question of
measurement is complicated by the observation of R. A. Bauslaugh, 'The
Text of Thucydides IV 8. 6 and the South Channel at Pylos', *JHS* 99 (1979),
1–6, that the stade, as used by Thucydides, was a variable measure (for
Thucydides, 140–260 metres). It is unclear what stade Polybius, or those who
dispute his measurements, was using. The text suggests that this may be an
early instance of the equation 8 stadia = 1 Roman *milia passuum*, which was
later to become normal. D. Engels, 'The Length of Eratosthenes' Stade', *AJP*
106 (1985), 298–311, redirects the focus away from the exact distance denoted
by a stade and towards the significance of attempts to measure and calculate
large distances, such as the earth's circumference, at all. For a more recent
treatment, see S. Pothecary, 'Strabo, Polybius and the Stade', *Phoenix* 49
(1995), 49–67.

numbers along the way, as the letters were timed to arrive at different dates according to the distance from Tegea. 'It resulted that no one knew to where he was marching, but knew simply the name of the next city on the list' (16. 36. 6).

The whole district of Media is treated in a broad geographical context (5. 44. 3–11). It is said to lie in central Asia, immediately evoking an image of the whole continent, and this image is continued in the comparison by which Media surpasses in size and the height of its mountains all other places in Asia. Polybius then locates the region more specifically with regard to the lands on all sides. To the east is a desert plain separating Persia from Parthia, reaching to the mountains of the Tapyri, not far from the Hyrcanian sea; to the south are Mesopotamia and the border with Persia, which is protected by Mount Zagrus; to the west are the satrapies, not far from the tribes whose territories go down to the Pontus; and to the north are various tribes and that part of the Pontus which joins the Palus Maeotis. The geographical context within which Polybius can place Media stretches literally hundreds of miles in all directions.

As I shall discuss later, Polybius' holistic approach to universalism is reflected in his 'geographical layering'. The simile linking, for example, the Alps with an acropolis depends on a conception of the part as microcosm of the whole.[70] The transitions between small- and large-scale geography span the entire distance from the written text itself to the whole world which it describes. The geography of the text is to be seen in references to its boundary (ἡ περιγραφή), to places in it which are suitable for the treatment of certain topics (ἁρμόζοντες τόποι), and to its finishing line (τὸ τέρμα τῆς ὅλης πραγματείας) (3. 1. 8; 5. 30. 8; 39. 8. 3). The text, as microcosm of the world, reflects the changing location of important events. After describing the actions of Rome and Carthage in Spain, Africa, and Sicily, Polybius promises to shift the story to Greece, as the scene of the action changed.[71]

The link between textual and large-scale geography is the

---

[70] On microcosm and macrocosm, see above, pp. 40–3.

[71] 3. 3. 1: μεταβιβάσομεν τὴν διήγησιν ὁλοσχερῶς εἰς τοὺς κατὰ τὴν Ἑλλάδα τόπους ἅμα ταῖς τῶν πραγμάτων μεταβολαῖς. 3. 57. 1 takes this relationship between textual and real geography to extremes, as discussed above, p. 94.

imagery of the city and of its various features, which, as I have
discussed, Polybius uses to elicit a picture of wider areas.
These examples of telescoping should be set alongside a further
network of similes and parallels, which reveal Polybius' affinities with Hellenistic scientific geographers like his contemporary, Hipparchus. Hipparchus is said to have believed that
the parallel through the Borysthenes was the same as that
through Britain, because the parallel of latitude through
Byzantium was that through Massilia, revealing a concern
with relative space similar to that of Polybius. The comparison
seems crude, since Britain covers several lines of latitude.
However, we must remember that Hipparchus' 'parallels'
(κλίματα) referred to zones rather than to lines, and also
appreciate that this kind of large-scale conception was quite
different from what could be discerned by the explorer geographers.

Hipparchus' analogical parallels, linking areas far apart and
evoking a broad geographical picture, are strongly reminiscent
of Polybius' comparison of the straits between the Pillars of
Hercules and between Abydus and Sestus, which I discussed
on p. 102. However, Polybius' geographical sophistication is
reflected in the fact that he brings to this analogy the factor of
scale. So a straight comparison in the style of Hipparchus is
combined with Polybius' own 'telescoping' technique. After
drawing the parallel between the two straits, he refines the
picture by stating that the width of the former channel is
proportionately greater than that of the latter, just as the
Ocean is larger than the Mediterranean: 'It is as though fate
built the two straits according to a kind of logic (πρὸς τινα
λόγον)' (16. 29. 8–9). This natural logic is foreshadowed in
Polybius' description of the silting of the Palus Maeotis and the
Pontus. He states that the distance for which alluvial deposits
are carried beyond the mouth of a river is directly proportional
to the force of the river's current.[72] In addition to this, the time
required for the Pontus to become a shallow, fresh-water lake
can be predicted, since it will be longer than that taken for the
Palus Maeotis in proportion to its greater capacity; and the

[72] 4. 41. 7: πρὸς λόγον ἑκάστου γίνεσθαι τὴν ἀπόστασιν τῇ βίᾳ τῶν ἐμπιπτόντων
ῥευμάτων.

greater size and number of its tributary rivers, with proportionately greater silting potential, must also be taken into account (4. 42. 4–5).[73] The logical world of the Pontic region is conceptually linked to that of the well-proportioned straits at each end of the Mediterranean, as the mouth of the Palus Maeotis is appropriately smaller than that of the Pontus, creating a chain of straits stretching from the Palus Maeotis to the Outer Ocean, and reflecting Polybius' broad geographical horizons (4. 39. 3–4).[74] The natural world may indeed display a certain logic here, but it is still for the author to point this out in his quest to bring the world to his readers' eyes.

Polybius' geographical interests range from the text, to the topography of regions, to their relative locations, and finally to the world itself. I shall discuss in the next section why the whole project demanded that Polybius take on the challenge of depicting for his readers not only individual sites, but also the world. But it is interesting first to examine the strategies he employed. It is worth noting that Polybius himself acknowledged the difficulties involved in really large-scale geography. He says that, although most Greek authors had tried to describe the most inaccessible parts of the known world, most were mistaken (3. 58. 2).[75] This was not grounds for criticism of earlier authors, but rather a result of the difficulties of travel and of communication, even if the journey could be made. 'For it was difficult to see many things at all closely with one's own eyes (αὐτόπτην γενέσθαι), owing to some of the countries being utterly barbarous and others deserted; and it was even harder to find out information about what one did see, owing to the difference of language' (3. 58. 8). In Polybius' day the situation had been radically altered by the conquests of

---

[73] The word λόγος is used also in this context.

[74] That Polybius had such a broad geographical perspective is reinforced by the fact that Pliny (*NH* 6. 206) cited his figure for the distance from the strait at the Pillars to the mouth of the Palus Maeotis (3,437 stades) (Pol. 34. 15. 2).

[75] The use of the phrase περὶ τὰς ἐσχατιὰς τόπων τῆς καθ' ἡμᾶς οἰκουμένης (3. 58. 2) is interesting. It most naturally means the most distant parts from the centre of the world in this context, but also carried other connotations. D. M. Lewis, 'The Athenian Rationes Centesimarum' in M. I. Finley (ed.), *Problèmes de la terre en Grèce ancienne* (Paris, 1973), 210–12, suggests that the ἐσχατιαί referred to *any* land that was inaccessible or difficult to cultivate, and so not necessarily always on the perimeter of our mental map of the world.

Alexander in Asia and of the Romans in all other parts of the world, making almost all regions accessible. But this did not answer the question of exactly how this newly expanded world could be brought to the mind of the reader. As Polybius himself says, 'it is not right simply to give the names of places, rivers, and cities', which meant nothing when referring to unknown lands, since the mind could not connect the words with anything already known to it (3. 36. 2).[76]

I have discussed the use of references to the past, as a means of eliciting information from the reader's mythological and historical mental geographies, as well as the use of similes, likening the topography of an unknown place to a feature familiar from city-life, and of geometrical figures. The last main geographical notion that I shall consider is the one which Polybius claims was the most commonly known, and it brings a third dimension to Polybius' geographical conceptions to add to those of place and two-dimensional space. This was the division and ordering of the heavens which yielded the celestial quadrants (3. 36. 6). The regions of the earth must then be classified according to their relationship to the sky. Fragments assigned to Book 34 testify to Polybius' interest in astrology and cosmology. He is said to have written a work entitled 'On the parts of the globe under the celestial quarter', and participated in the intellectual debate involving Eratosthenes and Posidonius concerning the climatic zones (34. 1. 7; 34. 1. 16–17). These preoccupations partly explain the importance of geometry in Polybius' geography and its expression, since the transition from sky to earth was carried out through geometrical shapes. The idea of measuring out the world in a geometrical way was not unique to the ancient world, but was taken up, for example, by the sixteenth-century Venetians. Cosgrove states that 'in late Renaissance Italy not only was geometry fundamental to practical activities like cartography, land survey, civil engineering and architecture, but it lay at the heart of a widely-accepted neo-platonic cosmology'.[77] Study of

---

[76] See also 5. 21. 4.

[77] D. E. Cosgrove, 'The Geometry of Landscape: Practical and Speculative Arts in Sixteenth-Century Venetian Land Territories', in D. E. Cosgrove and S. Daniels (eds.), *The Iconography of Landscape* (Cambridge, 1988), 254–76, at 256.

the heavens and parcelling up the landscape were thus closely linked, and expressed both the intellectual and political power of the ruling class.[78]

For Polybius, the next stage after dividing up the sky was to divide the known world in a similar way. It is interesting that, whereas Ephorus had matched the four quadrants of the sky with four divisions on earth, each dominated by an ethnic group, Polybius chose to set the three continents against the celestial pattern, a harder task.[79] He named the three continents and defined them in terms of natural features—the Tanais, the Nile, and the straits at the Pillars of Hercules. Each continent lay between two of these markers, could be described in terms of the celestial coordinates, and was further defined as lying, broadly viewed (καθολικώτερον θεωρούμεναι), to the north or south of the Mediterranean, the sea which, as we have seen, Polybius elsewhere set in the context of a series of linked water-expanses. It was not possible for Polybius to give a complete picture of the world, since there was still uncertainty about the north of Europe and the south of Libya. For these gaps he refers the reader to the possibility of future discoveries (3. 38. 2). However, the system of mapping the earth on to the heavens at least provided an additional means of locating unknown places in a fixed framework.[80] For instance, the triangle of Sicily was twisted into the correct orientation by reference to the coordinates of north, south, east, and west (1. 42. 1–7).[81]

[78] The arguments of post-modern geographers about the production of space are clearly of relevance here. See, for example, N. Smith, *Uneven Development: Nature, Capital and the Production of Space* (Oxford, 1984).

[79] For Ephorus see Str. 1. 2. 28. His pattern was followed precisely in the periplus attributed to Scymnus of Chios, a contemporary of Polybius (*GGM I*, 201–2); see ll. 170–4. For Polybius' division into continents, see 3. 37. 2–8, reflecting Eratosthenes' main terrestrial divisions.

[80] The method of describing location and relative position by reference to the sky is familiar from the fragments of Hipparchus. For him it was a question of which constellations were visible.

[81] A. V. Podossinov, 'Die Orientierung der Alten Karten von den ältesten Zeiten bis zum frühen Mittelalter', *Cartographica Helvetica*, 7 (1993), 33–43; and 'Die Sakrale Orientierung nach Himmelsrichtungen im alten Griechenland', *Acta Antiqua Academiae Scientiarum Hungaricae*, 33 (1990–2), 323–30, however, points out the variety of orientations given to maps in antiquity. Once the heavens had been divided, it was not automatically fixed how this would relate to orientation on the ground.

Since geographical considerations were important in Polybius' conception of history, he needed to develop methods of denoting place and space. Unlike time, which formed the underlying organizing principle, and for which Polybius adopted a single coherent system of reference, namely the Olympiadic structure of Timaeus, space was depicted in various different ways. It is striking how sophisticated Polybius' methods for conceiving and dealing with space were, in some ways surpassing those of the 'geographer', Strabo, and certainly refuting the view that no notion of abstract space existed in antiquity. The search for Polybius' geographical conceptions has led us to his vision that brings the world into a spatial relationship with the whole cosmos. I now turn finally to consider the nature of Polybius' universalism, problems of structure and conception, and some of Polybius' solutions.

'PIECEMEAL' (κατὰ μέρος) AND 'AS-A-WHOLE' (καθόλου): POLYBIUS' UNIVERSALISM

Universal historians strictly speaking are only those who deal with the history of mankind from the earliest times, and in all parts of the world known to them.[82]

This strong definition of universalism, involving the full temporal and spatial scope known to the author, was one to which few extant writers aspired. Diodorus Siculus perhaps came closest with his assertion that 'if someone were to start with the most ancient times and record as far as possible the affairs of the whole world, which have been handed down to memory, up to his own times . . . he would have to undertake a great task, yet he would have composed a work of the utmost value to those who are inclined to study' (1. 3. 6). Diodorus criticized the efforts of previous universal historians for not being sufficiently comprehensive.

---

[82] Alonso-Núñez, 'The Emergence of Universal Historiography', 173. I have discussed in 'Universal Perspectives in Historiography', in C. Kraus (ed.), *The Limits of Historiography: Genre and Narrative in Ancient Historical Texts* (Leiden, forthcoming), the nature of universal writing in the first century BC, as reflected in the works of Diodorus Siculus, Pompeius Trogus, Strabo, and Polybius.

Although the benefit which history offers its readers lies in its
encompassing a vast number and variety of circumstances, yet most
writers have recorded isolated wars waged by a single nation or a
single state, and only a few, starting with the earliest times and
coming down to their own day, have tried to record the events
connected with all peoples; and of the latter, some have not attached
to the various events the appropriate dates, and others have passed
over the deeds of barbarians; and some have rejected the ancient
legends because of the difficulty of the undertaking, while others have
failed to complete the project, their lives cut short by fate. Of those
who have made an attempt at this task, not one has continued his
history beyond the Macedonian period. For some have finished their
accounts with the deeds of Philip, others with those of Alexander, and
some with the Diadochi or the Epigoni, yet despite the number and
significance of the events subsequent to these and stretching to my
own lifetime which have been left neglected, no historian has tried to
treat all of them within the compass of a single narrative, because of
the enormity of the undertaking. (1. 3. 2–3)

Polybius, by contrast, wrote an account that had a definite
starting-point in the third century, and which was exclusive of
certain regions.[83] His failure to start his full account until 220
BC would thus earn the censure of both Diodorus and Alonso-
Núñez. However, Polybius, given the chance, might have
objected to the assertion that no universal historian before
Diodorus had treated the post-Macedonian period. Polybius
himself took a fairly strict view of what counted as universal
history, and he criticized those who claimed to have written
universal history by giving simply an account of the war
between Rome and Carthage in three or four pages (5. 33. 3).
Only Ephorus counted for Polybius as one who had previously
written a properly universal history (τὰ καθόλου γράφειν). But
Polybius speaks of his own project in these terms, and Strabo
makes clear that he agreed with Polybius' assessment of himself
as a universal historian, listing him alone with Ephorus at the
start of Book 8. In this final section I assess in what senses
Polybius can justly be termed a universal historian, and how

---

[83] Lacy, 'ἔθη καὶ νόμιμα', 84, asserts that 'the whole of book xxxiv was
devoted to the geographical description of the world then known'. I am not
convinced that the securely placed fragments allow us to make any such
assumption.

this may contribute to a study of the relationship between time and space, or history and geography, in his work.

It is important not to confound the differences in the logic and manifestation of universalism at its various levels. Time and space, history and geography as disciplines, 'real' history and geography, and historiography all reveal and require new nuances in our understanding of Polybius' universalism. Some interpretations offer attempts to fuse together time and space, others reveal conceptions of the world which are not dependent on these categories. The philosophical categories of time and space have parallels in the concrete world in that historical events and processes take place in space, transform it, and are affected by it. Just as time and space cannot exist independently, although they may be formulated as separate notions, so in reality there is a close interplay between environment and historical process, and I have already discussed Polybius' concern with these mutual influences. One manifestation of universalism, in so far as it may be taken to refer to a holistic view of the world, must lie in this lack of independence of time and space, and of geography and history, which between them provide a location for all human experience, as I have discussed in chapter I.

However, a different kind of universalism is suggested both by the fact that Polybius was motivated to start his account in the 140th Olympiad (220–216 BC) by the particular phenomenon of the union of world history, and by the fact that the main object of his enquiry was the extension of one historical power over almost the whole known world. Whether or not Rome had set out with the intention of taking over the world has been vigorously contested.[84] But it is undeniable that Polybius says that Rome had designs over the whole world (τὰ ὅλα), and thought that it could gain rule (ἀρχή) over it (1. 3. 6; 1. 3. 10).[85] The whole narrative was explicitly intended to show

---

[84] P. S. Derow, 'Polybius, Rome, and the East', *JRS* 69 (1979), 1–15, sets out and attempts to reconcile the various views, stressing the need for distinction between purpose and result.

[85] Rome's τῶν ὅλων ἐπιβολή ('aim of universal hegemony') is evoked again at 3. 2. 6, as a potential next move after subduing Italy, Sicily, Spain, the Celts, and Carthage. *Contra*, see 6. 50. 6, where Rome is said to have intended to rule only Italy, but ended up with the world.

how Rome 'made the inhabited world (οἰκουμένη) subject to it'
(3. 3. 9). Polybius indicates that at the battle of Zama the
Carthaginians were fighting for their safety and dominion of
Libya; the Romans for rule and dominion over the whole
world. The conquerors, whoever they were, would rule all
that fell within the realm of history (ἱστορία), but only to Rome
was this aim attributed (15. 9. 2; 15. 9. 5).

Rome was not the only power to whom the idea of world rule
had occurred. On a smaller, but still threatening, scale, the
embassy from Megalopolis to Antigonus in 225 BC complained
that the greed (πλεονεξία) of the Aetolians would not stop at the
boundaries of the Peloponnese, nor even at those of Greece
(2. 49. 3). Demetrius of Pharus advised Philip V to concentrate
on Illyria and Italy, since 'Italy . . . was the beginning of
conquest over the world (τῆς ὑπὲρ τῶν ὅλων ἐπιβολῆς), which
belonged to no one more than him' (5. 101. 10).[86] It is
interesting, although not surprising, that other rulers urged
Rome not to exceed the natural limits of empire. Antiochus
reminded the Romans of their human status and begged them
not to test fate (τύχη) too much, providing an alternative view
to the idea that the rise of Rome was somehow naturally
ordained (21. 14. 4).[87] But the Romans certainly exceeded all
others in their dominion and thus provided a stimulus for
Polybius' work.

He expressly sets out the huge spatial scope encompassed by
his work in a way which must complicate the question of
perspective and focus discussed above (pp. 98–101). He states
that he will not be like other historians, who deal with the events
of one nation, but will write up events in all known parts of the
world (2. 37. 4).[88] He contrasts the magnitude and significance of
his own project with that of Timaeus, whose work was not
comparable with those which dealt with the whole inhabited

[86] Philip is said to have been encouraged in the venture because he came
from a house which more than any other aspired to world dominion (5. 102. 1).

[87] I shall return to the question of how natural law and fate appear in the
History (pp. 125–6).

[88] Also 5. 31. 6: 'My plan is to write history not of particular matters, but
what happened all over the world.' Authors such as Livy (cf. Pref. 4) and
Dionysius of Halicarnassus (*AR* 1. 3. 6), with their explicit concentration on
the history of just one city, provide an Augustan formulation of the kind of
work to which Polybius objects.

world and universal history (ἡ οἰκουμένη καὶ αἱ καθόλου πραξεῖς)
(12. 23. 7). For Polybius there was a crucial difference between
his work, which was comprehensible both in its entirety and in
part, and a selection of individual accounts written 'bit by bit'
(κατὰ μέρος). The essential process of finding an overall
structure and sense in history could not be omitted (8. 2. 2).[89]
In order to convey the unparalleled work of fate, which
consisted in bringing the world under one power, only a unified
history of events (καθόλου τῶν πραξέων ἱστορία) would suffice
(8. 2. 2–6).

But Rome had *not* conquered the entire world, and Polybius'
narrative does not cover all parts of it. Even if he did deal with
global matters at length in the thirty-fourth book, his narrative
through the work is concentrated on certain areas, exactly as in
Diodorus, in spite of the claims of that author. Yet the
recurrence of references to 'the inhabited world' (ἡ οἰκουμένη)
suggests that at some level Polybius saw Rome, in particular, as
verging on truly global domination. The totality of that vision
is brought out by comparison with previous less comprehensive 'universal empires', such as that of the Macedonians
(1. 2. 5). Moreover, Polybius' geographical conceptions
extended far beyond the known world, even into the heavens.
At this point conceptual geography exceeded the bounds of
what had been achieved in history, and gave the work a
'universal' aspect in the true sense of the word.

I mentioned above that in order to bring to the reader's mind
unknown and large-scale geographical features Polybius compared them to parts of the city, and that this method relied on
the assumption that the individual architectural feature could
be seen as a microcosm of the wider world. Polybius conceived
of the world under Roman rule as a corporate whole, a single
unit, rather than being formed from independently acting
parts. The Alps could be envisaged as an acropolis to Italy
because the *overall* shape and relationship between the Alps
and Italy was similar to the *overall* shape and relationship of an

---

[89] This, of course, perfectly supports the arguments of those who would
distinguish history from mere temporal succession. See P. Ricoeur, 'Narrative
Time', in W. J. T. Mitchell (ed.), *On Narrative* (Chicago, 1981), 165–86, as
discussed above, p. 26. The sense of the overall shape of events transformed
chronicle into history.

acropolis to a city. For the image to work, the scene had to be viewed as a whole, as is clearly indicated by the use of both the prefix συν- and the dual form: συνθεωρουμένων ἀμφοῖν ἀκροπόλεως φαίνεσθαι διάθεσιν ἔχειν τὰς Ἄλπεις τῆς ὅλης Ἰταλίας ('When the two are viewed together, the Alps appear to stand to the whole of Italy in the relation of an acropolis to a city', 3. 54. 2).

The importance of the whole as opposed to its constituent parts is relevant not only to forming mental pictures of the wider landscape, but also to Polybius' entire project. The fact that Polybius formulated space in a holistic way is crucial to our understanding of the relationship between time and space in his work. Their convergence in Rome's aim of universal empire meant that the world now progressed as one unit. From 220 BC spatial separation no longer gave rise to different histories, so space could not be the primary matrix against which Polybius' account was written; rather it was subordinated to time. The progressive expansion of Roman rule further contributed to the domination of time over space, focusing on the idea of process, and drawing together the world into one unit.[90] Time now provided the spine of the corporate world, the axis along which it progressed, making geography a true subordinate to history. I shall return to this conceit, and to its implications for the subordination of space to time in Polybius.

However united the world might have been portrayed, the process of writing about it still required the author to draw together a work from disparate elements. Polybius argues for the union of history in a striking metaphor, contrasting his period with the ill-co-ordinated one of the past. 'Previously world events were, in a way, dispersed (σποράδας) . . . but since this date [sc. 218 BC], history has been a corporate whole (σωματοειδῆ), and the affairs of Italy and Libya have been interwoven (συμπλέκεσθαί) with those of Asia and Greece,

[90] Both Derow, 'Polybius, Rome, and the East', 4–6, and Millar, 'Polybius between Greece and Rome', 1, stress the non-spatial nature of *imperium*, and it is certainly the case that to press for a spatial definition of *provincia* would be to misunderstand the term. But I would argue that, in addition to the notions of command and obedience, Polybius *was* interested in the geographical aspect of Roman rule, in the looser sense of the zones in which domination was exercised. His strongly spatial, as opposed to place-orientated, view of the world is natural in a study of expansion and changing boundaries.

leading to one end' (1. 3. 3–4).[91] But I recall from chapter I the
fact that Polybius' near-contemporary, the author of the
periplus attributed to Scymnus of Chios, brought out the
difference between real history and historiography by his
application of precisely the same formulation to the disparate
nature of the information he must use now as relater of the
unified world. 'From several *scattered* histories, I have written
in summary for you of the colonies and city-foundations,
covering all the places that are accessible by sea and land
across almost the whole earth.'[92] The world might now be
united, but its narration must still be brought together from
different elements, in a way which belies the idea of the
microcosm/macrocosm, or 'part for the whole', conception as
seen in Polybius' geography.

Just as there was in fact a disparity between the real extent of
the unifying power of Rome's empire and the global extent of
Polybius' geographical conceptions; so too was the nature of
universalism in reality different from its intellectual and
literary manifestations. Universalism in the real world meant
that world history moved as one wave; universalism in historiography meant constructing a literary system that could reflect
this new reality, albeit imperfectly and from disparate elements, as Pseudo-Scymnus shows. The problem was later to
be formulated by Diodorus:

One might criticize historical narrative when one sees that in life many
different actions happen at the same time (κατὰ τὸν αὐτὸν καιρόν), but
that those who record them must interrupt the narrative and distribute

[91] Note the return of the weaving imagery.

[92] *GGM I*, 197, Scymnus ll. 65–8: ἐκ τῶν σποράδην γὰρ ἱστορουμένων τισίν |
ἐν ἐπιτομῇ σοι γέγραφα τὰς ἀποικίας | κτίσεις τε πόλεων, τῆς ὅλης τε γῆς σχεδόν |
ὅσ᾽ ἐστὶ πλωτὰ καὶ πορευτὰ τῶν τόπων. (Cf. Polybius 3. 59. 3: σχεδὸν ἁπάντων
πλωτῶν καὶ πορευτῶν γεγονότων, using precisely the same formula to express
the breadth of horizons brought by the combined conquests of Alexander and
the Romans.)

The idea that Polybius himself amalgamated local histories is suggested by
G. A. Lehmann, 'The "Ancient" Greek History in Polybios' *Historiae*:
Tendencies and Political Objectives', *Scripta Classica Israelica*, 10 (1989/
90), 75: 'It becomes quite obvious here that Polybius did often grasp at *local* or
regional histories to have concise information close at hand for a necessary
digression'. P. J. Rhodes, 'The Atthidographers', in *Purposes of History*, 73–
81, argues that local histories, such as those of Attica, were surprisingly varied
in nature, ranging from the historical to the antiquarian.

different times to simultaneous events, contrary to nature (τοῖς ἅμα συντελουμένοις μερίζειν τοὺς χρόνους παρὰ φύσιν), with the result that the written account mimics the events, but falls far short of the true arrangement (πολὺ δὲ λείπεσθαι τῆς ἀληθοῦς διαθέσεως). (20. 43. 7)[93]

It is a real historiographical problem that a chronologically ordered narrative cannot truly represent contemporaneous events.

There is an additional problem. If Polybius' assertion that history was now 'a corporate whole' were correct, then there would be just one story to tell, and the historiographical problem would be lessened, although not eradicated. But, as is clear, events in different parts of the world were not entirely intertwined so as to form a single coherent narrative, and Polybius' account naturally reflects this. The conceit by which the diversity of the world was encompassed in a single history lay in the fact that the process of Roman expansion was still taking place and the world was not yet united. This was surely in part responsible for Polybius' striking concern with the dynamic concept of space rather than with established and static place. For the period with which Polybius dealt, history was precisely concerned with the production of, and changes in, space. Both Timaeus and Diodorus (possibly following Ephorus) were concerned with moments when the histories of different places seem to be co-ordinated. Diodorus noted that the battle of Plataea occurred on the same day as the battle between the Greeks and Persians at Mycale (11. 34. 1); the Peloponnesian war in Greece and the first war between Dionysius and Carthage in Sicily ended roughly together (13. 114. 3); on the very same day, and even at the same time on that day, the battles of Chaeronea and that between the Tarentines and the Lucanians in Italy took place (16. 88. 3). Momigliano saw this preoccupation also in the fragments of Timaeus' work, for which Polybius provided the

[93] The use of the compound of θέσις is interesting, and recalls the stress on accurate location in Polybius' geographical descriptions. See E. Auerbach, *Mimesis: The Representation of Reality in Western Literature*, trans. W. Trask (Princeton, 1953), ch. 1, on the process of representation in Homer. He sees Homer's mimesis as being totally foregrounded and lacking 'perspective in time and place', but argues that Greek culture and literature soon took on the problem of historical change and the 'multilayeredness' of existence.

continuation.[94] However, this concern with examples of
synchronism precisely reveals the disparate nature of *most* of
the world's history.

Hence Polybius' concern with the ordering of the text. The
geography of the text itself, to which I have already alluded,
meant that there were appropriate places to which he could
assign material. He declined to discuss Britain and the Outer
Ocean partly because he wanted to assign 'the proper place and
time' to their treatment.[95] After telling of Rome and Carthage
in Spain, he promises to 'turn the scene of the story totally, as
the action shifted to Greece', making the geography of the
narrative match the changing location of the main action
(3. 3. 1).

The turning-point for the organization of the narrative
according to time and space was the 140th Olympiad. Up
until the third year of this Olympiad (218 BC) Polybius
argues that the events in different parts of the world should
be related separately. The events in Italy, Greece, and Asia
were still best explained individually, until the point at which
they became interwoven and began to tend towards one end
(πρὸς ἓν τέλος). By keeping the narratives distinct until the great
interweaving of events (ἡ συμπλοκὴ τῶν πράξεων) in 218, and
then giving a united account (κοινῇ) in chronological order,
Polybius argues that he will give more prominence to the
transformation of world history (4. 28. 2–6). In fact, when he
reaches this year in his account of Europe, he says that he has
come to a suitable place at which to turn the narrative to Asia
and confine himself to that area for the same Olympiad
(5. 30. 8).

---

[94] A. Momigliano, *Essays in Ancient and Modern Historiography* (Oxford,
1977), 51. In F 60, he notes the contemporaneous foundations of Rome and
Carthage; in F 150, the birth of Alexander on the same day as the temple of
Artemis at Ephesus was burned.

[95] 3. 57. 5: καὶ τόπον καὶ καιρὸν ἀπονείμαντες. Note the conceptual separation
of space and time, although the proper place in the text will inevitably occur at
the proper time, making the two indistinguishable. At 3. 59. 6 he again
promises to find a suitable place (ἁρμόζοντα τόπον) for discussion of little-
known lands, appropriately using a geographical metaphor. Cf. also 5. 98. 11
on finding a 'suitable time and place' (ἁρμόζοντα καιρὸν καὶ τόπον) for an
exposition of siege-tactics.

In order that my narrative may be easy to follow and clear, I think that nothing is more essential for this Olympiad [sc. 140th] than not to interweave events together, but to keep them distinct and separate as much as possible, until, on reaching the next and subsequent Olympiads, I can begin to write of events alongside each other year by year. (5. 31. 4–5)

Polybius here strikingly fails to live up to his programme. The year 218 did not affect the writing of history in the way he had envisaged; for that we must wait until the start of the next Olympiad.

However, even then, although events might have undergone an interweaving that united them in reality, Polybius' attempt to mirror this in the text does not result in the single account that spans vast areas. Indeed, he states his practice later as being to relate 'separately the events in each country for each year' (28. 16. 11). Towards the end of the work, this is repeated—'Keeping distinct all the most important places in the world (πάντας διῃρημένοι τοὺς ἐπιφανεστάτους τόπους τῆς οἰκουμένης) and the events that took place in each . . . I leave it open to the students to cast their minds back to the continuous narrative (τὸν συνεχῆ λόγον)' (38. 6. 5). The image of weaving is used of events in Polybius' narrative, concerning both reality and the process of historiography. He considered that the great length of his work was no hindrance to the reader since the books were 'as though connected by a single thread' (καθάπερ ἂν εἰ κατὰ μίτον ἐξυφασμένας) (3. 32. 2).[96] The inter-weaving of real events differed from their interweaving in historiography, reflecting the different manifestations of universalism as discussed above. The historian's creation of his text as a woven fabric involves drawing together the narrative of separate places, but, as Diodorus explained, this can only mimic reality and lacks its true arrangement.[97]

---

[96] Pédech, *La Méthode historique*, 507, notes that the term συμπλοκή ('weaving') was used by the atomists, Leucippus and Democritus, to denote the combination of elements, illustrating the real interweaving of the world into an organic whole at the most basic level, and again illustrating the importance of Ionian cosmology through Herodotus and on to the Hellenistic historians.

[97] Diodorus 4. 60. 1 and 4. 63. 1 use the same image of weaving a narrative (ἀναγκαῖον ...τὰ συμπεπλεγμένα τούτοις διελθεῖν: 'it is necessary . . . to go through the events which are *interwoven* with these').

I wonder whether it is possible to look beyond this to less polarized notions of unity and universalism. At least two alternatives are suggested within Polybius' text. The relation of a holistic view of the world to biography is the first of these. Polybius likens the effect of trying to gain an overall view of history from studying isolated accounts to imagining the whole living animal from having seen only its dissected component parts (1. 4. 7). The image is particularly interesting when set against Strabo's comment directed against Eratosthenes that the world must not be divided up into random piecemeal sections (ἄλλως κατὰ μέρος), but limb by limb (κατὰ μέλος) (Str. 2. 1. 30). Here we may recall the use of biological metaphor, explicitly applied to history itself in the justification for the start-date of Polybius' work. From the 140th Olympiad, world history was 'like a corporate whole' (σωματοειδής). So, geography, history, and historiography adhered to this principle of holism. The idea that writing history (or geography) may have affinities with biography is supported by the notion of the life-cycle of historical institutions, of customs, and of places. I shall discuss the life-cycle of places later, in relation to Strabo's *Geography*, but Walbank has pointed out the importance of biological patterns for Polybius' historical conceptions also.[98] Nowhere is this clearer than at the fall of Carthage, where the idea of the succession of empires is strongly evoked, and Rome's success is set in the context of the rise and fall of states (38. 22. 2).[99]

Polybius' interest in the way that historical processes yield constitutions following a natural biological pattern of birth, development, and decline is interestingly paralleled by his concern with the lives of individual actors in history. 'All that befell Rome and Carthage could be ascribed to one man and one life, I mean that of Hannibal (εἰς ἦν ἀνὴρ αἴτιος καὶ μία ψυχή, λέγω δὲ τὴν Ἀννίβου)' (9. 22. 1).[100] Concerning Philopoi-

---

[98] Walbank, *Polybius*, 142–4.

[99] See also 29. 21. 4. J. Hornblower, *Hieronymus of Cardia* (Oxford, 1981), 104–6, traces the common Hellenistic motif of pondering the mutability of fortune. The case discussed by Hornblower (Antigonus Gonatas and Pyrrhus) is significant because it came in the final cadence of Hieronymus' work, as in Polybius, suggesting a conscious imitation by Polybius.

[100] A crucial stage in the development of biography as universal history was the work of Theopompus, whose *Philippica*, ostensibly focused on one person,

men, Polybius places accounts of people above those of city-foundations on the grounds that it is men who actively play out events (10. 21. 3–4).[101] This appears to diminish the importance of place as an active player in history, but Wiedemann does something to reinstate places alongside human characters, nicely illustrating the overriding nature of the biographical form. Wiedemann ascribes the full incorporation of biographical sketches into historiography to Polybius, writing that 'the idea of including descriptions of an individual's character—in addition to those of the character of a city or area—in a historical narrative seems to have been Polybius' own contribution'.[102]

Biographies and life-cycles also introduce into the discussion the laws of nature. I mentioned above (p. 110) the way in which geographical phenomena obeyed a certain natural logic, which coherently linked the processes taking place across the world. The notion of the natural order, sometimes referred to as φύσις, and worked out by fate, offers another way of conceptualizing the unity of the world without explicit recourse to the categories of time and space.[103] Polybius states that what was particular to his period was that fate 'had guided almost all the affairs of the world in one direction and forced them to incline to one single end' (1. 4. 1). The unification of the world led Polybius to investigate 'when and from where the general and comprehensive scheme of things originated and how it led up to the end' (1. 4. 3). Elsewhere he states that the most important part of history is the investigation of the remote or immediate consequences of events and especially that of causes (τὰ περὶ τὰς αἰτίας) (3. 32. 6).

told the history of a whole age. It is telling that Pompeius Trogus adopted the title *Historiae Philippicae* for his Augustan universal history.

[101] Scipio Africanus' exploits are explicitly recounted against the background of his character (10. 2. 1).

[102] T. Wiedemann, 'Rhetoric in Polybius', in *Purposes of History*, 294. But cf. Thucydides' portrait of, for example, Pericles at 2. 65.

[103] That fate (τύχη) was the architect of the world's fortunes is brought out in 4. 2. 4, where the reason for the start-date of the work is that 'fate had, as it were, made new the whole inhabited world' (τὸ καὶ τὴν τύχην ὡσανεὶ κεκαινοποιηκέναι πάντα τὰ κατὰ τὴν οἰκουμένην). A particular example of this is the attribution of the natural logic of well-proportioned straits to the agency of fate (16. 29. 8).

The principles of causation and consequence and of interlocking events span the categories of time and space and apply
to both historical and geographical processes. Polybius' example that the war with Antiochus resulted from that with
Philip, which was a consequence of the war with Hannibal,
which in turn was a result of the war over Sicily, mirrors
exactly the constant flow of water from the Palus Maeotis, to
the Pontus, to the Propontis, to the Mediterranean, to the
Outer Ocean.[104] Both processes require a vision of some all-
encompassing universal law. Polybius' political theory also
involves the natural order; the dominance of the strong over
the weak, which first gave rise to a social order, is seen as 'the
truest work of nature' (φύσεως ἔργον ἀληθινώτατον) (6. 5. 8). The
whole cycle of political institutions ran according to the organization of nature (φύσεως οἰκονομία) (6. 9. 10).[105] We have
already seen how the organization (οἰκονομία) of the text was
the business of the writer (5. 31. 7); that of the world belonged
to fate. The idea of world unity through divine will, and the
centralizing tendency of fate, are strongly associated with Stoic
thought, which may provide yet another approach to the
formulation of Polybius' conception of the whole (τὰ ὅλα).[106]

But it would be a mistake to attribute these notions to a single
school of thought. As I discussed in chapter I, the Presocratic
philosophers had already put forward various models of a
symmetrical and unified cosmos, and Herodotus, so much of
whose world-view seems to have been owed to his fellow Ionian
Greeks, echoed the stress on a world ordered by symmetry
with, for example, his assertion that 'if there are Hyperboreans,
then there are others, Hypernotians' (Hdt. 4. 36). Indeed, the
importance to Polybius' *History* of the Herodotean historio-

---

[104] 3. 32. 7 for the string of historical consequences. Pédech, *La Méthode
historique*, 405–31, helpfully points out the way in which Polybius' use of
geographical parallels employs precisely the same technique as his system of
parallel lives and parallel constitutions. These all add up to what Pédech calls
'la méthode comparative' (p. 415).

[105] At 4. 40. 6 the inevitable silting-up of the Pontus is described as 'in accord
with nature' (κατὰ φύσιν); 4. 39. 11 gives preference to reasoning from φύσις.

[106] The principle underlying Diodorus' own universal history has been
seen by B. Farrington, *Diodorus Siculus. Universal Historian* = Inaugural
Lecture at Swansea (Swansea, 1937) as Stoicism, with its idea of a unified
universe.

graphical model, the capacious history later exemplified in the works of the *Annales* school and in the views of Jacoby, seems to be borne out by many aspects of the text. Not only, as I have tried to show, was Polybius far more interested in geographical issues than has sometimes been appreciated, bringing his *History* in that respect close to Herodotus' all-embracing model; not only was he writing a response to conquest, as Herodotus had done; but also the conceptual unity of both accounts and the world they describe is clear.

Universalism may be encompassed not only in the fusion of time and space, the co-extension of these across the known world, and the author's attempt to reflect this, however imperfectly, in his account, but also in the concepts of biography and of the natural order. It is interesting that Polybius' project used both the categories of time and space, and unifying notions that did *not* involve this polarized approach. This accords with his repeated stress on the need to view the world both 'bit by bit' (κατὰ μέρος) and 'as a whole' (καθόλου). His introduction was designed to convey a notion of the work to the reader καὶ καθόλου καὶ κατὰ μέρος ('both as a whole and bit by bit') (3. 5. 9); the enormity of the project necessitated careful attention to organization, so that the work might be clear καὶ κατὰ μέρος καὶ καθόλου (5. 31. 7); and in the epilogue he indicated his wish to summarize the whole subject (τὴν ὅλην), establishing καὶ καθόλου καὶ κατὰ μέρος the connection between the beginning and the end (39. 8. 3). All these passages concern the methodological problem of organizing a work of huge scope. The process of composition must be clear on two levels, both in its putting-together of constituent parts and in its overall conception.

The notion of microcosm and macrocosm, of the 'part for the whole', may offer one interpretation of what Polybius meant by this duality. The *History*, like the world which it related, could be understood to function logically both as a whole and in part, since each part was an integral component of the whole.[107] But

---

[107] There is also a sense in which the microcosm/macrocosm approach to history enabled the work to stand as a fragment of a wider whole, just as D. S. Levene, 'Sallust's *Jugurtha*: An "Historical Fragment"', *JRS* 82 (1992), 53–70, argues with regard to that work. So, for example, allusions to Xerxes extend the scope of the *History* to the fifth century BC.

it can be argued that this is also precisely how the purely spatial content of the work could be analysed. I have already mentioned that Claudius Ptolemaeus distinguished in the introduction to his *Geography* between chorography and geography. The passage is worth citing again in full, since it recalls many of the themes of this chapter, as well as revealing how strikingly comprehensive Polybius' notion of geography in history was: 'Chorography has as its aim the treatment of the subject piece by piece (ἐπὶ μέρους), as if one were to depict (μιμοῖτο) an ear or an eye by itself; but geography aims at the general survey (τῆς καθόλου θεωρίας), in the same way as one would depict the entire head' (*Geog.* 1. 1. 1).

As I have argued above, the language of the body recalls Polybius' own view of his work and the world it describes as an organic whole, with a life to be related. The notion of geography as a form of mimesis sets the enterprise neatly alongside Diodorus' task of historical mimesis (20. 43. 7), however imperfect that may be. Both geography and history are seen as forms of representation of the world, which might naturally fall within the compass of a single integrated work such as that of Polybius. Ptolemaeus' stress on geography as representation is accompanied by the importance of the visual. The geographer has to engage in θεωρία ('spectating' or 'viewing'), in a way which we have seen was crucial in Polybius' *History*. But just as Polybius' work, representing in a strongly visual way the changing world of Roman power, spans geography and history, so too Polybius' geography embraces Ptolemaeus' chorographical style (ἐπὶ μέρους) and his geographical approach (καθόλου). Not only did geography for Polybius function on both the small- and the large-scale, but the formula can be pushed yet further. Both as a separable component (μέρος), which interacted with history in various ways, and as an undifferentiated ingredient in Polybius' truly holistic view of the world (καθόλου), geography and space were integral to the *History*.

III

Posidonius: Geography, History, and Stoicism

INTRODUCTION

Posidonius of Apamea and of Rhodes earns his place in this study on several counts. In his own right, he was one of the most important intellectual figures of the early part of the first century BC. He was the leading Stoic of his day, and an expert in a vast range of fields—mathematics, physics, philosophy, history, and geography. In addition to this, he forms a neat chronological and textual link between Polybius and Strabo. Posidonius, like Strabo, wrote a continuation of Polybius' *History*, and he was a major source for Strabo in his *Geography*.[1] Posidonius held a high political profile in Rhodes, a crucial point in the network of communications across the Mediterranean world.[2] He had held the prytany in Rhodes and was sent on an embassy to Marius (Str. 7. 5. 8; Plut. *Mar.* 45. 7). Like Polybius, and to a lesser extent, Strabo, he had connections with the highest level of the Roman élite, which gave him a complex viewpoint on the development and consolidation of the Roman world.[3] His travels took him to Spain, Italy, Liguria, and Gaul in the West, to add to his personal experience of the eastern Mediterranean world.

I shall say more in the next sections about Posidonius' works, of which I have, for obvious reasons, focused on those traditionally characterized as 'geographical' and 'historical',

---

[1] For Posidonius' 'Events after Polybius' (τὰ μετὰ Πολύβιον), see *FGrH* 87 T 1; as a source for the *Geography*, see Str. 1. 1. 1; 8. 1. 1.

[2] Str. 14. 2. 13: Ποσειδώνιος δ᾽ ἐπολιτεύσατο μὲν ἐν ῾Ρόδῳ ('Posidonius held public office in Rhodes').

[3] For links with Cicero see T 29–34; on links with Pompey see T 35–9 in L. Edelstein and I. G. Kidd (eds.), *Posidonius I. The Fragments* (Cambridge, 1972).

attributing the majority of unacknowledged pieces of high-quality thought in authors such as Diodorus and Strabo to their superior predecessor, Posidonius. This process tends to take on a momentum of its own. As Diodorus and Strabo are stripped of their 'clever' passages, they become increasingly unworthy of such pieces and all the more likely to lose them. As Posidonius is accorded more of these intellectual highlights, he becomes proportionately more intelligent and all the more likely to have been the source of high-level discourse. It is precisely in opposition to such polarization of authors in terms of intellectual achievement into 'thinkers' and 'compilers' that I favour the practice of Jacoby and of Edelstein, followed by Kidd, in rejecting for their collections any passage not directly attributed to Posidonius in the ancient sources.

The problem of fragments is, however, also directly related to the challenge which I wish to pose to modern assumptions about the genre of ancient works. It is because so much has been made of so little that all the more care should be taken when assessing the broader nature of Posidonius' works. Brunt has argued for extreme caution in the degree to which we can assert anything about whole works from their fragments.[9] It is often unclear where citations start and end, how much has been paraphrased, and to what extent a passage is characteristic of the work as a whole. All of these problems will be exemplified when I consider the fragments individually, but the overall effect must be to enforce great caution in trying to draw any conclusions whatsoever about the nature of the complete works and about the contents of their separate books.

A particular difficulty arises in the case of Posidonius' *Histories*, since every single one of the fragments from this work which survive with a book number is preserved in just one source, Athenaeus' *Deipnosophistae*. Given our complete dependence on this one work for our view of the organization of the *Histories*, it seems appropriate to discuss briefly at least some of the problems arising.

Firstly, the textual tradition is fairly complex. A parchment manuscript (A), written probably in the tenth century, was brought to Venice from Constantinople in 1423. The mid-

⁹ P. A. Brunt, 'On Historical Fragments and Epitomes', *CQ* NS 30 (1980), 477–94.

fifteenth-century copy of this manuscript formed the basis of the Aldine edition of 1514, the only edition which preserves the book numbers of fragments cited, and the main source for the text. However, the manuscript lacked Books 1 and 2, much of Book 3 and the end of Book 15. For these, it was necessary to rely on other manuscripts, which may or may not have been dependent on A. In particular, much of what the modern textual critic can reconstruct for parts of the work not found in A is derived from epitomes.

Secondly, it is worth repeating that the book numbers are given in only one manuscript of Athenaeus (A). This explains to some extent the willingness of editors to emend any number that does not comply with his or her own view of Posidonius' work, on the grounds that numbers are notoriously corruptible and cannot in this case be verified by reference to any other text. This does not, however, provide a justification for where and why editors have wanted to make emendations in the first place. As I shall argue, the wish to emend has usually sprung from a desire to create a narrative which complies perfectly with chronological order.

Thirdly, the nature of the *Deipnosophistae* as a source for Posidonius' *Histories* must be taken into account. The relaxed context of learned leisure is hard to assess for accuracy of citation and choice of topic. The analogy of high-table dinner talk may have something to offer the answer to both questions; namely that the accuracy may be more apparent than real, and that the turns in the conversation are likely to be erratic, illogical, and certainly not intended primarily to illuminate or to give a full picture of any one source drawn into the discussion. Rather the focus of interest will be the occasion in hand, that is, dinner, and the references will be deliberately allusive, and not designed to provoke too thorough an investigation into their accuracy. Of course, the *Deipnosophistae* is far more packed with literary references and allusions than any real conversation would be, certainly over so long a period. However, the point is that, as our only source for the organization of the *Histories*, the peculiarities and conventions of Athenaeus' *Deipnosophistae* must at least be acknowledged.

The two major issues of accuracy and choice of subject both deserve consideration. The latter is quite clearly an important

factor when dealing with Posidonius' *Histories*. Athenaeus'
dinner party not surprisingly discusses food, drink, and associated customs at length, and it is in this context that many of
his references to Posidonius are to be found. Of fewer than
thirty citations, eighteen mention food or drink in some form,
either still to be eaten, or at the moment of being consumed, or
taking its toll afterwards. A further six concern revelry,
extravagance, or some other form of frivolity; leaving only
five which could not be described as immediately congenial to
the sympotic milieu of the *Deipnosophistae*. These are F 38 on
the enslavement of the Chians by Mithridates, F 61 on rabbits,
F 8 on the subordination of the Mariandynians to the Heracleots, F 17 on Celtic parasites, and F 23 on the Syrian
parasite. Of these, the first two are unusual in having no
book number attributed to them by Athenaeus; the other
three all have in common a concern over social organization.

But the overwhelming majority of citations made by Athenaeus of Posidonius' *Histories* concern precisely the central
theme of the *Deipnosophistae*—dining, revelry, and extravagance. This comes as no surprise, but it is worth recalling,
especially when using collections of fragments taken out of
their Athenaean context, how strongly determined by Athenaeus and his gastronomic preoccupations this makes our
picture of Posidonius' *Histories*. Of course, it could be, as
Hornblower has pointed out, that Athenaeus quarried Posidonius extensively precisely because his *Histories* were known to
be so rich in details on the subject of food.[10] It would not
indeed be unreasonable to expect a work with a strong ethnographic element to contain information on eating habits. To an
extent this picture of Athenaeus' deliberate selection of Posidonius' *Histories*, as a text which he knew to be ethnographic
and broad in its cultural interests, would support my view that
we should be prepared to find a strong Herodotean influence on
this work. However, it does seem that these Athenaean passages must still be distorting our view of the scope of the
Histories.

The other point concerns the literal fidelity of the citations.
The whole question of precisely how ancient authors used their

---

[10] S. Hornblower, *Greek Historiography* (Oxford, 1994), 48.

'sources' will be important in assessing Strabo's use of earlier historiographical texts, as I discuss in chapter VI. But it is clearly also relevant to any consideration of Posidonius from the opposite angle, the retrieval of the source. Pelling has argued in connection with Plutarch that the clumsy nature of papyrus consultation would have made the use of more than one source at a time very difficult.[11] The clustering of Posidonius citations at certain locations in the *Deipnosophistae* may support the view of Athenaeus also consulting the Posidonius papyrus on a few limited occasions. For Laffranque the notion that Athenaeus referred to works 'livre en main', secured the accuracy of his citations. The 'livre en main' technique, together with the frivolity of the setting, which gave Athenaeus no reason to distort his sources in order to present his own philosophical or intellectual message, supported the notion that Athenaeus was preserving a faithful record of Posidonius' *Histories*.

Pelling too has contended that Athenaeus' use of his sources was anything but careless. His earlier work on Plutarch argued for a complex process of composition from sources, elements of which may be applicable to Athenaeus. The dominant source open on the desk, and probably cited with relative accuracy, was only one of many types of reference to other texts. Pelling suggests that the main source would be supplemented by memory both of a general background of other texts, and of preliminary reading done specifically for the work in hand. So it is plausible that one passage from an author evoked the memory of several other citations, with no textual consultation involved, and the question of accuracy becomes a complex one.[12] Indeed Pelling has suggested that short-term memory may have been more important for Athenaeus than working face to face with a source, although it is hard to see what

[11] C. B. R. Pelling, 'Plutarch's Method of Work in the Roman Lives', *JHS* 99 (1979), 74–96.

[12] See M. Laffranque, *Poseidonios d'Apamée: Essai de mise au point* (Paris, 1964). C. B. R. Pelling, 'Fun with Fragments: Athenaeus and the Historians', in D. Braund and J. Wilkins (eds.), *Athenaeus and his Philosophers at Supper* (Exeter, 1999), develops a simpler process for Athenaeus, reproducing passages from short-term memory. For a similarly complex picture of oral and written memory in the citation of 'sources' see Hornblower, *Greek Historiography*, 56–64.

process other than direct consultation could account for Athenaeus' inclusion of book numbers in his references.

In addition, Pelling went on to use his picture of Athenaeus' closely interwoven and skilfully connected text to develop the important issue of where a fragment starts and ends. Both Laffranque and Pelling reach the conclusion that sources are hard to extrapolate from Athenaeus and that, once retrieved from this most idiosyncratic of settings, they are hard to contextualize and interpret. A glance at Pelling's discussion of how Athenaeus uses authors whose works are known from elsewhere, and how confused and distorted a picture we should gain from Athenaeus alone, must raise serious questions about what we can possibly attempt with the fragments of Posidonius' *Histories*. We can be sure neither of what constitutes the citation, nor of how accurately it is cited.

Given the many problems associated with texts which survive only in fragmentary form, extreme caution is required in any attempt to draw broader conclusions about the complete works. I intend to demonstrate that even meticulous editors and commentators can be lured towards generalizations about the lost works of Posidonius that rest on modern assumptions about the nature of 'geographical' and 'historical' works; assumptions which, as I hope is becoming apparent, have been challenged by historians and geographers in a way which should make us reassess our view of ancient authors.[13] The result may seem destructive, since much of what follows is an attempt to argue against previous approaches to this author. I have tried to relegate some of the polemic to Appendix B, but it could be argued that I offer little as an alternative to what I reject. My approach to Posidonius may appear pedestrian and unadventurous, but it is determined by a desire to respect the fragmentary nature of the works and not to force the evidence into rigid patterns. Even so, I may be convicted myself of falling into a similar trap of overemphasizing certain aspects of the material at the expense of others. However, if all we

[13] There is, of course, a danger in using the term 'modern' in the context of this argument. By 'modern assumptions' I mean those which underpin the way in which, for example, geography and history are taught as separate and distinct disciplines in British education. But the most modern approach may be to challenge this division.

conclude is that we cannot allow the accepted characterizations of Posidonius' works to remain unchallenged, that may at least halt the reconstruction of the works in some ways which are unwarranted.

More optimistically, the re-examination of the fragments, undertaken with greater awareness of the generic assumptions which have usually been applied and of the problems associated with these assumptions, may enable us to see new possibilities for broader interpretations of the lost works, to which standard conceptions of what constitutes a geographical or historical work have blinded us. In particular, the extant fragments of Hellenistic histories, while sharing all the problems of fragmentation themselves, may offer some insights into the possible range and scope of Posidonius' *Histories*. These fragments seem to have been rarely cited in commentaries and works on Posidonius, and yet offer a crucial aid to our understanding of the intellectual world of the late Hellenistic period, to which Posidonius belonged. By taking into account both this literary milieu of broad Herodotean historiography, alongside the widely accepted influence of Thucydides, and also the cosmological implications of Posidonius' Stoic philosophy, we may move towards a more satisfactory understanding of the works as fitting products of the age—that is, as different responses to the changes in world-view brought by Roman imperialism.

I shall deal with two lost works, the *Histories* and *On Ocean*, which illustrate the dangers of constructing the nature of whole works around scant evidence on the basis of modern notions of separate narrow disciplines of geography and history. I shall argue against the attribution of unplaced fragments to the works on these grounds, and show that if we look at the fragments actually assigned in the ancient sources to the *Histories* and *On Ocean* we gain a very different view of the character of those works, which may alter the way in which other fragments should be allocated. It seems that assigning these fragments on the basis of a picture gained from the placed passages themselves, even acknowledging the fact both that these offer mere glimpses of the complete original and that no reading is objective, is a more sound approach than allocating them simply according to our ideas of what a 'history' and a 'geography' should be.

Many of the debates in modern geography, which are causing scholars to re-examine the ways in which they analyse geographical and historical texts, are not readily applicable to Posidonius simply because we can tell so little about the overall design of fragmentary texts. As always the cue for questions should come from the evidence itself; it is a bonus if the issues raised in relation to modern material can play a part in guiding our study of the ancient texts. However, there are several major questions which I shall keep in mind while considering the extant fragments. Firstly, do the fragments of each work differ from or conform in content to what we might expect from a 'geography' and a chronological narrative? How different are the issues raised in the two works? Will an examination of the contents prove helpful in allocating unplaced fragments to each of them?[14] Secondly, is there any evidence in the fragments to help reconstruct the arrangement and nature of the works? Shall we be able to conclude that *On Ocean* was spatially organized, as we may assume a geography should be; and that we should see the *Histories* as a temporally dominated narrative? Or, did the works simply deal with different parts of the world, but concerning the same kind of issues and arranged in indistinguishable ways? Alternatively, will the Herodotean model of cultural historiography and Jacoby's interrelated prose styles prove helpful in understanding what remains of the lost works of Posidonius?

Firstly, I look at what is firmly assigned in the sources to each work. I demonstrate that the one surviving fragment of *On Ocean* conforms only to the most far-reaching and capacious definition of geography. I contend that the extant fragments of the *Histories* are either ethnographic in nature, or that, if they contain datable material, this may tell us nothing about the contents of the surrounding book. In particular, I argue that, even if we conclude that the *Histories* were broadly arranged according to time, still textual emendations made for the purpose of fitting the extant fragments into a temporally ordered narrative are unwarranted and futile.

Having considered the securely assigned passages, and

---

[14] As I discussed in Ch. I, the use of contents as guides to the 'geographical' or 'historical' nature of works is open to challenge.

argued on the basis of them for Posidonian works which were broad in scope, I turn to the unplaced fragments and re-examine the way in which they have been labelled by various commentators as 'historical' or 'geographical'. It is interesting that both Jacoby and Kidd adopted the principle of separating the securely located fragments from those for which the source indicates no specific original context, but that they did so in rather different ways. Finally, I consider Posidonius' wider view of the world, which may help us to look beyond matters of generic classification. Except in the case of passages not included in Jacoby's collection, I use his numbering for the fragments cited. For ease of reference and in order to support my arguments concerning the nature of the *Histories*, I have included all the fragments securely assigned to this work with translation and some comments in Appendix B.

ON OCEAN[15]

The amount of secondary literature which focuses on this work would never lead one to suppose that there is only one securely attributed extant fragment.[16] It is often referred to as Posido-nius' 'geographical' work, a denotation which, in the light of the various challenges to the definition of geography under discussion, should immediately raise questions.[17] What do

[15] From now on I shall use this translation of the title assumed for the work on the basis of Strabo's comments at 2. 2. 1. While accepting that it was very common for ancient works to be denoted by the word περί followed by the subject matter, it is particularly interesting in this case, since the work, as far as I can tell, also literally went 'around' the Ocean, at least on one shore. I shall return to the question of the work as a periplus text. I have chosen to reflect in my translation the lack of a definite article in the Greek. However, one may argue that the great Outer Ocean did not require an article by virtue of its being the only *significant* ocean (cf. βασιλεύς used without an article to refer to the Great King of Persia).

[16] F 28 (= Str. 2. 2. 1–3. 8). All references to Jacoby's or to Kidd's views will be taken from their respective commentaries on the fragment under discussion.

[17] Laffranque, *Poseidonios d'Apamée*, deals with *On Ocean* strictly within the confines of her chapter on 'Poseidonios Géographe', and makes her view of the work clear on p. 156; namely that all the information that we can have today on the geographical work of Posidonius is extracts from *On Ocean*, and that if he wrote another work in the same discipline, we know nothing of it.

scholars mean by saying that *On Ocean* was a geographical
work? Are they taking their definition from modern conceptions of the subject, and, if so, *how* modern? In other words, I
suspect that the description of *On Ocean* as 'geographical' relies
on notions of geography which do not take fully into account
the recent debates over the relationship between geography and
other disciplines, notably history. As I shall later show, the way
in which non-assigned fragments have been discussed and
consigned to the realm of geography, and so allocated a
speculative place in *On Ocean*, strongly suggests a narrow
definition of geography as a scientific discipline. I shall demonstrate that even in our one surviving fragment of the work,
there is evidence that *On Ocean* had a far broader scope than a
purely scientific account. The consequence of this is that either
we can maintain the description of the work as geographical,
but revise our idea of what 'geographical' means; or we can
keep the notion of geography as a scientific discipline, but
assert that *On Ocean* was not a purely geographical work.[18]

The fragment comes from Strabo's survey of his main
predecessors, to whom much of the first two books of his
work are devoted, and it is important to remember that it is
only Strabo's summary of some of Posidonius' theories, and
not a direct citation from *On Ocean*. As I mentioned above in
connection with Athenaeus and his use of Posidonius' *Histories*, it is far from clear where the Posidonian section starts
and ends, how accurate a reflection of the original work has
been preserved, how representative it is of the whole, and how
far its contents have been determined by Strabo's preoccupations and interpretations. I give the following summary of the
contents, rather than quote the whole passage.

(a) Strabo states that he will next discuss Posidonius' theories
from his treatise on the Ocean.
(b) He discusses the theory of zones, giving Posidonius' criticisms of Parmenides and Aristotle; then, Posidonius' own
division of zones in relation to celestial phenomena, and

---

[18] K. Reinhardt, *Poseidonios* (Munich, 1921), was already questioning the
ease with which Posidonius could be labelled a geographer, with no thought
given to the individuality of his approach. Reinhardt pointed out that the
geography of Strabo and that of Posidonius were very different things (59).

secondly, in relation to human geography. Strabo next criticizes Polybius' division into six zones on the basis of Posidonius' theory, although he notes inconsistencies in Posidonius' views also.

(c) The question of a circumambient Ocean is discussed, with Posidonius' arguments for its existence supported by the story of Eudoxus of Cyzicus and the voyage round Libya. Strabo criticizes Posidonius' method.

(d) Strabo mentions Posidonius' arguments about changes in the level of sea and earth, with the Atlantis story and the Cimbrian migrations adduced as evidence.

(e) Posidonius' figure for the length of the inhabited world is given.

(f) Various geographical divisions are discussed: by zones, by continents, by ethnographic variation. Strabo criticizes Posidonius' belief in geographical determinism.

(g) Strabo criticizes Posidonius' predilection for investigating causation.

By dealing with Posidonius at this point, Strabo sets him in the line of great geographers that included not only Eratosthenes and Hipparchus, but also Polybius. The first two are well known as examples of the mathematical geographical tradition, concerned with distances, lines of latitude, and measurements of the earth's circumference.[19] Reading beyond the Posidonian section of Strabo's discussion complicates the picture. The emerging image of Posidonius' *On Ocean* as being firmly rooted in a scientific geographical tradition might have allowed us to dismiss ethnographical passages of human interest as belonging to some other work such as the *Histories*. Such a scientific image might in turn have been shattered by the mention of the historian, Polybius. But both sides of the comparison, as well as their point of contact in Posidonius, resist such straightforward analysis.

Firstly, the distinction between scientific and human geography was insufficiently clear to allow us to interpret references to Eratosthenes and Hipparchus as signifying that Posidonius wrote an account devoid of human interest. Even

---

[19] D. R. Dicks, *The Geographical Fragments of Hipparchus* (London, 1960), provides an excellent discussion of these fragments.

the work of the 'scientific' geographer *par excellence*, Claudius
Ptolemaeus, reveals concern with what might be termed
'ethnography'. His latitudinal and longitudinal divisions of
the earth were ethnographically characterized. His description
of Taprobane and eastern India included ethnographical notes
on the size and appearance of the inhabitants, and the treatment of India provided details of the minerals and other
natural resources, such as diamonds and beryls (*Geog.* 7. 4).
The Fish-Eaters of Agatharchides and of Nearchus appear in
Ptolemaeus' descriptions of the west coast of Libya and of
southern India.[20]

It is clear both that so-called 'human geographers', the
authors of periplus texts, were interested in scientific observations, and that 'theoretical' geographers relied on the reports of
sailors, as well as taking an interest in ethnography. Ptolemaeus
included travellers' tales in his list of sources of information at
the start of the *Geography*: 'the history of travel, and the great
store of knowledge obtained from the reports of those who have
diligently explored certain regions' (1. 2). Given this, it is hard
to understand how the *Geography* could have been described in
the following terms: 'It set the standard for scientific spirit if
not for accuracy. Nowhere on his maps do we find wind gods,
vignettes, and monsters such as decorated maps up to the
modern period and nowhere in his text does he give space to
the tall tales of travellers such as the prodigies found in
geographies of Africa up to Livingstone's day.'[21]

Nearchus' description of the periplus from the mouth of the
Indus to the Persian Gulf further blurs the 'voyager / theore-
tician' divide. He points out that as he sailed southwards down
the coast of India, the shadows too fell in a southerly direction,
but that when the sun was at the midday point, there were no
shadows at all. Some of the stars were not visible and others
nearer the horizon. He concludes his observations with the
comment that similar phenomena occur at Egyptian Syene and
at Meroë, as well as in the far south (Arrian, *Indica*, 25). This is
precisely the kind of information used by the mathematicians

[20] See *Geog.* 4. 5 and 7. 3 for Fish-Eaters. At 7. 2 Ptolemaeus even mentions
man-eating tribes.

[21] W. H. Stahl, 'By their Maps you shall Know Them', *Archaeology*, 8
(1955), 152.

and astronomers, in conjunction with their own observations, to hypothesize over the placement of lines of latitude and the relative position of places. Nearchus' account of the division of Persia into different climatic zones—sandy and sterile by the coast, temperate and fertile to the north, and wintry and snowy yet further from the sea—recalls both the 'ethnographer', Agatharchides, and the zones or κλίματα of Hipparchus (Arr. *Ind.* 40. 2–4). The scientific interests of another traveller, Onesicritus, are reflected in his details on silting, flood-tides, and the effects of the sun on the skin. He asserted that the Aethiopians have a darker skin than the Indians because the sun's rays hit them more directly, not because the sun is nearer to them (Str. 15. 1. 24).[22]

Even Eratosthenes seems to have relied on the experiences of voyagers to help in his measurement of the earth's circumference, using the differing angle of incidence for the noonday sun on the day of the summer solstice at Alexandria and Syene. Having calculated that the land distance between these two places would be $\frac{1}{50}$ the circumference of the earth, he may still have been indebted for figures to the traveller, Philo, who made a voyage to Aethiopia and told of the relationship of the gnomon to shadows in the solstices and equinoxes (Str. 2. 1. 2).[23] On the latitude of south India, Strabo says that if, as both Eratosthenes and Philo believed following the account of Nearchus and the other Indian voyagers, both of the 'Bear' constellations set there, it cannot be on the same line of latitude as Meroë (2. 1. 20).[24] For the west, Eratosthenes was reliant on tradition. We are not told from whom Eratosthenes took his information on the western Mediterranean, but it seems likely that Pytheas may have been among his sources (Str. 2. 1. 41).

---

[22] It is interesting to see the scientific and ethnographical slants in geographical research so neatly combined here.

[23] Many of the distances used by the theoreticians were those given by the explorers. Eratosthenes' figure for the minimum length of India was 16,000 stades, the distance given in the ἀναγράφη τῶν σταθμῶν ('record of the staging-posts', Str. 15. 1. 11).

[24] It is striking that in Eratosthenes' *Geography*, one of the most theoretical works known and, it would seem at times, almost independent of physical experience of the earth, we still have references to the information brought by actual travellers. It is impossible to disentangle entirely the worlds of the periplus and of the mathematical approach.

But Hipparchus too confounds any clear distinction between
exploratory and theoretical geography. He described location
and relative position by reference to the visibility of constellations such as the different groupings of Cassiopeia and Perseus.
If one sails into the Pontus and proceeds around 1,400 stades
northwards, a point equidistant from the pole and equator is
reached. From here the star on the neck of Cassiopeia lies on
the arctic circle, while that on the right arm of Perseus is
further north. The scientific investigation necessitated recourse
to the tradition of practical exploration, destroying any attempt
to distinguish neatly between abstract and 'experienced' space
(Str. 2. 5. 41).

Just as the names of Eratosthenes and Hipparchus should
not symbolize purely mathematical geography, so too should
the mention of Polybius not dismiss scientific theories from our
minds. I have already discussed how Polybius' spatial conceptions and their expression owed a great deal to scientific
thought, and also that Polybius himself is attested as having
written a presumably astronomical work, *On the Habitation of
the Equatorial Region*. It should come as no surprise that Strabo
introduced him here in the context of a debate on physical
geography, criticizing Eratosthenes, questioning the reliability
of Pytheas as a source, and involved in the ongoing debate on
distances and measurement.

But where does that leave Posidonius? Although Polybius is
mentioned here by Strabo in a section dealing with *On Ocean*,
we should recall that Posidonius' *Histories* were described by
the Suda as following on from Polybius.[25] Although there is no
compelling reason why Posidonius should have followed his
chronological forerunner in any stylistic way, still the possibility remains that, just as Polybius' 'historical' work was engaged
in the scientific debates of the day, so too could Posidonius'
Histories have dealt with such matters.[26] This need not affect

---

[25] *FGrH* 91 T 2: ἰστέον ὅτι διαδέχεται τὴν Πολυβίου ἱστορίαν Ποσειδώνιος
Ὀλβιοπολίτης σοφιστής ('You should know that Posidonius, citizen of Olbia
and a sophist, followed on from the *History* of Polybius'). Kidd argues
convincingly for the identification of Posidonius of Apamea with the author
mentioned here.

[26] Although, as Prof. D. A. Russell has pointed out to me, the scale of
scientific discussion in Posidonius' *Histories* may have been minimal.

the way in which we look at *On Ocean*, but could open up new possibilities for the nature of the *Histories*, which will be important in dealing with unassigned fragments.

This fragment yields far more of interest than simply a discussion of its context, and the tentative suggestion that, although this particular reference seems to have been to *On Ocean*, it might not have been entirely out of place in Posidonius' *Histories*, and so illustrates the difficulty of placing unassigned fragments. Before setting out some of the main theories in *On Ocean*, Strabo attempts to characterize the work in a way which raises yet more problems of interpretation. 'In it he seems to deal mainly with geography (τὰ πολλὰ γεωγρα-φεῖν), partly in a way properly befitting (τὰ μὲν οἰκείως), partly more mathematically (τὰ δὲ μαθηματικώτερον). And so it will not be out of place for me to judge some of the things he has said, some of them now, some of them in the individual descriptions, as occasion offers, always keeping some standard of measure (μέτρου τινὸς ἐχομένους)' (Str. 2. 2. 1).

This enigmatic passage tells us something of Strabo's own idea of what geography comprised, and it is true that math-ematical geography in the sense of determining the size of the earth, distances on its surface, and the shape and orientation of countries, was not prominent beyond Strabo's second book. We may contrast this with Polybius, whose entire work was imbued with such information, in spite of the apparent relega-tion of 'geographical' material to a separate book. But, more relevant to this chapter is what we learn about Posidonius, namely, that *On Ocean* was not confined to scientific slants, that Posidonius would continue to be of importance to Strabo beyond the theoretical start of the *Geography* and on into his descriptions of individual places, and that once again we have reason to argue against those who would consign all ethno-graphical passages to the *Histories*.

Strabo's account of *On Ocean* is the only passage to be directly assigned to the work, but at least it gives a reasonable idea of the huge scope encompassed. It becomes clear from this description why Posidonius could appear in a list which included both Eratosthenes and Polybius, and why his work could be described by Strabo as dealing with more than 'mathematical' geography. The spherical nature of the earth and zone theory start Strabo's account, possibly indicating their prominence in Posidonius' work. Strabo signals assent to Posidonius' criticism of Aristotle and Parmenides, before moving on to Posidonius' own theory. Even in this apparently scientific exposition, Strabo reveals the human implications of Posidonius' theory. Five of his zones were useful for celestial purposes (χρήσιμοι πρὸς τὰ οὐράνια); but, in addition, for human purposes (πρὸς τὰ ἀνθρώπεια), it was helpful to add two narrow zones lying beneath the tropics. These zones were parched and sandy, produced only silphium and withered fruits, had no rivers, and were inhabited by creatures with woolly hair, crumpled horns, protruding lips, and flat noses (for their features were withered by the heat); this was where the Fish-Eaters lived (Str. 2. 2. 3). As Kidd points out, such strong ethnographical interest might not have been expected in this work. The Fish-Eaters did not simply represent primitive tribes in hot climes, but the generic ethnic distinction of a particular latitudinal zone.[27]

The attempt to combine the mathematical approach to geography with one that made sense in human terms was continued in Posidonius' criticism of Polybius' zone theory. Polybius' division into six celestial zones was rejected for a five-part division, founded 'both physically and geographically'.[28] Strabo explains that by 'physically' he referred to a division which was in accord with the celestial phenomena and with the temperature of the atmosphere; by 'geographically' he meant that the five-zone theory accorded with the division into habitable and uninhabitable regions. 'For geography seeks to define by boundaries that section of the earth which we inhabit by means of one of the two temperate zones' (2. 3. 1). This separation of τὸ φυσικόν ('the physical') and τὸ γεωγραφικόν ('the geographical') is particularly interesting in the light of reflec-

---

[27] On Fish-Eaters and other peoples characterized by their means of subsistence as stock representatives of different levels of civilization, see P. Janni, 'Fernando Colombo e l'INDIKÉ di Arriano', Geographia Antiqua, 1 (1992), 161–6, comparing the voyages of Nearchus and Christopher Columbus. The name, Ichthyophagi, had a generic value, and 'indicated not so much a particular people, as a level of human culture, the lowest' ('non indicava tanto un determinato popolo quanto un gradino della cultura umana, il più basso').

[28] Str. 2. 3. 1: δοκεῖ μοι καὶ φυσικῶς ἅμα καὶ γεωγραφικῶς εἰρῆσθαι.

tions on Polybius in chapter II. Posidonius might have been trying to produce a system which linked the two concepts, but, if my interpretation of Polybius' geographical and historical conceptions is correct, then τὸ γεωγραφικόν and τὸ ἱστορικόν ('the historical') would both inevitably fall within the realm and laws of τὸ φυσικόν. It could be argued that Posidonius meant by τὸ φυσικόν something different from 'natural law', but even if this term referred to celestial ordering and 'geographical' to terrestrial arrangement, these two were also brought together in Polybius' geographical conceptions.[29] The distinction recurs in Strabo's summing-up of Posidonius, and it could be that it was not part of Posidonius' formulation at all (Str. 2. 3. 8). His theories, in so far as they related to geography (ὅσα γεωγραφικά), would be discussed throughout Strabo's regional survey; but, in so far as they related rather to 'physics' (ὅσα φυσικώτερα), they would be discussed elsewhere or not at all. This passage clearly reinforces the idea that τὸ φυσικόν was somehow 'scientific', since that is how we should probably best describe the contents of Strabo's non-regional books. However, I am still unhappy about this interpretation.

As with so much of Posidonius, we are left with an unsatisfactory lack of clarity. It is not clear to what extent Strabo's own thoughts have filtered into the account. It would be of great interest if Strabo's assertion that geography's concern is with the *habitable* world were foreshadowed by Posidonius.[30] This would make Posidonius and *On Ocean* a true intermediary between the preoccupations of scientific geography and ethnography, dealing with global issues, but in so far as they affected man, and recalling Polybius' use of the celestial coordinates in his description of man's location on earth. Strabo insisted on a sphere for geography which was more restricted than that of Posidonius, rejecting the discussion of mountains in the Ocean as lying outside the province of geography. 'Perhaps we should pass on those matters to someone who proposes to write a

---

[29] Although Polybius did not explicitly map out the world in terms of zones (except perhaps in the thirty-fourth book), he did explain in detail his method for locating places unknown to the reader in terms of celestial coordinates.

[30] Str. 2. 5. 34: 'Geographers need not concern themselves with what lies outside our inhabited world' (τοῖς δὲ γεωγραφοῦσιν οὔτε τῶν ἔξω τῆς καθ' ἡμᾶς οἰκουμένης φροντιστέον); see also 2. 5. 5.

treatise on the Ocean.'[31] It would be difficult not to see in this a
reference to Posidonius' *On Ocean*, although the fact that
Posidonius' work of that name is the only one known to us
does not rule out the possibility that Strabo might have known
of other such writings. But the idea that *On Ocean* showed even
a limited interest in the human implications of its scientific
theories does something to re-characterize it from being a
treatise concerned solely with tidal theory and sea-levels to a
far more wide-ranging work.

This impression is reinforced by the next section of Strabo's
treatment of the work, dealing with the possibility of circum-
navigating Libya. This had been a preoccupation of geographers before Posidonius, but was clearly relevant to his theme
of the circumambient Ocean. Posidonius' account, as we have
it, of the circumnavigability of Libya, proving the unity of the
Ocean, culminates in the story of Eudoxus of Cyzicus, in
answer to all the unsubstantiated accounts of the circumnavigation given by earlier authors (Str. 2. 3. 4).[32] Four voyages are
mentioned, two starting from the eastern side of Libya, two
from Gades. It was the second voyage, during which Eudoxus
found off the east coast of Libya figureheads which had
apparently come from Gades, that encouraged him to believe
that the continent was circumnavigable, and inspired him to
attempt to sail from Gades to India.

The Posidonian account never actually shows that Eudoxus
succeeded in the circumnavigation, but Strabo draws it to an
end by saying 'so, from all these indications he [sc. Posidonius]
says that it is shown that the ocean flows in a circle round the
inhabited world' (2. 3. 3), an assertion which Strabo finds
'amazing' (θαυμαστόν). Strabo's objection is to Posidonius' use
of evidence, which was no more reliable than the tales of

---

[31] 2. 3. 3: δοτέον δ' ἴσως τῷ προθεμένῳ τὴν περὶ ὠκεανοῦ πραγματείαν ταῦτ'
ἐξετάζειν.

[32] Previous accounts included Herodotus' story of Neco, and Heracleides
Ponticus' story of Magos at the court of Gelon. Early interest in the
possibilities of sailing along the outer shore of Libya is attested by the
periplus of Hanno, king of Carthage, although this voyage probably reached
no further than modern Sierra Leone due to lack of provisions and fear of the
rivers of fire flowing into the sea, clearly a reference to volcanic activity. For
Hanno's voyage, see the edition by J. Ramin, *Le Périple d'Hannon: The
Periplus of Hanno* (London, 1976).

Pytheas and Euhemerus.[33] It is thus strange, as Kidd points out, that Strabo devotes more than 40 per cent of his discussion of Posidonius to this story, only to discredit it. Perhaps Kidd is correct to conclude that Strabo is pointing out a lapse in the research methods of an admired predecessor. However, from my point of view, the interest lies in the fact that Posidonius appealed not only to theories of tides and zones in *On Ocean*, but also to the evidence of travellers, even in the form of implausible or anecdotal tales.

The next Posidonian theme to be addressed in Strabo's critique is the issue of changes in earth-levels. Rather than discuss Posidonius' physics and natural philosophy, Strabo illustrates the theory through the disappearance of Atlantis, and the causes of the Cimbrian migrations. The passage is problematic, not least because it directly contradicts the theory attributed by Strabo elsewhere to Posidonius, and usually assigned as a fragment to the *Histories*, that the Cimbri moved owing to their nomadic and piratical nature, and not because of inundations, either gradual or sudden.[34] The contradiction has led to suggestions of emendation, but it seems that Strabo must have intended here at least to give the reason for the migrations as being flooding because of the juxtaposition of the Atlantis tale, and the stress on illustrating changing earth-levels.

There is no obvious way in which to solve this problem. However, it may be useful to consider the contradiction as an indicator of Strabo's habits in Posidonian quotation. We might recall Pelling's arguments concerning Athenaeus' use of sources, including Posidonius, and his suggestion that referring to sources involved a combination of techniques: consulting a single papyrus at a time while writing, and drawing on memory both of texts read specifically in preparation for the current project, and of works read for earlier projects, and of general

---

[33] We may recall Polybius' view on the use of such 'travellers' tales', somewhat at odds with his stress on autopsy (4. 39. 11). It is ironic that Polybius, the historian, rejected such evidence in favour of 'argument from reasoning' while Posidonius, writing a work that has been deemed 'scientific', was happy to support his theories with reported tales.

[34] The citation is given at Str. 7. 2. 1–2. Strabo nowhere indicates that he took this passage from Posidonius' *Histories*.

reading and learning that would form part of one's education. It is striking that Strabo's references to Posidonius are scattered through almost every book of the *Geography*, but that there is just one extensive passage of discussion, namely the fragment currently under consideration. If Pelling's picture is accurate also for Strabo, then it would appear that this extensive passage is the one for which Strabo had the Posidonius papyrus open on his desk, and that the notes scattered throughout the work represent individual items drawn up from Strabo's memory of reading undertaken either for the *Geography* or earlier for his own *Histories*, in which, like Posidonius, he carried on where Polybius had finished. We need not assume that Posidonius expressed different opinions on the Cimbrian migrations in his different works, although this cannot be ruled out; it may instead be a simple case of Strabo misremembering his source on one occasion.

From this, Strabo moves to a theme more obviously germane to geography, namely the length of the inhabited world, drawing Posidonius into the debate involving Eratosthenes, Hipparchus, Artemidorus, and Strabo himself. The final section of Strabo's summary of *On Ocean* takes us back to Posidonius' division of the world into latitudinal zones, which he is now said to have rejected in favour of a division into three continents. The reasons given for this change of mind have a strong ethnographical basis. As before, the apparently scientific nature of zone theory is imbued with an interest in human geography, and, here, also flora and fauna. Two oppositions are set up—between the influences of latitude and continent on the living things that inhabited a place, and between environmental determinism and the influence of custom, habituation, and education.[35] The whole passage is confused, and it is hard to be sure how much of it is really Posidonian. But we can at least conclude that *On Ocean* dealt with various ways of parcelling up the earth, and was concerned with the human aspect of this topic.[36]

---

[35] Str. 2. 3. 7: τὰ μὲν φύσει ἐστὶν ἐπιχώριά τισι. τὰ δ' ἔθει καὶ ἀσκήσει ('Some local characteristics are the result of nature, others of custom and training'). As we shall see, the problem was one which troubled Strabo himself.

[36] Laffranque, *Poseidonios d'Apamée*, 160, defines Posidonius' view of geography as having as its goal the understanding of human life in terms of

Kidd says that 'what began as a scientific attempt to define zones or geographical divisions has culminated in an account of human geography in relation to the vegetation, life and climate of a total environment' (II(ii). 272). The tone is misleading. We do not know anything like enough about *On Ocean* to talk about its development. The change that Kidd describes is not inherent in the work, but reflects the ways in which assumptions about its nature are challenged and forced by the extensive fragment to change. There is no evidence that the project was a scientific one which became compromised; rather, the compromise should be applied to the way the project is at first conceived in our minds. The relationship between the scientific and human strands is difficult to define. For Kidd, it lies in Posidonius' attempt to write explanatory ethnography, depending on the relationship between celestial and terrestrial phenomena.[37] The establishment of astronomical zones leads to discussion of how this affected the inhabitants of different regions.[38]

It is perhaps the idea that Posidonius was keen to explain, rather than simply to describe, which lay behind Strabo's observation, often seen as a criticism, that 'there is much enquiry into causes in him' (πολὺ . . . ἐστι τὸ αἰτιολογικὸν παρὰ αὐτῷ) (Str. 2. 3. 8). This has often been taken to refer to an excessive yielding to the influence of Aristotelian methods of rigorous observation and quantitative analysis. Laffranque, for example, stresses the importance of Aristotle, and asserts that Posidonius treated history as a science, as Polybius had tried to do, insisting on objectivity in historical explanation, rather than relying on marvels.[39] We may recall the importance of

differences in location, and of physical and social conditions. This acute awareness of the human side of the work makes it all the more surprising that she characterizes *On Ocean* elsewhere as a technical, scientific piece (p. 196).

[37] H. G. Thümmel, 'Poseidonios und die Geschichte', *Klio*, 66 (1984), 558–61, discusses the ethnographical and philosophical implications of Posidonius' zone theory. He argues that Posidonius, by taking the peculiarities of different peoples back to climatic factors, was stressing the importance of a life in accord with nature (κατὰ φύσιν).

[38] For a detailed exposition of the effects of both climate (in the sense of zone) and different landscapes within that climate, see K. Schmidt, *Kosmologische Aspekte im Geschichtswerk des Poseidonios* (Göttingen, 1980).

[39] Laffranque, *Poseidonios d'Apamée*, 141.

causes (αἰτίαι), both historical and geographical, to Polybius. But parallels for the uneasy coexistence of 'scientific' explanation and superstitious belief are attested in other Hellenistic historians. Artapanus' account of the Jewish Exodus from Egypt recorded how the people of Memphis said that Moses knew the tides of the Red Sea and so was able to lead the people across as a result of his scientific geographical knowledge; the people of Heliopolis, by contrast, said that the crossing was due to a divine miracle.[40]

Apart from this extensive treatment of *On Ocean* in Strabo, we have only one other reference which is usually taken to relate to the work. This is Pliny's list of sources for Book 5 of his *Natural History*, which included Posidonius, who wrote a περίπλους or a περιήγησις (T 19c = Pliny, *NH* 1. 5). Kidd objects to this as a description of the work as we know it. But we hardly do know it, and it is just as easy to argue *for* the work being a periplus of the Ocean as *against*. The section on the Cimbri and the circumnavigation of Libya could obviously come from a periplus text; the digression to Atlantis would be quite in keeping with the way in which earlier Hellenistic periplus writers made formulaic digressions from their strict progression around the coast to incorporate islands into the account.[41] Even the passage on the theory of zones could be worked into this vision of *On Ocean*. The Fish-Eaters appeared in numerous periplus texts, notably those of Agatharchides around the Red Sea and of Nearchus along the coast from India towards the Red Sea. The idea of different inhabitants occupying various zones along the journey was an integral part of this type of literature, and again supports the idea that there was a human aspect to *all* zone theory.[42] In my opinion, it is not

---

[40] *FGrH* 726 F 3 §35. The element of the divine is, generally, surprisingly absent from works on Judaea, and it is interesting to see it competing here with a scientific explanation.

[41] See, for example, the periplus attributed to Scylax of Caryanda, (*GGM I*). He treated islands by inserting them into the description of the coast as appropriate, marking the digression with the formula ἐπάνειμι δὲ πάλιν ἐπὶ τὴν ἤπειρον, ὅθεν ἐξετραπόμην ('I shall go back again to the mainland, from which I turned aside'; see also §13, §53, §58).

[42] For Agatharchides, the ethnographical arrangement of space was primary. He moved down the east coast of Africa, describing the different groups of people as he went—the race which lived near rivers and sowed sesame; the

implausible to suggest that *On Ocean* came in the form of a real or imaginary journey around the outer edge of the continents in as far as this was known, uniting the two strands of the Hellenistic geographical tradition—the scientific and periegetic.[43] I shall consider below how this might have related to the historical work, although the potential for a blurred boundary between the contents and nature of the two should already be apparent.

A greater awareness of the inadequacy of generic categorization may also offer further nuances to our picture of Strabo's use of Posidonius as a source. I take as an example his short description of the Parthian senate. The fragment tells us little about the senate, simply that it consisted of two parts—one made up of kinsmen, and the other of wise men and Magi—and that it appointed kings in accordance with the views of both groups (F 72 = Str. 11. 9. 3). Interest has focused on the Strabonian context, rather than on the contents of the fragment itself. Strabo declines to elaborate on the Parthian customs (νομίμα) here in his *Geography*, saying that he has already dealt with them in his *History*. The fragment attributed to Posidonius therefore comes as an additional note to the information given in Strabo's historical work. Theiler argues that the passage must have come from *On Ocean*, 'since Strabo would have read Posidonius' *Histories* for his own historical work, and now supplements from Περὶ Ὠκεανοῦ, which he used for the *Geography*'.[44] As Kidd comments, 'this is an uncertain argument' (II(ii). 958). Not only is it uncertain, but it rests on

race which lived in the marshes; the nomads who ate meat and milk; the coast-dwelling Fish-Eaters. See the excellent edition by S. M. Burstein, *Agatharchides of Cnidus: On the Erythraean Sea* (London, 1989).

[43] On the imaginary nature of ancient 'travel' literature, see C. Jacob, *Géographie et ethnographie en Grèce ancienne* (Paris, 1991), 73–84; *contra*, F. Cordano, *La geografia degli antichi* (Rome, 1992), 29.

[44] For the problem of Strabo's use of sources, see Laffranque, *Poseidonios d'Apamée*, 113, arguing that Strabo tended to name his sources. It seems that we can have no certain method for testing this, but the fact that Strabo cited only four sources for his account of Babylonia (Eratosthenes, Posidonius, Polyclitus, and unnamed historians), an area which he had not visited himself, suggests that Laffranque may be wrong. On the illogical nature of Theiler's conclusion that the only possible source was one read specifically for the work in hand, I recall Pelling, 'Plutarch's Method of Work'.

unwarranted assumptions about the possibility of using a historical work as a source for a geographical work, and vice versa.

The notion of writing a work that dealt with 'Events after Polybius' (τὰ μετὰ Πολύβιον) might give us some reason to look for parallelism between the *Histories* of Posidonius and those of Strabo. But Strabo listed large-scale histories as sources for his *Geography*, and it is possible that Posidonius' *Histories* might have been somewhat like those of Ephorus and Polybius, in other words a perfectly good source for the *Geography* (Str. 8. 1. 1). So, Posidonius' 'geographical' work was set by Strabo in a discussion culminating with Polybius' *History*, and his 'historical' work cannot be ruled out as a source for the *Geography*. Theiler's argument that the fragment on the Parthian senate must be from *On Ocean* cannot be allowed to stand unchallenged.

THE *HISTORIES*

The *Histories* are comparatively better represented in the extant fragments, with almost thirty passages assigned in the sources to this work, but the odd assortment of fragments makes it difficult to characterize the *Histories* accurately. As I mentioned above, the problem is exacerbated by the domination of the fragments by one figure, Athenaeus, whose gastronomic preoccupations must give a skewed picture of Posidonius' *Histories*.

The starting date of the work is given by the *Suda*, inasmuch as it dealt with 'Events after Polybius' (τὰ μετὰ Πολύβιον). The *Suda* also tells us where the *Histories* ended, but not in a way which can be securely interpreted. It went up to the Cyrenaic wars and Ptolemy in fifty-two books, but it is virtually impossible to determine a date for this war, and Ptolemy could be any one of four people. The latest date definitely included was 86 BC, and it has been argued that the fifty-two books would have run out by that time, assuming that the number of years treated in each book remained fairly constant. There is, however, no compelling reason to believe that this was the case. One of the most striking features of Hellenistic histories, to which I shall return in chapter VI, is the way in which certain points in time were privileged in coverage over others. In spite of this, Laffranque believes that the extant fragments of Posidonius' *Histories* point to an annalistic structure, which would explain the absence of dates, since they would be redundant.[45] On this kind of argumentation, we could make a case for the vast majority of Hellenistic histories, which have survived in an extremely fragmentary state, being annalistic in design, since they too show no evidence of dates. The suggestion may prove to be correct, but the argument itself seems unconvincing.

Strasburger argues for a much later finishing date, so that the work would include Pompey's campaigns in the East.[46] The issue arises from T 11 (= Str. 11. 1. 6), in which Strabo says that Posidonius wrote 'an account of him/it' ($\tau\dot{\eta}\nu$ $\dot{\iota}\sigma\tau o\rho\dot{\iota}\alpha\nu...\tau\dot{\eta}\nu$ $\pi\epsilon\rho\dot{\iota}$ $\alpha\dot{\upsilon}\tau\dot{o}\nu$). Kidd is, it seems, right to reject the possibility that $\alpha\dot{\upsilon}\tau\dot{o}s$ refers to the Ocean, rather than to Pompey. The usual view is that the *Histories* ran out long before Pompey's eastern campaigns; and hence the suggestion that Posidonius wrote a Pompeian monograph, although there is no more positive evidence for a separate work devoted to Pompey's exploits. Therefore it is impossible to judge with any certainty the terminal date of the *Histories*, especially since none of the extant fragments is in any sense programmatic or methodological. Nor is it possible to date accurately all the fragments, or even to identify the people mentioned in them, so any attempt to fix an end-date cannot rest on the supposed latest date referred to in the fragments.

The whole question of dating and chronology is raised by Kidd in his discussion of the fragment concerning the enslavement by Mithridates of the Chians (F 38), who were handed over in fetters by their own personal slaves to be settled in the territory of Colchis.[47] Kidd comments that this almost certainly comes from one of the last books of the work, dealing with the Mithridatic war. He is probably correct, and Jacoby

---

[45] Laffranque, *Poseidonios d'Apamée*, 121.

[46] H. Strasburger, 'Poseidonios on Problems of the Roman Empire', *JRS* 55 (1965), 44.

[47] For this, and all other fragments included in Appendix B, I shall not indicate the source here, but only in the Appendix. Otherwise, I shall indicate the source when the fragment is cited in the chapter.

too places the passage towards the end of his chronologically arranged section of historical fragments which contain no reference to a book number. However, Kidd's point illustrates the fact that assumptions about the nature of 'historical' works are deeply embedded and may need to be reassessed. He assumes that the *Histories* must have followed a strictly chronological pattern, so that if a fragment mentions a set of circumstances approaching the supposed end-date, it must have come from a late book.

The foundations of this assumed structure can be challenged with reference both to other authors and to the fragments of Posidonius themselves. Diodorus stressed the need for a year-by-year account, but resorted to a region-by-region account for the first six books.[48] Appian openly adopted a geographical arrangement for his historical work.[49] Indeed, Posidonius may have been directly influenced by the model of Ephorus, and Appian influenced in turn by Posidonius. Alonso-Núñez has argued that Posidonius' *Histories* moved through a largely geographical progression, in which each area was given a distinct treatment.[50] He has argued similarly for Pompeius Trogus' universal history, that its concern with the succession of different empires led to a strong sense of geography within the work, although the arrangement was predominantly chronological.[51] As we saw with Polybius, no history that deals with more than one place can adhere constantly to a strictly chronological arrangement. Nor is it easy to imagine any historical work from which no fragment would be 'out of

---

[48] Book 1 deals with Egypt; 2 with Assyria, India, Scythia, Arabia, and the islands of the Ocean; 3 with Aethiopia and Atlantis; 4 with the Greek gods, the Argonauts, Theseus, and the seven against Thebes; 5 with the islands and peoples of the West, Rhodes, and Crete; 6 is fragmentary.

[49] Appian rejected a synchronic treatment of all parts of the Roman world for a nation-by-nation approach: συγγράφω κατ᾽ ἔθνος ἕκαστον ('I give my account people by people') (*Preface*, 13). The titles of individual books are revealing—4 is ἱστορία Κελτική ('an account of Celtica'); 5 is νησιωτική ('an account of the islands'); 6 is Ἰβερική ('an account of Iberia'). For a suggestion of the same kind of regional arrangement in Ephorus' universal history, see R. Drews, 'Ephoros and History Written κατὰ γένος', *AJP* 84 (1963), 244–55.

[50] J. M. Alonso-Núñez, 'Die Weltgeschichte bei Poseidonios', *Grazer Beiträge*, 20 (1994), 87–108.

[51] J. M. Alonso-Núñez, 'An Augustan World History: The *Historiae Philippicae* of Pompeius Trogus', *Greece and Rome*, 34 (1987), 56–72.

order'. Besides, there is a further problem specific to fragmentary texts in that the extremely dislocated nature of what remains means that it is impossible to know whether our fragments are part of the 'main chronological narrative', or were actually part of digressions, lists of *exempla*, corroborative or contrasting cases. Given this practical difficulty, Alonso-Núñez may have argued the case for the spatial organization of Posidonius' *Histories* too far. However, his view does something to redress the balance which has long been in favour of an excessively rigid annalistic work.

It is through relying on the assumption that the extant fragments of the *Histories* must form a strict chronological order that certain textual emendations or suggested emendations, particularly concerning book numbers, have been made, a point which is illustrated in Appendix A and discussed more fully in Appendix B. As I have already mentioned, the simple fact that we cannot know what constituted the 'main narrative' would render hazardous any attempt to alter book numbers in the extant fragments in order to make their subject matter conform to the narrative of the book.[52] If we were to abandon this model for the *Histories*, we would not only avoid the need for otherwise unwarranted emendations, but also allow our conception of the character of the work as a whole to be modified in ways which would affect the treatment of fragments not assigned in the sources specifically to this work. What might appear to be a pedantic point of textual criticism has far-reaching implications for our understanding of Posidonius' *Histories* and the nature of late Hellenistic historiography in general.

I first examine those fragments which can be securely located within the *Histories* as belonging to particular books, and argue that these have often been forced into a chronological order which does not accurately reflect the extant material. I start with those fragments whose contents are commonly agreed to be timeless in nature. For some of these, attempts at chronological contextualization have been made, but, in my view, unconvincingly. I then present the fragments whose contents

[52] Although book numbers appear in only one manuscript of Athenaeus, and are notoriously prone to corruption, this seems to me no reason to emend them on the basis of unwarranted assumptions.

do allow chronological contextualization, but which still do not entitle us to reconstruct the entire framework of their book. Having summarized all that I think we can actually know about the narrative structure of the *Histories*, I argue that this offers no reason to emend book numbers which have been considered doubtful. These approaches rest on the unwarranted assumption that what remains of the *Histories* must conform to strict chronological order. Although it would be inaccurate and oversimplistic to identify such a style precisely with Thucydides, I would argue that the excessive dominance of Thucydides in treatments of mainstream Hellenistic historiography, at the expense of the digressive Herodotean model, is at least partly responsible for attempts to reconstruct Posidonius' lost *Histories* as an unswervingly annalistic narrative. Appendix A lists the fragments assigned by the sources to each book, together with their supposed dates, geographical scope, and an indication of their contents. A text and translation of all these fragments, together with a more detailed survey and discussion of interpretations by various scholars, are to be found in Appendix B.

The very first fragment which comes with a securely assigned place in the *Histories* conforms precisely to a digressive Herodotean reading of Posidonius. This description of the banqueting customs of the Romans and Etruscans (F 1) is impossible to date, and the indefinite ὅταν should warn us not to try. The passage concerns repeated customs, and we do not know why they have been evoked at this point in the work, although various attempts at historical contextualization have been made. The passage on pistachios grown in Syria and Arabia (F 3), and that concerning wild turnips and carrots in Dalmatia (F 19), are also timeless. Although the former has been explained in terms of Posidonius as a 'moral' historian expressing anti-luxury sentiments, and the latter in the context of certain historical events, it seems that both could be better understood as snippets from regional accounts, which may or may not be associated with the general movement of the theatre of events to a new part of the world.[53] All of these fragments

---

[53] On the question of pistachios as a luxury item, LSJ cites only the

simply indicate the inclusion in the *Histories* of ethnographic and geographical information.

The difficulties involved in trying to contextualize ethnographical or geographical passages is exemplified in the fragment on the proliferation of rabbits to be found on an island between Dicaearcheia and Neapolis (F 61). Jacoby's suggestion that this passage may have belonged to Posidonius' Spanish history, since Spanish rabbits were notorious, is important in its rejection of the assumption that the contents of a fragment must comply with the subject matter of the 'main narrative'. On that 'main narrative' reasoning, the Neapolis localization would suggest that the fragment came from a part of the *Histories* dealing with events in southern Italy. A suitable campaign could be found to act as the stimulus for such a comment; the fragment may indeed have come from a section on the *origines et situs* of an area new to the narrative. But Jacoby's alternative, that this fragment came from a part of the work whose main narrative was located elsewhere, has far-reaching implications. Firstly, he takes it for granted that a discussion of rabbits could have formed part of a Spanish history; that details of geography, flora, and fauna, or ethnography would have been integral to Posidonius' *Histories*, characterizing that work quite differently from a broadly Thucydidean narrative with a strong annalistic and political slant. Secondly, Jacoby acknowledged the phenomenon of exemplification or of stepping outside the narrative progression. The direct correlation between fragment and context, and the consequent deduction that the date and subject matter of a fragment reflects that of the surrounding book are importantly called into question here.

Among the hints of ethnography in the fragments, we should include those dealing with social structures, such as the voluntary self-subordination of the Mariandynians to the Heracleots in return for subsistence provision (F 8), or the phenomenon of the 'King's friend' (F 5). For the former we have no idea in what historical circumstances the system arose; the latter was presumably an ongoing state of affairs. Both are

Posidonian passage for βιστάκιον, which suggests that we cannot actually tell from Greek literary sources the estimation in which they were held, or how common they were.

clearly impossible to fix to a particular date, although again such attempts have been made. Similarly, descriptions of the luxurious lifestyle in Syria (F 10 and F 20), dinner customs among the Celts and Germans (F 15, F 16 and F 22), details on different types of cup (F 25) and on Celtic parasites (F 17) are both impossible to fix in time and indicative of the nature of the *Histories* as a work of broad interests and scope.

It emerges that of the twenty-seven fragments collated by Jacoby as having their provenance in the *Histories* of Posidonius with their book number explicitly stated, almost half give absolutely no indication of their temporal context. We may speculate as to why any particular piece of information or anecdote was included in Posidonius' work, and suggest possible narrative contexts by which its inclusion may have been prompted; but we cannot use such speculation as the basis for reconstructing our vision of the progress and narrative arrangement (οἰκονομία) of the work. These fragments tell us nothing about chronological frameworks, but a great deal about the varied nature of the work and about its ethnographical slant. It is, of course, possible that such passages about the customs of different peoples appealed to later writers, and may be over-represented in Athenaeus, particularly given the limited subject matter of the *Deipnosophistae*. However this does not alter the fact that Posidonius' work itself may have been of great ethnographical scope, a suggestion which is supported by Athenaeus' comment (F 15) that Posidonius 'recorded many habits and customs from many peoples' (πολλὰ παρὰ πολλοῖς ἔθιμα καὶ νόμιμα ἀναγράφων).

I turn now to those fragments whose subject matter can be partially or wholly attached to a chronological setting. As with the ethnographic passages, more detailed discussion is to be found in Appendix B, and I concentrate here simply on the implications for the characterization of the *Histories*. In particular, I recall the difficulty associated with the fact that we have no idea of the status of the extant passages *vis-à-vis* the primary contents of a book, that is, whether or not they are digressive. I have therefore adopted a cautious approach to what we can derive from these datable fragments concerning the wider arrangement of the work.

It is indicated (F 2) that Posidonius described in Book 3 a

war between Larissa and Apameia, but the precise conflict in question is uncertain, and much of the argumentation in the commentaries seems to have been determined by the expectation that, at this early stage in the work, we should be looking for a war soon after 145 BC. It would be dangerously circular to use this to argue for any particular start-date. Also flawed is the assumption derived from the passage (F 4) on Hierax of Antioch that Book 4, from which this fragment comes, must have dealt with the period between the assumed start-date of the work and the time of the next datable fragment (from Book 7), namely the eastern embassy of Scipio between 144 and 139 BC (F 6). Some fragments can be dated through their reference to specific conflicts, such as the first Sicilian slave-war (F 7), or broadly through their attachment to a particular reign (F 9 and F 11 on Antiochus VII Sidetes; F 21 and F 23 on Antiochus Grypus; F 26 on Ptolemy I Alexander).

The description of the wealth of Luvernius (F 18) is important because it illustrates further the difficulties involved in using datable fragments of the *Histories* to construct a chronological framework, which can be used to explain the introduction of ethnographical passages and to which all fragments must be fitted. Jacoby separated this from the passage on the customs of the Celts (F 15). However, Kidd linked the two as one continuous passage in Posidonius and claimed that, having identified the reference to Bituis (father of Luvernius) with events of 121 BC, the defeat and annexation of the Averni and the Allobroges, he had provided the 'historical context of Posidonius' ethnography in Bk 23' (II(i). 314). It is easy to leap to such a conclusion, but the Greek makes clear that the ethnographical information in F 15 was the point of interest in its own right. Furthermore, Bituis is only mentioned at all in his role as Luvernius' father. So historical, datable events do not necessarily provide the reason for the inclusion of ethnographical information, nor can they be automatically regarded as forming the main narrative. In this case, the datable allusion to events in 121 BC is secondary to a note on Luvernius' wealth. The date does not provide a chronological context for the fragment, but relates simply to the incidental information on the identity of Luvernius. It is unhelpful for reconstructing the individual book, let alone illuminating the framework of the entire *Histories*. Examples such as this should warn us once more against assuming that datable fragments can necessarily inform us about the work's overall arrangement (οἰκονομία).

It is clear from Appendix A that the extant fragments appear to lead broadly to the conclusion that the *Histories* followed a chronological order. It is indeed likely that this was the case. However, many anomalies exist. The fact that, for example, Books 28 and 34 both appear to be datable to a particular period of a few years tells against a strict progression through time. We simply do not have enough fragments to link them into a coherent sequence, and certainly lack grounds on which to reconstruct the organization of the 52–book *Histories*. There is clearly insufficient evidence for absolute certainty that Posidonius, writing 'Events after Polybius' (τὰ μετὰ Πολύβιον), must have followed the same organizational principles as his predecessor.

The rigidly annalistic approach is further weakened by its failure to accommodate fragments which deviate from the neat order. Such an approach has been responsible for suggested textual emendations in F 12, 13, 19, and 24 in order that the datable elements of these fragments might be allocated a suitable place within the *Histories* as a whole. The arguments are set out in detail in Appendix B, and here I simply summarize the conclusions so as to reveal the weakness in this approach. F 12 concerns the royal treatment of Seleucus following his capture by King Arsaces. This has been considered problematic, since the most famous example of a Seleucid king to be treated in this way was Demetrius II Nicator *c*.140 BC, and yet this date is deemed too early to appear in Book 16 from which the fragment is taken. The suggested solutions are either to retain the name Seleucus, but to insert an indication that this was the son of Antiochus VII Sidetes, who invaded Media in 129 BC (a more 'suitable' date for Book 16) and was taken prisoner, or to assume that Athenaeus intended to write about Demetrius II Nicator, and so to emend the book number to 6. A similar problem arises in connection with F 24 on Heracleon of Beroia, the commander of Antiochus Grypus. The manuscript declares that the passage comes from Book 4; Kidd announces that this is 'chronologically impossible'. He accepts Bake's emendation which places the fragment in Book 34, presumably on the grounds that this would be a suitable place in the *Histories* for a passage concerning the early 90s BC. Both of these fragments have evoked a weak argument which rests simply on the assumption that the contents of extant fragments should be made to conform to chronological order.

F 13 on Himerus, left in charge of Babylon in the early 120s BC, has been subjected to similar emendation for chronological reasons. Athenaeus states its provenance as Book 26, but this has been disputed on the grounds that it should follow close on the heels of F 11 (from Book 16), in which the death of Antiochus VII Sidetes in 129 BC is mentioned. However, as I argue in Appendix B, a close reading of F 11 does not permit the conclusion that Antiochus' death itself actually fell in Book 16. In addition, we have no reason to assert that any reference to the 120s must necessarily be given a place in the *Histories* alongside the death of Antiochus. Furthermore, as is the case also with F 12 and 24, such an argument rests on the belief that a brief fragment automatically informs us about the contents of the surrounding book.

F 19 provides a final example of the way in which the relentless attempt to force the fragments of the *Histories* into a neat chronological order has led to unwarranted emendations. This passage (from Book 27) concerns the existence of wild turnips and carrots in Dalmatia, and its treatment has involved at least two methodological flaws. The first step is to find a historical circumstance which might have elicited this piece of information. The obvious answer is to link it to the triumph of L. Caecilius Metellus Delmaticus over the Dalmatians in 117 BC. However, that date is seen as chronologically problematic in Book 27, and it has been suggested that the book number be emended to 24. The difficulties are obvious. Firstly, we have no sound reasons for motivating the mention of regional flora by means of a military triumph. Secondly, our knowledge of the work as a whole is so limited as to prevent us from knowing whether or not such a triumph was discussed, or simply alluded to in passing, in any particular book.

It is possible to criticize the argumentation which underlies such emendations, but the point may be made most effectively by reference to F 14 on Harpalus the Macedonian. In the cases mentioned above, the solution to accommodating fragments which step outside chronological order is to emend the text, usually in the form of the book number, which is admittedly vulnerable. However, F 14 cannot be dealt with in this way. Since the figure of Harpalus from the fourth century BC so obviously falls outside the assumed chronological scope of the entire work, the line of argument automatically adopted in the commentaries is that he must have been introduced as an analogy to a contemporary. But this precisely reveals the dangers of assuming that datable fragments can give us an accurate picture of the temporal scope of their surrounding books and so of the work as a whole, and supports my point; namely, that we cannot safely reconstruct a framework for the *Histories* by stringing together the tiny extant fraction of what was once a 52–book work. It is methodologically inconsistent to allow some fragments to be mainstream, and representative of their book, while others are relocated through emendation of the text and others discarded as analogous simply because they so obviously do not fit anywhere. The existence of such anomalies as the presence of Harpalus and of the fragments which can be made to adhere to a preconceived order only through recourse to textual emendation does not deny the strong possibility that the work had a broadly chronological structure. It simply reminds us that the fragmentary nature of the work cannot but leave us largely in the dark about form and contents, and makes textual emendation a highly contentious exercise.

However, this is all extremely negative and might lead to the unwelcome conclusion that we should simply abandon the attempt to make sense of a work which earned the reputation for being one of the greatest of late Hellenistic historiography. I shall now try to suggest some more positive approaches to interpreting the scattered remnants of the *Histories*. If Murray is correct to emphasize, alongside the importance of Thucydides, the great and continuing influence of Herodotus on Hellenistic historiography, then we should be open to the possibility of finding a digressive and discursive strain in Posidonius' *Histories*, in which a re-evaluated world-view is set out in response to the new power of Rome. With this more broadly conceived work in mind, we may even move towards the notion of Posidonian *Histories* in which not only time but also space was an important organizational matrix. Such a work may still follow a broadly temporal plan, but one involving numerous flashbacks, foreshadowings, and elements which cannot be located in time at all—the ethnographic and the geographical.[54] We should not expect that all extant fragments of such a work would adhere to a chronological order. This model seems to account for the extant fragments better than one in which they are constantly forced into a strict chronological narrative, with ethnographical and geographical elements existing only as anomalies to be explained away by reference to one or other political or military event.[55]

The suggestion was made by both Jacoby and Malitz that Books 1 and 2 comprised an ethnography of Rome and Italy, providing a reasonable context for the fragment on feasts in the temple of Hercules. Kidd's characterization of the early books as a history of Syria also points towards a partially regional arrangement of material, rather than an uncompromisingly chronological account of all the world to fall within the scope of the *Histories*. Indeed, such a vision would accommodate one of the fragments which Kidd deems chronologically impossible as it stands. F 24 is out of chronological order in Book 4, but fits well into the Syrian context of the early books of the work.

Syria dominates the extant fragments. Indeed, if it were not for the Celtic material in Book 23, the Germans in Book 30, and the Mariandynians around the Pontus in Book 11, we could argue that the work was almost exclusively focused on the south-eastern Mediterranean world. This may come as no surprise, given Posidonius' close connections with both Apameia in Syria and Rhodes, a crucial point in the eastern Mediterranean network.[56] However, we do know that the

[54] As described by O. Murray, 'Herodotus and Hellenistic Culture', *CQ* NS 22 (1972), 200–13.

[55] Indeed in some cases, such as the fragment about the proliferation of rabbits on the island which Posidonius passed on his voyage from Dicaearcheia to Neapolis (F 61), or the turnips in F 19, it is hard to see how any attempt at historical contextualization could be justified.

[56] On the importance of Posidonius' Rhodian connections, see Laffranque, *Poseidonios d'Apamée*, 128; Thümmel, 'Poseidonios und die Geschichte', 560, argues that the collapsing world of the East was crucial in forming Posidonius' view that Rome provided the only possibility of rescue from tyranny. More

geographical scope was wider than this, and the fragmentary nature of the work will prevent us from knowing to what extent the perceived Syrian bias reflects the balance of the original work, or is an accident of survival.

The fact that Syrian material appears throughout the work tells against an overriding spatial organization, recording the whole account of each region at once. In any case, that is hardly what we would expect unless we were to abandon altogether the notion of history as an account through time. But, as the text stands, the fragments concerning different regions *are* conspicuously grouped, most noticeably in the case of Syria, where the relatively large number of extant fragments allows us to see some pattern.[57] Laffranque develops the possibility of a 'Mithridatic' history, which would have included the story of Athenion, texts on Marius, the fragments on Chios and on the Scythians, as well as Pompey's dealings with the region.[58] Jacoby's commentary on the *Histories* reveals a strong belief in this regional arrangement. He set out the securely assigned fragments in order to indicate the way in which the *Histories* appear to have been made up of a succession of regional accounts, perhaps like the tales (λόγοι) of Herodotus.

I–II	Rome in 145; Roman life; Italian ethnography
III–VI (?)	Syrian history from start of universal empire of Demetrius II Nicator (145) to Parthian overthrow
VII	Egyptian history from accession of Physcon (145) to embassy of Scipio (140)
VII(–XI?)	History of the West; first slave war
(XII?–)XVI	Syrian history to death of Antiochus Sidetes

generally, T. R. S. Broughton, 'Roman Asia Minor' in T. Frank (ed.), *An Economic Survey of Ancient Rome IV* (Baltimore, 1938), 519–25, explains that the decline of Rhodes, because of Rome's encouragement of the slave-trade through Delos instead of Rhodes, resulted in the escalation of piracy in the Mediterranean, revealing Rhodes' crucial role in suppressing brigandage. Strasburger, 'Poseidonios on Problems of the Roman Empire', attributes this view of Rome's culpability to Posidonius, but does not explain on which fragments he bases this opinion.

[57] The following clusters appear: 3–4 Syria; 5–7 the East; 14–16 Syria; 23 Celtica; 28 Syria; 34–36? Syria.

[58] Laffranque, *Poseidonios d'Apamée*, 116–18.

	(129); perhaps to death of Demetrius Nicator (125)
XVII–XXII	? Syrian history
XXIII–?	First Transalpine Celtic war (122/1)
XXVII	Dalmatian war (119/7)
XXVIII	Syrian history under Antiochus Grypus (after 122)
XXX–?	History of the West to time of Cimbrians
XXXIV–?	Syrian history under Antiochus Grypus (c.109)

Just as is seen in the third column of the table in Appendix A, Jacoby's chart illustrates the way in which large sections of the *Histories* appear to have been devoted to giving an account through time of a particular part of the world. A glance at Malitz's contents page reveals the same pattern. His treatment of 'Die Fragmente in ihrer Folge' (1. Landes- und Volkskunde Italiens 2. Spanien und die spanischen Kriege 3. Sklaven und Piraten 4. Gallien und die Gallier 5. Die Völker des Nordens 6. Die Attaliden 7. Die Ptolemäer 8. Die Seleukiden 9. Die Juden 10. Das Zeitalter des Mithridates 11. Rom) illustrates his belief that Posidonius' *Histories* involved long narratives in each area. The overall structure may have been to progress through time, but we have no evidence that Posidonius dealt with all theatres of events year by year.

The table in Appendix A illustrates that, as the text has been transmitted in the manuscript, the chronological pattern is considerably interrupted. It is only with recourse to textual emendations that the order is significantly neatened, apparently indicating that the motivation for the emendations is precisely to result in a chronologically organized narrative. It is not possible to say anything with certainty about the arrangement of this work. But freeing ourselves from the unrelenting search for chronological contexts may make us receptive to other factors in the fragments and to alternative ways of reading and reconstructing the lost original. For example, F 10 on degenerate luxury in Syria need not evoke a postulated date of the 130s–120s BC (Kidd), on the basis that Book 16 dealt with that period. A more interesting feature of the fragment is its stress on the importance of *place* and geographical determinism. It was the abundant supply of produce from the land (ἡ τῆς χώρας εὐβοσία) which yielded the luxurious lifestyle of the Syrians, a factor which was constant through time, and reflects the importance of environmental determinism in antiquity.

Given the extremely fragmentary nature of the evidence, it would be just as unsound to suppose a regionally determined account as any other arrangement. Jacoby was right to stress that 'In general, the arrangement of the whole is questionable' ('Überhaupt ist die Ökonomie des Ganzen fraglich').[59] In any case, a strong conclusion that the work was spatially organized is not supported by what little evidence we have, and it is important not to follow methods which I have criticized elsewhere. F 22 on German ethnography, for example, breaks up a series of passages on Syria, just as F 24 disrupts a chronological sequence. However, we may at least consider for the *Histories* an organizing principle like that of Pompeius Trogus' *Historiae Philippicae*, whereby the narrative moved broadly forwards through time, but did not adhere to the synchronic interwoven model of Polybius and Diodorus. Alonso-Núñez has moved further along this line and has suggested that the spatial and temporal organizing principles may, for both Posidonius and Pompeius Trogus, have been almost equally important. Of Posidonius' *Histories* he suggests that each book had a thematic unity which related to a particular geographical area, and that within each thematic unity we find a chronological ordering of the fragments.[60] As I suggested above, this reading probably pushes the evidence too far to one extreme of the organizational spectrum; it seems that some compromise between the approaches of Alonso-Núñez and of the 'strict annalists' would best account for what evidence we have.

Alonso-Núñez's observations on the parallels between Posidonius and Pompeius Trogus also pinpoint interesting differences in the spatial, and consequent historical, conceptions of these two authors. He suggests that Posidonius' universal history may have moved in a circle from Rome, then east, south, west, north, east, and back to Rome, while Pompeius Trogus' narrative moved broadly in a linear progression from

[59] Jacoby, *FGrH*, *Kommentar* II C, 155.
[60] Alonso-Núñez, 'Die Weltgeschichte bei Poseidonios', 89.

east to west.[61] If circularity was a feature of Posidonius' world-
view, this would accord both with his Stoicism, as we shall see
later, and with the conceptual centrality of Rome in his
Histories, which contrasts with Pompeius Trogus' deliberate
rejection of Rome as the centre of his world, although it is not
clear how this should be reconciled with Posidonius' apparent
eastern bias.[62] I shall return in chapter IV to the notion of a
circular world, constructed around a Roman centre, as seen in
Strabo's *Geography*. But it is important to note here this
possible similarity in spatial conceptions between Posidonius'
Histories and Strabo's *Geography*, which would deal another
blow to the logic of Theiler's argument that 'Strabo would
have read Posidonius' *Histories* for his own historical work, and
now supplements from Περὶ Ὠκεανοῦ, which he used for the
Geography' (see above, p. 153). Universal history could be
written in different ways, and it is important not to assume that
there is only one model to impose when faced with a fragmentary text. The process of juggling with time and space to bring a
representation of the world to the reader could result either in a
narrative which privileged the temporal over the spatial (as in
Polybius and Diodorus), or the spatial over the temporal (as in
Strabo's *Geography*), or balanced the two more evenly, as
might have been the case in Posidonius' *Histories*.

So far, from a survey of the fragments assigned to specific
works in the ancient sources, we can draw a few conclusions.
The first and most important must be to acknowledge that we
can assert very little with confidence about either *On Ocean* or
the *Histories*. However, some attempt to characterize the works

---

[61] Ibid. 103.

[62] On the geographical constructions of opposition literature, see J. M.
Alonso-Núñez, 'L'opposizione contro l'imperialismo romano e contro il
principato nella storiografia del tempo di Augusto', *Rivista Storica dell'Antichità*, 12 (1982), 131–41. He sees the *Histories* of Timagenes and Pompeius
Trogus as accounts in which 'The historical process is not seen exclusively
from the perspective of Rome as the centre of the world' ('Il processo storico
non è visto in assoluto dalla prospettiva di Roma come centro del mondo',
134). Alonso-Núñez argues that Trogus was probably influenced by Timagenes' historical scheme, with the Graeco-Hellenistic world as the central
axis, picking up on Timagenes' interest in the Hellenistic kings (p. 135). Both
incorporated Roman imperialism into a much broader historical process.

is worthwhile, if only so as to formulate an approach to the fragments which are *not* given a specific context. The characterization of *On Ocean* as a work of scientific, mathematical geography, and the rejection of the periplus structure, views it too narrowly.

The fragments of the *Histories* have, in turn, been interpreted in too restrictive a way. There is every reason to believe that the work ranged widely across many topics—historical, ethnographical, and geographical.[63] The *Suda*'s note that the work dealt with 'Events after Polybius' does not mean that Posidonius was bound to exactly the same format and organizing principles, as Jacoby noted: 'Sie [sc. die Fragmente] zeigen natürlich im allgemeinen zeitliche Abfolge; aber die verbreitete Annahme, daß P. sich auch in der Anordnung des Stoffes an Polybios angeschlossen habe . . . ist damit nicht bewiesen' ('They [sc. the fragments] of course reveal a generally chronological order; but the broad acceptance that P. followed Polybius in the organization of material . . . is not thereby proven').[64] If we are prepared to read the fragments of Posidonius' *Histories* in the wider context of Hellenistic historiography, where ἱστορίαι were very obviously no more than 'pieces of research', the nature of works was extremely varied, and Herodotus' influence was strongly felt, we may perhaps avoid unnecessary emendations. Any reading even of a fully extant text requires a deliberate choice over which elements to stress. The problem is far more acute in the case of such a seriously fragmentary text as the *Histories* of Posidonius. What matters is not so much the nature of the choice—many versions will produce interesting and enlightening readings—but rather that the framework of interpretation is chosen consciously and subsequently acknowledged.

---

[63] Laffranque, *Poseidonios d'Apamée*, 122, acknowledges the huge range of material relevant to the *Histories* and sees them as a 'general history'.

[64] Jacoby, *FGrH, Kommentar*, 155. An excellent parallel is Xenophon's 'continuation' of Thucydides, pointed out to me by Prof. D. A. Russell. The start of his *Hellenica* is famous for its self-consciousness as a continuation: μετὰ δὲ ταῦτα . . . ('after this . . .'), but equally telling is the end of the work, where the notion of a continuous historiography is clearly indicated: ἐμοὶ μὲν δὴ μέχρι τούτου γραφέσθω· τὰ δὲ μετὰ ταῦτα ἴσως ἄλλῳ μελήσει ('Let it then be my task to write up to this point; as for what happened next, perhaps it will be of concern to someone else', 7. 5. 27).

LOCATING UNPLACED FRAGMENTS

Nowhere is this more the case than with the majority of fragments, which have been handed down with no specific ancient context, leaving the way open for a multiplicity of interpretations. The manner in which these unplaced fragments are categorized and treated is largely dependent on each commentator's characterization of the lost works. Those fragments which might be considered geographical or historical in nature have been divided by Kidd into the following generic categories: mathematical geography, tides and hydrology, seismology, geology and mineralogy, geography, and history. Kidd gives little explanation of why he has created so many fields of study and, in particular, why he considers the first four categories to be distinct from geography itself. Given the modern notion of separate disciplines of geography and history, it is easier to understand his distinction between these two areas, although I shall argue that many of the allocations of fragments are arbitrary and debatable. One might say that Kidd has simply organized the material in a way that makes it easy to find, and this is certainly the case. The danger with such categorization is that it encourages the notion, firstly, that Posidonius might have conceptualized material according to these categories, and secondly that the group to which fragments are assigned reflects their original location. That is, fragments found in the first five sections came from *On Ocean*, the 'scientific' 'geographical' work; and those from the historical category came from the *Histories*. I hope to have shown that the fragments securely assigned to those works defy such characterization. A final misconception to arise from these categories, combined with the narrow views of geography and history often propagated, is that we may be tempted to postulate a series of specialized works to account for fragments on subjects such as mineralogy. I would argue that no such works need be postulated.

Roughly the same group of fragments as Kidd would include in the categories described above were treated instead by Jacoby in a way which derived from his broader notion of both the historical and the geographical. He divided the unplaced fragments into only three categories: historical facts and events, lands and peoples, and geographical fragments, although the last set was grouped according to contents, in a way which foreshadowed Kidd's approach. Jacoby's edition still upheld the notion that historical events might reasonably be thought to derive from the *Histories* and geographical information from *On Ocean*, but the middle category of ethnographical material allowed for considerable generic flexibility between the works. Yet Kidd's decision to categorize the fragments simply according to contents, and to discuss the possible location in one work or another of each fragment individually, also has clear merits. I start my discussion of these fragments with the passages commonly agreed to be 'geographical'.

There is a great deal of overlap between Jacoby's 'geographical' fragments and Kidd's different types of 'geographical' passage, and the contents of many of these could plausibly come within the scope of a work *On Ocean*. Several passages concern the theory of zones, described by Kidd as 'mathematical geography' and reminiscent of Strabo's characterization of *On Ocean*: 'In it he seems to deal mainly with geography, partly in a way properly befitting, partly more mathematically' (Str. 2. 2. 1). Posidonius' interest in theories such as that on the division of the earth into zones is attested in sources other than Strabo. Cleomedes, for instance, criticized Posidonius for arguing that in the torrid zone there was a temperate and inhabited region (F 78 = Cleomedes, *De motu*, 1. 6. 31–3).[65] The fact that Strabo cited Posidonius' *On Ocean* on the length of the inhabited world contributes further to the impression that, in spite of the ethnographical interests already discussed, the work was concerned in part with the general size, shape, and layout of the earth (F 28 = Str. 2. 3. 6). Several of the unassigned fragments deal with the shape of the earth and its circumference.[66] The concern with the wider world in *On Ocean* is entirely appro-

---

[65] A similar theory is attributed to Posidonius in a passage not included by Jacoby (E–K F 211 = Symeon Seth, *De utilitate corporum caelestium*, 44).

[66] F 98a (= Agathemerus, *Sketch of Geography*, 1. 2) for the earth as sling-shaped; F 98b (= Eustathius, *Commentarii in Dionysium Periegetam*, 1) for the fact that the earth is not strictly circular; F 97 (= Cleomedes, *De motu circulari caelestium*, 1. 10. 50–2) for Posidonius' method for measuring the circumference of the earth.

priate in a work which may have concentrated on the outer
edges of the known world—the outer ocean—and was necessarily interested in broader definitions of what constituted the
globe.[67] There is, however, no reason to exclude this 'mathematical geography' from the *Histories*, or indeed from any other
work. Strabo is said to have cited Posidonius on the length of
the parasang, but, as Polybius has shown, such matters were as
relevant to history as to geography.[68]

The large number of fragments on tidal theory and hydrology might at first seem to fall within the scope of a geographical
work, and it is, of course, reasonable to suppose that they could
have come from *On Ocean*. While there is no reason to exclude
them from the *Histories*, for some fragments there is little
doubt as to their origin in *On Ocean*. Passages on the uniform
behaviour of the Ocean and the tides (F 82a = Str. 1. 1. 8–9), on
tidal ebb and flow (F 82b = Str. 1. 3. 12), and on Posidonius'
criticism of Homer's views of Ocean (F 83 = Str. 1. 1. 7) all
seem fairly safely assigned to this work.[69]

It seems likely that fragments concerned with Gades and the
Pillars of Hercules would also have been part of an account of
the Ocean.[70] It is interesting to see how often Posidonius and

[67] If the work incorporated as much of the outer circuit of the continents as
was known, then F 100 (= Pliny, *NH* 6. 57) on the orientation and climate of
India would fit the scheme. See also on the relative location of India E–K F
213 (= Solinus, *Collectanea rerum memorabilium*, 52. 1–2).

[68] E–K F 203 (= Anon. *Sylloge tacticorum*, 3. 2–3). Here, Eratosthenes and
Strabo are cited for variations in the number of stades in a mile; Xenophon,
Strabo, and Posidonius for the parasang. As Kidd (II(ii). 730) points out, in
our text of Str. 7. 4. 4, it is Polybius, the 'historian', who is cited for the stade,
rather than Eratosthenes.

[69] F 86 (= Str. 3. 5. 9) on tidal behaviour at Gades introduces the theories
of Seleucus of Babylon on the tides in the Indian Ocean. If these were part
of *On Ocean*, it would support my suggestion that the work may have
incorporated any available information on the whole outer circuit of the
continents.

[70] J. M. Alonso-Núñez, 'Les Informations de Posidonius sur la péninsule
ibérique', *L'Antiquité Classique*, 48 (1979), 639, claims that the Iberian
peninsula appeared in both the *Histories* and *On Ocean*. I can find no firm
evidence for this region appearing in any of the fragments securely assigned to
the *Histories*. However, Alonso-Núñez's comment that ethnographical material might have accompanied an account of the effects of Roman rule on
Celtiberia seems plausible and increases the difficulty of placing fragments in
one or other of the works.

Polybius are set alongside each other in passages which deal with this part of the world, and which are assumed to come from Posidonius' 'geographical' work. He attacked Polybius' view of the wells at Gades and his tidal theory, using arguments based on observation and inference (F 85 = Str. 3. 5. 7–8).[71] If we were to adopt a strongly generic approach, it would appear strange that Posidonius engaged in polemic with a historian in a scientific work.[72] But Polybius, as I have argued, was not bound by our preconceptions of defined fields of study; nor should we expect Posidonius to be.

Other than those dealing directly with the Ocean, it is impossible to find a certain context for most fragments on tides and hydrology. On the view that one work was geographical and one historical, these fragments would fall within the former. But if we acknowledge the effect of ethnographical material in the *Histories* and of less scientific elements in *On Ocean*, the question becomes more complicated. There is no reason why Strabo could not have taken Posidonius' estimate of the depth of the Sardinian Sea from the *Histories*, especially since we know that Posidonius mentioned at least one voyage within the Mediterranean in this work (F 91 = Str. 1. 3. 9); nor why the fragment (F 79 = Str. 17. 1. 5) on the Nile floods could not have come from an account of Egypt in the *Histories*.[73] Fragment 80 (= Str. 17. 3. 10) on the paucity of rivers in Libya, which Posidonius connects with lack of rainfall, is still more problematic. Did it come from a part of the narrative focused on this area, or from *On Ocean*? This would not fit with a strict periplus model, but could have been part of a digression from the journey round Africa, or have been incorporated into a section on global geography—possibly seen as a consequence of lying at a southerly latitude.

---

[71] It is interesting that both Polybius and Posidonius made the same claims to autopsy. Posidonius travelled to Gades to observe the tides and distinguished between autopsy, reported information, and derived theory. See also F 86 (= Str. 3. 5. 9).

[72] For other possible examples of this polemic, see F 89 (= Str. 5. 1. 8) on the Timavus, and F 49 (= Str. 3. 3. 4) on the river Bainis in Lusitania. Kidd identifies the source against whom Posidonius reacts as Polybius, who may have taken his information from D. Iunius Brutus Callaicus, who campaigned in Lusitania in 138/7 BC.

[73] F 4 and F 7 reveal that Egypt fell within the scope of the work.

The generic ambiguity of these fragments is acknowledged by both Jacoby and Kidd. The former sometimes suggests that the *Histories* might have been the original location of fragments categorized as 'geographical', revealing a broad conception of what is 'historical', and often coinciding with the way the fragments would be assigned on the model 'outer-ocean : inner-sea', although this does not imply that Jacoby would have agreed with this characterization of the works.

Although Kidd chooses not to gather together those fragments which he thinks might have come from *On Ocean*, he tends towards the notion that geographical phenomena should be consigned to this work on the grounds of content.[74] But they could equally well fit into a 'historical' work of the kind which we know included notes on pistachio production and the flora and fauna of various regions. Jacoby's suggestion that Posidonius' account of the stony Plaine de la Crau probably came from the Celtic section of the *Histories* illustrates precisely this point, only to be countered by Kidd's comment that the passage may have been from *On Ocean* or from some scientific work giving explanations of marvels (παράδοξα) (F 90 = Str. 4. 1. 7).[75] But why postulate the existence of such a work, when these explanations were already a normal part of Hellenistic historiography?

The same kinds of argument could be applied to many of the fragments. How can we determine a context for the information that an earthquake in Phoenicia damaged Sidon, and affected areas from Syria to Greece? Strabo mentions it in a passage on various floods and the effects of earthquakes on land-formation (F 87 = Str. 1. 3. 16). But elsewhere, Strabo uses precisely this kind of information in his brief *histories* of individual cities, and it seems that Posidonius may have mentioned it in a passage focused on Sidon, rather than in a strictly scientific context. Could this have come from one of the

---

[74] This is the case in F 88 on the volcanic eruption in the sea between Panarea and the Liparaean islands; and with E–K F 228 (= Seneca, *Naturales quaestiones*, 2. 26. 4–7) on a similar incident in the Aegean, although Kidd expresses uncertainty in both cases.

[75] Jacoby said of this fragment, classified by Edelstein and Kidd as 'mathematical geography', simply that it 'could come from the *Histories*'. Jacoby proposed as a location Book 23, on the first Celtic war of 122/1 BC.

Syrian sections of the *Histories*?[76] A striking parallel for discussion of earthquakes in a Hellenistic history is to be found in C. Acilius' treatment of how Sicily came to be disjointed from the Italian mainland by the great flood (*FGrH* 813 F 3). Many features of the passage are significant, not least of which is the fact that this 'geographical' passage comes from a 'historical' work. But we should go on to note that Acilius' geography has a temporal side, in so far as the geography of the present day is different from that of the past. Thirdly, the geography of Italy is linked to a particular event which had far-reaching historical and geographical repercussions. The great flood is generally not referred to in Greek geographical sources, but in accounts of the history of Judaea, Egypt, and Babylonia, where it is used as a chronological marker for calculating large time-spans.[77] There is no reason why Posidonius too should not have discussed earthquakes and their impact in his *Histories*.

In the field of mineralogy and geology, the passages cited from Posidonius give little or no clue as to their place in the original works. The lava on Mt. Etna and the effect of volcanic ash on the soil (F 92), the classification of naphtha in Babylonia (F 94), the porous clay in Iberia (F 95) all fell within Posidonius' interests. It is the fragment on the corrupting effect of gold and silver which has attracted most attention in this subsection of the geographical fragments (F 48 = Athen. 6. 233D–4C).[78] Athenaeus cites Posidonius on the collection of alluvial ores by the Helvetii and other Celts, the way in which the Alps flow with silver in forest fires, and mining, the method by which most gold and silver is extracted. This leads to a series of examples of the way in which the greed for precious metals has corrupted peoples, notably the Spartans and the Scordistae, a Celtic tribe linked elsewhere by Posidonius with the Cimbri.[79] The source of the material has been much

---

[76] Similarly, could the earthquake in F 87a, which Posidonius says destroyed many cities and 2,000 villages in Parthia, have come from the account of Parthia in the *Histories*?

[77] See the king-list given by Eusebius of Egyptian dynasties 'after the flood' (μετὰ τὸν κατακλυσμόν) (*FGrH* 609 F 3b).

[78] The same story is told in Eustathius, *Commentarii ad Homeri Odysseam*, 4. 89.   [79] See Dobesch, *Das europäische 'Barbaricum'*, 52.

debated. Theiler postulated the existence of a separate work entitled *On Gold and Silver*, but there is no reason whatsoever to accept this, especially given the diverse nature of the works we already have. Kidd suggests that the examples came from a single series in the *Histories*, hanging together through the ethical theme, and this would reflect the fact that the examples are grouped together by Athenaeus into a single passage. But an alternative solution is that of Jacoby, who thought that the passages came from various regional accounts in the *Histories*— the Celtic ethnology, the Iberian passages, the *Cimbrica*, and so on—in which mineral wealth and its social implications could have played a part.[80]

It is interesting that Jacoby placed this fragment on the corrupting effects of mineral wealth in his section on 'countries and peoples' ('Länder und Völker'). This perfectly illustrates the importance in his vision of Greek prose writing of Herodotean-style λόγοι, equivalent to the *origines et situs* of writers such as Pompeius Trogus, in which a land, its inhabitants, and their history would be described. We know many examples of such passages being part of '*Histories*' and we shall see with Strabo how they could be integral to a 'geographical' work. Jacoby presumably did not want to commit himself to a decision over whether these fragments belonged to *On Ocean* or to the *Histories*, because, with a capacious definition of 'geography' and 'history', they could clearly belong to either or both of these works.

This ethnographical category is helpful in many of the cases where Kidd expresses anxiety over how best to proceed. For example, on the fragment concerning remarkable trees in Spain, he comments: 'Since the extract is reported by Strabo, the source is probably *On the Ocean*, but we cannot be sure, since the *History* also contained details of natural history' (F 54 = Str. 3. 5. 10). Jacoby had addressed this ambiguity by placing the passage in his intermediary section, concerned with regional accounts. Similarly, Kidd included in his geographical section Athenaeus' citation on the Persian king, who would drink only Chalybonian wine, with the result that the Persians transplanted the vines to Damascus; but Jacoby had placed it in

[80] Jacoby, *FGrH*, *Kommentar* F 48.

the 'Länder und Völker' (F 68 = Athen. 1. 28D). Precisely the
same pattern is true for the dead monster in Coele Syria,
described as 100 feet long, with scales each as large as a
shield (F 66 = Str. 16. 2. 17). Kidd terms this a Posidonian
marvel (παράδοξον), and in a sense it is; but such creatures were
not far from being treated as part of historical reality in
Hellenistic accounts of the Near East. In particular, the
emergence of creatures from the sea to contribute to the
development of civilization was an important feature of the
early history of Babylonia. The occasions on which the
creature, Annedotos, came out of the sea were told by Abydenus and more fully by Berosus of Babylon. In the first year
after the creation of the world, a creature, called Oanne, with
the body of a fish, but the head and feet of a man, appeared
from the Persian Gulf on to the land bordering Babylonia. It
had a human voice, and taught men the alphabet, a system of
laws, architecture, agriculture, and all the arts. According to
Berosus there was no time of greater invention (*FGrH* 680 F 1
§ 4). We should not be too quick to dismiss this kind of material
as lying outside the realm of serious history.

Just how open-minded we should be about the potential
scope of each work is reinforced by the fragment in which we
find an account of the foundation of Gadeira, based on the
oracle given to the Tyrians (F 53 = Str. 3. 5. 5). The
importance of Gades in *On Ocean* may at first lead to the
assumption that the place was of interest to Posidonius only
from a scientific point of view, and Kidd groups this passage
with the other scientific geographical fragments. However, the
passage illustrates the inseparability of geography and history
in Posidonius' work. The underlying story was a narrative of
the foundation of Gadeira, but the problem facing Posidonius
was geographical—where exactly were the Pillars of Hercules
at which the foundation was to be made? Kidd remarks
interestingly that Posidonius' preferred version of the answer
might have been influenced by his own geographical background, for, as a Syrian, he chose the pillars in the temple of
Hercules Melkart.[81] If this fragment is from *On Ocean*, as I

---

[81] But, as Prof. F. Millar suggests, we may question whether or not
Posidonius would have thought of himself as a Syrian, or whether his
strong Rhodian connections would have provided an alternative identity.

think is likely given its concern with the Pillars of Hercules, which standardly marked the start of the Outer Ocean in ancient geographical thought, then it would offer a good example of how that work ranged more widely than the field of mathematical geography.

It is interesting that Jacoby's specifically 'geographical' fragments overlap with those of Kidd's categories which we might term 'scientific'; that is, those dealing, for example, with hydrology, geology, and mathematical geography. By contrast, in all but one of the instances I have so far discussed, where Jacoby's 'Länder und Völker' solved a possible generic ambiguity, Kidd assigned the passage to his 'geography' section. So, in a sense, both Jacoby and Kidd created a separate category for less scientific geography, or regional description. But, while Kidd was to keep these segregated from the 'historical' fragments, for Jacoby, as we shall now see, they would form a large ethnographical group together with much that Kidd classed as historical.

I mention first those passages which Jacoby, like Kidd, saw as primarily historical in nature, that is, those which dealt with specific events and people. Of these the most famous is the extensive passage in Athenaeus about the tyranny at Athens of the philosopher, Athenion, in the year 88 BC during the Mithridatic war (F 36 = Athen. 5. 211D–215B). This is one of the few 'narrative' passages, making it important to scholars trying to write the history of the period, but less interesting than an ethnographical passage from the point of view of common ground between geography and history. I mention merely the way in which this fragment, like some of those specifically assigned to the *Histories*, has been interpreted in terms of the 'moralist's view of historiography' (Kidd, II(ii). 886), by which Posidonius, alone among the extant sources, stressed the tyranny of Athenion over that of Aristion because Athenion offered the chance to show how dangerous uncontrolled emotions could be under the rule of the reverse of a philosopher-king.[82]

On Hercules-Melkart see J. Gagé, 'Hercule-Melqart, Alexandre et les Romains à Gadès', *Revue des Études Anciennes*, 42 (1940), 425–37.

[82] Aristion would at first seem to be the more obvious focus of attention,

This group of fragments gives a sense of Roman history which is almost entirely absent from passages securely assigned to the *Histories*, a fact which is due to the different modes of citation employed by different authors.[83] It is no accident that the preoccupations of Athenaeus, whose practice in Posidonian citation was to refer systematically to his source by name, title, and book number, dominate our picture of the *Histories* gained from fragments assigned to books. But Athenaeus had little reason to refer to the events and personalities of Roman history in his *Deipnosophistae*. Instead, we rely largely on Plutarch to provide us with such insights into the *Histories*, and Plutarch's methods for referring to his sources were much less specific than those of Athenaeus, resulting in the clustering of these Roman fragments in Jacoby's section of passages 'without book-title'.[84]

We have, for example, from Plutarch a vivid description, attributed to Posidonius, of Marius' mental apprehension at the end of his life (F 37 = Plut. *Mar.* 45. 3–7); Plutarch also cites Posidonius on Scipio's summoning of Panaetius, when the Senate sent him on a diplomatic mission to Egypt and the Middle East (F 30 = Plut. *Mor.* 777A). It is not always clear, however, whether the focus was Rome itself or a place affected by Rome. Posidonius tells of Nicias of Engyion in Sicily, trying to persuade the town to change its allegiance from Carthage to Rome, and in the process expressing doubt about the epiphany of goddesses for which Engyion was renowned, with the result that he fled to Marcellus for safety. However, it is not certain whether this was part of an account of the deeds of Marcellus,

since he was by far the most powerful tyrant of Athens and was in power at the crucial time of Sulla's siege and capture of the city.

[83] See, for example, the note in F 40 (= Plut. *Brutus*, 1) that Posidonius attacked the view that the Iunii Bruti were not descended from L. Iunius Brutus, the first consul and traditional founder of the Republic. Or the etymological notes concerning famous Romans: F 42a and 42b (Plut. *Marc.* 9. 4–7; Plut. *Fabius Maximus*, 19. 1–4) on how the Romans called Fabius their Buckler and Marcellus their sword; F 41 (= Plut. *Marc.* 1. 1–3) on how M. Claudius Marcellus was the first of his house to be given that *cognomen*, meaning 'martial'.

[84] On Posidonius as a major source for Plutarch, see B. Scardigli, *Die Römerbiographien Plutarchs* (Munich, 1979), 39–40; on Plutarch's use of sources, see Pelling, 'Plutarch's Method of Work'.

or of the history of Engyion, or of the spread of Roman influence (F 43 = Plut. *Marc.* 20. 1–11). When he was cited on Marcellus' exaction of 600 talents' tribute from Celtiberia, was the context a study of the man and his actions, or of the place and its fortunes under Rome? (F 51 = Str. 3. 4. 13).[85] The comment was juxtaposed with Posidonius' criticism of Polybius for having pandered to Tiberius Gracchus over his success in Spain, favouring an Iberian, rather than a Marcellan, context, and indeed Jacoby placed this passage in his section of 'Länder und Völker'. Kidd was perplexed by the fact that both of these events (152/1 BC) fell outside the chronological scope of the *Histories*, and could not decide on a Posidonian context. He here came closest to giving up on the strict chronological arrangement which had been implicit in his assessments so far, and conceded that both might have come in the context of the Celtiberian war of 143–133 BC.

Just as many of the 'geographical' fragments were treated by Jacoby as ethnographical in nature, being distinguished from scientific themes by their assignation in his collection to a section on peoples and places, so too did Jacoby include in this section many of the fragments which Kidd would treat as 'historical'. Not surprisingly, this is true of the many occasions on which Posidonius revealed his interest in the behaviour and customs of the Romans and of other peoples, an interest which sometimes involved tracing their development over time. We shall see in chapter V a similar interest in the evolution of peoples, places, and their habits in the *Geography* of Strabo, revealing how unsatisfactory are strictly generic approaches to these works.

Posidonius' comments on the development of customs over time are sometimes hard to disentangle, as in the case of Athenaeus' description of Roman virtues (F 59 = Athen. 6. 273A–275A). However, the passage on Scipio Africanus' mission to 'settle the kingdoms throughout the world (κατὰ τὴν οἰκουμένην)', in which he showed great restraint in taking only

---

[85] A similar problem is raised by F 44 (= Plut. *Marc.* 30. 6–9). Was the statue of Marcellus in the temple of Athena at Lindos mentioned as part of the *res gestae* of Marcellus, sacker of Syracuse, and *Roman* conquests, or from an account of Rhodes? Here Jacoby decided that the fragment was historical rather than ethnographical.

five slaves, is securely attributed to Posidonius.[86] As Kidd points out, Scipio was hardly 'ancient history' for Posidonius. Therefore this fragment's context, which sets Scipio among virtuous 'old' Romans, must belong to Athenaeus, showing once again how difficult it is to contextualize and interpret small fragments of text. However, Posidonius elsewhere clearly structured his information on this topic in a temporal progression, from early times down to his own contemporaries. 'Earlier on the inhabitants of Italy were so sparing in their needs that even in our own time well-off people make their sons drink water mainly and eat whatever there is' (F 59).[87]

It is clear that this kind of information verges on the ethnographical, and indeed it may have been part of the 'Roman and Italian ethnography' postulated by Jacoby and Malitz for Books 1 and 2. The hard lifestyle of the Ligurians, and the story of the Ligurian woman who paused from her work digging trenches to give birth, then returned immediately to continue digging, are equally impossible to define as geographical or historical (F 57a = Str. 5. 2. 1; F 58a = Str. 3. 4. 17). Often details of lifestyle and customs seem to have been included with no historical motive that we can discern. The display of severed heads by the Celts, as Kidd says, probably came from the Celtic ethnography of Book 23 (F 55 = Str. 4. 4. 5); the eating habits of the Germans presumably from Book 30.[88] Friendship toasts among the Carmani might, according to Kidd, have been part of an eastern ethnography, and if this is correct then we could set it alongside the discussion of how the etymological connection between the Erembians and the Arameans reflected their kinship.[89] This formed part of a larger treatment of the shared features of Mesopotamian peoples in language, lifestyle, and physical

[86] Note the broad geographical context of this piece of history (F 59). Polybius is named with Posidonius as a source for this fragment, a problem since the embassy was probably in 140/39 BC, outside the scope of Polybius' work.

[87] The structure πρότερον . . . καθ' ἡμᾶς and its variations are very common in Strabo. See G. D. Massaro, 'I moduli della narrazione storica nel libri di Strabone sull'Italia meridionale', in *Strabone II*, 81–117.

[88] E–K F 277b (= Eustathius, *Commentarii ad Homeri Iliadem*, 13. 6).

[89] F 72 (= Athen. 2. 45F); F 105a, 105b, and E–K F 281b (= Str. 1. 2. 34; 16. 4. 27; Eustathius 2. 783).

appearance. Was it a geographical passage, linked with the theory of zones and climatic effect on the inhabitants of different parts of the world, or the kind of information that we might expect to find as background to a historical event in the area, or simply part of a regional account?

Jacoby's category of 'Länder und Völker' provides a helpful bridge between the traditional view of the interests of the *Histories* and those of *On Ocean*; the clear area of overlap urges that capacious, rather than narrow, definitions of each work will prove more satisfactory. Just as there are fragments in Kidd's 'geography' sections which could have come from the *Histories* if they were a general account of the Mediterranean world, so too are there passages in the 'history' section which would not be out of place in *On Ocean* if it dealt generally with the outer ocean. The rites of the Samnite (or Namnite) women on the island off the mouth of the Loire, in the Atlantic Ocean, would fit well into this context (F 56 = Str. 4. 4. 6).[90] There is also a detailed description of how, when the women were re-thatching their temple on a particular day each year, any woman whose load of thatch slipped was torn apart by the others. Such detail gives a strong sense of the diversity of customs from place to place.

Posidonius' description of the Cimbrian migrations is another example of a 'historical' fragment which could have come from *On Ocean*. The suggestion, mentioned above, that the migrations were caused by a great tidal wave is here rejected for a theory based on the piratical and nomadic nature of the people, which took them as far as the Cimmerian Bosporus, to which they gave their name (F 31 = Str. 7. 2. 1–2). Kidd comments that 'this is the most important indication that Posidonius saw the explanation of historical events in the characters of the people rather than in the proximate causation of occurrences'.[91] This links the Cimbrian passage with the

[90] Str. 4. 2. 1 says Namnite; Ptolemaeus 2. 8. 6 says Samnite, but 2. 8. 8 Namnite.

[91] Note the interest shown by Agatharchides in the causes of mass-migration. He says that animals have often been the cause—either locusts or deadly winged lice, which burrow under the skin and kill the victim, or scorpions or venomous spiders. The phenomenon was not confined to Africa, says Agatharchides, recalling similar migrations caused by mice in Italy, farrows in Media, and frogs among the Autariatae (*GGM I*, 111–95 § 59).

Athenion fragment which has been seen as another example of character as a factor in historical causation.[92]

From a geographical point of view, the Cimbrian fragment is interesting for its mention of Cleitarchus, who is introduced in connection with the idea that the cavalry (which cavalry?) fled at the sight of the great flood. Kidd suggests that this was said not of the Cimbri, but of Alexander's army as it approached the Indus Delta.[93] But he raises the possibility that Cleitarchus might have mentioned the Cimbri too, or that Posidonius might have used the Alexander story as a parallel. If so, this would be interesting in connection with the criticisms of Seleucus' theory about tides in the Indian Ocean, and might be used to support the idea that *On Ocean* really was concerned with the whole of the encircling ocean.

On Ocean has generally been viewed as a scientific work. The fragments securely assigned to the *Histories* have often been dealt with in a way which depends on a conception of history as a rigidly chronological narrative. However, both works defied such strict characterizations. The problems are extremely similar to those encountered when dealing with Hecataeus, whom I mentioned in chapter I (pp. 60–2). There too we found a 'geographical' work and a 'historical' work, but the fragments assigned by the sources to one or other of these did not allow the characterization of either as anything other than extremely broad in scope; and this, in turn, created problems for an attempt to place the unassigned fragments in one work or the other. So too with Posidonius, an examination of the fragments not assigned to books simply reinforces the view that the two fields overlapped considerably.

Kidd's treatment of these 'floating' fragments reveals a much broader conception of history than his exposition of the

---

[92] D. E. Hahm, 'Posidonius's Theory of Historical Causation', *ANRW* II 36.3, 1325–63, discusses the combination of individual and group behaviour in historical causation. He sees the Athenion fragment as a good example of this combination, with history determined by Athenion's character and the communal reaction of the crowd at Athens. It was, according to Hahm, the importance of the group or society that made ethnography a crucial part of Posidonius' *Histories*.

[93] This is supported by Q. Curtius Rufus 9. 9.

Histories as they stand would suggest, and he quite rightly does not suggest locations for them bound by generic considerations. How can we reconcile his narrow chronological narrative with the fact that he considers as 'historical' a passage on the solidification of asphalt in the Dead Sea, or a discussion of how the Hyperboreans came to inhabit the Italian Alps?[94] Jacoby's middle category of passages concerned with depicting lands and peoples might be described as ethnography in the sense of regional history, or as λόγοι in the Herodotean mould, or as comprehensive accounts of the customs, history, beliefs, and environment of various peoples. All of these descriptions clearly straddle generic definitions, and encourage greater flexibility both in reconstructing the lost works and in dealing with unassigned fragments. I turn finally to consider how we may try to make sense of *On Ocean* and the *Histories* in the context of Posidonius' reputation as a philosopher and within their historical setting.

STOIC 'SYMPATHY' (συμπάθεια): POSIDONIUS'
UNIVERSALISM

How satisfactory is the model of Posidonius' works which would include a *Histories* that described the Mediterranean world in all its aspects, and an *On Ocean* that did the same for the Outer Ocean and the limits of the inhabited world, including its overall shape and character? One potential problem has already emerged in the form of the Cimbri. For they started on the shores of the Outer Ocean, and moved through Europe, gathering support as they went, until they reached Italy, where they were finally defeated by Marius in 101 BC. A similar link between the outer and inner seas is seen in a small fragment on

---

[94] F 70 (= Str. 16. 2. 34–45); F 103 (= Scholion on Apollonius Rhodius 2. 675). On the Hyperboreans in general see J. S. Romm, *The Edges of the Earth in Ancient Thought: Geography, Exploration, and Fiction* (Princeton, 1992), 60–7. Romm does not mention Posidonius as a source for the location of these people. In 'Herodotus and Mythic Geography: the Case of the Hyperboreans', *TAPA* 119 (1989), 97–113, Romm discusses the Herodotean location of these people, concluding that Herodotus used a mixture of reasoning from probability (τὸ εἰκός) and arguments from both climatic and geometrical symmetry to support their existence.

the length of the 'isthmus of Gaul', measured from the Atlantic, north of the Pyrenees, to Narbo (F 34 = Str. 4. 1. 14).[95]

These fragments linking the outer and inner oceans tell against a strict division of spheres of interest. They may even show that Posidonius saw a parallel between the two, which might be reflected in the way the two areas were written about. In this final section I wish briefly to explore the universality of Posidonius' world-view, in an attempt to move away from notions of geography and history, or even of inner and outer oceans. It would be contrived to expect the same manifestations and conceptions of universalism in Posidonius as in the works of Polybius or Strabo, but all lived at various stages in the establishment of a notionally global power, and it would not be surprising to find this reflected in the works of all three.

The place of Rome in Posidonius' thought has been the subject of several articles, of which Strasburger's is probably the best-known. I have already mentioned some of the fragments in which Roman history and people seem to be at the centre. Verbrugghe's reading of the Sicilian slave-war in Posidonius focuses attention exclusively on Roman history and power, arguing that the details of the account reflect mainland Italy, rather than Sicily, and that the physical location of the narrative is irrelevant.[96] It would be easy to imagine one aspect of the *Histories* being a concern with the growing power of Rome, although we have little evidence on which to base any view about Posidonius' large-scale conceptions.

Schmidt's book, although infuriating in its failure to cite evidence for the views expressed, hints at a helpful alternative view of the world to that dominated simply by the progress of Roman rule.[97] She sees the importance of the ethnographical passages as being linked with Rome's mission to rule the inhabited world. It was only by understanding the subject-peoples that Rome could hope to rule them fairly. Like Verbrugghe, she stresses the Romanocentric nature of Posidonius'

---

[95] Strabo sets this in the context of the river-system of Gaul, providentially laid out, but there is no reason to attribute that also to Posidonius.

[96] G. P. Verbrugghe, 'Narrative Pattern in Posidonius' *History*', *Historia*, 24 (1975), 189–204, esp. 197–8.

[97] Schmidt, *Kosmologische Aspekte*, 97–104.

world-view, but she adds a vision of Rome's centrality in a way
which I think has greater potential for an understanding of
Posidonian universalism, that is, expressed through its tenure
of the privileged middle of the climatologically arranged earth.
I shall return to consider the notion of a unified world whose
leaders inhabit the cosmologically appointed centre when I
discuss Strabo's geographical and historical conceptions. One
feature of Polybius' universalism which I mentioned briefly
was its seemingly Stoic aspect, expressed through the notion
that fate unified the world temporally and spatially (p. 126). It
is to this side of Posidonius that I now turn.

Several fragments have evoked the interpretation that Posidonius was moralizing in his role as philosopher-historian. The
fragments on eastern luxury are particularly prone to this
reading.[98] But most come from Athenaeus, and we cannot
assume that Posidonius shared his preoccupation with luxury
and degeneracy. The term φιλόσοφος, or philosopher, was often
applied to Posidonius, and Thümmel states with confidence
that Posidonius saw himself as such ('sich als Philosoph ver-
stand').[99] But this, in itself, is not enough to convince me that
we should interpret all his works in a moral light. Strabo
famously introduced his *Geography* as a work of philosophy,
although few would thus be led to argue that this work had the
moral basis often assumed for the *Histories* of Posidonius.[100]

Rather than see the title 'philosopher' as a cue for a
moralizing interpretation, we should look at what *kind* of
philosopher Posidonius was. A frequent alternative to φιλόσοφος was 'the one from the Stoa' (ὁ ἀπὸ τῆς Στοᾶς), signifying the

---

[98] But see also F 59 (= Athen. 12. 542B), on the luxury of Damophilus, the
Sicilian Greek who stirred up the slave-war of the mid-130s BC, which
Verbrugghe, 'Narrative Pattern', sees as expressing a warning to Rome: 'do
not abuse your power'.

[99] Thümmel, 'Poseidonios und die Geschichte', 559. I. G. Kidd, 'Posidonius as Philosopher-Historian', in M. T. Griffin and J. Barnes (eds.),
Philosophia Togata: Essays on Philosophy and Roman Society (Oxford,
1989), 38–50, discusses the concept of the philosopher-historian in both
ethnographical and more strictly historical fragments.

[100] The philosopher is the very first concept to be mentioned in the first
sentence of Strabo's vast work: τῆς τοῦ φιλοσόφου πραγματείας εἶναι νομίζομεν
. . .καὶ τὴν γεωγραφικήν ('I believe that the field of geography is also part of the
philosopher's task', 1. 1. 1).

strand of philosophy for which Posidonius was, and is, best known.[101] The importance of Posidonius, the *Stoic* philosopher, is backed up by one of the testimonia (T 12a = Athen. 4. 151E). 'Posidonius the Stoic in the *Histories* which he composed not inconsonantly with the philosophy which he has adopted . . . says . . .' (Π. ὁ ἀπὸ τῆς Στοᾶς ἐν ταῖς Ἱστορίαις αἷς συνέθηκεν οὐκ ἀλλοτρίως ἧς προῄρητο φιλοσοφίας . . . φησί . . .). The interpretation of this testimonium has caused many problems to translators and editors. But it does seem to mean that the *Histories* were consonant with Stoicism, and we need to see which tenets might be applicable.[102]

Stoicism certainly had a strong ethical aspect, and it is quite possible that, given Athenaeus' own preoccupation, it is to this that he refers here. However, it seems to me that, alongside the search for moralizing tendencies in the 'historical' and 'geographical' works of Posidonius, it is profitable to consider them both in terms of Stoic ideas about the wider world and the cosmos. Many of these, of course, had a far longer history in the cosmological assumptions of the Presocratic philosophers, some of whose theories I have already discussed. We have some examples of Posidonius' thoughts on these matters in the fragments classified by Kidd under 'physics'. One of the most striking is the fragment preserved by Diogenes Laertius on the idea of the cosmos as a living creature (ζῷον), which vividly recalls Polybius' notion of universal history as 'corporate' (σωματοειδής) and his wish to avoid a disparate picture of the world, which would be like a dismembered animal (p. 124).[103] Posidonius' creature was animate, thinking, and

---

[101] For examples of this phrase, see F 2, 3, 8, 15, 19. Posidonius is just ὁ φιλόσοφος in F 61 and 25.

[102] We should, of course, heed the warning given by A. D. Nock, 'Posidonius', *JRS* 49 (1959), 1, that Stoicism itself was full of individual divergence, and not a neatly defined set of tenets.

[103] E–K F 99a (= Diog. Laert. 7. 142–3): ὅτι δὲ καὶ ζῷον ὁ κόσμος καὶ λογικὸν καὶ ἔμψυχον καὶ νοερὸν καὶ Χρύσιππος ἐν α φησὶν Περὶ προνοίας καὶ Ἀπολλόδωρός φησιν ἐν τῇ Φυσικῇ καὶ Ποσειδώνιος ('Chrysippus in book 1 of his *On Forethought*, Apollodorus in his *Physics*, and Posidonius all say that the cosmos is a living creature, logical, animate, and intelligent'). It is, of course, typical of our knowledge of Posidonius that Diogenes should have cited the titles of all his sources except for Posidonius' work. See Polybius 1. 4. 7 for the world and its history as a living creature.

rational. The idea of the world as a 'logical creature' (ζῷον
λογικόν) again calls to mind Polybius and the natural logic to
which both geographical and historical processes adhered. The
idea of a unified, living universe was also behind some of the
etymological explanations given for the name of Zeus, who
governed everything. Posidonius is named, along with Crates
of Mallos, Chrysippus, and anonymous others, in a note which
derives 'Zeus' from the verb 'to bind' (δεῖν), and 'to live'
(ζῆν).[104] The single, animate universe was closely bound to
the Stoic doctrine of συμπάθεια, by which events and processes
were interrelated, mutually influential, and inseparable. Cicero
attacked the theory, referring to the *coniunctio naturae . . . quam
συμπάθειαν Graeci appellant* (E–K F 106 = Cic. *De div*. 2. 33–5).

But of what relevance is this to *On Ocean*, the *Histories*, and
the attempt to move away from generic classifications of these
works? I should like to suggest that Posidonius ὁ ἀπὸ τῆς Στοᾶς
would not have thought of a 'geographical' work and a
'historical' work as being two totally separable entities, since
all processes were interrelated and under the sole direction of
fate. This is clearly reflected in the impossibility of finding a
straightforward characterization of each work. *On Ocean* was
not purely scientific; the *Histories* had room for material that
was not part of a straight chronological narrative. It is also true
that a division between the works in terms of one which dealt
with the Outer Ocean and one with the inner sea is inadequate.
The world, as one animate being, could not be divided up into
areas which either operated or could be conceived of independently.[105]

The importance of Stoic doctrine to Posidonius' conception
of the world is plainly visible in a passage from Priscianus the
Lydian on the behaviour and conditions of the seas, straits, and
rivers, and assigned by Kidd to the realm of tides and
hydrology (E–K F 219 = Prisc. *Solutiones ad Chosroem*, VI).
In this Posidonius is cited as an authority on tides and author
of the idea that the Outer Ocean moved in relation to the lunar
cycle, while the inner sea moved in unison with it; they were

---

[104] E–K F 102 (= John of Lydia, *De mensibus*, 4. 71. 48).

[105] See Alonso-Núñez, 'Die Weltgeschichte bei Poseidonios', 90, on the
links between universalistic concepts and the Stoic notion of the unity of
mankind.

joined only at the Pillars of Hercules, and acted in sympathy
with one another, like a harbour to the sea. The Latin used to
express this relationship is extremely interesting in the light of
Posidonius' Stoicism, and I quote it in full: 'dicunt [sc.
Posidonius and Arrian] enim moveri exteriorem Oceanum ad
lunae ambitum, *compati* vero interius mare; iuxta columnas
⟨enim⟩ ei Herculis solummodo coniunctum quasi portus pelago
compassione afficitur et alios motus speciales accipit.' We could
hardly find a clearer expression of the way in which the Stoic
world moved as one, in a distinctive manifestation of universalism.[106]

A question remains: if the world was one inseparable unit,
and if we can reasonably argue that 'geography' and 'history'
were categories that Posidonius would probably not have
conceptualized, then how, if at all, are we to relate the two
separate works—*On Ocean* and the *Histories*? The issue will
recur in relation to Strabo, and various possible answers might
be offered in both cases. It is easy to explain the existence of
different works about the world by a single author simply in
terms of the literary tradition. One of the more profitable ways
of distinguishing between generically different works is to
think of their organizational principles. According to Kant,
geography is description according to space; history according
to time. I have argued persistently against the way in which
Posidonius' *Histories* have been treated as a text organized on
strictly temporal lines, and for a work which may have involved
more regional arrangement than has sometimes been conceded.
However, this is the point at which to reintroduce the parallel
suggested to me by Professor D. A. Russell; namely, that the
Histories may have been organized in a similar way to the work
of Pompeius Trogus, with a narrative that moved forward
through time, but supported by extensive regional accounts,
giving the work a strong spatial aspect. Possibly, then, one
could argue simply that Posidonius chose to write *On Ocean* as
a geographical work with a spatial, possibly periplus, structure;
and the *Histories* as a historical work in which time predominated over space in the overall organization.

[106] The whole passage is reminiscent of Polybius' 'sympathetic' water-
expanses, stretching from the Palus Maiotis to the Atlantic Ocean. See above,
pp. 110–11; 125–6.

But time, space, and organization were clearly not all that distinguished the two works. Although both dealt with the same united world and were linked through Stoic συμπάθεια, different material receives different stress in each work, and I would not like to put forward the view that the *Histories* were simply *On Ocean* rearranged, or vice versa. As I set out in chapter I, other, less schematic, approaches to the writings of the late Hellenistic period may prove helpful. One alternative might be to return to the Polybian notion of seeing the world and its description 'both as a whole and piecemeal' (καὶ καθόλου καὶ κατὰ μέρος). *On Ocean* may have been written as a description of the limits of the world as it was known at that stage, an overview of what comprised the world καθόλου; the *Histories* as an account of the past and present of the peoples within that world, described κατὰ μέρος. In that case, the suggestion that Strabo would have been interested only in *On Ocean* would become even more untenable, since, as I shall discuss in chapter V, his *Geography* was full of precisely such descriptions of peoples and places through time.

However, I should like to suggest a further possible relationship between the two works which helps us to understand them in combination as the products of an individual and of an age. We have every reason to suppose, both from Posidonius' repeated identification as a Stoic philosopher and from his view of the world as revealed in certain scientific and philosophical fragments, that he would have been interested in the literary construction of a unified world. However, this is precisely in accord also with the requirements and preoccupations of an age in which Rome's world dominion was becoming firmly established.[107] One need, as in other post-conquest phases, was for the scope and limits of the new world to be set out; the size, the shape, and the habitable zones of the physical globe which was becoming almost synonymous with

---

[107] See Hornblower, *Greek Historiography*, 47: 'For Polybius, Rome's rise to empire was a wonder. For Posidonius of Apamea . . . Rome's empire was an established fact.' S. C. Humphreys, 'Fragments, Fetishes, and Philosophies: Towards a History of Greek Historiography after Thucydides', in Most, *Collecting Fragments*, 207–24, stresses Posidonius' united vision of Roman history, mirroring the unity of the physical world, although she sees the ongoing process of expansion as an important factor (p. 215).

Roman imperial aspirations.[108] These were some of the themes
treated in *On Ocean*. The all-encircling Ocean not only
provided an evocation of global geographical conceptions
from Homer onwards, but it was also the most potent symbol
of world dominion.[109] This had been the outer limit of
Alexander the Great's intended conquests, and it was in
terms of the Ocean that Pompey and Caesar, towards the end
of Posidonius' life, were formulating the imperial aspirations of
their own Roman power.[110] The scope of the new world was
perfectly encapsulated in a work *On Ocean*; in which both the
intended extent of real Roman power, and the ambitious
intellectual and scientific horizons of the age, were represented.
However, it is possible to go further and suggest that Posidonius' contribution to rewriting the late Hellenistic world was
twofold. The new world of Rome, stretching to the Ocean, also
involved the conquest of many peoples, a historical process
which must itself be outlined, and which brought with it the
need to depict recently encountered peoples, places, and
cultures. This was possibly the task of the *Histories*, forming
a link between the historical dynamism of the expanding world
of Polybius and Strabo's descriptions of the lands and peoples
which comprised the newly established world of Rome.

[108] For just some examples of the globe as equivalent to Rome's dominion,
see C. Nicolet *Space, Geography and Politics in the Early Roman Empire* (Ann
Arbor, 1991), figs. 5, 6, 7, 8, 12.
[109] The relevance of the Ocean to attempts to define the οἰκουμένη, which
the Romans saw as their dominion, is brought out by Reinhardt, *Poseidonios*,
126: 'das Problem der Oikoumene war zuletzt die Weltmeerfrage' ('the
problem of the inhabited world was ultimately the question of the Ocean').
[110] I shall discuss this in detail in Ch. VI.

IV

Strabo and Space

INTRODUCTION

My third and final example of the all-encompassing ethnographical, geographical, historical works written in the late Hellenistic period in response to Roman imperialism is the *Geography* of Strabo. Since I shall not turn to the *Geography* as a complete project until chapter VI, a very brief introduction of Strabo and his writings may be helpful at this stage. I hope that it will become apparent that any attempt to give a neat biography of Strabo and a summary of his projects is open to debate and qualification, but I shall nevertheless offer some contextualization and give a framework of the *Geography*, which has survived almost intact.[1]

Strabo came from Amaseia, a Greek city in Pontus, and lived probably from the 60s BC to the 20s AD. Belonging to a family which had enjoyed close connections with the Mithridatic dynasty, Strabo also, like Polybius and Posidonius, had access to the Roman élite, and accompanied Aelius Gallus on his Egyptian expedition of the mid-20s BC. He was thus caught between, or was rather a participant in, two worlds, the Greek and the Roman, and I shall argue that this complex identity is reflected in the geographical and historical conceptions which guide his description of the world.

As a literary figure, it is worth remembering that Strabo was primarily a historian. His 47-book *History* now survives

[1] I have discussed the issues of Strabo's biography and self-presentation more fully in 'In Search of the Author of Strabo's *Geography*', *JRS* 87 (1997), 92–110. See also S. Pothecary, 'The Expression "Our Times" in Strabo's *Geography*', *Class. Phil.* 92 (1997), 235–46, in which Strabo's background and historical contextualization are discussed. The issue of when Strabo's *Geography* was actually composed will be discussed below (pp. 284–5), but I treat it here as a work of the late Augustan/early Tiberian period.

in only nineteen fragments (*FGrH* 91), but was clearly the major of Strabo's two works. It was at the very least ambitious, being described by the *Suda* as a continuation of Polybius (τὰ μετὰ Πολύβιον), precisely parallel to Posidonius' *Histories*, but the exact scope of the work is not at all certain.[2] Only three ancient readers of Strabo's *History* are attested— Josephus, Plutarch, and Tertullian—after which the *History* disappeared from the tradition, possibly overshadowed by the work of Nicolaus of Damascus.[3] The *Geography* fared no better initially. It would be remarkable if Pliny the Elder, Pausanias, and Ptolemaeus all knew of the work, but deliberately ignored it. Strabo receives no mention in Agathemerus' *Sketch of Geography*, written in the first or second century AD, a fact which strongly suggests that the text lay in obscurity at this period.[4] In fact, there are few references to Strabo's *Geography* in the first five centuries after it was written. That we know the text at all is due to its lucky survival through the great sixth-century transference from papyrus to parchment, an example of which is preserved in the Strabo palimpsest (*Π*)—the earliest known text of part of the *Geography*.

The nature of this initially obscure geographical work, by an author who was first and foremost a historian, is the subject of the next three chapters. The structure of the *Geography* is fairly straightforward: two books discussing the tradition and the general shape of the world, followed by a description of individual regions, starting in Spain and moving clockwise around the Mediterranean to Mauretania:

---

[2] A. Diller, *The Textual Tradition of Strabo's Geography* (Amsterdam, 1975), 3, suggests that Strabo's *History* went up to the 20s BC, but did not include Aelius Gallus' expedition, presumably because this was discussed in the *Geography*.

[3] See Diller, *Textual Tradition*, 7, for the suggestion concerning Nicolaus.

[4] See A. Diller, 'Agathemerus, *Sketch of Geography*', *GRBS* 16 (1975), 59–76. R. Syme, *Anatolica: Studies in Strabo* (Oxford, 1995), 357, comments: 'There is no evidence that he ever published the *Geography*. On the contrary, it seems to have lurked in obscurity for long years.' Syme's comment is, of course, ironically prophetic of the fate of his own work on Strabo. For a more detailed appraisal of Syme's work, see the review by K. J. Clarke in *Gnomon* (forthcoming).

I–II	Theoretical prologue; correction and discussion of predecessors, especially Homer; general geography
III	Iberia
IV	Gaul; Britain
V–VI	Italy; Sicily
VII	Northern Europe; areas south of the Istros; Epirus; Macedonia; Thrace
VIII–X	Peloponnese, southern and central Greece, islands
XI	Start of description of Asia; areas north of the Taurus; Parthia; Media; Armenia
XII–XIV	Asia Minor peninsula
XV	India; Persia
XVI	Areas between Persia, the Mediterranean, and Red Sea
XVII	Egypt; Libya

I argue later in this chapter that the general geography which characterizes the first two books becomes overshadowed by the accounts of individual places through the rest of the work, and I discuss the way in which the periplus structure is transformed. For the moment, it remains simply to indicate and justify my approach to Strabo.

Given my title, 'Between geography and history', it might seem natural to divide my treatment of Strabo into 'Strabo the geographer' and 'Strabo the historian', and it could be argued that those are the descriptions that will emerge from the next two chapters. I could then conclude that Strabo's *Geography* involved him being both a geographer and a historian at once. But these labels seem to me confusing because of the different connotations attached to them both in the past and now. I shall conclude by arguing that both Strabo's *Geography* and his *History* fell between geography and history, but what I shall really mean is that ancient notions of the terms γεωγραφία (geography) and ἱστορία (history) both incorporated aspects of the modern subjects of geography and history; in other words, that separable subjects of geography and history, as defined in the narrow, modern sense, do not map exactly into the ancient world. If I formulate my approach to the *Geography* in terms of 'geography' and 'history' this seems to make linguistic, if not logical, nonsense of the fact that Strabo also wrote a separate *History*.

Because of the problem of shifting meanings attached to these words, I have chosen to examine separately the way in which Strabo deals with and formulates spatial and temporal factors in the *Geography*, while keeping in mind that these elements went to make up a single work. There are several difficulties inherent in my approach. Firstly, as I argued in chapter I, time and space are hard, if not impossible, to deal with as separable entities, and it is questionable whether such an imposition should be made on Strabo's work. Secondly, by looking at 'Strabo on space' and 'Strabo on time' one might seem to impose an interpretation of geography as space and history as time before we have even started. If 'between geography and history' turns into a study of space and time, and not, for example, of present and past, then I have already said something about my assumptions about the nature of geography and history. But, by examining Strabo's use of and attitudes to space and time in a single γεωγραφία, I hope to demonstrate that a limited notion of 'geography' as a spatial term, although perhaps the most satisfactory way of distinguishing it from temporally determined history, does not begin to explain the motivation for Strabo's work and its modes of expression.

Finally, the fact that Strabo wrote a historical work as well as his *Geography* might at first make a traditional generic classification seem reasonable. Why not look in the *Geography* for Strabo the geographer as opposed to the historian, when the works seem to have been divided in this way? My answer is simply to reiterate that Strabo's 'geographical' work contains a great deal that we might term 'historical', and it seems likely that his 'historical' work contained a good deal of 'geography'. If the *History* had survived, we would expect to see something of both Strabo the geographer and Strabo the historian there too, as in the *Geography*, although perhaps in a different combination. I am trying to show that a limited, modern, notion of 'geography' and 'geographers' does not account for the text of Strabo's *Geography*; that Strabo's notion of γεω-γραφία incorporated much that we might not term strictly geographical. I wish at this point to move away from the terminology of my title and to avoid separate discussions of 'geography' and 'history' in the *Geography* because *everything* that I am about to consider was 'geography' in Strabo's view.

STRABO AND THE GEOGRAPHICAL TRADITION: SPATIAL SYSTEMS

The fact that periplus texts occupy most of Müller's first volume of *Geographici Graeci Minores* suggests that for him they lay at the heart of Greek geographical writing. The relationship between such texts and real exploratory voyages has been the subject of some debate, and I have already discussed in chapter I some of the links between geography and fiction. Jacob's assertion that these texts were simply literary constructs examining the nature of non-Greek *alterité* is countered by Cordano's belief that the literary periplus texts were firmly rooted in the accounts given by sailors of their voyages, and that there were probably, in addition to the long journeys of the extant texts, also descriptions of much shorter stretches of coastline.[5] Given the long history of exploration and the resultant literary output, it is hard to be convinced by Jacob's theory, which in any case still needs to provide a motive for the periplus form given by authors to their constructions of 'the other'.[6]

[5] C. Jacob, *Géographie et ethnographie en Grèce ancienne* (Paris, 1991), 73–84; F. Cordano, *La geografia degli antichi* (Rome, 1992), 29. Jacob sees also Agatharchides' *On the Erythraean Sea* as an intellectual exploration of *alterité* and a questioning of what constitutes civilization (p. 146); this view may be supported by the observations by S. M. Burstein, *Agatharchides of Cnidus: On the Erythraean Sea* (London, 1989), 17, that Agatharchides does not mention autopsy as a requirement for a potential successor to his project, and that his contacts with the élite of second-century BC Egypt must have given him 'access to documentary sources on a scale almost unparalleled among major Greek historians'. A much later, anonymous, account of the same sea, edited by L. Casson, *The Periplus Maris Erythraei* (Princeton, 1989), gives much of the same material as Agatharchides, but the perspective is that of a merchant, rather than that of an ethnographer, and the reality of the author's experience is not in doubt.

[6] P. M. Fraser, 'The World of Theophrastus', in S. Hornblower (ed.), *Greek Historiography* (Oxford, 1994), 167–91, illustrates a quite different medium through which the opening-up of the world could be expressed.

The form of the coastal voyage entails that this kind of
account was dominated by linear space, prone to calibration,
in so far as it is liable to have built into it distances, expressed
numerically.[7] Although Strabo did not include periplus
authors in the 'canon' at the start of his work, the *Geography*
was itself organized largely according to a periplus structure.
By starting his description of the world in Iberia and continuing round the Mediterranean in a clockwise direction, finishing
in north-west Africa, Strabo was following the structure
adopted, for example, in the periplus texts attributed to
Scymnus of Chios and Scylax of Caryanda, and, as far as can
be discerned from the extant fragments, in Hecataeus' *Periegesis*.[8] In any case, the literary nature of Strabo's project
necessitated some kind of linearity in the description. Unlike
pictorial accounts, which could give a sense of contemporaneity, Strabo's written account of the world had to have a clear
sequence. In this section I shall start by discussing aspects of
the periplus texts which are shared by Strabo's *Geography*, as
well as considering how limited or varied are the spatial
concepts associated with this technique.

Strabo announces that, just as Ephorus used the coast as his
measuring-line (τῇ παραλίᾳ μέτρῳ χρώμενος), he will use the sea
as his guide around Greece (8. 1. 3).[9] This immediately
conjures up a linear image, an impression which is reinforced

Fraser explores how Theophrastus' botanical works can be seen as a 'mirror of
the great changes that the world had recently undergone' (p. 169). The variety
of ways in which the East became known to the Greek-speaking world is
endless. T. S. Brown, 'Suggestions for a Vita of Ctesias of Cnidus', *Historia*,
27 (1978), 1–19, discusses how Ctesias came to know and write about Persia
through his time there as court-physician, having been taken prisoner by
Artaxerxes. M. Cary and E. H. Warmington, *The Ancient Explorers* (London,
1929), 140–9, stress the growth in knowledge which resulted from the
campaigns of Alexander.

[7] The same obviously applies to road itineraries. It is striking quite how
interested Polybius was in milestones and distance—preoccupations which are
relatively absent from Strabo's text.

[8] For Scymnus and Scylax, see *GGM I*; for Hecataeus, see *FGrH* 1. An
example of a modern periplus which follows precisely the same structure, as
indicated in its title, is P. Theroux, *The Pillars of Hercules: A Grand Tour of
the Mediterranean* (London, 1995).

[9] He calls the sea his τόπων σύμβουλος (guide to places).

by the allusion to measurement. It is, however, interesting that when Ephorus is invoked as a source for the Peloponnese in the second-century BC periplus of the Mediterranean attributed to Scymnus of Chios, what results is not a linear perspective, but a two-dimensional one, in which space is defined according to dominant peoples.[10] The Peloponnese is treated as a microcosm of the world, with the area divided into the celestial coordinates and the dominant people of each quadrant recorded. The Sicyonians live in the north, the Eleans and Messenians dominate the west, the Laconians and Argives hold the south, and the Acteans the east. So we are left uncertain as to how Ephorus' own geographical conceptions were formulated. There is, however, some reason to believe that the geographical view of Ephorus given by Scymnus may be closer than the linear approach suggested by Strabo. Earlier in the periplus Scymnus departs suddenly from the linear structure to give his text a global aspect in a way which foreshadows the description of the Peloponnese. The Celts are said to be the largest people in the west, the Indians to hold almost all the land in the east, the Aethiopians to dominate the south, and the Scythians the north. Each quadrant of the celestial coordinates is characterized by a dominant set of inhabitants, and astronomy and anthropology combine to define the world. Although Scymnus does not cite Ephorus as a source here, the similarity with Ephorus' world-view as noted by Strabo elsewhere is striking. Strabo says that Ephorus in his treatise on Europe divided the heavens and the earth into four, and gave each section of the world a dominant population group—Celts, Scythians, Indians, and Aethiopians (1. 2. 28). So our original apparently simple allusion to a linear structure may be more complex than it at first seems.

One of the main features of the linear periplus texts is the calibration of distance, expressed in terms of both space and time. In the periplus attributed to Scylax of Caryanda, for the first few chapters all distances are given in terms of the number of days' and nights' sailing. When the Tyrrhenian coast is reached, this is partly replaced by a measurement in stades, although the temporal method of giving distances remains

---

[10] See *GGM I*, Scymnus l. 472 for Ephorus; ll. 516–23 for the Peloponnese.

common.[11] This author refined the 'day-and-night' system to the degree where small fractions of a day were used, as in the case of the crossing from Sason to Oricus—a sea-journey of one-third of a day. Similarly, the journey time from the Bulini tribe of Illyria to the river Neston is given as 'a long day'.[12] The section on Europe ends with an exposition of the author's method for reckoning up the total sailing time along that coast. It is suggested that we take a night's sailing to be equal to that of a day and that we assume 50 stades' travel in a day, giving a total for the journey of 153 days.

These expressions of distance are interesting in terms of the interaction of time and space, for their preoccupation with space as well as place, and for their sense of 'experienced' space and of relative position.[13] The notion of distance over space being measured in temporal terms counters the argument of some social geographers that the conceptual precedence of time over space is a modern phenomenon. I have already mentioned Harvey's argument that modern society has placed a high value on time, so that it must be privileged over space, making us sacrifice the experience of travelling through space.[14] The use of time to measure space in the ancient periplus texts may simply reflect that 'time taken' was the most straightforward way to measure journeys at sea; but it also shows that the conceptual privileging of time over space does not necessarily result from the need to speed up time. Indeed, the very fact that the space between places is represented by a measure of time stresses the act of journeying.

The distinction between *temps vécu* and *temps mesuré* (and their spatial equivalents) is one which, as I shall argue, does not correlate exactly with a division between ancient and modern ways of viewing the world, in spite of those who argue that the ancients had no notion of abstract space and time. However, in the case of the periplus texts, the 'lived-in' nature of both space

[11] *GGM I*, Scylax §17.

[12] *GGM I*, Scylax §26, §22.

[13] We may recall Y.-F. Tuan, 'Space, Time, Place: A Humanistic Framework', in *Making Sense of Time*, 14, who defined place as 'pause in movement', which fits the periplus scenario extremely well. But space, as it gains in familiarity, is scarcely distinguishable from place.

[14] D. Harvey, *The Condition of Postmodernity: An Enquiry into the Origins of Cultural Change* (Oxford, 1989), 265. See above, p. 14 and n. 26.

and time *is* brought out by the use of the first person to refer to those participating in the voyage. The experience of passing through space is central to the exposition. This creates problems for the idea that place alone can be defined as 'lived-in space', as discussed by modern geographers, although the 'places' too have a strong sense of being lived in, owing to the amount of ethnographical material. Langton's distinction between 'spatial geography' and 'place geography' provides a useful way of describing the different approaches taken by Polybius and Strabo.[15] But the periplus texts represent something between the two. Merrifield's suggestion that space and place could be bound by 'emplotment'—the narrative binding our experiences of different places to cover space—is perfectly exemplified in the periplus texts, whose main concern is precisely with the narrative of travelling across space from place to place.[16]

Albeit in a way which is dimensionally limited, the periplus authors reveal a conception of relative location through their interest in plotting out a real or imaginary journey between fixed points, with places defined primarily through their position in the list.[17] One of the strongest impressions of travel comes in Dicaearchus' description of Greece, a periegesis rather than a periplus, and extant in only three substantial

[15] J. Langton, 'The Two Traditions of Geography. Historical Geography and the Study of Landscapes', *Geografiska Annaler*, 70B (1988), 17–25. Both types of approach are, he concludes, equally valid; both are found in the ancient material.

[16] See A. Merrifield, 'Place and Space. A Lefebvrian Reconciliation', *TIBG* NS 18 (1993), 516–31, cited above, p. 37 with n. 97. Jacob's argument for the fictional nature of some periplus journeys might have implications for the idea of 'espace vécu', except that the intended impression is of a real journey in which space is crossed through time, whether or not the journey actually took place. But, on the relationship between fictional and 'real' space and time, see above, pp. 23–5.

[17] I have already mentioned Brodersen's paper, in which he discussed the connection between written lists and visually conceived space, and argued that the map of Agrippa was not a visual representation but a list of places along itineraries. The list was, he argued, the predominant way of conceiving space in the ancient world. Although his point is partially vindicated by the periplus texts, this does not entail that there was no notion of visual space in antiquity. I have already set out in chapter I some of the evidence for visual representations of the world, and argued in chapter II that Polybius' geography was strongly visual. I shall argue, furthermore, that such visual space is evident in the periplus texts themselves.

fragments.[18] The first fragment deals with Athens, Oropus,
Tanagra, Plataea, Thebes, Anthedon, and Chalcis. The reader
is taken along this pleasant route to Athens and shown everything of interest both on the way and in the city itself. We are
told of the great buildings in Athens, the produce of the area,
and the characteristics of the Attic people as opposed to those
of the Athenians themselves (1. §1–4). The route from Athens
to Oropus is described as a journey of one day for a person
without baggage and the steepness of the route is compensated
for by plenty of resting places (1. §6). By contrast and
inexplicably, the distances between Oropus, Tanagra, and
Plataea are given in terms of stades rather than days' travel.

Strabo's language is sometimes reminiscent of that of the
periplus writers. Expressions such as 'as one sails from Nisaea
to Attica, five small islands lie before one', and 'the voyage,
starting from the country of the Chaones and sailing towards
the rising sun' evoke the immediate experience of real travel
(9. 1. 9; 7. 7. 5).[19] The extent to which Strabo adopted the
interests of the periplus writers both in the journey along linear
space and in distance is of relevance to the purpose of the
Geography, and also to the type of spatial conceptions which
dominate his description. In fact, if we recall Polybius' interest
in distance, Strabo 'the geographer' is surprisingly silent.
Strabo is expected to be concerned with distance and linear
space not only because those are fields which we assign to
modern geography, but also because some scholars have
assumed that he was writing a manual for Roman governors,
who might indeed find a literary version of itinerary maps
useful. If Strabo set out to write this kind of geographical
manual, then he failed. In a memorable sentence he describes
negatively the type of geography which might be most useful to
commanders and officials, namely, the distance between places,
regretting that 'in the case of famous places it is necessary to
endure the tiresome part of such geography as this' (14. 1. 9).[20]

---

[18] For Dicaearchus (or Athenaeus), *Periegesis of Greece*, see *GGM I*. All
following numbers in the text refer to Müller's chapters.

[19] The use of the phrase 'towards the rising sun' (πρὸς ἀνίσχοντα ἥλιον) is
particularly striking. See also 16. 4. 2: 'The whole journey is towards the
summer sunrise (πρὸς μὲν ἀνατολὰς θερινάς).'

[20] The case in question is the difference in distance between Miletus and

Scholars, such as Jacob, have been reluctant to accept this non-utilitarian nature of Strabo's account, arguing that geography must provide dimensions since 'elle est l'instrument de la conquête, mais aussi d'une politique d'administration'.[21] The justification for this view can be derived from Strabo's own preface, in which he aims the work at Roman rulers and strongly advocates the practical usefulness of geography. 'The geographer should take care of these [sc. the useful] matters rather than those [sc. the famous and entertaining]'; 'The greater part of geography is directed at political requirements (τὰς χρείας τὰς πολιτικάς)'; 'Geography as a whole has a bearing on the activities of commanders (ἐπὶ τὰς πράξεις . . . τὰς ἡγεμονικάς)' (1. 1. 19; 1. 1. 16). But Caesar's *Bellum Gallicum* should introduce a note of caution into any attempt to place narrow limitations on what kind of geography might seem appropriate to a military commander. Caesar's account incorporates military and strategic information together with ethnographic and geographical descriptions, confounding certain assumptions about what might have appealed to generals and officials. His purpose in writing, namely to gain support in Rome for his own political career, may have been quite different from that of Strabo, but the readership of the two works, the cultured member of the Roman élite, the potential commander or governor, remained the same.

Syme, however, expected Strabo to provide detailed information on routes, strategic points, and communications, only to be disappointed. Syme's own interest in this kind of geography comes through in his account of Anatolia. His sense of large-scale geography, strategic points, and communications is nowhere better exemplified than in his account of Termessus.[22] But Syme was constantly frustrated when he

---

Heraclea, and between Miletus and Pyrrha, which is considered τὸ περισκελὲς τῆς τοιαύτης γεωγραφίας. περισκελής means 'hard', or 'difficult', with a connotation of 'unpleasant' or 'irritating' when used of medicines (LSJ).

[21] Jacob, *Géographie et ethnographie*, 149: 'It [sc. geography] is the instrument of conquest, but also of a political system of administration.'

[22] See Syme, *Anatolica*, 193: 'Termessus occupies a strong and secure position at the head of a valley on the southern flank of the defile through which passes the road out of Pamphylia to Isinda and Cibyra—the main road to the valley of the Maeander. That would be enough to explain the strategic

turned to Strabo for help on these points. Strabo's spatial
misconceptions were inexcusable to Syme. Strabo's inadequate
account of the river Tigris, for example, was a result of his
'clumsily combining, or rather juxtaposing, heterogeneous and
often incongruous information'. His knowledge of the Tigris
compared unfavourably with that of other authors, was 'ele-
mentary and archaic', and these limitations led to his overlooking 8,000 square miles of land.[23] I shall return to Strabo's
lack of a sense of two-dimensional space, which Syme was right
to attribute to the *Geography*, but for the moment simply
suggest that the work could still be 'useful'. Strabo's statement
of intent is mismatched with the work itself if we take it to refer
to itineraries and strategic positions, but the intention might
still have been fulfilled if we allow for a different interpretation.
By presenting a picture of the world as it was now, as well as its
transformations into that state, Strabo could claim to be
educating the ruling Romans on the nature of their subjects
and potential enemies, providing an account of the lands and
peoples which were of interest to the Roman ruling élite.[24]

We shall see in the next section how Strabo rewrote the world
by transforming the use of linear concepts of space in conjunction with a different spatial model. First, however, I shall
examine ways in which even the periplus texts departed from a
strict linear sequence, thus themselves providing alternative
spatial models. I have already mentioned the remarkable passage
of Scymnus in which a picture of the whole world is suddenly

importance of Termessus. There is something more. The defile is also an exit
from Pamphylia into central Anatolia.'

[23] Ibid. 29; 39.

[24] G. W. Bowersock, *Augustus and the Greek World* (Oxford, 1965), 123–8,
suggests that Strabo was part of the general influx of Greek literati towards
Rome, which included Dionysius of Halicarnassus and Timagenes and
formed a group around the aristocracy. This situation may encourage the
view that Strabo's work was primarily intended to be useful for those who
would govern the empire. The addressee is seen as the 'man of state' (ὁ
πολιτικός), engaged in politics, but in the broad sense of 'the cultured and
superior men who managed the affairs of state' (p. 128). C. Van Paassen, *The
Classical Tradition of Geography* (Groningen, 1957), 9, supports this view of
the dualistic nature of the intended reader, but he adds that 'one could read
for φιλόσοφος Greek, and for πολιτικός Roman', a notion to which I shall return
in chapter VI.

evoked. The periplus attributed to Scylax of Caryanda shows one way of breaking the linear progression to incorporate islands into the account, simply inserting them into the description of the coast as they occur, and invariably ending with the formula 'I shall return to the mainland from which I digressed'.[25] Scylax also foreshadowed the clearly ethnographical geography of later writers such as Agatharchides of Cnidus, revealing an interest in people rather than places, and so with whole areas rather than individual cities or villages. As we shall see, Strabo's concern was predominantly with the cities (πόλεις) of the world, although he did devote some attention to the treatment of non-urban peoples, and these non-πόλις occasions are precisely when he became interested in space as opposed to place.[26] Scylax, at the end of his description of Europe, departs again from the linear sequence, and also broadens the scope of spatial conceptions from the city-to-city scale to a comparison between the size of the Palus Maeotis and the Pontus.[27] The broad horizons, well beyond the scope of the periplus, are maintained in a description of the Scythians as reaching from the outer sea beyond Taurica to the Palus Maeotis. Finally we are told of the Syrmatae, a race which lived by the river Tanais and, with it, bounded Asia and Europe. Thus the periplus gives rise to a vision of such large-scale geographical areas as continents.

Dicaearchus' periegesis of Greece, in spite of its strong sense of travel along a linear journey, is not devoid of wider geographical ideas. His detailed account of Mount Pelion links the mountain to the surrounding area. One of the rivers flowing off the mountain connects it via the Pelian grove to the sea and the views from the summit are used to orientate the mountain. One side faces Magnesia and Thessaly, the west and the Zephyr; the other looks towards Athens and the Macedonian bay, a method of description (that is, by orientation) which recalls Polybius on Media.[28] In the third fragment the boundaries of Hellas are

---

[25] ἐπάνειμι δὲ πάλιν ἐπὶ τὴν ἤπειρον, ὅθεν ἐξετραπόμην: *GGM I*, Scylax §13, §53, §58.

[26] But Strabo rarely shows a real interest in terrain, one of the first topics to feature in modern geographical accounts of a region. By contrast, see Polybius 5. 22. 1–4 on the terrain around Sparta; 5. 59. 3–11 for Seleuceia.

[27] *GGM I*, Scylax §68.

[28] *GGM I*, Dicaearchus 2. §7–9; Pol. 5. 44. 3–11.

discussed, raising the issue of defining geographical units, a problem which was to tax the brains of geographers throughout antiquity and beyond.[29]

I shall discuss the question of focus more fully in the next section, but it is already worth mentioning that the broadly linear form of the periplus and its apparently internal and ever-changing perspective do not exclude the idea of viewing the world from a single point. The notion of standpoint accounts for one of the less obvious ways in which the periplus perspective coloured Strabo's description. He treats the coastline of the area facing Euboea before moving inland, and uses a similar technique with the coast of the Troad and Aeolia, keeping the interior as the second element of the description (9. 2. 14–15; 13. 3. 6). This ordering is made explicit—'since I have gone through the Trojan and Aeolian coasts together, it would be next in order to run through the interior'. The use of the sea as the point of reference from which the land is described has been discussed by Nicolai.[30] He assesses the possible location of the Aorsi and Siraci tribes on the basis of the meanings of ἄνω and κάτω, rejecting the possibility that these could refer to high and low-lying areas, in favour of the meanings 'inland' and 'near the sea'. By pointing to other instances in Strabo's text where the adverbs take the latter meaning, such as 1. 3. 22 where ἡ ἀνωτέρω πᾶσα μέχρι τοῦ ἰσημερινοῦ ('all of the "higher" region as far as the equator') clearly refers to the whole of Africa moving *inland* as far as the equator, Nicolai puts forward a convincing interpretation of the use of these words with regard to the Aorsi and Siraci. The argument is important for two reasons. Firstly, it stresses the periplus viewpoint adopted by Strabo in many of his descriptive passages. Secondly, it brings out the centrality of the Mediterranean in Strabo's view of the inhabited world (οἰκουμένη), reminding us that affiliation to periplus texts did not have a linear spatial

---

[29] As C. Bearzot, 'La Grecia di Pausania. Geografia e cultura nella definizione del concetto di Ἑλλάς', *CISA* 14 (1988), 90–112, discusses, the boundaries of Hellas were still debatable in Pausanias' day. One of the problems was the discrepancy between administrative, political, and cultural limits.

[30] R. Nicolai, 'Un sistema di localizzazione geografica relativa. Aorsi e Siraci in Strabone XI 5, 7–8', in *Strabone I*, 101–25.

view as its only consequence. For Strabo to describe Asia Minor from the Mediterranean viewpoint required a deliberate decision since, as a native of Amaseia, he would naturally have seen the Aorsi and Siraci from a quite different angle.

The other main strand of Hellenistic geography known to us was the so-called scientific tradition represented by figures such as Eratosthenes, Hipparchus, and Strato of Lampsacus. I have discussed in connection with both Polybius and Posidonius the view that it is misleading to think of scientific geography as divorced from ethnography or periplus literature; but for convenience I shall isolate some of the concerns revealed in the extant writings of these authors, and consider Strabo's treatment of these themes. His debt to the scientific geographical tradition is obvious from the prologue to his work, in which Hipparchus is one of the prominent figures. The fact that Strabo devoted Book 2 to a discussion of mathematical geography reveals a considerable degree of interest and knowledge in this type of research. But what would affiliating his *Geography* with the authors listed above entail? Strato's sea-level debates are known to us from the *Geography*.[31] The theories of Eratosthenes and Hipparchus are expounded and criticized at length. But how did Strabo's practice through the rest of the text relate to them?

The use of geometrical figures as aids to geographical understanding, so important to Eratosthenes and Hipparchus, was taken up by Polybius, as we have seen. Strabo too used such figures, but only to a limited extent. Britain, Italy, Sicily, and the Nile Delta were, for example, triangular, although Strabo expresses some reservation over the possibility of describing Italy by means of a single figure (4. 5. 1; 5. 1. 2; 6. 2. 1; 17. 1. 4); India was shaped like a rhombus (15. 1. 11). But more crucially, the whole scope of Strabo's world was different from that of the scientists. The quest to measure out the globe was explicitly rejected by Strabo in favour of studying the inhabited world. While Eratosthenes discussed the shape not only of the inhabited world (οἰκουμένη), but of the whole earth (ἡ σύμπασα γῆ), and Posidonius extended his sphere of interest to the outer Ocean, Strabo contested that 'geographers

---

[31] Cited at 1. 3. 4–5 and discussed by J. O. Thomson, *History of Ancient Geography* (Cambridge, 1948), 155.

need not concern themselves with what lies outside our
inhabited world' (2. 5. 34).[32] This zone of study was reduced
even further elsewhere: 'The geographer seeks to relate the
known parts of the inhabited world, but he leaves alone the
unknown parts of it—just as he does what lies outside it'
(2. 5. 5). Strabo was interested primarily in the inhabited
parts of the world because they formed the stage for, and
even influenced, human action, in a way which was consistent
with his concentration on places rather than the uninhabited
space between them.[33] As I have discussed in chapter I, the
concern with the world which humans have made for themselves is shared by both geographers and historians, and is
perfectly illustrated by the Herodotean *histoire humaine*.

One of the theories inherited by Strabo from the Hellenistic
geographical tradition and treated in the *Geography* concerned
the climatic zones formed by the equator and parallel lines of
latitude. Posidonius attributed the five-zone scheme to Parmenides; Polybius added a sixth, according to Strabo, giving a neat
symmetry to the hemispheres. Posidonius himself complicated
the conception of climatic zones by introducing ethnic criteria
(2. 2. 2–3. 2).[34] This was another geographical model discussed
by Strabo in his introductory books but scarcely taken up in his
own account of the world. Hipparchus' attempts to determine
which places lay on the same lines of latitude find no place in
Strabo's view of the world, although they are included in his
summary of the geographical tradition (2. 1. 20).[35]

---

[32] Strabo gives the limits of this field as the parallels through the
Cinnamon-producing country and through Ierne in the north. When talking
of Laconia, Strabo puts a limit to how much should be said 'about a country
which is now mostly deserted' (8. 4. 11).

[33] 1. 1. 16: χώρα γὰρ τῶν πράξεών ἐστι γῆ καὶ θάλαττα, ἣν οἰκοῦμεν ('for the
location of events is the land and sea which we inhabit'). I shall return to the
problem of how this statement can be reconciled with my view that Strabo
saw nature as more than a passive backdrop for history.

[34] I have discussed the contributions of Polybius and Posidonius to the
theory of zones above, pp. 112, 145–7, 182–3.

[35] Hipparchus took as a basis for his system of lines of latitude and
longitude a principal latitude through the Pillars of Hercules and the Gulf
of Issus, and a main meridian through Alexandria. He then drew parallels of
latitude through well-known places and thus created zones called κλίματα.
Strabo, however, used the term κλίμα to refer to the lines of latitude
themselves.

The continents offered yet another way of dividing up the earth and were also discussed by Strabo. I have mentioned the influence of Eratosthenes on ideas about continental divisions, and also Strabo's objections to the artificiality of Eratosthenes' system of vertical seals. In the introduction to his treatment of Asia Strabo favoured the division according to natural boundaries, which Eratosthenes had applied to the inhabited world as a whole (11. 1. 1). As I have noted (p. 205), the notion of continents was of interest to the periplus authors. Both Scylax and Scymnus gave the river Tanais as the boundary of Asia and Europe.[36] But a geography describing the individual places in the known world would have little cause to make much of huge continental units.

One occasion on which Strabo *does* refer to the continents is in the penultimate chapter of the whole work, picking up on the kind of geography which he discussed at the start. In the meantime Strabo has set out his own vision of the world in which geometry, continents and wide-scale geography are subordinate. Jacob has argued that Strabo adopted *all* preceding traditions, and in a sense this is true. He sees the general, wide-scale geography of the first two books followed in the rest of the work by a periplus structure. But Jacob skews the picture by deliberately 'dégageant simplement le fil du parcours au détriment des informations apportées sur chacun de ces lieux'.[37] Of course, by removing the extensive historical descriptions of each place, we shall be left with something approaching a bare linear structure. But this entirely distorts the overall impression, which is predominantly of a world made up of individual and discrete places. As I discuss in the next section, these places are linked not so much to each other as to Rome.

Of course Strabo was not hopelessly ignorant when it came to the broader geographical conceptions of the tradition. His first two books set out the 'scientific' geographical framework for the rest of the work; the description itself follows a broadly periegetic order. But I shall now move on to consider what was really distinctive about the way Strabo constructed his world.

[36] Scymnus called the river τῆς Ἀσίας ὅρος. See *GGM I*, Scymnus l. 874.

[37] Jacob, *Géographie et ethnographie*, 154: 'simply separating the thread of the journey to the detriment of information adduced on each of these places'.

The end of the work gives a clue as to the model for which I shall argue. When Strabo finally returns to the continental divisions, having scarcely mentioned them since the second book, it is in a way which is transformed to reflect his preoccupations. Strabo's interest in the continents is entirely related to the extent of Roman rule. After describing the initial spread of Roman influence through Italy, Strabo then tells what parts of each continent Rome does and does not rule (17. 3. 24).[38] As with every other spatial conception in the preceding tradition, the continents are brought into play in the *Geography*, but as part of a fresh vision of the world, dominated by a new spatial model, to which I now turn.

STRABO'S CIRCULAR MODEL: A WORLD BUILT
AROUND ROME?

In the following two sections I examine the conception of the world as a whole which emerges from the *Geography*. Having considered some of the spatial models which were part of the preceding geographical tradition, and which Strabo largely neglects after the introductory books on the theory of geography and its scholarly tradition, I shall now try to describe what Strabo's own spatial world-view might have been. I argue that his world was constructed according to a circular model in a way which was historically determined by the consolidation of the Roman empire. I use the term 'circular' not to refer to that specific geometrical shape as opposed, for example, to an ellipse, but rather to suggest that the world of the *Geography* was, by contrast with the wandering linearity of the periplus tradition and with the mathematical abstraction of the scientific treatises, a world constructed with a periphery and a primary centre. This picture will necessarily be subjected to considerable modification, in particular through the incorporation of other focal points besides Rome itself, but I shall deal first with the broad conception of a Romanocentric world.

The question of circularity is not dependent on an understanding of the spherical nature of the earth among the

---

[38] Interestingly, the continents are introduced here in an anti-clockwise direction—Europe, Libya, Asia—the opposite of the progress of the work as a whole, although, in each instance, Europe is given precedence.

ancients, although that notion was well established. Eudoxus of
Cnidus, a fourth-century forerunner of Hipparchus and Eratosthenes, invented a system of twenty-six concentric spheres
around the earth on which the different planets could spin on
differently orientated axes to explain the irregularities in their
movements. He was also responsible for the earliest known
figure for the circumference of the earth, which Thomson
suggests he calculated by measuring the height of a star at
two places roughly on the same meridian.[39] Eratosthenes
measured the earth's circumference almost two centuries
later using the differing angle of incidence for the noonday
sun on the day of the summer solstice at Alexandria and Syene
(Str. 2. 5. 7). His understanding of the spherical nature of the
earth is further attested in his belief that anyone sailing west
from Iberia would reach India, hindered only by the size of the
intervening ocean, an idea with which he pre-empted Christopher Columbus by about two millennia (Str. 1. 4. 6).

This indicates that the ancient geographers were accustomed
to thinking of a spherical earth. But did this correspond to a
circular 'mapped earth'? The notion of the encircling Ocean
around a circular inhabited world was hotly disputed in
antiquity. Herodotus had criticized those who 'depict Ocean
as flowing round an earth which is rather circular as though
traced by compasses', taking the idea of circularity to extremes
for his rhetorical effect.[40] However, the related debate concerning whether the inhabited world, albeit not perfectly
circular, was surrounded by a single Ocean would continue
to rage through the second century BC. The tale of Eudoxus of
Cyzicus, related by Posidonius and then by Strabo, encouraged
a belief in an all-encompassing Ocean, since Eudoxus
attempted to sail right around Libya (Str. 2. 3. 4). Hipparchus,
Eratosthenes' second-century BC critic, argued against the view
that the inhabited earth was an island surrounded by a uniform
Ocean, and contended that, even if the Ocean behaved uni-
formly throughout, this would not necessarily mean that the
Atlantic flowed in one stream forming a complete circle. Both
Strabo and Eustathius cite Hipparchus as claiming that the

[39] Thomson, *History of Ancient Geography*, 115–17.
[40] Herodotus 4. 36: οἳ Ὠκεανόν τε ῥέοντα γράφουσι πέριξ τὴν γῆν, ἐοῦσαν
κυκλοτερέα ὡς ἀπὸ τόρνου.

current out of the Strait at Byzantium sometimes actually stands still, acting as though independent of the tides, a theory which would seem to deny the continuous nature of the earth's waters (Str. 1. 3. 12; Eust. *Ad Dion. Peri.* 473). But Strabo reverted to the idea of the Homeric encircling Ocean, and remained unconvinced by Hipparchus (1. 1. 9).

So, some notion of a circular world was current, but had come under serious criticism and challenge. Strabo needed to reassert the Homeric model. The all-encircling Ocean suited Strabo's historical view of a united world; and need not imply strict circularity, but simply a centre–periphery model. Indeed Strabo's world could not conform to a strictly circular model, its focal point of Rome being considerably left-of-centre. But first, what of the visual representation of this world? I mentioned in chapter I some of the evidence for mapping in antiquity. Eratosthenes' map of the known world was notorious and was severely criticized by Hipparchus. But it was Anaximander's sixth-century attempt which was seen as a landmark by the Roman geographer, Agathemerus, who called Anaximander 'the first to have the audacious idea to depict the inhabited world on a table'.[41] Strabo's own description of how to relate a spherical reality to a plane surface seems to suggest that he envisaged a rectangular inhabited world (οἰκου-μένη). Following the theory of Crates of Mallos, he accepted the division of the earth into four quadrilaterals, one of which contained the known world (2. 5. 6).[42] He suggested that the best representation of the world would be on a spherical globe, but if that were not possible it should be drawn on a plane surface. Strabo's repeated reference to the rectangle (τὸ τετρα-πλεύρον) in which the οἰκουμένη lay, might seem to suggest that the world itself that he described was also rectangular, but he never states that τὸ τετραπλεύρον actually represented the οἰκουμένη itself. Rather, it *contained* the inhabited world, which could still be, and I shall argue was, broadly circular.

Given the range of spatial conceptions formulated by other authors and mentioned by Strabo himself, the use of the circular conceptual model of the world invites discussion.

---

[41] See Cordano, *La geografia degli antichi*, 46.

[42] The οἰκουμένη was an 'island in the aforementioned rectangle' (νῆσος ἐν τῷ λεχθέντι τετραπλεύρῳ).

The creation of worlds around central points of focus recurs throughout the *Geography*. After conquering the Medes, Strabo says, Cyrus and the Persians noticed that their native land was situated somewhat on the edges (ἐπ' ἐσχάτοις που) of the empire and so moved their royal seat to Susa (15. 3. 2). Strabo notes elsewhere that Alexander moved his capital from Susa to Babylon on the grounds that the site was preferable, lacking the extreme heat of Susa (15. 3. 10).[43] As I mentioned in chapter I, the need to avoid geographical and climatic extremes, which were in any case usually linked, was firmly established in ancient thought.

As I shall argue, Rome formed the main focus for Strabo's conception of the world, but the notion of *other* foci leads us first to the interesting thesis of Thollard, in which he asserts that the work was arranged around the opposition of civilization to barbarism.[44] It is hard to say how specific we can be, and how specific Strabo himself was, about the standard against which he measured barbarism. Barbarous behaviour was geographically determined in so far as absence of contact with civilized societies such as Rome hindered the process of civilization. Isolation (ὁ ἐκτοπισμός) was a feature of barbarian nations, but this was by no means the only influencing factor. And to what extent was Rome to be seen as the only centre of civilization? In Gaul, Roman rule led to the cessation of barbarian customs and sacrifices, all the practices that were 'not current among us' (παρ' ἡμῖν) (4. 4. 5). But who were we (ἡμεῖς)? The Romans? The people of Strabo's Pontic region? Simply the adherents to the life of the Graeco-Roman city? Or Strabo's assumed readership?

As I hope to show in this and the following chapter,

---

[43] Early Babylonian maps of Mesopotamia, with Babylon at the centre, form a precise parallel for the centrality of Rome in Strabo's world. See R. A. Butlin, *Historical Geography: Through the Gates of Space and Time* (London, 1993), 91.

[44] P. Thollard, *Barbarie et Civilisation chez Strabon: Étude critique des Livres III et IV de la* Géographie (Paris, 1987). Jacob, *Géographie et ethnographie*, 161, suggests that we should replace the idea of a decreasing level of civilization as we move from the centre at Rome with a decrease correlating to the distance from *any* centre of civilization. This must be true to some extent, and might be used to explain the prominence of India in the *Geography*, in spite of its freedom from Roman impact.

questions of focalization are more complicated in the *Geography* than has generally been recognized, and there is more than one identifiable focus in the work. The northern shore of Libya would be the coast 'on our side' (ἡ καθ' ἡμᾶς παραλία) to almost *anyone* in the known world (17. 3. 24); at a slightly more specific level, the *Roman* empire is summed up at the end of the work as 'our inhabited world' (ἡ καθ' ἡμᾶς οἰκουμένη) (17. 3. 24); on a much smaller scale, Strabo refers to himself individually as 'we' (ἡμεῖς), and possibly also implicates his intended readership of the cultured man of state (ὁ πολιτικός) in this denomination. All of this complicates our use of the term in determining those against whom the barbarians were being judged, although it is also important to recognize that *alterité* is itself a much more subtle concept than simply the polar opposite of whatever consitutes 'us', and that identifying 'us' would not provide an easy answer to the question of who is barbarian.[45]

Strabo professed to start his description with the Mediterranean, and particularly Europe, because that was where deeds of action, constitutions, and arts were most concentrated and where government was good (2. 5. 26). So, Thollard's model of a world conceptualized around the opposition of barbarism and civilization is consistent with the notion of Rome and the Mediterranean as the central focus. But, according to Thollard, Strabo's professed privileging of the civilized Mediterranean in the ordering of his work is extended on a smaller scale throughout. So, although the general principle of movement is from west to east, Turdetania is dealt with before Lusitania, and Narbonensis before Aquitania and the rest of Celtica. One might argue that the periplus principle would lead us to expect inland Celtica to be treated after coastal Narbonensis, but it is harder to explain why Narbonensis should precede the more westerly Aquitania. Within this framework, civilization plays a part in determining the starting-point for the description of a

---

[45] See the comments of E. Hall, *Inventing the Barbarian: Greek Self-Definition through Tragedy* (Oxford, 1989), especially in the epilogue on 'The Polarity Deconstructed', for the inadequacy of a straight opposition between 'them' and 'us'. The whole complex question of acculturation is treated by A. Momigliano, *Alien Wisdom: The Limits of Hellenization* (Cambridge, 1975).

region—Lugdunum, for example, for the territory of the Belgae. Thollard concludes that 'la structure s'adapte au sujet, et non le contraire'.[46] This is useful in so far as it warns us against placing Strabo firmly in the tradition of periplus writing where the structure was relatively inflexible. But Thollard's thesis is limited in that he implies that the periplus and the opposition of barbarism and civilization are the only methods of orientation for the text.

As both Thollard and Van der Vliet stress, the notion of continuum and gradation, from civilized to utterly barbarous, accommodates a corresponding spatial conception better than does a straight opposition. Although the Romans were in a sense accustomed to using clear-cut boundaries such as rivers to delineate themselves from 'non-civilized' peoples, a certain degree of blurring was necessarily built into the picture in order to accommodate the incorporative aspect of Roman imperialism. The barbarian enemy had to be capable of becoming a Roman citizen, and even a senator in the future, making the idea of continuum preferable to that of polarity. In Thollard's view, Strabo was interested in different levels of barbarism, although the movement of history was almost always in the direction of civilization.[47] Van der Vliet sees a Posidonian influence in Strabo's rejection of a simple opposition in favour of an appreciation of the differences between various barbarous races.[48] The Celts and Germans are, for example, compared and contrasted in terms of physical appearance and lifestyle (7. 1. 2). But this sensitive appreciation of the subtleties in different barbarian lifestyles seems hard to reconcile with the view of both Van der Vliet and Sechi that Strabo's depiction of barbarian peoples was designed to legitimate Roman imperialism.[49]

[46] Thollard, *Barbarie et Civilisation*, 75: 'the structure is adapted to the material available and not the other way round'. Against this we may set Jacob's assertion that detail was never allowed to hinder the overall arrangement—Strabo aimed always to preserve in spirit the global structure *(Géographie et ethnographie*, 152).

[47] Thollard, *Barbarie et Civilisation*, 19–20. The Scythians provided a counter-example to the move towards civilization (7. 3. 7).

[48] E. Ch. L. Van der Vliet, 'L' Ethnographie de Strabon: Idéologie ou tradition?', in *Strabone I*, 37–8, for Strabo's debt to Hellenistic ethnographical ideas.

[49] Van der Vliet, 'L'Ethnographie de Strabon', 82, identifies Strabo's

Strabo's real alternative to the continental divisions, to the geometrical approach, and to the theory of latitudinal zones as methods of conceptualizing the world, was a model based on the centrality of the Mediterranean, Italy, and Rome.[50] It was not only administrative and cultural systems which privileged the centre of the inhabited world, but also nature and climate. In scientific mode, we hear that the physicists say that the universe and the heavens were spherical, with the earth at the centre, and that 'bodies with weight tend towards the centre' (ἐπὶ τὸ μέσον) (2. 5. 2). This scientific explanation is repeated in philosophical terms towards the end of the work. 'The work of nature (φύσις) is that all things converge to one, the centre of the whole (τὸ τοῦ ὅλου μέσον), and form a sphere around this (σφαιρουμένων περὶ τοῦτο)' (17. 1. 36). For Strabo, nature was providence (πρόνοια). So the forces of fate and history worked in conjunction with the laws of atoms in the realm of physics to draw everything towards the centre of the universe and then of the world.[51] A study of Strabo's text reveals this process in action. Both temporally and spatially we shall see that everything moves towards the centre of the cosmos—Rome.[52]

The strong sense of movement towards the effective centre of the world, Rome, dominates the text, but I wish first to consider the possibility of *outwards* movement, and the dynamic implications of Strabo's model. Rome's sphere of influence is seen in Strabo's final survey of the empire as having spread in concentric circles centred at the capital—

attitude to barbarians as one of disgust 'from the point of view of the civilized and superior conqueror' ('du point de vue conquérant civilisé et supérieur'). See also M. Sechi, *La costruzione della scienza geografica nei pensatori dell' antichità classica* (Rome, 1990), 224, on the non-civilized nature of barbarian peoples as justification for military expeditions.

[50] This contrasts with the non Romanocentric geographical conceptions, which Alonso-Núñez argues underpinned the 'opposition' universal history of Pompeius Trogus. See above, pp. 168–9 with n. 62.

[51] The Stoic influence is very clear; Strabo's remarks are strongly reminiscent of Posidonius. It is significant, as Prof. D. A. Russell has pointed out to me, that Strabo introduced his work as one of philosophy.

[52] The picture is not clear-cut. One complicating factor is the tension between Rome's centrality and its omnipresence throughout the empire. Not a region goes by without some mention of Roman influence, Roman battles, or Roman leaders.

from Rome to Italy to the areas lying around Italy in a circle
($\kappa\acute{\upsilon}\kappa\lambda\omega$) (17. 3. 24). Roman influence in the form of cultural and
political change is attested throughout the work. But the time
of dynamic expansion lay in the past for Strabo. Traina argues
that Polybius had already given a Romanocentric picture of the
empire.[53] But in reply I would argue that, whereas Polybius'
picture was of expanding Roman power, and his account of its
encroachment across the world is extremely vivid in dynamic
spatial terms, Rome as a fixed physical entity in a crucial
position comes across much more clearly in Strabo's work. It
is not that Strabo's model lacks movement, but that its inward
nature leads to a sense of geographical equilibrium rather than
of spatial dynamism. Strabo was interested in the workings of
the empire and the relationship between individual places and
Rome, but the Roman world of the late Augustan and early
Tiberian period, when the *Geography* was probably being
written, was no longer expanding significantly, making
change in space a less pressing concern than description of
place.

This equilibrium is reflected in Vitruvius' picture of Rome's
position at the centre of the world, which gave it the balanced
nature necessary for the leader of a world empire.[54] This
geographical location partly explains the predominance of
Italy, and in particular of Rome, for Vitruvius. The superiority
of the centre of the known world over the edges is expressed by
Strabo in terms similar to those used by Vitruvius, arguing for
Rome's success by virtue of its privileged central location in the

[53] G. Traina, *Ambiente e paesaggi di Roma antica* (Rome, 1990). Traina sees
the idea of Rome as the capital of the empire as delineated during the last two
centuries of the Republic, particularly through the works of Cato and
Polybius. 'Catone e Polibio sono due momenti separati, ma complementari
per definire il ruolo dell' Urbe come centro dell' oikoumene' (Cato and
Polybius are two separate moments, but ones which are complementary in
defining the role of the city as centre of the inhabited world) (p. 53).

[54] Vitruvius 6. 1. 10–1: *vero inter spatium totius orbis terrarum regionisque
medio mundi populus Romanus possidet fines . . . Ita divina mens civitatem populi
Romani egregiam temperatamque regionem conlocavit, uti orbis terrarum imperii
potiretur* ('But the Roman people possesses territories in the true *mean* within
the space of all the world and the region of the earth . . . Thus the divine mind
has allocated the state of the Roman people an outstanding and temperate
region, so that it might gain a world empire').

world, giving Rome the kind of temperate climate which had motivated Alexander's move to Babylon (see p. 213). Before embarking upon his description of Aethiopia, Strabo comments that 'in general, the extremities of the inhabited world, which lie along the part of the earth that is intemperate and uninhabitable because of heat or cold, must be defective and inferior to the temperate part' (17. 2. 1).

As so often, it is appropriate to recall the elements of Presocratic thought and the theories of the Hippocratic writers and of Herodotus. The importance of balance between opposites underlay the Ionian cosmology of Anaximander and Anaximenes. Herodotus' world, as I mentioned in chapter II, was one of symmetry and balance. This is particularly clear in his description of the Ionian founders of the Panionium, who 'of all those that I know, have founded cities in the most beautiful setting of climate and season. For the country to the north of them is not the same in these respects, nor to the south or the east or the west, for some of it suffers from cold and wet, and some from heat and drought' (1. 142). Such sentiments are found again applied to Ionia in the Hippocratic corpus. 'The situation most conducive to growth and gentleness is when nothing is forcibly predominant, but equality (ἰσομοιρίη) in all respects prevails' (*Airs, Waters, Places*, 12).[55] The theme of environmental determinism, which I discussed in chapter I, is common to both the Ionians of the sixth and fifth centuries BC, who found the perfect balance in their own part of the world, and the 'Roman' authors of the first century BC, whose ideal location was predictably Rome itself. It is, however, interesting that for Herodotus and the Hippocratic author of *Airs, Waters, Places* the political consequences are rather different from those envisaged by Vitruvius and Strabo. As I shall argue in chapter VI, with certain qualifications, life in a balanced and temperate place such as Rome enhances one's chances of securing hegemony. But for Herodotus, as I mentioned in connection with Polybius, the delightful setting of the Ionians rendered them unable to rule (9. 122). Exactly the same view is expressed in *Airs, Waters, Places*: 'bravery, endurance, hard work, and high spirit could not arise in such conditions

[55] The criteria are very close to those of Herodotus; lack of heat, drought, cold, and excessive wet.

[sc. those of climatologically privileged Ionia] . . . but pleasure must rule supreme' (12).

In spite of the sense of equilibrium seen in Vitruvius' and Strabo's accounts of Rome, one of the most striking impressions of the world gained from Strabo's text is that of a constant deluge of resources towards its capital. These come in various forms—human, material, and intellectual. The centrality of Rome and its attraction of the human resource is reflected in the ideology of the *Res Gestae* where Augustus describes the whole of Italy flooding into Rome to vote on and witness his appointment to the position of *pontifex maximus*.[56] It is noteworthy how spontaneous much of the movement of people towards Rome is in Strabo's account also, in stark contrast to the compulsory movement of peoples enforced by Rome. The city exerted a magnetism on the people of its empire. The main group of people depicted by Strabo making their way towards Rome is that of envoys, seeking to make requests of the emperor.[57] The Aedui of Gaul are mentioned as the first of the peoples in that region to ask for the friendship and alliance of Rome (4. 3. 2).[58] Artemidorus of Ephesus went on an embassy on behalf of his native city to win back for the goddess the sacred revenues from the Selinusian lakes, which had been taken by the Attalids, restored by Rome, then usurped by the *publicani*. The success of this petition sheds a favourable light on Roman rule, with the Romans (we are not told exactly who) ready to right some of the injustices resulting from the greed of the *publicani* (14. 1. 26).

Another example concerns an envoy sent from the Cycladic island of Gyarus to request from Octavian a reduction in tribute payments. This is one of the relatively few occasions where we have a first-hand account, since Strabo himself was on the boat that gave the envoy a lift to Corinth, where Octavian was staying on his way back to Rome to celebrate

---

[56] *Res gestae divi Augusti*, 10. 2: *cuncta ex Italia ad comitia mea confluente multitudine* ('as the crowd flowed in from the whole of Italy to my election').

[57] See F. G. B. Millar's petition-and-response model of the principate, developed in *The Emperor in the Roman World* (London, 1977).

[58] For Tacitus' account of the senatorial debate over the admission of the Aedui, a later stage of development in the relationship with Rome, see *Annals*, 11. 23–5.

Actium (10. 5. 3). Furthermore, we have Strabo's account of
how Nicolaus of Damascus also came across envoys on his
travels. In this instance the envoys were sent by King Poros of
India to ask for the *amicitia* of Augustus and to offer free
passage through his country (15. 1. 73).[59] Strabo stresses the
irresistible pull exerted by the emperor on peoples who were
not even under his rule, and whose difficult journey led to the
death of some members of the embassy.

One last point may be made about the movement of people
towards the emperor. After Petronius had garrisoned the city
of Premnis against Queen Candace of Aethiopia, he received
ambassadors from her, but told them to go to Augustus with
their requests. 'They asserted that they did not know who
Caesar was or where they should have to go to find him.'
Petronius gave them escorts and they found Augustus on
Samos and secured their requests (17. 1. 54). This episode is
interesting in so far as it hints at the multi-focused nature of the
work and of the way it reflects the world. Both Rome and the
emperor were centres of attraction for goods and people, and
much of the time they coincided geographically. However,
there were occasions when Rome was *not* the centre of
power. Goods might continue to pour towards Rome, but
people wishing to petition the emperor might be forced to
seek him elsewhere.[60]

The material influx to Rome is explicable in terms of its large
population consuming more than the area could supply, and
Strabo provides many examples of this process. Consumables
such as meat were transported along the river Arar towards
Rome and textiles brought from Patavium (4. 3. 2 and 4. 4. 3;
5. 1. 7). A plant used for filling mattresses ($\tau\acute{\upsilon}\phi\eta$), papyrus, and
reeds came from the Tyrrhenian lakes (5. 2. 9); Falernian,
Statanian, and Calenian wines from Campania (5. 4. 3). Even

---

[59] This passage also demonstrates the flow of goods to Rome in the form of
gifts brought to the emperor by hopeful embassies. The gifts brought by the
Indian envoys displayed the exotic nature of the country—huge vipers, a
river-tortoise, and a partridge larger than a vulture.

[60] This provides an interesting counter to the example given by S. Ardener
(ed.), *Women and Space. Ground Rules and Social Maps* (Oxford, 1993), 3, of
people defining space—'The Court is where the king is'. In the early Roman
empire, capital and emperor might be separately located.

water was transported to supply Rome's demands, being drawn from Lake Fucinus along the Aqua Marcia aqueduct (5. 3. 13). All of the trade from Iberia was with Rome and Italy, leading to the minerals of the region being called by Posidonius 'storehouses of nature or a never-failing treasury of an empire' (3. 2. 5).[61] Ironically the Iberians were given no enjoyment of this wealth; the empire being supplied was not that of the Iberians, but had been appropriated by Rome. Sicily is described in strikingly similar language, for this time the treasury of an empire was made explicitly 'the treasury of Rome' since the island sent all its surplus produce to that city.[62]

Leaving aside the implicit question of whether Iberia and Sicily should be forced to fund another state's empire, we have so far seen no explicit censure of Rome's draining of its conquered lands. The subject becomes more pertinent when we consider Strabo's portrayal of rock and mineral reserves flowing to Rome. The rock-quarry at Gabii serving Rome with this resource along the Via Praenestina evokes no comment (5. 3. 10). However, the Roman desire for gold resulted in the gold-mines of the Alpine Salassi being taken over by *publicani*.[63] Marble was another mined resource to be drawn to Rome. Proconnesus furnishes a rare example of Strabo *not* mentioning Rome as the marble's destination. In this case the marble was used within its native region around Cyzicus (13. 1. 16). Marble from Luna and Scyrus, however, did come to Rome (5. 2. 5; 9. 5. 16). Yet it is only in discussing Phrygian marble that Strabo makes any explicit moral comment. This commodity was transported with great difficulty and at large expense. It was due to present Roman extravagance (διὰ δὲ τὴν νυνὶ πολυτέλειαν τῶν ῾Ρωμαίων) that huge pillars were now mined instead of small stones (12. 8. 14). There is a sense of Roman greed, demanding resources which required wealth and expertise to transport.

Another asset drawn to Rome involved aspects of cultural or social life. Rome not only took in human and material resources, but also borrowed ideas from elsewhere. The laws of

---

[61] 3. 2. 9 for Iberia's minerals as a ταμιεῖον ἡγεμονίας.

[62] 6. 2. 7 for Sicily as ταμιεῖον τῆς ῾Ρώμης.

[63] 4. 6. 7 for ἡ πλεονεξία τῶν δημοσιωνῶν ('the greed of the *publicani*'); 4. 6. 12 for gold-mining in the rest of Italy.

Hermodorus of Ephesus are said to have been taken to Rome,
and Etruria was the source for the triumphal and consular
adornment, the fasces, various Roman rites, and the art of
augury (14. 1. 25; 5. 2. 2). All of these resources could be
'shared' by their original owners with Rome. However, many
cultural assets could be brought to Rome only at the expense of
people around the empire. Apellicon's library of Aristotelian
works was removed by Sulla on his capture of Athens and
became part of the intellectual drain to Rome (13. 1. 54). But
the most prominent aspect of Rome's cultural pilfering of its
empire in Strabo's text is the appropriation of art treasures
from around the world. The statue of Hercules came from
Tarentum to the Capitol in Rome (6. 3. 1); the statue of the
goddess was demanded from the temple at Pessinous, as was
that of Asclepius from Epidaurus (12. 5. 3); the painting *The
Fallen Lion* was taken by Agrippa from Lampsacus to Rome
(13. 1. 19). The regularity with which Strabo draws attention
to Rome's demands on the cultural heritage of other places
might suggest that he disapproved of Rome's attitude. Yet
Strabo himself was part of the flow of intellectuals to the
capital, and he justifies Rome's actions on several occasions.
The removal of the *Labours of Hercules* from a precinct on the
coast near Alyzia in Acarnania by a Roman commander is
viewed positively since the picture was being saved from
neglect (10. 2. 21). The plunder of art treasures from Corinth
by Mummius is not condemned, since it is connected with his
generosity in sharing the booty (8. 6. 23). Rome is sometimes
depicted as taking works of art which had special significance
for its early history. Apelles' picture of Aphrodite rising from
the sea, taken from Cos and dedicated by Augustus to Julius
Caesar, is an example of a situation where Rome is seen as
taking something to which it had a claim because of its
associations with Venus (14. 2. 19).[64]

The question of Rome as the focal point to which all
resources converge is crucial in gaining some idea of Strabo's
perspective. As I have already noted, centrality need not, and
indeed cannot, be taken in the strictest sense of the word, since
far more of Strabo's world lay to the east of Rome than to the

---

[64] The Coans were also given a 100–talent tribute remission in return for
the painting.

west. By saying that Rome was centrally placed in Strabo's conception of the world, I refer to its position at the point where the various lines of movement of goods, people, and ideas met. Perhaps one of the reasons why we gain an inadequate sense of the relationship between places in the empire is that Strabo is more interested in their relationship with Rome than with each other. His treatment of Gaul in Book 4, for example, is heavily structured by the river network, and in particular by its potential as a trade-route from the Ocean to the Mediterranean through some of the richest land in the western empire. All routes go through the centre of the web. The linearity of the periplus is redirected, so that each place is linked, not to the next along the journey, but to the capital of the empire.

Pericles' vision of Athens, as portrayed by Thucydides, places that city in a similarly central position, drawing in resources from around the world (ἐκ πάσης γῆς) (2. 38). However, this view of Athens' place in the world is constructed and described from the centre, and also differs from Strabo's Rome in so far as, in terms of ideas, Athens is not a consumer, but an exporter (a παράδειγμα at 2. 37; and a παίδευσις for Greece at 2. 41). Defoe provides a more striking parallel for Strabo's picture, developing his view of London as he moves around the British Isles. He persistently notes that the produce of each place he describes is sent to London, and builds up a picture of Britain in which every place has its own link to the capital, but not necessarily to anywhere else. The model is made explicit early in the work: 'It will be seen how this kingdom, as well as the people, as the land, and even the sea, in every part of it, are employed to furnish something, and I may add, the best of every thing, to supply the city of London with provisions.'[65] Similarly, Strabo's political view is inextricably bound up with the way in which his geography of the world is constructed. We might perhaps expect Strabo, if he were describing Rome's actions from the point of view of a provincial, to be more resentful of Rome's drain on all that lies within the empire and yet he repeatedly reinforces its role as central consumer with

---

[65] D. Defoe, *A Tour through the Whole Island of Great Britain*, (3 vols.; London, 1724–6—page refs. are to the Penguin reprint of 1986), 54. For a few examples, see pp. 83, 95, 118, 119, 128, 130, 137, 147, 166, 182, 207.

little hint of censure. As Jacob says: 'Il ne dissimule pas son admiration pour la Ville de Rome, . . . pour la personne d'Auguste, le régime politique qu'il a instauré et l'administration de l'Empire, qui répand les bienfaits de la civilisation sur la plus grande partie de la terre habitée.'[66]

One way in which Strabo's view of Rome may be assessed is in terms of his attitude towards rivals to its supremacy, particularly given his family's associations with the Mithridatic dynasty, one of the casualties of Roman imperialism. Various cities appear in Strabo's work as potential rivals of Rome. Not all threatened Rome's overall supremacy, but their superiority in particular areas might have been seen to challenge the capital, and so to provide alternative focal points. Naples, for example, is presented as a repository of Greek culture, a welcome retreat from the pressures of Rome (5. 4. 7). Suetonius' picture of the last days of Augustus' life comes to mind at this point, since it was here, absorbed in the city's Greek ambience, that Rome's first *princeps* died (Suet. *Aug.* 98).[67] Another way in which cities might rival the centre of the empire was to share aspects of its topography. Mylasa, for example, is described as a great city with its own *Sacra Via* for religious processions, partially obviating the attraction to Rome of the peoples of the empire. Rome's magnetism over its subjects was due partly to its uniqueness (14. 2. 2).[68]

In the case of Rhodes, praised for its excellent facilities and administration, and acting as an anti-pirate state in parallel with Rome, Rome's response was to provide a relationship of

---

[66] Jacob, *Géographie et ethnographie*, 147: 'He doesn't disguise his admiration for the city of Rome, . . . for the figure of Augustus, the political régime which he instigated, and the administration of the empire, which spreads the benefits of civilization over most of the inhabited world.'

[67] Suetonius says that, during his last days, Augustus insisted that the Romans on Capri should speak Greek and dress like Greeks, and that the Greeks should do the opposite. The question of interplay between Greek and Roman will later become of relevance to Strabo.

[68] An example of a city sharing political structures with Rome was Gades, which had its own *equites* (3. 5. 3). The uniqueness of Rome is brought out most effectively in Virgil, *Eclogue*, 1. 19–25, where Tityrus acknowledges that he was wrong to think of Rome as simply larger than any other city. Rather, it was qualitatively different as well, like a cypress raising its head above the guelder roses.

amicitia (14. 2. 5). The privileged status of this city is brought
home by the detail that its architect was the same as that of the
Piraeus—the different fates of the two places could not be in
starker contrast, with one destroyed by Sulla and the other
benefiting from Rome's friendship (14. 2. 9). Strabo, however,
attests a range of more ambiguous approaches to rivals. The
first involved pilfering of the kind discussed above. Massilia
appears as a centre of education for Romans, heir to Athens'
role as a focus for philosophers. Its status is complimented and
at the same time belittled by Rome's imitation of Massilia with
its own *xoanon* of Artemis on the Aventine (4. 1. 5). The
architecture of a provincial city was in a sense no longer its own
when it was liable to be transferred in conception to Rome. A
similar fate befell the temple of Aphrodite on Mount Eryx in
Sicily, which provided the model for the temple of Venus
Erycina in front of the Colline Gate (6. 2. 6). Places around the
empire became sources of inspiration for Rome. We might
have expected that Rome, like Pericles' Athens, would itself be
the model for other cities. Instead, the overwhelming impression in Strabo is of Rome drawing on others.

This siphoning of ideas and cultural symbols to Rome, part
of that city's general drain on the resources of its empire, was
not the only way of dealing with rival centres. Another was to
cast doubt on their claims to importance. Delphi is the prime
example, interesting because the doubt is specifically Strabo's
own in this case. Strabo could not avoid the idea of Delphi as
the centre of the inhabited world, but he attributes this idea to
others—'it was *believed* to be the centre of even the inhabited
world and people *called* it the navel of the earth' (9. 3. 6).

Smyrna was a model city which Strabo found it hard to
criticize. There was, however, one respect in which the people
of Smyrna had failed, that is, in their lack of a proper underground sewage system (14. 1. 37). The provision of a water-
supply, efficient drainage, and sewers is said in Strabo's
description of Rome to have been an example of the greatest
foresight of the Romans that set them above the Greeks (5. 3. 8).
So, Smyrna failed on the very point at which Rome excelled,
suggesting that nowhere, however promising, could really
threaten Rome's supremacy. We might contrast Rome's intol-
erance of rival centres with the attitude taken by the Persians:

'Although they adorned the palace at Susa more than any other, they esteemed no less highly the palaces at Persepolis and Pasargadae' (15. 3. 3).[69]

The mention of Persia again brings us to the question of the succession of empires, and the notion that Rome was only one in a line of world powers. The Persian kings, according to Polyclitus, built dwellings for themselves on the acropolis at Susa and had storage places for the tribute they collected, as memorials of their administration (ὑπομνήματα τῆς οἰκονομίας) (15. 3. 21). We may recall Rome's public display of its imperial aspirations in the theatre of Pompey where permanent reminders of his triumph were displayed—the inscriptions of his triumphs, trophies, and statues representing fourteen subject nations.[70] Persia, like Rome, drained resources from its subject nations. The produce of each country was drawn in, and the wealth of the kings led them to ever greater extravagance, demanding wheat from Assus in Aeolis, Chalymonian wine from Syria, and even water from the Eulaeus (15. 3. 22). The Persian parallel provides a gentle hint that Rome's own power might be temporally limited.

The theory of the succession of empires has been thoroughly studied by others. I mentioned it in chapter I, and shall return to it in chapter V.[71] But it is worth noting that the implications are not solely temporal, since there were parts of the world which Rome had not yet wrested from the control of other empires. Strabo's list of Asian rulers does not end like the others, culminating in Rome's supremacy, but with the Parthians.[72] Indeed, the word Παρθναίοις is the last of the

[69] The Persians kept their treasures and tombs at these centres for the practical reason that they were better fortified, as well as because the places were ancestral (προγονικός).

[70] See C. Nicolet, *Space, Geography, and Politics in the Early Roman Empire* (Ann Arbor, 1991), 38, for Pompey's theatre and the imperialism on show there; see pp. 41–7 for the interesting suggestion that a similar display of personifications of subject nations occupied the upper storey of the porticoes in the Forum Augustum, lined up above the *summi viri*.

[71] D. Mendels, 'The Five Empires: A Note on a Propagandistic *Topos*', *AJP* 102 (1981), 330–7; J. M. Alonso-Núñez, 'Die Abfolge der Weltreiche bei Polybios und Dionysios von Halikarnassos', *Historia*, 32 (1983), 411–26; ibid., 'Die Weltreichsukzession bei Strabo', *Zeitschrift für Religions- und Geistesgeschichte*, 36 (1984), 53–4.

[72] See 11. 13. 5 for the list of rulers of Asia—Syria, Armenia, Persia,

book dealing with that region (Book 15). Strabo neatly structures the final sentences into a chronological sequence of
empires, which reaches a climax with the dominant power of
the present time, Parthia. Persia, so similar to Rome, enjoyed
hegemony over Asia for 250 years, and then became subject to
other kings—'first to the Macedonians, but now to the
Parthians' (πρότερον μὲν Μακεδόσι, νῦν δὲ Παρθυαίοις) (15. 3. 24).[73]

The threat of Parthia in the East was a recurrent theme in
Augustan poetry and Parthia's empire was seen by Strabo as an
explicit rival to Rome. It shared marriage customs with Rome
and rivalled Rome in terms of land and tribes ruled. Even
though the Parthians were barbarians, they were 'equals of the
Romans' (ἀντίπαλοι τοῖς 'Ρωμαίοις) (11. 9. 1–2). This same
equivalence between Rome and Parthia is explicitly stated in
the Augustan universal history of Pompeius Trogus.[74] Our
version of Book 41 starts: 'today the Parthians rule the East, the
world being partitioned, as it were, between them and the
Romans'. The parallelism between the two imperial powers in
Strabo is suggested geographically by the fact that they shared
a boundary, that of the river Euphrates (16. 1. 28). The
competition between Parthia and Rome was further emphas-
ized by the Medians' relationship of *amicitia* with Rome at the
same time as their paying court to Parthia, placing the two
empires on a similar footing (11. 13. 2).[75] All the peoples in that
part of the world, says Strabo, were now subject to the power
of the Parthians. Their influence was so great that if they fared

Macedonia, and Parthia. Rome is strikingly absent from the end of this list
representing the present state of affairs. This picture is repeated at 16. 1. 19
where the Parthians are described as having resolved the permanent power-
struggle between Media, Armenia, and Babylonia, by ruling over the Medes
and Babylonians, although not the Armenians.

[73] M. Clavel-Lévêque's study of the temporal structure of Strabo's
description of Gaul in 'Les Gaules et les Gaulois: Pour une analyse du
fonctionnement de la *Géographie* de Strabon', *Dialogues d'Histoire Ancienne*,
1 (1974), 75–93, heightens our awareness of the significance of Parthia here.
Gaul's *Roman* present was paralleled in Asia by a *Parthian* present.

[74] It is certain that this particular view must have belonged to Trogus,
rather than to his epitomator, since by Justin's day, Parthia had been taken
over by the Sassanids.

[75] Perhaps indicative of disapproval on Strabo's part for the Medians'
attitude towards Parthian power is his use of the verb θεραπεύουσι, carrying
connotations of 'fawning'.

well, so did all their subjects (15. 3. 12). Yet in his summing up
of the Roman empire at the end of Book 6, Strabo was able to
state that even Parthia was now subject to Rome, having sent to
Rome the trophies which they set up in honour of their defeat
of the triumvir, Crassus, in 53 BC and handed over all authority
to Rome. Parthia forms the climax of Strabo's account of the
spread of Roman influence and leads him to discuss the
difficulty of governing such an empire, to be handled by only
one man, acting like a father—a clear reference to Augustus'
assumption of the title *pater patriae* in 2 BC (6. 4. 2).

To conclude this section, it may be worth comparing
Strabo's view of rivals with that of Polybius. According to
Nicolet, Polybius' statement that he was interested in how
Rome came to rule the inhabited world (οἰκουμένη) in fifty-
three years cannot mean that Rome dominated that entire area,
but that she was present in each region 'and—at this date—had
no serious rivals'.[76] This is a reasonable deduction for the
world as it must have appeared in the second century BC,
when Rome was constantly gaining power. However, by
Strabo's day such a view was hard to sustain. The Romans
had not proved themselves able to conquer everywhere they
went and it was clear that there were peoples well described as
'rivals' (ἀντίπαλοι). The difficulty for historians whose task was
to represent the Augustan world of Roman power would be
how to deal with Rome's failure to achieve total supremacy.

STRABO OF AMASEIA

I have set out Strabo's Roman world as one where the city of
Rome was placed at the conceptual and practical focal point, in
spite of the threat of rival powers. But Strabo was of eastern
Greek origins, coming from the edge of the area controlled by
Rome, so this Romanocentric view of the world is unexpected.
One caution concerning focalization has been raised earlier in
relation to Polybius, namely the confusion between spatial and
ideological standpoints. The acknowledgement of different
kinds of perspective is taken further by Jacob, who argues, in
connection with the periplus of Hanno, for the creation of a text

[76] Nicolet, *Space, Geography, and Politics*, 30–1.

to a certain cultural viewpoint as an alternative focalization to that brought by the experience of the voyager.[77] Is it the case that Strabo's world was spatially built around Rome, but ideologically or culturally focused elsewhere, perhaps in the Greek East? I have argued in the previous section that Strabo not only portrays Rome as the hub of the empire, but also appears to condone this state of affairs, suggesting that he was not ideologically opposed to Roman dominance in his world. In the case of Rome, spatial and ideological centrality seem to go hand in hand, but I now turn to consider whether there is anything in the text which might suggest a more nuanced construction of Strabo's world, perhaps reflecting his own origins.

The manner in which most autobiographical information appears in the text is elliptical. This reticence does not, however, extend to Strabo's place of birth. He mentions his home city for the first time in connection with the course of the river Iris, which 'flows past the very wall of Amaseia, my native place (ἡ ἡμετέρα πάτρις)' (12. 3. 15). However, the city is not described until later, where it is introduced simply as 'my city' (ἡ ἡμετέρα πόλις), Strabo relying on the reader to remember that this is Amaseia (12. 3. 39). Josephus' citations of Strabo's historical work, in which he called Strabo 'the Cappadocian' (ὁ Καππάδοξ), take us further, but also complicate the issue of identity.[78] Amaseia was part of the Pontic realm in Strabo's day, at the same time as being in Cappadocia.[79] This complex identity is reinforced by a tenth-century testimonium of Constantine VII Porphyrogenitus, who cited Strabo four times and described him as 'a Cappadocian by race, from the city of Amaseia'.[80] So Strabo's birthplace was Amaseia, and this is

---

[77] Jacob, *Géographie et ethnographie*, 76.

[78] Josephus, *AJ* 13. 286; 14. 35; 14. 104; 14. 111; 14. 138; 15. 9.

[79] The shifting regional boundaries make neat identifications impossible, but such fluidity was, in any case, common in the ancient world. J. Moles, 'The Interpretation of the "Second Preface" in Arrian's *Anabasis*', *JHS* 105 (1985), 165, interestingly points out the lack of specificity in a phrase such as ἡ ἡμετέρα πόλις, which can be used of a place other than one's actual native city. Dio of Prusa called Apamea, with which he had family connections and of which he was an adoptive citizen, his πατρίς (41. 2; 41. 3; 41. 6).

[80] See Diller, *Textual Tradition*, 81, on Constantine VII Porphyrogenitus, *De thematibus*, 2. 6 where he describes Strabo as Καππαδόκης ὢν τὸ γένος ἐξ Ἀμασείας τῆς πόλεως.

what he calls 'my city', but he could also be described racially as a Cappadocian.

I shall discuss Strabo's temporal standpoint in chapter V, but for the moment I take it as read that he was growing up in Asia Minor in the aftermath of the Mithridatic wars and Pompey's settlement at a time of relative peace, but considerable upheaval, in the area.[81] As Rostovtzeff points out, the draining of resources in both Greece and Asia Minor during the wars against Sulla, the imposition of a 20,000-talent demand on Asia made by Sulla as part of his settlement with Mithridates at Chersonesus in 84 BC, and the condition that Mithridates' power be confined to the Pontic area, meant that Asia Minor was in severe financial difficulties.[82] Lucullus' pacification of Asia—he is described by Plutarch as having filled Asia with 'good government and peace'—must have helped the economic situation a little, as must the subduing of the pirates by Pompey (*Luc.* 23.1). The pirates had been a major hindrance to trade and communications since Mithridates had raised their power in the first war against Rome.[83] Indeed, as Broughton shows, piracy had been an increasingly difficult problem during the second century as the powers, such as Rhodes, which had tried to check it went into decline.[84] The

[81] The still precarious nature of life in Asia Minor is apparent from the study by S. Mitchell, *Anatolia: Land, Men, and Gods in Asia Minor, i: The Celts in Anatolia and the Impact of Roman Rule* (Oxford, 1993). For an example of the need to please the ruling power see p. 36 on the Galatians, who fought alongside Pompey at the battle of Pharsalus, but then switched to support the victorious Caesar. Deiotarus of the Galatians is found on Caesar's side at the battle of Zela in 47 BC.

[82] The contemporary speeches of Cicero reveal how difficult the situation in Asia was. See esp. *Pro Murena*, 31–4; *De imperio*, 31–2.

[83] M. Rostovtzeff, *Social and Economic History of the Hellenistic World II* (Oxford, 1941), 945 and 953.

[84] T. R. S. Broughton, 'Roman Asia Minor', in T. Frank (ed.), *An Economic Survey of Ancient Rome IV* (Baltimore, 1938), 519–25. That Rome was responsible for this decline and so indirectly for the rise in levels of piracy is brought out by H. Strasburger, 'Poseidonios on Problems of the Roman Empire', *JRS* 55 (1965), 40–53. However, as Strasburger explains, Posidonius also gives other reasons for the growth of piracy—the Ptolemies were helping pirates against the Seleucids, as were the Rhodians. Rome's contribution to the problem was its encouragement of the slave-trade via Delos, which helped the market in captured people and promoted Delos above Rhodes. Strasburger stresses that Posidonius' attitude towards Pompey

attempt in 102 BC of M. Antonius (grandfather of the triumvir) had little lasting effect, and in 100 BC a law was passed calling on allied cities and nations to refuse pirates entrance to harbours, a measure which simply encouraged alliances with Mithridates. A series of Romans tackled the problem of piracy. A. Terentius Varro, legate of L. Licinius Murena, the governor of Asia who led the Roman forces in the second phase of the Mithridatic wars, headed an expedition in 82 BC paid for by all the cities of the province. In 78 BC P. Servilius Vatia took on the task, only to be replaced in 74 BC by M. Antonius Creticus (son of the *praetor* of 102 BC and father of the triumvir).[85] It was, however, only with the advent of Pompey that the pirate situation was brought under control. In Plutarch's account we hear that the Romans could no longer tolerate the fact that the Mediterranean was 'impossible to sail or travel on'.[86]

I discuss in chapter VI the law drawn up by Gabinius in 67 BC giving Pompey 'power' (δύναμις) over all men, and its implications for the conceptual geography of the first century BC. Here I wish simply to consider whether Strabo's eastern origins are reflected in his attitude to the activities in the area of major players such as Pompey and Lucullus. Pompey's achievement and the ease with which he succeeded where so many others had failed are stressed not only by Cicero, who had clear reasons for emphasizing Pompey's success, but also by both Plutarch and Appian.[87] Plutarch underplays the difficulties encountered by Pompey in his account of how the

and Rome was ambiguous, against those who see Posidonius as an apologist for Roman expansionism.

[85] Strabo's comment at 12. 6. 2 that he saw P. Servilius Isauricus is fraught with chronological problems, since Isauricus died in 44 BC. I shall return to the problem in chapter V.

[86] Plut. *Pomp.* 25. 1: ἄπλουν καὶ ἄβατον. We may compare precisely the opposite view on the accessibility of the world held in the previous century by both Polybius (3. 59. 3): σχεδὸν ἁπάντων πλωτῶν καὶ πορευτῶν γεγονότων; and Scymnus (ll. 67–8): τῆς ὅλης τε γῆς σχεδόν | ὅσ᾽ ἐστὶ πλωτὰ καὶ πορευτὰ τῶν τόπων. See *GGM I*.

[87] See Cic. *De imperio*, 34–5 for the speed of Pompey's success against the pirates; 43–5 for the power of his reputation among Rome's enemies, but it is clear why Cicero argued this line in 66 BC when trying to persuade the people of Rome to extend Pompey's powers through the *lex Manilia* to cover the war against Mithridates.

pirate strongholds surrendered within three months and brought an end to the war (*Pomp.* 28. 2). Appian recounts the speed with which Pompey was able to subdue the pirates of Cilicia simply by his reputation (τὸ κλέος αὐτοῦ) (*Mith.* 96). His settlement of the pirates inland is seen as the most humane treatment he could have been expected to give.

This praise for Pompey is missing from Strabo's account. He simply states that Dyme and Soli in Cilicia had received colonists from among the pirates shortly before his own time (8. 7. 5).[88] His account of Pompey's expedition against the Iberian and Albanian peoples of Asia does nothing to enhance Pompey's image. The military encounter with the Albanians is recounted in the middle of Strabo's description of their idyllic lifestyle and their honesty (11. 4. 5). No comment is passed on Pompey's rearrangement of Mithridates' Pontic kingdom and its territories, nor on his completion and renaming of Mithridates' dynastic foundation of Eupatoria as Magnopolis (12. 3. 1; 12. 3. 30). His building-up of Cabeira into a city—Diospolis— is thrown into the background by its further adornment at the hands of Queen Pythodoris and its second change of name to Sebaste (12. 3. 31). Overall, Strabo's failure to pass convincingly either a positive or negative judgement on Pompey's actions make it difficult to assert that his geographical origins have coloured his reaction to this aspect of Roman intervention in the East.

Lucullus receives surprisingly little attention in Strabo's account. Indeed, we hear of him only nine times in the whole work. Three of these instances concern his plundering of art objects to Rome, precisely the kind of reference which makes *Rome* the centre of attention, and deflects interest from the East.[89] The other references to Lucullus concern his military role in the Mithridatic war—besieging Amisus (12. 3. 14), helping Cyzicus against Mithridates (12. 8. 11), driving Tigranes out of Syria and Phoenicia (11. 14. 15), giving the

---

[88] The information is repeated at 14. 3. 3 with the added detail that Soli was renamed Pompeiopolis.

[89] For these acts of plunder see 7. 6. 1 (statue of Apollo from the Apollonian isle in the Pontus); 8. 6. 23 (Lucullus' dedication of Mummius' plunder from Corinth in his Temple of Good Fortune); 12. 3. 11 (globe of Billarus and statue of Autolycus, founder of Sinope, from that city).

fortress Tomisa to the ruler of Cappadocia who helped him
against Mithridates (12. 2. 1)—and finally his handing over
control of the war in the East to Pompey (12. 5. 2). Lucullus'
siege of Amisus comes as part of a list of foreign interventions
in the city and so attracts no great attention; his help to Cyzicus
came late (ὀψέ) and was overshadowed in its effectiveness by the
famine which fell upon the Pontic king's army. A more
decisively negative picture emerges from Strabo's account of
the Senate's reaction to the relative achievements of Lucullus
and Pompey. Pompey managed to persuade the Senate not to
honour the promises of rewards to the people of Pontus given
by Lucullus, since it would be unfair for one man to win the
war and another to distribute the prizes (12. 3. 33). Yet this
attitude is attributed to Pompey and not endorsed by Strabo
himself. As with Pompey, it seems that Strabo had no strong
views on the actions of Lucullus in dealing with his native
country, or at least none that are expressed in this work.[90]

The long-term geographical significance of the Mithridatic
wars is brought out by Appian. He describes the resources of
Mithridates VI Eupator as including all the pirates from Cilicia
to the Pillars of Hercules, from one end of the Mediterranean
to the other (*Mith.* 119). Appian's whole work ends with a
description of the fate of Pontus after the fall of Mithridates.
Although it was initially given to Mithridates of Pergamum to
rule, a praetor was soon sent by Rome to govern both Pontus
and Bithynia as one province. Appian concludes that the result
of the Mithridatic wars was to extend Roman hegemony from
Spain and the Pillars of Hercules to the Pontus, Egypt, and the
Euphrates, making Pompey's *cognomen* 'Magnus' truly appropriate. Only the coast from Cyrene to Egypt was missing from
a complete circuit of the Mediterranean.[91] The threat that
Mithridates himself, in conjunction with Sertorius, might
win an empire that would join the Atlantic Ocean with the
Pontus was voiced in the 60s BC by Cicero (*Pro Murena*, 32).
Appian's description of the fulfilment of this ambition by

---

[90] It is, of course, possible that the history of the Greek East would have
been extensively treated in the *History*, making its relative absence from the
Geography less striking.

[91] Appian, *Mith.* 121: περίοδον τῆς ἐντὸς θαλάσσης ('a circuit of the inner
sea').

Rome reveals how momentous were the geographical implications of the victory over Mithridates.

The importance of this series of conflicts in determining the
Roman world that Strabo knew cannot be overestimated.
However, Strabo's interest in the recent history of the Pontic
region is revealed in passages other than those focused on
Pompey and Lucullus. His involvement with the opposing
side, the Mithridatic dynasty, stemmed not only from his
place of origin, but also from its connections with his mother's
family. Moaphernes, his mother's uncle, came into prominence
as governor of Colchis just before the kingdom was dissolved
and so suffered along with Mithridates—we are given no clear
indication of what Strabo means by this remark (12. 3. 33).
Strabo's maternal grandfather, Dorilaus, was also unlucky in
his involvement in Mithridatic politics. Seeing that Mithridates was doing badly in the war with Lucullus, he caused
fifteen Mithridatic garrisons to revolt to Lucullus so as to be on
the winning side. Unfortunately, when Pompey took over the
command, he counted as enemies all those who had sided with
Lucullus, so Strabo's grandfather never received the reward he
expected (12. 3. 33).

All of these connections, according to Pais, make a court post
for Strabo not unlikely, setting him in a position like that of
Nicolaus of Damascus. Strabo's 'great respect for Augustus
and for Rome' would thus be a reflection of the obsequious
attitude of subject monarchies, and is not necessarily indicative
of Strabo's own view of Roman rule, or of the existence of a
Roman patron. Pais put forward the suggestion that Strabo's
work was composed expressly for Queen Pythodoris and her
family. Pythodoris' husband, Polemon, ruled over the area in
which Strabo lived until it became a provincial region in 7 BC
after Polemon's death, leaving Pythodoris in charge of the rest
of Pontus. 'In the entire *Geography* no other ruler is mentioned
so frequently as Pythodoris. With the exception of Augustus,
Tiberius, and the governors of Egypt, Strabo compliments and
eulogizes her alone.'[92]

This view clearly has its problems. As Anderson points out,

---

[92] E. Pais, *Ancient Italy*, (trans. C. D. Curtis) (Chicago, 1908), ch. 26
'Strabo's Historical Geography', esp. pp. 421–6.

we have no evidence for such an official position for Strabo.[93]
In spite of Pais' assertion that Pythodoris is prominent in
Strabo's account, the text does not uphold this. Certainly her
wisdom and statesmanlike attitude are praised. She is described
as a 'wise woman and qualified to preside over affairs of state
(γυνὴ σώφρων καὶ δυνατὴ προίστασθαι πραγμάτων)' (12. 3. 29). Yet
Strabo mentions her by name only five times in the whole
work. This could not by any account be considered a prominent position, and does not begin to outweigh the references to
Augustus and Tiberius, whom Pais sweeps aside as exceptions.
Pais's stress on the Pontic perspective of Strabo overplays
extremely scant evidence.

But the Mithridatic dynasty was important as a rival of
Rome, and it is interesting to see how its treatment by
Strabo compares with that of the rival cities and powers
discussed above (pp. 224–8). Strabo presents the two empires
of Pontus and Rome as parallel in some respects. Both are part
of the list of powers whose conquests furthered geographical
knowledge (1. 2. 1). Both were involved in the suppression of
barbarism. Neoptolemus, Mithridates VI Eupator's general, is
said to have put down the barbarians, and Old Chersonesus
adopted Mithridates as its protector against barbarian attack
before the coming of the Romans (7. 3. 18; 7. 4. 3). Rome had
defeated Mithridates by Strabo's time, but it may be of
significance that the site of Rome's victory over him, Chaeronea, is described by Strabo as also the site of Macedonia's
defeat of Greece, possibly hinting that Rome too might in the
future suffer the same reversal of fortune as that which had
befallen Macedonia (9. 2. 37).

One of the cities which underwent cultural plundering at the
hands of Rome was Sinope, a special case for Strabo since it
was the metropolis of the Mithridatic dynasty with which the
family of Strabo himself had connections, and is thus of great
interest if we are considering how this eastern Greek viewed
Roman rule. Strabo describes Sinope as blessed by both nature
and man's intervention, whereas the site of Rome, we may

---

[93] J. G. C. Anderson, 'Some Questions Bearing on the Date and Place of
Composition of Strabo's *Geography*', in W. H. Buckler and W. M. Calder
(eds.), *Anatolian Studies presented to Sir William Mitchell Ramsay* (Manchester, 1923), 1–13.

recall, was blessed only by man's work, and not advantaged by
the natural order.[94] This would be enough to turn it into a
threat to Rome's image of superiority. But Strabo's picture of
the contest between Rome and Sinope as centres for empire is
predictably ambiguous.

Lucullus, who plundered Sinope, displayed remarkable
restraint, it seems at first, taking only two items (12. 3. 11).[95]
Their removal, however, cut at the heart of Sinope's identity.
By taking the statue of Autolycus, Lucullus was removing the
legendary founder of the city, revered as a god. The sphere
(σφαῖρα) of Billarus receives no elaboration in Strabo's work.
There is, however, evidence to suggest that this refers to a
spherical representation of the earth.[96] If this was the case, then
the significance of its removal was increased. If the sphere of
Billarus was anything like a Pontic forerunner to Agrippa's
map in Rome, representing the extent of the empire at present
and aspirations for its future, then it is clear why Lucullus
might want to remove this symbol of Mithridatic imperial-

---

[94] But we shall see in chapter VI that this assertion is somewhat compromised by the geographical advantage enjoyed by Rome and Italy at the
temperate centre of the earth.

[95] E. Rawson, *Intellectual Life in the Late Roman Republic* (London, 1985),
40, suggests that the plundering by Lucullus was in fact greater than Strabo's
account shows and that the Library of Lucullus in Rome was formed from the
booty from Mithridates' palace. Plutarch's *Lucullus* predictably supports
Strabo's view that Lucullus was restrained in the way he took booty from
Asia Minor. At 14. 2 he describes the complaints from Lucullus' soldiers that
the peaceable bringing-over of the cities of Bithynia and Galatia was yielding
them no rewards. However, this restraint is somewhat inconsistent with the
end of Plutarch's account, in which Lucullus is presented as revelling in the
life of luxury and using wealth 'as though it were a barbarian prisoner of war
(αἰχμαλώτῳ καὶ βαρβάρῳ)' (41).

[96] The word σφαῖρα is used by Strabo of the world as a part of the cosmos,
of *this* globe, and also of the globe constructed by Crates and recommended by
Strabo at 2. 5. 10 as a model of how to relate a two dimensional picture of the
known world to its real spherical shape. LSJ cite this passage as an example of
σφαῖρα referring to a geographical globe. Hultsch's article in *R-E* iii has little
to say about what the globe of Billarus actually was. He envisages it as a globe,
rotating on its axis and symbolizing on the earth the daily rotation of the vault
of the sky and maybe also the paths of the planets. Hultsch, however, cites no
source other than Strabo and gives no evidence for his interpretation of the
globe, thus offering no compelling reason to take it as an astrological device
rather than as a representation of terrestrial affairs.

ism.[97] This picture is speculative, but if it bears any relation to reality at all, it would provide a neat removal by Rome of items which symbolized the whole history of the rival Pontic empire—past, present, and future.

Strabo's treatment of another region relatively close to home, the Cimmerian Bosporus, again gives little hint of a particularly Pontic viewpoint.[98] One of its themes, as Bosi discusses, is that of barbarism and civilization, around which Strabo could have chosen to construct his world-view. Pre-Mithridatic Tauris had been dominated by barbarians, whose tribute demands eventually forced the previous dynasty of Parisades to relinquish power to Mithridates I. The barbarians are categorized by Strabo into farmers and nomads who exacted tribute from the settled farmers (7. 4. 6). Bosi argues that Posidonius' ethnographical material strongly influenced this part of Strabo's text, and the categorization of peoples by their method of subsistence is reminiscent of the Hellenistic ethnographical tradition.[99] The idea of the fight against barbarism is one which Strabo attributes to Mithridates. Forts built on his orders allowed his forces to fend off the Scythians more easily (7. 4. 7). The role of defender of Greek city-culture against the threat of barbarism is one that we know the Mithridatic dynasty was still appropriating in the time of Mithridates VI Eupator. McGing views the latter as a king with a strong Hellenic image which involved protecting Greek civilization

[97] For Mithridatic imperial ambitions see B. C. McGing, *The Foreign Policy of Mithridates VI Eupator King of Pontus* (Leiden, 1986), 82, where he cites Florus 1. 40 saying that Mithridates intended to rule the whole of Asia and Europe; and p. 102 on Mithridates' adoption of the Alexander image of world conqueror. Mithridates VI dominated the Pontic coast with his rule, lacking only the coast of Bithynia and the part of the north-east coast above Colchis.

[98] Strabo's accounts of this region (7. 4. 3–8; 11. 2. 3–12) are discussed by F. Bosi, 'La storia del Bosforo Cimmerio nell'opera di Strabone', in *Strabone II*, 171–88.

[99] See, for example, Agatharchides' account of the peoples living around the Arabian Gulf in *On the Erythraean Sea*. When Strabo himself described this region, he virtually repeated Agatharchides' account with no additions, adopting along with other literary conventions the distinction of peoples by food-source. Strabo's passage on the name of the Red Sea (16. 4. 20) accurately repeats Agatharchides' explanations given at the beginning of his work.

from the assault by the new barbarians from the west—the Romans.[100] Sallust's *Letter of Mithridates*, in which the Romans are called 'robbers of peoples' (*latrones gentium*), illustrates the attachment of the image of barbarism to Rome at this time.[101]

This is a striking role reversal for Rome, the imposer of civilization upon the barbarian races of its empire, and given that such ideas were current, we might have expected Strabo to pick up on them in a gesture of support for his native dynasty's fight against the imminent Roman rule. As Bosi shows, however, no such simple image is presented by Strabo. For just as he does not make clear his views on Mithridatic attempts to take on the role of civilizing force against the barbarian peoples of the Pontic region, nor does he attribute the role of brigand to Rome, or present Rome as the outright enemy of native rule in this area. Indeed, he brings out the *intervention* of Rome in the accession of Polemon to the Pontic and Bosporan throne; he was promoted by Antonius and offered the throne at Panticapaeum by Augustus and Agrippa after the death of Asander and the advent of a usurper, Scribonius (12. 8. 16).[102]

So, just as Strabo is remarkably neutral in his treatment of Pompey and Lucullus and their conflicts with his native dynasty in the Mithridatic wars, so too is this ambiguity in allegiance reflected in his comments on piracy and brigandage. Strabo's failure to make clear his stance on whether Mithridates or the Romans were to be seen as the opponents of piracy is mirrored throughout the work. The tribes between the Tagus and the Artabrians were stopped from their life of brigandage by the Romans, and were made not only peaceful but even 'civilized' (πολιτικός) by Tiberius (3. 3. 5; 3. 3. 8); Augustus tackled the same problem among the Iapodes (4. 6. 10). I have already mentioned the concerted attack by a series of Romans against the pirates and brigands of Asia

---

[100] McGing, *Foreign Policy of Mithridates*, 89 and 99. McGing discusses the image of Mithridates as a second Alexander, wishing for world conquest and drawing support from Greece by his professing to be anti-barbarian.

[101] Sallust, *Letter of Mithridates*, 22. Tacitus, *Agricola*, 30 provides a parallel for the questioning of the Roman image, proclaiming the Romans *raptores orbis* ('plunderers of the world').

[102] See also Dio 54. 24. 4 for the same story.

Minor. But Sextus Pompey helped the pirates during the Sicilian revolt (5. 4. 4); Rome's demand for slaves via Delos led to an increase of piracy in the Aegean (14. 5. 2); and the degeneracy of the Scythians is put down to Rome's corrupting influence, including the introduction of a seafaring life (7. 3. 7). So Strabo rejects the possibility of presenting Rome as unambiguously opposed to piracy, but equally does not propound the image of Mithridates as the defender of Pontic civilization against the piratical Romans.

Another theme in Strabo's description of the Cimmerian Bosporus, which reflects one of the principles of Mithridates VI Eupator's reign and may have a bearing on Strabo's perspective, is that of East and West united. Strabo as a native of the Pontic region was interested in its commercial contacts, both as a productive centre and as a trade-route, linking not only geographically disparate parts, but also bridging cultural gulfs. In Bosi's words, Strabo sees the Bosporus 'come centro di produzione granaria e come luogo di incontro fra i Greci e il mondo nomade'.[103] This interest in points of contact between different cultural worlds reflects the Mithridatic image of integration between East and West.[104]

The unity of Strabo's vision makes it all the harder to accept Lasserre's argument that Strabo reflected his eastern perspective in differentiating between Roman rule in the East and the West. Lasserre distinguishes between the progress of civilization through Roman conquest in the West, and Strabo's treatment of the Roman encroachment on the last refuges of independent Hellenism. Colonization in Asia Minor meant repression, not pacification. He takes it that Rome was to be seen as an occupying force, Strabo an outsider—'le Grec d'Asie qu'il est pouvait admettre sa condition de sujet de l'empereur . . . sans étouffer en lui toute nostalgie de liberté'.[105] It is

---

[103] Bosi, 'La storia del Bosforo Cimmerio', 186: 'as a centre of corn-production and as a meeting place between the Greeks and the nomadic world'. See Strabo 7. 4. 6 for the richness of the produce of the eastern Crimea.

[104] Seen, according to McGing, *Foreign Policy of Mithridates*, in the adoption of the image of Perseus (as a Greek hero with Persian associations) on coins of Mithridates IV and Mithridates VI (pp. 35 and 94 respectively).

[105] F. Lasserre, 'Strabon devant l'Empire romain', *ANRW* II 30.1, 892–3 for East v. West; 896 for Strabo on the outside: 'The Asian Greek, which he

noticeable, although not surprising given what we now know about the origins of Strabo and his family, that explicit autobiographical references tend to be concentrated in the sections of the work dealing with Asia Minor, rather than spread throughout the work. Strabo's eastern origins may be betrayed by occasional reflections of the ideologies of the Pontic dynasty, but it is hard to say that he really creates a Mithridatic world-view.[106] The ambiguity of his picture of the Pontic region and its recent history seems explicable in terms of his circumstances, not simply as an inhabitant of the Mithridatic kingdom, but as someone caught between allegiance to his native land and a strongly perceptible sympathy for the spread of Roman culture, involvement with the Roman élite, and admiration for Roman rule.

The problem of the author's geographical focus and his spatial viewpoint is, in any case, complicated by the question of his various travels. The wanderings of the Odyssean Strabo are no less problematic than those of Polybius in a similar guise. The extent of Strabo's travels in Greece have been the subject of much debate. While Pais claims that Strabo knew little of Greece and had rarely visited it, Waddy argues that he had in fact visited more places than he explicitly claims.[107] One

is, could admit his position as subject of the emperor . . . without extinguishing in himself all nostalgia for liberty'. However, for a nuanced view of Romanization in the Greek East as a process of acculturation rather than imposition, see G. Woolf, 'Becoming Roman, Staying Greek: Culture, Identity and the Civilizing Process in the Roman East', *PCPS* 40 (1994), 116–43.

[106] But I would not go as far as to assert that his place of origin is irrelevant to our understanding of him as author of the *Geography*, following by analogy the assertion of M. Foucault, 'What is an Author?', in P. Rabinow (ed.), *The Foucault Reader* (Harmondsworth, 1984), 106, that 'If I discover that Shakespeare was not born in the house that we visit today, this is a modification which, obviously, will not alter the functioning of the author's name. But if we proved that Shakespeare did not write those sonnets which pass for his, that would constitute a significant change.' It matters more than this, I think, that Strabo came from Amaseia, not least because it is one of very few pieces of autobiographical information that he chooses to give us.

[107] L. Waddy, 'Did Strabo Visit Athens?', *AJA* 67 (1963), 296–300, argues against the view that Strabo saw nowhere in Greece at first hand except for Corinth. He points out the careful way in which Strabo treats sources including his own autopsy, rarely trusting casual or isolated pieces of

place that Strabo does claim to have visited is Corinth, where he saw the Roman restoration work (8. 6. 21). Wallace contends that Strabo's own experience of the place is evident in his account of the view from Acrocorinth, a novel way of arranging his description of the area, which breaks from his dependence on the periplus structure or on Homer's Catalogue, whereas elsewhere he 'follows the haphazard Homeric Catalogue line for line'.[108]

Some clear references to Strabo's travels occur throughout the work. He claims to have accompanied Aelius Gallus up the Nile and had detailed information about his expedition to Arabia Felix (2. 5. 12). He saw temple-servants in Cappadocia and the stunning narrowing of the river Pyramus as it reaches the Taurus (12. 2. 3; 12. 2. 4); he gives details of the journey from Asia to Rome, by sea to Brundisium and then by road to Rome, a route which Strabo himself must have taken several times (6. 3. 7).[109] Pais claims that Strabo 'declares that he visited the entire inhabited world, from the shores of the Euxine to the borders of Ethiopia, and from Armenia as far as Populonia in Etruria', but this is simply incorrect.[110] Strabo does claim to have travelled to these places, but *not* that they constitute the whole inhabited world. In fact, Strabo goes so far as to say that these are the only parts of the world he has

information. A fleeting visit to a place is not considered sufficiently important to be mentioned. Strabo probably passed through Athens on one of his journeys from Asia Minor to Rome, but did not consider himself sufficiently well acquainted with the place to claim autopsy as he does for Corinth. The description that Strabo gives of Athens fits well with the devastation that it suffered at Sulla's hands in 87/6 BC; the city described also by Servius Sulpicius Rufus to Cicero in 45 BC as *nunc prostrata et diruta* (*Ad fam.* 4. 5. 4). This view is supported by Strabo's comment concerning Eratosthenes (1. 2. 2) that to write about the Mediterranean without seeing Athens would lay one open to criticism.

[108] P. W. Wallace, 'Strabo on Acrocorinth', *Hesperia*, 38 (1969), 498.

[109] F. Coarelli, 'Strabone: Roma e il Lazio', in *Italia Antica*, 75–91, has discussed Strabo's knowledge of Latium. He concludes that Strabo had a good knowledge of the Via Appia, of Ostia, Antium, Sperlonga, Tivoli, Praeneste, Tusculum, Lanuvium, Aricia, and several other places close to Rome (pp. 79–80); but that his knowledge of the Via Latina was patchy. The area between the Viae Appia and Latina is particularly badly covered, reinforcing the non-continuous nature of space in the work.

[110] Pais, *Ancient Italy*, 417–18.

visited—for the rest he has had to rely on what other travellers have said (2. 5. 11).

The successive physical locations of Strabo do not, however, represent the only alternative to a purely Roman focus for the work. An examination of the phrases used to denote events which related to Strabo himself suggests a new possibility for the spatial focus of the *Geography*. Through self-referential phrases we gain a subtle picture of where we might locate Strabo as an author, and it is interesting to find that this is quite different from either of the most obvious foci—Rome and the Pontic region. Many of the oblique self-references in the *Geography* are orientated to locating the author in time more than in space, but one particular phrase meaning 'in my time'—καθ' ἡμᾶς—is used in a way which carries more specifically spatial implications, and it is to this phrase that I now turn.[111]

By far the largest category of references to which καθ' ἡμᾶς is applied is the life and works of the intellectuals of the Greek East. It is striking that over two-thirds of its occurrences are found in Books 12–15, dealing with Asia Minor, particularly the Hellenized coast. This geographical bias in the distribution cannot be adequately explained in terms of Strabo's background in Amaseia, which is rather far removed from the parts covered by the phrase. Of the relevant occurrences, two-thirds are connected with the intellectual activity of the area, rather than with political events. As Strabo moves from city to city, he lists their famous alumni after describing the places themselves. Those writers and philosophers who are Strabo's peers are described as καθ' ἡμᾶς. Strabo certainly does not ignore political aspects of the present day in this region; far from it, as we shall see. It is thus all the more significant that he distinguishes between political events, which are described impersonally as νῦν ('now'), and the intellectual life of the Greek East, which is given a temporal indicator linking it directly with the author and his own self-representation.[112]

---

[111] I have set out the arguments in Clarke, 'In Search of the Author', 107–8.

[112] καθ' ἡμᾶς is used of contemporary intellectuals from Mytilene 13. 2. 3; Pergamum 13. 4. 3; Antioch on the Maeander 13. 4. 15; Miletus 14. 1. 7; Nysa 14. 1. 42; Rhodes 14. 2. 13; Cnidus 14. 2. 15; Halicarnassus 14. 2. 16; Cos 14. 2. 19; Mylasa 14. 2. 24; Seleuceia on the Calycadnus 14. 5. 4; Tarsus 14. 5. 14.

The specialized use of καθ' ἡμᾶς in relation to particular notes in Strabo's account of the Asia Minor coast provides an important insight into the geographical outlook which the author created as part of his own persona. That is, while he centred the world which he described on the city of Rome, to which all regions were linked through the constant flow in that direction of goods, people, resources, and ideas, for himself, in his capacity as an author, there was an additional, maybe even alternative, location in the intellectual circles of Asia Minor. The issue of whether this is a 'spatial' or an 'ideological' location seems to me to miss the point. By aligning himself intellectually with the world of the Greek East, Strabo creates a mental image of the world in which our eyes are drawn not only to Rome, but also to Asia Minor, where the author places himself and his educational milieu. The focus is spatial in so far as it has a notional location on the map, but also ideological in so far as the author's background inevitably informs his outlook. Furthermore, the double focus has certain implications for the way we view Strabo's presence within or absence from the text, since, if the author and text have separate geographical foci, the author may gain an identity which is independent of the text. How this affects the 'objectivity' of the account is a topic that has been discussed at length by modern geographers.[113]

Strabo never names himself, and he does not follow in the tradition of most Greek historians in building up a coherent prefatory autobiography, although it is possible that he had already done this in his own *History*. In formal terms, he is relatively absent from his text, and the distancing effect of this is backed up by his normal practice of using the first-person *plural* to refer to himself. This may have a similar effect to the passive voice adopted by modern scientists in order to make the presentation of their results seem more objective, less prone to human interference, interpretation, and error.

It is neither possible nor even desirable to insert Strabo precisely into the modern debate. He is largely absent from his account of the world, but not like modern geographers in a post-colonial reaction; and although it is interesting for us to

---

[113] See above, pp. 33–6, with Clarke, 'In Search of the Author', 92–8.

try to 'situate' his knowledge of the world, my reasons for doing this are not those initially formulated by the feminist geographers. I am not attempting to show the limitations of his viewpoint in the hope that someone will write the 'anti-Strabonian' world to redress the ideological balance. That is clearly a fruitless way to approach an ancient text. If anything, Strabo himself should have been the prime candidate to write a version of the Roman world from a marginal viewpoint. As I hope to have shown, he failed to rise to the occasion. But Strabo's relative lack of personal involvement in the main description does not give grounds for belittling his knowledge as coming from a limited, unacknowledged viewpoint. Rather, his creation of a second spatial focus for himself, distinct from the focus that he gives to the world he describes, opens up new possibilities of interpretation and gives a far more accurate picture of the background against which the project was undertaken. This focus is not autobiographically determined in the sense of being connected with Strabo's native Pontic region, but is linked specifically to the intellectual milieu in which Strabo was educated and in which he formed his view of the world, in relation both to his own experience and to the tradition of writing about the world that had been developing, in his opinion, since the time of Homer.

V

Strabo and Time

THE PROBLEM OF TIME: A CHANGING WORLD

As I discussed in chapter I, one of the major distinctions proposed between geography and history lies in their temporal focus. Although the logic behind this does not stand up to scrutiny, the notion still remains strong in our minds and, for once, the problem is not one of anachronism. Strabo himself repeatedly asserted that geography should deal with the present day. However, as I shall argue, the majority of Strabo's *Geography* was, in fact, concerned with the past rather than the present. In the last chapter I considered 'Strabo and space', his use of different spatial systems, and the placing of himself and his work in a 'geographical' tradition which had as its primary concern the description of space and place. I shall now turn to the question of 'Strabo and time', which can be justified on several grounds. Firstly, Strabo himself raised problems over the temporal aspect of geography; secondly, space and time together are matrices against which the world is commonly described; thirdly, I wish to show that geography, and particularly Strabo's *Geography*, does have a significant time-element extending beyond the present, thus confounding one traditional view of the distinction between geography and history.

Strabo's view of the temporal focus of his account defies simple analysis. On Thessaly he says, 'I must omit all that is really ancient and mythical, and tell what seems appropriate' (9. 4. 18); on the Getae, 'let ancient matters be omitted; the state of affairs in my time is as follows' (7. 3. 11); later, 'Posidonius says that the ancient theory of atoms originated here (at Sidon) with Mochus, before Trojan times, but let us leave out ancient matters . . . In my time . . .' (16. 2. 24). From these statements Strabo seems clearly to have set out the temporal focus for a geographical work as being the present Roman world.[1] But, quite apart from the fact that this is not borne out by the text, Strabo himself qualifies this objective, and at times openly contradicts it.

Strabo sets out his general principle as being that 'it is necessary for the man who deals with the description of the earth (τὴν τῆς γῆς περίοδον) to tell of things as they are now . . . and also some of the things that have happened in the past, especially when they are noteworthy' (6. 1. 2).[2] About the Pontic region, he says 'I must speak in detail about how things are now, but also touch on a few things concerning earlier events' (12. 3. 1). But these disclaimers do not account for the vast proportion of material about the past, concerning not only the Pontic region, but almost every place mentioned in the work.[3] It is my purpose in this chapter to investigate the role of time, both past and present, in the *Geography*. I shall consider the strategies adopted by Strabo for indicating time; in particular, to what extent he was concerned with precisely when something happened, or was rather interested simply in the fact that a particular state of affairs preceded or followed another.

As we have seen, Strabo both stresses his concentration on the present and the inappropriateness of discussion of the past in a geographical work, and at the same time says that he will include historical material: an ungenerous reading might conclude that he was simply incompetent. Strabo's profession to exclude the past is problematic, but not wholly surprising. The idea that geography deals with the present and history with the past has similarly been a common theme in the debate among

[1] D. Defoe, *A Tour through the Whole Island of Great Britain* (London, 1724–6; refs. are to the Penguin reprint of 1986), again provides a fascinating parallel for Strabo's text. Defoe states in the preface (p. 45) that 'the situation of things is given not as they have been, but as they are; . . . all respects the present time, not the time past'. Like Strabo, Defoe abandoned this aim almost immediately.

[2] For an excellent treatment of the past in the work of another ancient geographer, Pausanias, see K. W. Arafat, *Pausanias' Greece: Ancient Artists and Roman Rulers* (Cambridge, 1996).

[3] There are some notable exceptions to this. The descriptions of India, the Arabian Gulf, and much of Aethiopia seem to have few temporally determined features of any kind, either past or present.

modern geographers about the focus of their subject.[4] In any case, Strabo had already written a history, at least partly dealing with the past, and which he expected the readers of his *Geography* to know. But it is hard to imagine what a description of the world which had no temporal aspect would be like. So what are we to make of the professed concentration on the present, when it is clear from the text that this aim was abandoned by Strabo just as by those modern geographers who have considered the issue?

I discussed in relation to Polybius and Posidonius the parallels between geographical and historical processes, which make time an essential matrix of geography as well as of history. Even physical geography, which might seem more permanent than human geography, cannot be contemplated without room for discussion of change.[5] Strabo's interest in physical change was, in fact, surprisingly limited, although he took its occurrence for granted and expected the reader to do the same. That some parts of the earth were now inhabited, while they had previously been covered by sea, or vice versa; that fountains had dried up, while others had sprung forth—all this was a natural part of life (17. 1. 36). Strabo preserved the arguments of Strato of Lampsacus, Polybius, Eratosthenes, and Posidonius concerning changes in the physical world.[6] However, if physical geography required discussion of the past, then all the more so did human geography, with its need to explain density of population in particular places due to the creation of cities, and the ethnic make-up of regions through mass-migrations. This was the past in which Strabo was most interested, bringing his *Geography* close to what we might term 'human geography' and to the kind of all-encompassing account of the human world

[4] I recall H. C. Darby, 'On the Relations of Geography and History', *TIBG* 19 (1953), 6: 'The geography of the present day is but a thin layer that even at this moment is becoming history.' *Contra* Darby, J. B. Mitchell, *Historical Geography* (London, 1954), 12: 'the historian does not become a geographer when he studies the present'. See above, p. 15 with nn. 29 and 30, for these arguments.

[5] See above, p. 16, for the importance of this element of change in the world in Vidal de la Blache's approach to geography and history in the late 19th cent.

[6] The views of these intellectuals on, for example, changing sea-levels, the overflowing of seas, and the discovery of sea-fossils inland are to be found throughout Books 1 and 2.

exemplified by Herodotus' *Histories*, which I discussed in chapter I.

Strabo himself tried to explain why he needed to include such a sizeable amount of ancient material in the *Geography*. The whole question of geographical extinction was given prominence, predictably in connection with a people, the Aethices, who 'are said to be extinct now'. Strabo defines extinction (ἔκλειψις) as having occurred either when the people have vanished and their country has been deserted, or when the ethnic name (τὸ ὄνομα τὸ ἐθνίκον) has been lost and the political organization changed (9. 5. 12). It is interesting that Strabo seized on this problem and attempted a definition. There are certainly many examples of real ἔκλειψις in the work. Peoples came and went, making the introduction of material about the past all the more difficult.[7] It is clear that Strabo needed to formulate some way of dealing with the fact that the world described by his predecessors had now gone.

There could be no predecessor for whom this was more true than the earliest 'geographer', Homer.[8] Homeric geography was particularly problematic for Strabo, because Homer talked 'not about things as they are now, but of ancient matters, which time has mostly obscured' (8. 1. 1). The world that Homer knew was not only different from Strabo's Augustan world, but also hard to retrieve because it was so distant in time.[9] Strabo gave his own explanation for why he did not simply leave aside the Homeric problem—'I am comparing things as they are now with those told of by Homer, for it is necessary to make this

---

[7] A variation on this idea is the inappropriate survival of city-names derived from local circumstances. Plataea near Lake Copais took its name from its lakeside position; the settlement then moved, but kept the name (9. 2. 17).

[8] At 12. 3. 26 Strabo counters criticisms of Homer, arguing from the fact that the world had changed since he composed. 'It is not surprising that Homer does not mention Heracleia, Amastris, and Sinope, since they had not yet been synoecized.'

[9] The point is made at 8. 5. 3 that many places in Homer's Catalogue no longer existed, or had changed names. The theme of recovery of the past was prominent in Diodorus' universal history. He stressed that inaccuracies should be forgiven since historians are only human (ὡς ἂν ἀνθρώπους ὄντας) and the truth of antiquity hard to discover (τῆς ἐν τοῖς παροιχομένοις χρόνοις ἀληθείας οὔσης δυσευρέτου) (13. 90. 7). See 3. 72. 2: the ancestry of Silenus, first king of Nysa, remained unknown because of its antiquity (διὰ τὴν ἀρχαιότητα).

comparison because of the fame of the poet and because we have all been brought up together on him.' Strabo goes on to say that no subject has been satisfactorily treated until there is nothing in it which conflicts with the Homeric picture (8. 3. 3). The process Strabo describes was, in practice, sometimes reversed. Strabo's picture of Greece and the Troad seems to use Homer as a base, and to add details from later ages as relevant. However, it does give us some idea of the importance of Homeric geography in the world-view of Strabo and of his readership. If their knowledge of the world came from the Homeric epics, then that had to be incorporated into Strabo's account. This is confirmed a few chapters later.

Perhaps I would not examine ancient matters (τὰ παλαιά) at such length, but would merely tell how things are now, if there were not connected with these matters a tradition handed on (παραδεδομένη φήμη) to us from childhood; and since different people say different things, I must make a judgment . . . It is the most famous, the oldest, and the most experienced men who are believed; and since Homer has surpassed all others in these respects, I must inquire into his account and compare it with the present. (8. 3. 23)[10]

So, discussion of the vanished Homeric world could be justified because this was the picture which had most informed the mental geography of Strabo and the reader, although this hardly accounts for the vast and varied material about the past in the work.[11] The Amazons provide a different instance of how accounts of the past had impinged significantly upon the present readership, to the extent that it was not only interesting, but necessary, to draw attention to a past world. Strabo explains that with most peoples, myth is kept apart from history, which desires the truth, whether ancient or recent, but with the Amazons, the same stories were told both in

[10] My view of Strabo's relationship to Homer has been greatly enlightened by conversations with Yuval Shahar. I look forward to the publication of his work.

[11] As F. Prontera, 'L'Italia meridionale di Strabone. Appunti tra geografia e storia', in *Italia Antica*, 103, notes, the *Geography* is an odd mixture of chorography and history of origins, which is dictated by the importance of Homeric epics. The Homeric world-view impressed on the geography of places an inevitable historical trend, which meant that Greek geography was forced to be interested in the history of geography.

antiquity and now, and the present stories told about them reinforce belief in the ancient accounts (11. 5. 3). Whether we are meant to contrast myth and history, or ancient and modern history, is somewhat unclear, although it appears that Strabo is, to some extent, associating ancient history with myth. His point is that the Amazons were different from most peoples because there had been no real development in accounts about them. But Strabo had identified a problem in the fact that time altered both the world and the accounts given of it. The Amazons were exceptional in that tales told about them in the past were just as relevant as more recent accounts, but they raise a crucial, and more general, point which I discuss further below, namely that the picture of the world which Strabo presents is one made up of perceptions and traditions.

In most places, time radically changed the landscape, the population, the urban structures, lifestyle, language, and political systems.[12] Occasionally, and not surprisingly, given the scope of his project, Strabo seems to have included information about the past, not because he wanted to show development through time, but simply because he was drawing on old sources. This was one of the problems associated with a tradition. Individual studies often point to the fact that Strabo's material is out of date, such as the note on military levies by the Senate in the description of Cisalpine Gaul.[13] This process appears in the text as a feature of the present, that is, Augustan, age, but by that time it would have been an imperial, rather than a senatorial, function, and Strabo's note must refer back to the period before Marius' reforms.[14]

[12] One of the few fields for which this was not true to the same extent was cult. G. Camassa, 'Problemi storico-religiosi dei libri di Strabone relativi all'Italia', in *Italia Antica*, 191–206, discusses how Strabo was concerned with the continuation of myth and cult into the present.

[13] G. E. F. Chilver, 'Strabo and Cisalpine Gaul: an Anachronism', *JRS* 28 (1938), 126–8, discussing Str. 5. 1. 11. 'The whole chapter on Cisalpine Gaul, though valuable to us, was out-of-date when written' (p. 128).

[14] See P. Funke, 'Strabone, la geografia storica e la struttura etnica della Grecia Nord-Occidentale', in F. Prontera (ed.), *Geografia storica della Grecia antica* (Rome, 1991), 174–93, discussing a similar problem concerning Strabo's account of north-west Greece. For this part of Greece the first stages of Roman domination would be virtually unknown were it not for Strabo's text. So, how can we tell whether Strabo is up to date in his account, or not?

A clearer example of anachronism is given by the description of Crete. Here, however, the anachronism works in the other direction. The plausibility of Strabo's administrative divisions for the island, decided by King Minos, has come under the scrutiny of modern scholars.[15] Strabo's tripartite division does not seem sensible geographically and is deemed by Stergio-poulos as totally arbitrary and unjustified. The Homeric evidence is of little help as it distinguishes five races on the island. Archaeology has revealed many palace-like residences on the island, with no three obviously prominent. Stergiopoulos' theory is that Strabo starts from the Roman advent in 67 BC, which brought unity of administration with a governor and capital at Gortyn, and retrojects this single figurehead on to the legendary administrator, Minos. The attempt at stability made by Cydonia, Cnossus, and Gortyn following the destruction of Lyttus, and the subsequent success of these three cities, perhaps account for the supposition that Crete was once divided into three administrative districts. Thus in this case the historical confusion leads to a contemporary situation being reflected in the account of a previous age.[16]

So, on the grounds both that the world had undergone significant changes and that sources from the past informed the mental geography of himself and his readership, Strabo provided some justification for including details about a world, or worlds, that no longer existed. But is this enough to explain his abandonment of the aim to focus on the present, the proper field of geography, as he saw it? Having looked at some of Strabo's professed objectives and explanations of the historical content of his *Geography*, it seems that the best way to assess the apparent disparity between theory and practice is to look at how the past is introduced, and what roles it plays in the description.

---

[15] C. D. Stergiopoulos, 'Strabon et la division administrative de la Crète', *Revue Archéologique*, 31–2, 6th ser. (1949), 985–92, on Strabo 10. 4. 8.

[16] The way in which Strabo's picture of the world refers to so many periods of history leads R. Nicolai, 'Scelte critico-testuali e problemi storici nei libri V e VI della *Geografia* di Strabone', in *Italia Antica*, 267–86, to see textual emendation on the grounds of anachronism as a last resort.

TEMPORAL SYSTEMS: ABSOLUTE AND RELATIVE

Firstly, however, I consider the various temporal systems
found in the *Geography*, as well as some of those that were
rejected. Just as different ways of indicating and conceptualizing space were either adopted, rejected, or transformed, so
some method for calibrating time in the *Geography* had to be
devised. In particular I shall consider how coherent that
method was, and how similar it was to the dating systems
used by universal historians, such as Diodorus and Polybius,
which I discussed on pp. 10–13. Was Strabo really concerned
to explain precisely when anything happened, or was the
interest in time subordinate to spatial considerations, support-
ing the characterization of history and geography as concerned
with time and space respectively?

In answer to the question posed above, the similarity
between the dating-systems used by Polybius or Diodorus
and those found in Strabo's *Geography* is negligible. Strabo
does not date by Olympiads, archons, or consuls.[17] He thus
rejects in this work the systems adopted by the universal
historians (including perhaps himself in his own historical
work), which could be applied across space and were largely
unconnected with the events which they were used to date. I
consider later the implications of this for an understanding of
Strabo's geographical conceptions, but for now turn to see
what Strabo *does* use to indicate time.

I start with the system of chronological markers formed by
well-known points in history. There are three main examples
of this phenomenon; two from the distant past, and one from
very recent history.[18] The Trojan war appears regularly with a
temporal function. Sardis' foundation, for example, was 'more
recent than the Trojan war, but ancient nevertheless'
(13. 4. 5).[19] The voyages of the Phoenicians took place 'slightly

---

[17] But he states, exceptionally, that C. Antonius founded one of the cities
which make up the Tetrapolis of Cephallenia when he went into exile 'after
his consulship which he held with Cicero' (10. 2. 13).

[18] Precisely fitting the 'hour-glass' model of Hellenistic historiography. I
shall return later to this question of privileging periods of the past.

[19] For more examples of the Trojan war as a measure of time, see 13. 1. 22;
12. 8. 6.

after the events at Troy' (μικρὸν τῶν Τρωικῶν ὕστερον), a fact
which forms part of the argument that the ancients made
longer sea-journeys than later travellers (1. 3. 2).[20] As will
become apparent, the effects of the post-Trojan migrations
played a crucial role in creating the world as described by
Strabo.[21] Just once, Trojan times (τὰ Τρωικά) are replaced by
the Iliadic war (ὁ Ἰλιακὸς πόλεμος), but this can be explained by
the context (13. 1. 7). Here Strabo is explaining that the whole
of a particular stretch of coastline was subject to Troy and
Priam during the Trojan war, and was itself called Troy. To
describe this period as τὰ Τρωικά would be confusing at the
very least, since, for this area, τὰ Τρωικά had taken on a
permanent *spatial* dimension, whereas in the context of any
other city, the phrase would refer simply to the famous period
of the war. Another slight variation is the use of the heroic age
as an indicator of time. Susa was described as having been
important 'in antiquity, in the time of the heroes' (15. 3. 2).

The mythical return of the Heracleidae, like the Trojan war,
had great ethnographical consequences and was also used to
indicate time. Strabo comments at 12. 8. 4 on the confusion of
peoples due to the many migrations and colonizations of the
Trojan period.[22] He reveals that the effects of the return of the
Heracleidae were just as far-reaching, and he uses the event as a
chronological hook on which to pin other great migrations and
ethnic changes. For example, at that time, the Achaeans
emigrated from Laconia to Ionia, leaving the Peloponnese to
Dorian domination (8. 5. 5). Also at the time of their return the

[20] At 1. 2. 31 we are told that there was no canal from the Arabian Gulf to
the Nile 'before Trojan times'. This is directly contradicted at 17. 1. 25, with a
note on Sesostris' attempt at such a canal 'before Trojan times' (πρὸ τῶν
Τρωικῶν).

[21] At 3. 2. 13 he mentions that there were still traces of the wanderings of
Trojan heroes in the region of Iberia. At 6. 1. 2 we see Greeks returning from
Troy making their mark on the settlements of the Adriatic coast of Italy,
starting ἀπὸ τῶν Τρωικῶν.

[22] Note, however, that quarrels over land occurred also *before* Trojan times
(πρὸ τῶν Τρωικῶν), when the Pelasgians and Cauconians were wandering
around Europe. Rhodes and Cos were both already inhabited before Trojan
times (12. 8. 6). The Trojan period should not be privileged too much in the
other direction either. Strabo set the migrations immediately following the
Trojan war in the context of *later* migrations, attacks, and foundations
(12. 8. 7).

Ionians moved to join the Carians in Epidaurus (8. 6. 15).
Attica too was affected: many people were driven out of their
native lands, and Attica was full of exiles, which worried the
Dorian Heracleidae. They attacked Attica, only to be driven
back from all except the Megarian territory, on which they
founded the city of that name (9. 1. 7).[23]

One feature of this early period, which Strabo treats
extensively and which provides a striking example of non-
city history, is the development of the Olympic festival.[24] This
forms an important link between Strabo's chronological markers and the Olympiadic time-system regularly used by Greek
historians, such as Timaeus, Polybius, and Diodorus, although
Strabo himself does not exploit the link elsewhere for dating
purposes. The Eleians, we are told, were not prosperous during
the Trojan period, or before it, having been humbled by the
Pylians and afterwards by Hercules, when King Augeas was
overthrown. But later still, 'after the return of the Heracleidae',
the opposite was the case, for the Aetolians, having returned at
the same time under the leadership of Oxylus, enlarged Coele
Elis and gained control of Olympia. These were the founders of
the Olympic games, and celebrated the first Olympiads, but
from this time on until the 26th Olympiad, the Eleians were in
charge of the temple and the games.[25]

Alongside the semi-mythical events of the Trojan war and
the return of the Heracleidae, the battle of Actium seems an
incongruous chronological marker, being a real historical event
that occurred in Strabo's own lifetime. Strabo does not use it
as regularly as the other two, but he uses it sufficiently often
for it to be regarded as one of the important fixed points in
history. Large numbers of veterans were, for example, settled
at Patrae 'after the battle of Actium' (8. 7. 5). The embassy
from Gyarus, mentioned above (p. 219), went to see Octavian

---

[23] This information ties in with 6. 2. 4 on the relationship between the
foundation of Megara and those of Naxus, Croton, and Syracuse. All of these
events happened after Trojan times (μετὰ τὰ Τρωικά) and all after the death of
Codrus, which fits in with Strabo's placing of the return of the Heracleidae
after the Trojan war.

[24] The development of the festival and games is to be found at 8. 3. 30.

[25] At 8. 4. 1 the Trojan war also seems to predate the return of the
Heracleidae. At 13. 1. 3 an interval of sixty years is proposed.

at Corinth, on his way to celebrate his victory in this battle
(10. 5. 3). The attack on the Romans by Adiatorix, the
Galatian, who received from Antonius the Heracliot part of
Heracleia Ponticus, took place 'shortly before events at
Actium' (μικρὸν πρὸ τῶν Ἀκτιακῶν) (12. 3. 6); after Octavian's
victory at Actium, Adiatorix was killed. The consequences of
Actium for the cities of Asia Minor can be seen in the case of
Amisus. After being given by Antonius to the kings, it was
freed again by Octavian after his victory, and restored to good
government (12. 3. 14). The final reference to Actium comes in
Strabo's summary of Egyptian history from the death of
Alexander to the present day, where it is used to mark the
end of Egypt's rule by drunken violence (17. 1. 11). It is not
surprising that the regions whose past is most commonly
marked out by reference to the battle are Egypt and Asia
Minor, Antonius' official sphere of influence. These were
clearly the places which had most to gain or lose by the
outcome of the battle. Perhaps we could conclude that these
three chronological points—the Trojan war, the return of the
Heracleidae, and the battle of Actium—had one important
feature in common, namely their implications for the way
Strabo's world looked. The first two resulted in large-scale
migration. Actium determined the course of another great
phase in Roman history, the principate, and had far-reaching
consequences, particularly for the East.

Chronological markers offer a fairly crude measure of time,
especially when the dates of the markers themselves are
uncertain. They are, however, more precise than using words
like 'earlier' or 'later'; or simply contrasting some imprecise
point in the past with the present state of affairs through the
pair 'previously : now' (τὸ παλαιόν or πάλαι : νῦν or νυνί). Yet
these vague temporal indicators are extremely common in the
Geography. The Allobroges, for example, used to wage many
wars previously (πρότερον μέν), but now (νῦν δέ) they were
farmers (4. 1. 11); the Iapodes, who were previously (πρότερον)
well-supplied and strong through piracy, had now been van-
quished by Augustus (4. 6. 10). The Siceli and Morgetes,
according to Antiochus of Syracuse, inhabited the region
around Rhegium in antiquity (τὸ παλαιόν), but later (ὕστερον)
they crossed to Sicily (6. 1. 6); the name of Sicily itself was

formerly (πρότερον) Trinacria, but later (ὕστερον) Thrinacis
(6. 2. 1). This is a standard way of signalling change over
time, and it seems that, since the precise time is clearly
irrelevant, Strabo's focus is on the facts that change has
occurred but that the old name, location, or inhabitants are
still significant factors in the identity of the place.

This basic structure is often refined. The past (τὸ παλαιόν) is
sometimes subdivided into early and late antiquity. Eratosthenes said that early Mediterranean voyages were made
in the name of piracy, but that later in ancient times (ὕστερον...τὸ παλαιόν) people were afraid to travel (1. 3. 2). Strabo's
answer to this is that the truth of the assertion depended on
what was meant by 'people in the past' (οἱ πάλαι); how far back
'the past' really was. The number of stages identified by
relative expressions of time is often greater than two.
Comum used to be of moderate size (1), but Pompeius
Strabo settled a Roman colony there (2); then (εἶτα) Gaius
Scipio added 3,000 colonists (3); εἶτα Julius Caesar added 5,000
more (4) (5. 1. 6). The sequence often, but not exclusively,
ends with the present situation. The Samnitae previously
(πρότερον μέν) made expeditions to Ardea; after this (μετὰ δὲ
ταῦτα) they ravaged Campania; and now (νυνὶ δέ) they have been
totally subdued by Sulla and others (5. 4. 11).

One variation on the theme is that of the succession of
empires or individual rulers over a region. Asia was prone to
the successive take-over by great powers, which structured its
past in a way which was particularly appropriate to a geographical account. We are told few details about the dates
involved. This is a relative historical pattern, revealing that x
ruled; then y; then z. Greater Armenia is described as having
ruled the whole of Asia in the past (τὸ παλαιόν) after having
broken up the empire of the Syrians; later (ὕστερον δέ) the
Armenians were deprived of their power by Cyrus and the
Persians; and now Parthia was in command (11. 13. 5).[26] The
Troad had a long 'ruler-history'—after the fall of Troy, the
Phrygians and Mysians were supreme; then later (εἶθ' ὕστερον)
the Lydians, Aeolians, and Ionians; next (ἔπειτα) the Persians
and Macedonians; and finally (τελευταῖοι) the Romans (12. 4. 6).

---

[26] A few chapters later, Strabo enlarges the sequence to include the Medes.

Both sequences significantly end with the present day, a point to which I shall return.

The growth of Rome from its beginnings as a city to its acquisition of a world empire provides an extreme example of how these chronological indicators were accumulated. After the foundation of the city, it was ruled by kings for many generations (ἐπὶ πολλὰς γενεάς), until the reign of Tarquinius Superbus. Then the city gradually expanded until it was lost to the Gauls, an event dated more precisely than almost any other in the work to 'the nineteenth year after the naval battle at Aegospotami', at the time of the Peace of Antalcidas. It is no surprise to find that this precision was not Strabo's own, but an acknowledged debt to Polybius.[27] The subsequent growth of Rome, following its recovery from the Gauls, was charted in successive phases, signified by 'firstly' (πρῶτον μέν) for the initial expansion to incorporate the Latins, and then by three instances of 'then' (εἶτα). This system tells little about the precise chronology, but it does effectively reflect the continual expansion of Roman power. The Hannibalic invasion then led to the second Punic war, and the third occurred 'not much later'. At the same time the Romans gained much of Libya and Iberia. The sequence continues, with the world gradually conquered—one area, and later (ὕστερον) another, and last of all (ὑστάτους) another. Strabo further breaks down the conquest of Celtica into clearly marked phases—firstly piecemeal (πρότερον κατὰ μέρος), later (ὕστερον) by Julius Caesar, and after this (μετὰ ταῦτα) by Augustus. The description ends with an extremely brief summary of the state of the empire in Strabo's time.

This passage raises the question of how Strabo indicates the difference in time between any one preferred chronological

---

[27] 6. 4. 2: ἔτει ἐννεακαιδεκάτῳ μετὰ τὴν ἐν Αἰγὸς ποταμοῖς ναυμαχίαν, κατὰ τὴν ἐπ' Ἀνταλκίδου γενομένην εἰρήνην. See Pol. 1. 6. 1–2: ἔτος μὲν οὖν ἐνειστήκει μετὰ τὴν ἐν Αἰγὸς ποταμοῖς ναυμαχίαν ἐννεακαιδέκατον . . . ἐν ᾧ Λακεδαιμόνιοι μὲν τὴν ἐπ' Ἀνταλκίδου λεγομένην εἰρήνην πρὸς βασιλέα τῶν Περσῶν ἐκύρωσαν ('it was, therefore, the nineteenth year after the sea-battle at Aegospotami . . . the year in which the Spartans ratified the so-called peace of Antalcidas with the Persian king'). Note that Polybius is more specific than even Strabo's most precise chronological reference. Polybius elaborates on the Peace of Antalcidas, and also remarks that this was the sixteenth year before the battle of Leuctra and during the siege of Rhegium by Dionysius the Elder.

marker and the events narrated. This difference is often not specified, but Strabo sometimes denotes time difference simply by a number of years, although not with Polybius' precision.[28] Even the early history of Rome could be pinned down to a time-scale in years, although the numbers were clearly round figures. The stories about Amollius and his brother, Numitor, are placed '400 years' after the time of Aeneas and King Latinus (5. 3. 2). The generation also appears frequently as a unit of time. Tyrtaeus said that the first conquest of Messenia took place at the time of their fathers' fathers (κατὰ τοὺς τῶν πατέρων πατέρας) (8. 4. 10). This is clearly an instance where Strabo is simply adopting the formula used by his source, but the application of 'familial time' sometimes includes also self-referential phrases. The orator Menippus Catocas was born in Stratoniceia 'at the time of our fathers' (κατὰ τοὺς πατέρας ἡμῶν) (14. 2. 25). Laodiceia was small in the past, but had become large 'in our time and that of our fathers' (12. 8. 16).[29]

Strabo's chronology of the Ionian colonization employs almost every method of indicating time that I have mentioned (13. 1. 3). The Aeolians sent colonies to Ionia four generations before the great colonization from Athens, but they were delayed and so took longer. The initial expedition was led by Orestes; he was succeeded by his son, Penthilus, who arrived in Thrace sixty years after the Trojan war, at around the time of the return of the Heracleidae to the Peloponnese. It took two more generations for the expedition to reach Lesbos.

Another example of the build-up of a relative chronology for events concerns Taras in southern Italy. The foundation of Taras takes us back to the eighth century and near to the time of the Messenian wars. Its history, as given by Strabo, includes details from almost every century between then and Strabo's own time (6. 3. 4). The Tarantini were once (ποτε) powerful; their later (ὕστερον) wealth and prosperity led to poor government, so they sent for Alexander the Molossian to lead their

---

[28] The Roman victory over the Sallyes occurred in the 'eightieth year of the war' (Str. 4. 6. 3); the conquest of Iberia was not completed until the '200th year [sc. after it was started], or even longer' (3. 4. 5).

[29] See also 8. 6. 20 on the Cypselids who ruled Corinth 'for three generations' (τριγονίας); 10. 4. 18 on Lycurgus, the Spartan lawgiver who lived five generations after Althaemenes.

wars against the Messapians and Lucanians (fourth century), and even earlier (ἔτι πρότερον) for Archidamus (fifth century), and then (εἶτα) for Pyrrhus, when they formed a league with him against the Romans (early third century). At the time of the wars with Hannibal (late third century) they lost their freedom, but later received a colony of Romans, and now lived in peace (first century). Strabo shows a steady degree of interest throughout the history of the city, but this account also raises the issue of the order of information, since the fourth-century intervention of Alexander the Molossian is followed rather than preceded in the account by Archidamus' actions in the fifth century.

Strabo regularly, but for no apparent reason, abandons chronological sequence in describing events. Potidaea was founded by Corinthians, and later called Cassandreia after Cassander, which moves us significantly forward in time to the Hellenistic age. But the account then moves far back in time to explain that even earlier giants lived here in Phlegra, but that these were subsequently destroyed by Hercules on his way back from Troy (Fr. 7. 25). Again, strict chronological sequence is abandoned, and from the present, we move to the remotest point in the narrative of this place before filling in the gap.[30] This disregard for chronological order is seen also in the case of Laodiceia, small in former days, large in Strabo's own time, damaged by siege in between these two points by Mithridates Eupator. The city was made great partly through the wealth of its citizens; formerly (πρότερον) by Hieron, later (ὕστερον) by Zeno the rhetor and his son, Polemon, who became king of Pontus and Bosporus, which he was given earlier (πρότερον) by Antonius; and after this (μετὰ ταῦτα) by Augustus (12. 8. 16). Sometimes history turned full cycle in the fortunes of a city. Cnossus was praised by Homer and his successors; for a long time it was supreme on Crete; later (εἶτα) it was humbled, and Lyctus and Gortyn took supremacy; but later still Cnossus recovered its ancient dignity as metropolis (10. 4. 7).

---

[30] G. D. Massaro, 'I moduli della narrazione storica nel libri di Strabone sull'Italia meridionale', in *Strabone II*, 81–117, discusses the question of the structuring of the south Italian past excellently, but perhaps ignores the fact that the past was not always related in a straight line.

This survey of the techniques which Strabo uses to indicate time in the *Geography* leads to some preliminary conclusions which will be developed later in this chapter and in chapter VI. Strabo is not obsessed in this work with precise chronological details, nor with the construction of a coherent system which might be universally applied, nor does he necessarily adhere to chronological order in his account of places. Rather, as we shall see in the next section, he is concerned with particular moments of transformation in the past which have remained important for the present identity and perception of a place.

THE PAST IN THE *GEOGRAPHY*

I now turn to consider the nature of the past in the *Geography*. Was Strabo indiscriminately interested in any information that was available to him, in the mould of the ancient compiler? Or does he reveal his own agenda for describing his view of the world of the past? I divide references to the past into different categories, although this obscures something of the overall effect. Firstly, I consider literary history, including that of his own text, which is extensive enough to have a complex history of its own, and that of the whole tradition, starting from Homer, and in which Strabo participated. Secondly, I consider the history of cities mentioned by Strabo, and the way in which the past of settlements is structured into significant stages concerned with foundation, refoundation, renaming, and destruction, that is, the various ways in which cities are born and die, and so appear on and disappear from the world-map. Finally, I move to non-city history, and its differences in structure from that of the cities.

Textual time: Strabo and the tradition

Some of the most self-referential temporal reflections in Strabo's *Geography* occur in connection with his own text and with the way in which it fitted into the tradition of geographical writing. There is a history of the text itself, and a history of geographical writings, both of which give the text a temporal dimension which is independent of the historical events that appear within it.

There are far too many instances of internal textual time to mention all of them, but a few examples will give a sense of the kind of history that is involved here. Strabo often professes to be proceeding 'in order' (ἐφεξῆς), not quite equivalent to Diodorus' repetition of the phrase 'at the appropriate moment' (ἐν τοῖς οἰκείοις χρόνοις), meaning that everything has a place in the text and that he cannot recount what he knows about an event until he reaches its appointed time;[31] but Strabo does employ similar techniques of postponement. The subject of the Cauconians, for example, arises because of the tomb of their founder, Caucon, in the territory of Lepreum. But Strabo says that he will tell more about the people, when he comes to their region, preserving the order of the text (8. 3. 17). Again, of the Paphlagonians, he says that he will discuss them later, but talk now about the Pontic region (12. 3. 9).[32]

The opposite of postponement, regression, is equally important to the ordering of the text. Keeping the description satisfactorily arranged was not easy, and Strabo occasionally has to go back on his tracks to pick up from an earlier point. This is particularly problematic when he has moved inland for any length of time, losing the thread of the predominantly periplus structure. At 13. 1. 1, having dealt with the Phrygian tribes, he explicitly moves backwards (ἐπανιόντες . . . πάλιν) to the Propontis to continue the journey down the coast. The language of return is highly reminiscent of Diodorus' need to recount the earlier history of his present theme. For Diodorus the return was temporal, for Strabo it was a geographical regression, but for both the mode of expression was the same. The necessity to go back also occurs when Strabo has summarized a region, and then wants to fill in the details, as happens in his description of the Ionian cities.[33] After giving a brief account of the whole wave of colonization that resulted in the foundations, he then returns to describe each city in detail,

---

[31] For examples of this phrase, see Diodorus 4. 23; 5. 6; 5. 21; 5. 84; 13. 96; 20. 2.

[32] Troy too is postponed until later in favour of telling about Olympus at 12. 8. 8; and the inland Dardanians are put off until later so that the coast may be dealt with first (7. 5. 7).

[33] We have already seen how this pattern of an overview, followed by a more detailed discussion of what happens between the limits of the theme, is frequently adopted by Strabo in relating the history of individual places, sacrificing strict chronological order.

starting with the places where the foundations first occurred, that is, with Miletus and Ephesus (14. 1. 4). Sometimes previous parts of the text are alluded to without a lengthy digression. When Strabo describes the Aethiopians in Book 17, he recalls that they have already been discussed earlier (ἐν τοῖς πρότερον), in his account of the Arabian Gulf (17. 2. 1).

These passages give some idea of the text's own temporal structure through which Strabo moves backwards or forwards, and which is denoted by the same temporal indicators as the real history described in it. Thus he creates a complex, two-tiered, temporal system, involving both literary and historical time. But this is further complicated by the way in which Strabo refers to the history of the literary tradition which he followed. I have already discussed some of the spatial models implicit in the geographical tradition within which he wrote, and the way that a new spatial focus in Strabo's relationship to other authors of the Greek East emerges from his use of certain self-referential temporal phrases. But there is also a purely temporal dimension to the question. We have to deal with not only historical time, and the time of Strabo's text itself, but also the literary time that is external to the *Geography*.

References to literary predecessors were far more common in ancient literature than in modern writing, and debts to the tradition were embraced rather than feared as a sign of lack of originality.[34] Thus it is totally without surprise that Strabo started his work by evoking the history of his subject so far, starting from its founder, Homer. The fact that Strabo's work followed in the footsteps of great literary figures from the past could only add to its prestige. Our first instance of a clearly graded development appears in the first chapter and refers to

---

[34] D. Ambaglio, 'Strabone e la storiografia greca frammentaria', in *Studi di storia e storiografia antiche per Emilio Gabba* (Como, 1988), 73–83, notes the way in which Strabo tended to acknowledge openly his debt to other writers, but also points out the difficulties involved in determining to what extent we can read the original author from Strabo's citations and how much has been filtered through intermediary sources. By examining Strabo's treatment of Herodotus, whose text we know independently, Ambaglio argues for caution when trying to reconstruct lesser-known, or fragmentary, texts. L. Prandi, 'La critica storica di Strabone alla geografia di Erodoto', *CISA* 14 (1988), 52–72, also argues that Strabo's knowledge of Herodotus may have come through Callisthenes.

the history of geography itself. 'The first to discuss the subject were . . ., those after them . . .' (1. 1. 1).[35] Soon after this, Strabo names the author of the first map as Anaximander. The history of cartography is picked up again in Book 2 in connection with discussion of Eratosthenes, and Hipparchus, where these are set against the evidence of the ancient maps (2. 1. 4).

Strabo was keen also to establish a chronology for the development of other literary genres. Poetry came first, and there then followed authors such as Cadmus, Pherecydes, and Hecataeus, who initiated the transition to prose (1. 2. 6). Of his own time Strabo says that history and philosophy were the predominant literary forms. Geography is given no clear place in this scheme, but we are surely being encouraged to consider the *Geography* as part of a literary continuum, a view reinforced by the list of authors who reveal ancient knowledge of the world. Homer is understood as the 'inventor' ($\pi\rho\hat{\omega}\tau\sigma\varsigma$ $\epsilon\dot{\nu}\rho\epsilon\tau\acute{\eta}\varsigma$) of the tradition, but his account of, for example, the Scythians or Hippemolgi can be legitimately backed up by information given in the works of Herodotus on Darius' expedition, of Chrysippus on the kings of the Bosporus, of Anacharsis and of Abaris (7. 3. 8).[36] The use of historical accounts in support of the geography gleaned from the Homeric epics gives some indication of why Strabo included *all* literary forms in his account of the development of geography.[37] This is confirmed in the preface to Book 8, where Strabo

---

[35] At 2. 1. 11, Strabo asks us to compare earlier and later geographers ($o\dot{\iota}$ $\pi\alpha\lambda\alpha\iota\sigma\dot{\iota}$ and $o\dot{\iota}$ $\ddot{\upsilon}\sigma\tau\epsilon\rho\sigma\nu$). The fact that both groups agree (2. 1. 14) on the fertility of India somehow guarantees the truth of the assertion.

[36] The dates of these authors range from the 8th to the 3rd cent. BC. The continuation of the excursus through to the age of Alexander and the Hellenistic period enables us to build up something of a history for the process of discovering information about foreign peoples.

[37] The problem of what exactly we might expect from different types of work is raised again in connection with the Curetes. At 10. 3. 7–9 Strabo says that they have tended to be treated as a theological subject. The name of works on them—$Kου\rho\eta\tau\iota\kappa\acute{\alpha}$—leads one to suppose that the accounts will be the histories of the people of Aetolia and Acarnania, whereas they were really more like the accounts of the Satyrs, Bacchae, or Sileni. Strabo's knowledge of local histories is revealed at 11. 2. 14, where he says that the order of tribes will be given as by those who write $\tau\grave{\alpha}$ $M\iota\theta\rho\iota\delta\alpha\tau\iota\kappa\acute{\alpha}$.

turns his attention to Greece. The geography of Greece was treated first by Homer, then by authors of periegeses and periplus texts, and by those writing general histories, such as Ephorus and Polybius, and in scientific treatises, by Posidonius and Hipparchus (8. 1. 1). It is tempting to read this list as a bibliography for the work, although Strabo does not say that he has drawn extensively, and certainly not exclusively, on these previous accounts. However, he does at least seem to be setting out a geographical tradition.

One of the problems associated with the literary tradition is that the world changes. Strabo warns that one should take care when consulting 'the ancient histories, for more recent writers put forward many new beliefs, with the result that they even contradict them' (8. 3. 31). I have already mentioned some of Strabo's comments on the lost world of the past, and the problems this brought to the use of Homer as a source. Much of the description of the Troad and other parts of Asia Minor and Greece involved working through the version of the area which emerged from the Homeric epics. Strabo complains that 'writers after Homer lead to confusions of names and tribes because of the continual migrations, changes of political administration, and the mixing up of tribes', making it difficult for people now (οἱ νῦν) (9. 5. 21). Real changes in the world and their representation in the geographical literary tradition simultaneously enriched and complicated Strabo's undertaking.

The birth and death of cities: πόλις-history

The history of cities is one of the most common manifestations of the past in Strabo's geographical description, and is centred on specific defining moments in the history of a city, rather than a more general interest. Strabo would surely have agreed with the striking statement of Tuan that 'city is history incarnate'.[38] In particular, Strabo was concerned with the process by which places came into existence in a historically meaningful sense. Sites were there before, but, as was observed about the land of Narnia (p. 19), what could be said about them until they were structured by the presence of permanent

---

[38] Y.-F. Tuan, 'Space, Time, Place: A Humanistic Framework', in *Making Sense of Time*, 15.

settlements?[39] We shall see later that Strabo does deal with areas which were not structured in this way, but that this evokes a very different kind of narrative, which is less temporally specific. An exhaustive treatment of city-history, the stories of the many πόλεις, in the *Geography* would far exceed the limitations of this section, so I select a few recurring themes.

The earliest city-foundations, those said to have been accomplished by demigods and heroes, form a huge group. The foundation *par excellence* in Strabo's account is that of Rome itself, and it is no surprise to find more than one version given. Alongside the Romulus and Remus story is set an alternative foundation account, in which Rome appears as an Arcadian colony, founded by Evander with Hercules' help. Strabo tells of the development of the city, and includes additions to the fortifications over time, as well as simple contrasts between the past and the present. The first inhabitants decided, both for themselves and for their successors, that the city should rely on manpower from the start, rather than on the site itself. Whereas the ancient inhabitants dealt with the practical side of urban life, those who came after were concerned with adorning the city (5. 3. 2–8).

Equally, southern Italy had several cities founded by figures from the mythical past. Petelia was settled by Philoctetes, and was populous even in Strabo's day (6. 1. 3). Metapontium was founded by Pylians sailing with Nestor from Troy (6. 1. 15).[40] The influence of Diomedes over Italy was attested in the foundation of Canusium, Argyrippa, and possibly Sipus (6. 3. 9). Perhaps unsurprisingly, the southern part of Italy

---

[39] This included military as well as civilian functions. Strabo mentions many places as naval bases, or bases for land operations. See 3. 3. 1: Moron as the base for D. Iunius Brutus Callaicus against the Lusitanians (mid. 2nd cent. BC); 6. 2. 3: Messene as a naval base for the Roman fleet in the Sicilian war against Carthage; 13. 3. 5: Elea as a naval base for the Attalids; 14. 5. 2: Coracesium in Cilicia as a base for Diodotus Tryphon, when he tried to make Syria revolt from the kings.

[40] Nestor's party became dispersed on the return from Troy to the Peloponnese, leading to the foundation of Pisa by a splinter group, the Pisatae. The city is described as once rich, and even now not unrenowned (5. 2. 5). The connections between different heroic foundations is a theme to which I shall return.

was more prone than areas further north to the visits of heroes wandering around the Mediterranean. No such heroic foundations were established in, for example, Gaul or Britain.

In Greece the foundation of Argos by Danaus receives a good deal of attention. The rule over this city was later shared between the descendants of Danaus and the Amythaonides, emigrants from Pisatis and Triphylia, resulting in the creation of a second capital at Mycenae (8. 6. 10). In the beginning ($\kappa\alpha\tau$' $\dot{\alpha}\rho\chi\dot{\alpha}s$) Argos was predominant, but later Mycenae took over. But this change of fortune was later reversed, for after the Trojan war Mycenae was reduced, especially on the return of the Heracleidae.[41] Later still, Mycenae was razed to the ground by the Argives themselves, with the result that there was now no trace of the city.[42] The history of this foundation is interesting because it became two places, seemed in danger of disappearing altogether under the influence of the second capital, and then had the good fortune to survive after all. The whole story indicates, if nothing else, how precarious the life of an ancient city was, even one as long established as Argos. The case of Troezen was not altogether dissimilar, in so far as the foundation of one city led to another. Troezen and Pittheus were sons of Pelops. At some point, Troezen founded a city which took his name; Pittheus succeeded him as king. But the site had not been unoccupied before they arrived. Anthes, its previous owner, was forced out and set sail to found Halicarnassus (8. 6. 14).[43]

---

[41] This process is described in further detail at 8. 6. 19. Mycenae was founded by Perseus. It later fell to the Pelopidae, founders of Troezen (8. 6. 14), and then to the Heracleidae. After the battle of Salamis, the Argives destroyed Mycenae, giving a date of post-480 BC for the final destruction.

[42] The fact that the Trojan war occurred so far into the history of Argos reveals quite how ancient a foundation it was, pre-dating the many cities established by heroes returning from Troy.

[43] Strabo promises here to tell us more about the foundation of Halicarnassus in his description of Caria. The story is forthcoming (14. 2. 16), but slightly contradictory. Here we are told that the city was founded by Anthes *and the Troezenians*, as though Anthes were leading the people of Troezen on a colonizing expedition, rather than having been ejected from his land by them. The problem lies partly in the version at 8. 6. 14, since it is inconceivable that Anthes did not take any fellow-colonizers with him, making Halicarnassus start life with only one inhabitant. This instance where two colonization stories are actually available for comparison leads to

An unusual example of a heroic foundation was the village of Helus in the Peloponnese, established by the son of Perseus. The heroic founder and the importance of the settlement might seem initially to be mismatched, except that we are also told that the place was once a city, providing an example of why the past must be included in Strabo's account (8. 5. 2). The vicissitudes of the history of settlements were such that places of real importance and status in the past could run the risk of being entirely omitted.

Euboea was particularly rich in this kind of history. The various names of the island were attributed to the involvement of heroes, such as 'Ellopia' after Ellops, Ion's son, who was also responsible for founding Ellopia in Oria (10. 1. 3).[44] The main cities on the island, Eretria and Chalcis, had a history that stretched back to pre-Trojan times. They were founded 'before Trojan times' (πρὸ τῶν Τρωικῶν) by Athens. Then 'after the Trojan period' (μετὰ τὰ Τρωικά), Aiclus and Cothus set out from Athens to settle inhabitants in each respectively (10. 1. 8).[45] This is confusing, since it is not clear what kind of foundations pre-Trojan Eretria and Chalcis would have been if they had not yet received inhabitants. The initial foundation was called a κτίσις; the later phase was οἴκισις. It seems reasonable to suppose from the different terminology that different processes are to be envisaged, but precisely which ones is unclear.

Sometimes the Homeric account of cities around the time of the Trojan war confused the issue further, not least because this was a period of rapid colonization and growth of new settlements.[46] On Crete, for example, Homer is cited as saying at one

the question of how many of the other accounts are confused as to who exactly was involved and their reasons for founding a city at all.

[44] This evokes a sub-history of Ellopia, whose inhabitants migrated to Histiaea under pressure from Philistides after the battle of Leuctra. But, according to another account, Histiaea was colonized by Athenians from the deme of that name.

[45] Eretria and Chalcis soon become strong enough to send out their own colonies—to Macedonia, Italy, and Sicily at the time of the rule of the Hippobotae.

[46] At 3. 4. 3 we catch a glimpse of the work of Asclepiades of Myrlea on the post-Trojan colonization of the Mediterranean. Sorting out the effects of the migration of Trojan heroes was one of the great preoccupations of the Hellenistic period.

stage that the island had a hundred cities; elsewhere that it had ninety (10. 4. 15).[47] The reason for the discrepancy was that ten of the cities were founded 'after the Trojan war' by Dorians following Althaemenes the Argive, and referred to Homer's own time, rather than to the time of the Trojan war itself. Althaemenes turns up again at 14. 2. 6 in the account of the colonization of Rhodes, where he is better contextualized than in the earlier passage.[48] We are told that of the Dorians who founded Megara after the death of Codrus, some stayed in Megara, some went to Rhodes and others joined in the colonization of Crete with Althaemenes the Argive. This is set in a more detailed framework still, since Cnidus and Halicarnassus had not yet been founded, recalling the foundation of the latter by Anthes, who had been ejected from the site of Troezen by its own founders.

The earliest phase of foundations could not be attributed entirely to single heroes; some were carried out by named groups rather than individuals. Although it is hard to envisage a colonization that did *not* involve more than one person, there is a difference between knowing only that a place was a Milesian foundation, and knowing the name of the founder (κτίστης), not least because of the importance of the cult of the individual founder in ancient cities.[49] But more examples of early foundations in Strabo are attributed only to a group than are ascribed to an individual hero.[50]

Emporion is one of many cities described as a Massilian foundation (Μασσαλιωτῶν κτίσμα) (3. 4. 8),[51] and Massilia itself

---

[47] The Homeric references are to *Il.* 2. 649 and *Od.* 19. 174.

[48] The cities on Rhodes are interesting in their own right as foundations of such characters as the children of the Heliadae—Lindos, Ialysus, and Cameirus (14. 2. 8). The alternative to this version was that these cities were named after the daughters of Danaus.

[49] As revealed in Strabo's account of Sinope. Lucullus struck an effective blow at the city's identity by removing the statue of Autolycus. See also 16. 2. 5 on Antiocheia where Nicator settled the descendants of Triptolemus and was henceforth worshipped as a hero.

[50] One interesting instance, in which the name of the foundation was derived from the name of its founder, is Menebria in Thrace. Strabo explains how the name was formed from Menas, the founder, and 'bria', the Thracian word meaning 'city', a rare example of the introduction of foreign words (7. 6. 1).

[51] Nicaea and Antipolis were founded by Massiliotes as strongholds against barbarians (4. 1. 9).

had a set of founders, the Phocaeans, who followed an oracle given by Ephesian Artemis (4. 1. 4). Cumae is said to have been a 'most ancient foundation', indeed the oldest of all Sicilian and Italiote cities, set up by the Chalcidians and Cumaeans (5. 4. 4). Southern Italy was, not surprisingly, well endowed with these early foundations, just as it had many cities linked to named heroes. Neapolis was originally a Cumaean foundation; it was later recolonized by Chalcidians; later still it admitted some of the Campani (5. 4. 7). It thus not only illustrates the theme of group foundation, but also provides an example of the numerous places whose history, according to Strabo, consisted of moments of rebirth. This is perhaps the most striking feature of the group foundations mentioned in Strabo's text. These cities more than the others seem to have undergone redefinition and refoundation at the hands of successive occupants.

Herculaneum was inhabited by Osci, then (εἶτα) by Tyrrhenians and Pelasgi, after this (μετὰ ταῦτα δέ) by Samnitae (5. 4. 8). Temesa was founded by Ausones, later (ὕστερον δέ) by Aetolians, who were thrown out by the Brettii, who in turn were overthrown by Hannibal and then the Romans (6. 1. 5). Each time a city's inhabitants were changed, the place took on a new identity, sometimes accompanied by a change of name, as in the case of Hipponium, a Locrian foundation, which was renamed Vibo Valentia by the Romans when they took the place (6. 1. 5).[52] An interesting example of this process concerns Aegina. The most important phase in the island's history is mentioned first—its thalassocratic stage, during which it contended with Athens for the prize for valour at the battle of Salamis (8. 6. 16). But we are then told about its earlier history, in which it started life called Oenone; was colonized successively by the Argives, Cretans, Epidaurians, and Dorians; then turned into cleruchies by Athens; and then taken from Athens by Sparta and returned to the ancient colonizers (οἱ ἀρχαῖοι οἰκήτορες). But who were they? The Argives, Cretans, Epidaurians, or Dorians?

Because of the way in which Strabo explicitly sets various colonizations in a more general context of ancient migration it

---

[52] See also 6. 1. 13 for Thurii renamed Copiae; 6. 2. 3 for Catana, a Naxian city, later renamed Aetna; and Messene, which had once been a Naxian foundation called Zancle.

is possible to draw up a coherent chronology for some of the early foundations. Locri Epizephyrii was founded by colonists from Locri on the Crisaean Gulf only a little after (μικρὸν ὕστερον) the foundation of Croton and Syracuse (6. 1. 7).[53] This context is further built up a few chapters later, with details about the foundation of Syracuse by Archias, who sailed from Corinth at around the same time as Naxos and Megara were colonized (6. 2. 4). Archias went to the Delphic oracle about the colonization at the same time as Myscellus, the founder of Croton. Strabo thus links five foundations—Megara, Naxos, Croton, Syracuse, and, a little later, Locri Epizephyrii. But this is not all, for Archias, on his way to Sicily, left behind Chersicrates to colonize what is now called Corcyra, but was previously called Scheria. Chersicrates was meant to join in a settlement (συνοικιοῦντα) with the Liburnians, who were already there, but instead ejected them and settled the place alone (οἰκίσαι), as indicated by the disappearance of the prefix συν- between the plan and its fulfilment. The story was complicated even further by the collaboration that *did* take place between Archias and some of the Dorians who were meant to be participating in the foundation of Megara. A disillusioned group was on its way home, but met up with Archias at Zephyrium, and joined him in the establishment of Syracuse (κοινῇ μετ' αὐτῶν κτίσαι τὰς Συρακούσσας).

Thus, different foundations are caught up in a complicated web and make it possible, if not straightforward, for the determined reader to construct a fairly coherent narrative for the earliest phase of history dealt with by Strabo, in a way which is inconceivable for most of the subsequent periods. It is possible to reconstruct this phase in terms not only of group colonizations, but also of heroes associated with the Trojan war, and of the Homeric epics.

But after travelling round the coast of Asia Minor, Strabo mentions hardly a single other city-foundation by a hero from the Trojan period. This omission is a striking feature of his description of the Fertile Crescent, and it is only really broken when we reach Carthage and the story of Dido (17. 3. 15). It is not, however, surprising when we recall the pattern of founda-

---

[53] Croton and Syracuse were founded respectively in 710 and 734 BC.

tion stories in the Hellenistic regional histories. In these the
Fertile Crescent, stretching from Egypt to Persia, is characterized and distinguished from the rest of the world partly because
of its non-Greek foundation myths, which are specifically *not*
associated with heroes from the Trojan war. Rather than
placing alongside the Greek heroic foundations the equivalent
stories relating to the Fertile Crescent—myths involving the
migrations resulting from the great flood, the Exodus of the
Jews from Egypt, and the dispersal of the sons of Abraham—
Strabo fails to mention the earliest phase of colonization in
these regions.[54] One possibility is that he simply did not know
of these stories. However, it may be that, by contrast with
Josephus who attempted to synchronize the two sets of foundation stories, Strabo's omission indicates that the myths were
incompatible in the context of his project to write a coherent
account of the whole world, a point to which I shall return in
chapter VI.

So far I have discussed how Strabo enables us to put
together some kind of narrative, in the course of which the
early cities appear on the map and make up the first important
stage in city-history. But how much space in the narrative is
given to later foundations, and is it possible, as with some of
the very early phases, to gain a sense of synchronism?

Strabo is not silent on the fact that Ostia was founded by
Ancus Marcius, Ancona by Syracusans fleeing from the tyranny of Dionysius, Pyxus by Micynthus, ruler of Messene in
Sicily, but these foundations are not really given any satisfactory context, and make little impact (5. 3. 5; 5. 4. 2; 6. 1. 1).
However, the Hellenistic period emerges from Strabo's text as
one in which new cities were built, as opposed to being simply
renamed and refounded.[55] We hear of Thessalonica, founded

---

[54] A striking reference to the great flood, and I think unique in Strabo,
comes at 13. 1. 25, where he cites Plato's theory of the three kinds of
civilization that evolved after the flood. Firstly the hills, then the foothills,
and thirdly the plains were inhabited; and later the coasts and islands too, as
man dared to move to lower ground. The three stages were exemplified by the
Cyclopes, Dardania under Dardanus, and life in the plains under Ilus, the
traditional founder of Ilion.

[55] By contrast, we hear of hardly any foundations from the classical Greek
period. Rhodes, founded at the time of the Peloponnesian war, is a notable
exception (14. 2. 9).

by Cassander, and named after his wife, the daughter of Philip. Thessalonica was to be the new home of the inhabitants of the towns in Crusis and on the Thermaean Gulf, which Cassander had destroyed (Fr. 7. 21).[56] Greek cities in Media founded by the Macedonians in the aftermath of Alexander's conquests are also listed (11. 13. 6).[57] The impact of the Hellenistic monarchs on the geography of Asia comes through very clearly from Strabo's description. Secondly, we should not forget the victory cities of the first century BC, including two Nicopoleis—Octavian's post-Actium city, and Pompey's city in Lesser Armenia (7. 7. 5; 12. 3. 28).

This is my attempt at a synchronic view, drawing together geographically disparate, but contemporaneous, events, and it is important to remember that Strabo himself does not articulate his work in this way. The conclusion from the last section revealed Strabo's lack of precision over chronology and the order of events in time. But does this extend to his treatment of city-history? How specific a vocabulary does Strabo use to indicate the various stages of foundation, refoundation, synoecism, and renaming of cities? How does he indicate the diachronic nature of his accounts of particular cities? We have already seen in relation to Eretria and Chalcis that we need to distinguish between κτίσις and οἴκισις, with the difference probably lying in the involvement of significantly greater numbers of settlers for οἴκισις. This distinction receives further support from the description of the city of Dardanus in the Troad. The city was said to be an ancient foundation (κτίσμα ἀρχαῖον), which was moved around by successive kings; firstly to Abydus, and then back to the old site. Strabo formulates this later relocation of the city's inhabitants as ἀνῴκιζον πάλιν εἰς τὸ ἀρχαῖον κτίσμα ('they moved back into the ancient foundation') (13. 1. 28). In other words it is clear that κτίσις refers to the actual laying out of a site, which remained as the κτίσμα whether or not it was inhabited. The οἴκισις refers to the

---

[56] The foundation is mentioned again in fr. 7. 24.

[57] See also 11. 10. 2 for the foundation of Antiocheia by Antiochus Soter in the 3rd cent.; 12. 4. 2 for the foundation of Nicomedia by the Bithynian king, Nicomedes I; 16. 2. 4 for Antiocheia, Seleuceia in Pieria, Apamea, and Laodiceia, the great Seleucid Tetrapolis founded by Seleucus Nicator and named after members of his family.

inhabitants and is potentially separable from the process of foundation.[58]

We have also seen that the application or omission of the prefix συν- in connection with the verb οἰκέω was a way of distinguishing foundations that involved collaboration between two or more groups, and those that were the work of a single set of people. Initial foundations are further defined by being termed an ἀποικία ('colony') or a κατοικία ('settlement'). The difference between these seems to lie in the stress put on the place of origin of the inhabitants, as the prefixes indicate. We are told about a κατοικία called Buprasium in Greece, about which we have only the information that it no longer existed, and hear nothing about its founders (8. 3. 8).[59] But Leuctrum was an ἄποικος, and we are told that its founders were the Leuctri from Boeotia (8. 4. 4).[60] Similarly, the settling of Cilician pirates by Pompey in Soli was an act of κατοίκισις—the pirates had no fixed place of origin (14. 5. 8). It is noteworthy that the greatest achievement of Miletus is said by Strabo to be the number of its ἀποικίαι (14. 1. 6). This seems a cogent reason for believing that the designation ἀποικία reflected as much about the metropolis as about the new settlement.

This all concerns the beginnings of cities. However, Strabo also uses a specific vocabulary of later addition and refounda-tion. The recolonization of Corinth by Julius Caesar, after its long desertion, required 'extra inhabitants' (ἔποικοι) (8. 6. 23).[61] The arrival of Thracians on Euboea involved recolonizing (ἐποικῆσαι) the island, and renaming it (ἐπονομάσαι) (10. 1. 3).[62]

---

[58] This is confirmed at 8. 3. 25, where we hear that Cyparissēeis still existed, but was not inhabited. The place had a life that was independent of its inhabitants.

[59] The only counter-example that I have found is Stratoniceia, a κατοικία of the Macedonians (14. 2. 25).

[60] See 9. 4. 6 for Pharygae settled by ἄποικοι from among the Argives. Strabo repeatedly describes the great colonization of Asia Minor from Athens as ἀποικία, again perhaps stressing the place of origin.

[61] The fates of the cities of Corinth and Carthage ran in parallel, in terms not only of their destruction in the same year, but also of their rejuvenation under Julius Caesar. At 17. 3. 15 we hear that he sent ἔποικοι to Carthage at the same time as to Corinth.

[62] It is the consistent use of the prefix ἐπι- in connection with phases of history subsequent to the original foundation that makes me uncertain as to

Another place affected by different phases of development was Amisus, originally a Milesian foundation (12. 3. 14). The second stage in the city's history is missing from the text, and all we know is that it involved Cappadocians; but the third phase involved the process of ἐποίκισις by the Athenians under the leadership of Athenocles, and a change of name (μετονομα-σθῆναι) to Peiraeus.[63] Later still, Mithridates Eupator adorned it with temples and 'founded an additional part' (προσέκτισε μέρος). The precise significance of the prefix προσ-, as opposed to ἐπι-, is uncertain, but it seems likely, judging from the meaning of the prepositions, that προσκτίσις would refer to a new and additional quarter of the city being built, whereas ἐποίκισις might refer to a more integral change, involving the absorption of new citizens into the existing framework, a distinction which would fit well with the way in which Strabo seems to have used the basic roots of the two words οἰκε- and κτίζ-.

It is important to consider whether or not this vocabulary of foundation and colonization applied to settlements other than cities.[64] In particular, I shall look at the class of settlements which turned from village to city, or city to village, and which thus reveal the impossibility of categorizing settlements pre-

why, in the case of Eretria, the Loeb translator takes the prefix to mean 'on top of'. At 10. 1. 10 the razing of ἡ ἀρχαία πόλις ('the ancient city') by the Persians is followed by the foundation of the present city. The verb used is the perfect passive ἐπέκτισται, surely not necessarily meaning, as the Loeb gives it, that 'present Eretria is founded on it' (sc. the site of the old city), but simply 'present Eretria was founded subsequently'.

[63] The prefix μετά- is very rarely found attached to words of settlement and colonization, as opposed to naming. However, the mass-migration of the Seleuceians from present-day Holmi to Seleuceia on the Calycadnus, after its foundation, was described as μετοικία presumably because they literally did just exchange their place of residence (14. 5. 4). Exceptionally, the attempt to rename places met with serious opposition, and might even fail. Lysimachus tried to rename Ephesus after his wife, Arsinoë, but the ancient name (τὸ ἀρχαῖον ὄνομα) prevailed (14. 1. 21); Ptolemy Philadelphus tried to rename Patara in Lycia after his wife, Arsinoë, but again the plan failed (14. 3. 6).

[64] At 12. 7. 3, for example, we hear that Selge 'was founded as a πόλις for the first time by the Spartans, but [was founded] even earlier by Calchas'. In other words, there was such a thing as a non-πόλις foundation at an earlier stage. For another example of foundation vocabulary used of non-πόλις history, see 13. 1. 14 and the founder (ἀρχηγέτης) of the Ophiogeneis tribe.

cisely in a work which spans the period from the heroic age to the time of Tiberius across a wide range of societies and cultures.[65] Examples of the transition in both directions are numerous, although, despite the many instances of cities being added to and upgraded, there are more instances of urban decline into villages (κῶμαι) than elevations to the status of city (πόλις).[66]

Mediolanium in northern Italy was 'once a village . . . now a noteworthy city'.[67] Arsinoë in Acarnania previously existed as a village called Conopa, and was then founded as a city by Arsinoë, wife of Ptolemy II (10. 2. 22). A slightly different pattern applied to the settlement of Zela, 'which was governed by kings, not as a city, but as a sacred precinct of the Persian gods, ruled by a priest'. Pompey added land and called it a πόλις (12. 3. 37). The village of Gordium in the mountainous interior of Asia Minor was promoted from its village status in a process of enlargement and renaming (to Iuliopolis) by the bandit-leader Cleon (12. 8. 9). The same story was true on a grander and more elaborate scale for Ilium in Strabo's time (13. 1. 26–7). For a while this was only a village (κώμη), but Alexander went there after his victory at the river Granicus in 334 BC and adorned the temple of Athena, called the place a πόλις, added buildings, and freed it from tribute. Later he promised to make it not only a city, but a great one. But when the Romans first crossed over to Asia to deal with Antiochus III, the great city was not to be found. Instead, Demetrius of Scepsis, who visited the place around that time, found a κωμόπολις; presumably the name is intended to reflect the decline in the city's status. It was later improved, only to face ruin again at the hands of Fimbria, who took it by siege in the first Mithridatic war. The cycle of destruction and renewal had continued right up to Strabo's own time, with improvements by Sulla and Julius Caesar.

[65] It must be remembered that becoming a city was not the only promotion that a village could hope for. The ancient village of Mylasa in Caria became a royal residence (βασίλειον) under the Hecatomnids (14. 2. 23).
[66] See Thucydides 1. 10 for the possibility that a city as important as Sparta might one day be deserted.
[67] 5. 1. 6: πάλαι . . . κώμην, νῦν . . . ἀξιόλογον πόλιν. See also 12. 3. 38 and the village of Phazemon, which was transformed into the city of Neapolis.

Cures, on the other hand, was 'now a small village . . . but once a famous city', and the original home of two kings of Rome—Titius Tatius and Numa Pompilius.[68] Fregellae suffered the same fate as Cures—'now just a village, but once a noteworthy city' with dependencies.[69] Strabo describes the whole of Boeotia, with the exception of Tanagra and Thespiae, in these terms of decline. Thebes in Strabo's time did not 'preserve the character even of a noteworthy village', although it had at one stage claimed the supremacy of Greece (9. 2. 5).

Cities and villages moved from one status to another and could easily be wiped off the face of the map altogether.[70] Many examples of city-deaths are found; sometimes this destruction was permanent, sometimes the city could be revived, as we have seen in the cases of refoundation. Alexander appears as the anti-founder in Bactria and Sogdiana, establishing eight cities, but destroying others, including Cyra, the last foundation of Cyrus, and also the city of the Branchidae, whom Xerxes had settled there (11. 11. 4).[71] Aemilius Paulus Macedonicus did an equally devastating job with the cities of the Epirotes, destroying seventy of them after the subjugation of Perseus (7. 7. 3). Strabo included not only examples of the cities which gradually declined, passing through the state of being a village on their way out, but also those which suffered sudden obliteration.

The alternative: non-πόλις history

The history of cities and smaller settlements dominates Strabo's account. But what about the history of those who did not live in noteworthy settlements, and the evolution of various

---

[68] 5. 3. 1: νῦν μὲν κωμίον . . . ἦν δὲ πόλις ἐπίσημος. Note the diminutive, which serves to emphasize quite what a fall the place has suffered since the time when it was the provenance of kings.

[69] 5. 3. 10: νῦν μὲν κώμη, πόλις δὲ ποτε ἀξιόλογος γεγονυῖα. See also 5. 4. 13 on Picentia—once the metropolis for the Picentes, νυνὶ δέ they live in villages (κωμηδόν).

[70] See, for example, 8. 6. 13 and the village of Eiones, which became a naval station, but later disappeared altogether. The cities of Arcadia had been so devastated that they were hardly worth mentioning (8. 8. 1).

[71] But this was contrasted by Strabo with the fact that previously the peoples of Bactria and Sogdiana were little more than nomads (11. 11. 3). So, for cities to be present at all was some advance on the previous situation.

peoples (ἔθνη)? Could the same narrative structures be applied, or was something totally different required? To recall the most basic model of city-history—the account mentioned the first foundation and any subsequent destructions and refoundations, giving not a continuous narrative, but a summary of each crucial and separate stage in the city's life. It is obvious from the start that the model of foundation and refoundation would not be easily applied to non-city history.

Much of the non-city history is concerned with the establishment of peoples (ἔθνη). The Heneti of Paphlagonia reached Italy with Antenor from the Trojan war, bringing the art of horse-rearing with them (5. 1. 4).[72] Strabo gives no reference to a settlement, but the people had a history nevertheless. Their life in Italy could be traced back to the period of the Trojan war, and their changing fortunes were indicated by the contrast between their former fame (πρότερον) and their present obliteration (νῦν). They were even linked to the tyrant of a city, Dionysius of Syracuse, who bought horses from them. The Adriatic coast of Lucania had a history that can be divided into pre- and post-πόλις phases. Before the Greeks came, the area was inhabited by the Chones and the Oenotri, but this soon gave way to a city-history started by the Samnitae, who settled a colony (ἀποικία) of Lucani here (6. 1. 2).

Strabo's interest in ethnic history is indicated by his discussions of the various methods of defining peoples, and their development over time. There had been many tribes in Greece, but those that went back to the earliest times were only as numerous as the dialects. Strabo defines ἔθνη partly in linguistic terms, and he is careful to note that the present multiplicity of dialects cannot be assumed for earlier periods, revealing that the linguistic identity of a people could change over time. Ionic and Attic were essentially the same in origin; Doric and Aeolic were similarly identical at first (8. 1. 2). Changing urban landscapes had a non-πόλις equivalent in the ethnic map, with its constantly changing boundaries. The Apuli were now

---

[72] The story of Antenor's migration was also treated by Livy 1. 1. 2–3. See 13. 1. 53 for another reference to the stories of Antenor and Aeneas, in which Aeneas carried on westwards, leaving Antenor in the Adriatic, and also an alternative version, which denied the migration of Aeneas and asserted that he never left Troy.

no different from the Peucetii and the Daunii, but in antiquity they were separate (6. 3. 11). It is more difficult to reconstruct the vicissitudes and redefinitions of ἔθνη than those of cities, and the transitions are likely to be less easy to pinpoint to a particular moment, but changes did take place and it was Strabo's task to trace how the peoples, no less than cities, came to be in their present state.[73]

The regions of northern Europe were predictably more productive of non-πόλις history than were the urbanized areas of Italy. Strabo refers to the migration of the Mysi from Europe to Asia. Only a small group remained and changed their name to the Moesi (7. 3. 2–4).[74] The verb used is μετωνομάσθαι; the process is exactly what we find in the history of cities, and gives rise to the same kinds of confusion. But, in spite of this similarity, the history of the Mysi has a quite different tone from that of a city. We are informed not about moments of crisis in the past, but mainly about the customs of the people. Even Aelius Catus' transference of 50,000 Thracians across the Istros to join the Moesi lacks any reference to the vocabulary of colonization. The Thracians simply 'now live' (νῦν οἰκοῦσιν) there (7. 3. 10).

The ancient history of the Peloponnese provides some kind of counter-example (7. 7. 1). Strabo's description makes no reference to the creation of cities, but lists the various pre-Greek tribes which inhabited the area. He enumerates the peoples brought by the heroes, and says that, even in his day, most of Greece was held by barbarians. This interest in the development of and changes in the ethnic make-up of the world necessitated a non-πόλις history.[75] But we find, strikingly, that

[73] At 9. 5. 8 he states that 'the boundaries and organizations of tribes and places are always changing'.

[74] The idea that tribes, like cities, change name is reinforced at 7. 3. 12. The Daci were called Dai in the past (τὸ παλαιόν). This was the kind of temporal development appropriate to them. At 12. 3. 20 Strabo discusses many more changes in the names of tribes in Asia Minor, a phenomenon which occurs 'particularly among barbarians' (μάλιστα ἐν τοῖς βαρβάροις).

[75] The same type of ethnic history was attached to Armenus, Jason's companion, who appears several times in the *Geography*, such as at 11. 4. 8. Armenus and his followers settled in Armenia, which was named after him; 11. 14. 12; 11. 14. 13. For a fuller version of the story, see Justin, *Epitome of Pompeius Trogus*, 42. 2. 6– 3. 9.

the vocabulary of settlement and foundation, which was
applied to the cities, recurs in this most un-'political' context.
The whole of Greece was in antiquity, according to this
account, a settlement of barbarians (κατοικία βαρβαρῶν). Even
here, in the midst of the barbarian tribes, the vocabulary of the
πόλις breaks through.

Strabo argues strongly against those who believed that
writing the history of barbarian, or non-urbanized, peoples
was of minimal value. He says that there was little interest
shown by historians in the Scythians and Celtoscythians; nor
had much serious historical attention been paid to the ancient
affairs (τὰ παλαιά) of the Medes, Persians, or Syrians, because
of the prevalence of myths surrounding them (11. 6. 2). This
was a balance that Strabo was trying to redress in the Geography.[76] Strabo was interested not only in the history of cities
and peoples, but also in that of institutions, such as the
Olympic festival, which he discusses at length (8. 3. 30).[77]
The extensive accounts of various royal lines also fall within
the category of non-πόλις history. Strabo's history of Pergamum is a history of its rulers rather than of the place. It
launches straight into the question of the origin of the kings
and how they came to an end (13. 4. 1–2).[78] The account is
unusual for its degree of interest in the reigns of the successive
monarchs. Quite exceptionally, the length of each reign is given
in years, so that we get a complete, unbroken picture of the

[76] The Jews had a history which was not connected with urbanized life.
Strabo includes the story of Moses as an important prophet, rather than as the
founder of a nation. Jewish history for Strabo was not a story of migration and
foundation, but a moralizing tale of a good people turned bad. He sums up the
entire Exodus in three words—ἀπῆρεν ἐκεῖσε ἐνθένδε ('he went away from there
[Egypt] to there [Judaea]', 16. 2. 35), marking a radical change from the
foundation myths of the Hellenistic accounts of the Jews, and reinforcing the
view that the historiographical incompatibility of Hellenistic foundation
stories from the Fertile Crescent with those from the rest of the Hellenistic
world proved problematic in the attempt to write a universal geography.

[77] The extensive description of the development of the Achaean League falls
into the same category as the Olympic festival (8. 7. 1–3). The various occasions
on which it had proved a vital player in the politics of the Mediterranean, as
when it acted as arbitrator after the battle of Leuctra, are listed by Strabo.

[78] The kings of Egypt receive a similar treatment from the time of
Alexander's death to the battle of Actium and their full incorporation of the
region into the Roman domain (17. 1. 11).

Attalid dynasty, right up to the point at which Attalus
Philometor named the Roman people as heirs to his throne
and the region was turned into a province.

So, the past is integral to the *Geography* in various ways.
There is a sense in which the text itself takes place through time,
and has its own chronology and order. In addition, the text is set
in the context of a literary tradition which runs from the
Homeric epics to the present day and includes not only strictly
geographical works, but also any other genres which might
contribute to Strabo's project. Alongside this literary past, both
internal and external to the text, there is a real, historical past
which must be dealt with for two reasons: firstly, because the
world of the past is the world which underpins the tradition
continued by Strabo; and secondly, because Strabo was interested in seeing how different parts of the world had been
transformed through time. The transformation of the world is
most clearly seen in the life-cycle of cities, and these 'city-
biographies' dominate Strabo's account, giving us a parallel for
Posidonius' accounts of the animate universe and for Polybius'
history of the world, which he likened to a living creature. But
Strabo was writing about the whole known world, and,
although he structured the work through the cities, he also
recognized the importance of non-πόλις history. I think that
Strabo would have agreed with the sentiments expressed by the
modern geographer, Ogilvie: 'I feel that, just as with the
countryside, we cannot understand the cities as they are without
knowing the vicissitudes they have experienced in the past.'[79]

At the end of the second section of this chapter I suggested
that Strabo's methods for indicating past time revealed an
interest not in precise chronology, but in processes of change
and development in individual places. Having considered in
more detail what kinds of past are prominent in the *Geography*,
it is possible now to go further in understanding precisely why

---

[79] A. G. Ogilvie, 'The Time-Element in Geography', *TIBG* 18 (1952), 14.
See the comment of P. Pédech, 'La Géographie urbaine chez Strabon',
Ancient Society, 2 (1971), 251, that the history of a town in a geographical
treatise is not fully justified except if it explains its present state. Pédech's
opinion of Strabo's historical descriptions of settlements is extremely critical:
he complains that one would have preferred broadly developed treatments of
these towns to the boring listing of miserable villages and a number of
vanished settlements (p. 252).

so much information about the past was included in a work
explicitly focused on the present. The use of great events such
as the mythical dispersal of heroes or the much more recent
battle of Actium as markers of the past is mirrored by Strabo's
concentration on crucial moments of transformation in the life
of cities, from their foundation (often mythically based) up to
the present day. Even coverage is not the aim; rather Strabo
concentrates on the moments in history which have given the
place its identity. The notions discussed above (pp. 17–18) that
a sense of place only comes with time; that place is 'lived-in'
space, making human involvement necessary for the development of a place's identity; and that the passage of time is what
makes an inhabited space into a place, all reveal why the past
was crucial to Strabo in describing the world of his own day.
The world he wished to present was made up of inhabited
places, as he states explicitly, and what had made them into
places was their history. The stories told about the past were
precisely what gave a place its present identity. Cities and
permanent settlements had so much more to offer Strabo than
empty landscapes or nomadic peoples because they had a more
clearly structured social memory, a shared set of ideas about
what their place was like and how it had become so.

THE PRESENT IN THE *GEOGRAPHY*

I started this chapter with Strabo's striking profession that the
geographer should concentrate on the present. Strabo himself
offers a more nuanced description of the task than those which
I cited then. 'Whatever in ancient history escapes me I must
leave unmentioned, for the task of geography does not lie in
that area, and I must speak of things as they are now', as did
Defoe: 'If antiquity takes with you, though the looking back
into remote things is studiously avoided, yet it is not wholly
omitted, nor any useful observations neglected.'[80] Both Strabo
and Defoe saw the primary focus of their geographies as an
exposition of the present, but would not exclude the past where

---

[80] 12. 8. 7: ὅ τι δ' ἂν διαφύγῃ τῆς παλαιᾶς ἱστορίας, τοῦτο μὲν ἐατέον, οὐ γὰρ
ἐνταῦθα τὸ τῆς γεωγραφίας ἔργον, τὰ δὲ νῦν ὄντα λεκτέον; Defoe, *A Tour through
the Whole Island of Great Britain*, Preface, p. 43.

that could elucidate their theme. Furthermore, I hope to have shown the way in which Strabo's interest in the past may be reconciled with his intention to describe the world as it was in his day, since the present identity and perception of places consisted precisely in stories about the past. Just as Strabo constructed his spatial conceptions around the centrality of Rome, so too was the temporal aspect of his work determined by the Roman world of Strabo's day, and the past of the *Geography* may be seen as a reflection of the present.

But what kind of present does Strabo offer more explicitly to the reader? In the last chapter I tried to locate the work and its author in space, which proved difficult because of the multi-focal nature of the *Geography*: the world is described in such a way as to create a focus on Rome, but Strabo himself had a native attachment to the Pontic region, as well as an intellectual base in the Greek cities of Asia Minor. Locating the author and his work in time is no more straightforward.[81] The long-standing bio-graphical question of Strabo's dates centres on the problem that certain references in the *Geography* imply that he was born in the mid-6os BC, while others show that he must still have been alive and writing in the mid-2os AD, giving him a life-span long enough to cause concern for his biographers (17. 3. 7; 17. 3. 9).[82]

Looking for the temporal focus of the actual content of the *Geography* is problematic since it concerns different periods, and just as Strabo never explicitly sets out the spatial concep-tions underlying his work, nor does he state the temporal scope either of his own life, or of the composition of the *Geography*. But there are oblique signs of what the present means for him. Earlier in this chapter I considered temporal indicators used by Strabo to structure the past of the places he describes. Here I extend this to the phrases used of his own time. Were these any more specific than those applied to the distant past? Could they help to determine a temporal standpoint for either Strabo

---

[81] See K. Clarke, 'In Search of the Author of Strabo's *Geography*', *JRS* 87 (1997), 102–5.

[82] The inclusion of the death of Juba II of Mauretania shows that Strabo must have been alive at least until AD 23; the earlier chronological limit is more problematic, but hinges on Strabo's statement at 12. 6. 2, that he saw P. Servilius Vatia Isauricus, who died in Rome in 44 BC, making a birth-date for Strabo in the late-6os BC likely.

himself or the work's composition? I shall also look briefly at some of the historical events of Strabo's lifetime which are mentioned in the *Geography*, to see if these reveal any particular focus of interest.

Firstly, the apparently specific phrase 'shortly before us' (μικρὸν πρὸ ἡμῶν) is used twice to refer to other intellectuals, which immediately detracts from its possibilities for precision, since any part, but not the whole, of their lifetime could be meant.[83] The two people concerned are Apollonius of Tyre, 'who published a chart of the philosophers of the school of Zeno and of their books', and Antiochus of Ascalon, 'the philosopher, who was born shortly before our time' (16. 2. 24; 16. 2. 29). There is some danger of circularity in using the lives of intellectuals in order to determine what is meant by a phrase in Strabo, since such figures seem to have been dated themselves on the basis of dates assumed for Strabo.

The other three uses of the phrase are more specific, but still problematic. The settlement of pirates by Pompey at Dyme, the rule of Paphlagonia by several people before the Romans, and the rule over Mauretania by kings of the house of Bogos and Bocchus before Augustus gave the land to Juba—all happened 'shortly before us' (8. 7. 5; 12. 3. 41; 17. 3. 7). So this phrase places the author firstly after 67 BC; then either in 63/2 BC, when Pompey added the coastal part of Paphlagonia to Pontus and Bithynia, or in 6 BC, when inland Paphlagonia was added to the province of Galatia. The rearrangement of 63/2 BC is clearly more likely to be the event alluded to, and confirms the implications of the passage concerning Dyme. But the transition of Mauretania to the rule of Juba, chronologically problematic in itself, takes us to the period around 30 BC, which is incompatible with the fact that the author of the *Geography* accompanied Aelius Gallus on his Egyptian visit around this time, presumably as an adult.[84] So the phrase 'shortly before us' (μικρὸν πρὸ ἡμῶν) allows us to draw no precise conclusions about Strabo's present.

---

[83] As Chris Pelling has suggested to me, the use of various forms of ἡμεῖς in phrases such as this may be intended to embrace the audience as well as the author, rendering hopeless any detailed argument about Strabo's biography based on them.

[84] See N. K. Mackie, 'Augustan Colonies in Mauretania', *Historia*, 32 (1983), 332–58.

'In our fathers' time' (ἐπὶ τῶν πατέρων τῶν ἡμετέρων and ἐπὶ τῶν ἡμετέρων πατέρων) is also used vaguely. Laodiceia was large in the time of the author's father (12. 8. 16); the Erasistratean school of medicine was established then (12. 8. 20); and Menippus Catocas, according to Cicero the best orator in Asia, was born in this period (14. 2. 25). Even if we could be certain of any of these dates independently, the fact that they would fall within the span of a whole generation could not possibly allow them to be used in arguments over temporal focus.

At the other end of the chronological spectrum, 'recently' (νεωστί) proves to be just as unhelpful. It is applied to Sextus Pompey's activities on Sicily in the mid-30s BC, the burning-down of the temple of Ceres in Rome (31 BC), Octavian's settlement of troops at Patrai (c.30 BC), and Aelius Gallus' expedition of 25/4 BC (6. 1. 6; 8. 6. 23; 8. 7. 5; 16. 4. 22). However, Tiberius' help to the earthquake cities such as Sardis, the appointment of Zenon as king of Greater Armenia (AD 18), and the death of Juba II of Mauretania (AD 23) are also 'recent' (13. 4. 8; 12. 3. 29; 17. 3. 7). If νεωστί covers a span of around sixty years, it can scarcely be an accurate guide to the author's biography.

But the issue of what counts as recent does raise the question of the date when the *Geography* was written. No small amount of effort has been put into devising timetables for its composition. Pais, most influentially, suggested that the *Geography* was started soon after the *History* and completed by 7 BC, but was then reworked following the arrival of Germanicus in the East and the subsequent reduction of Cappadocia and Commagene to Roman provinces. He also saw the death of Augustus as a stimulus for the revision of the work. 'With the succession of Tiberius the new political form which had been created by C. Caesar was permanently established.' Pais supported his view of the method of composition by pointing out that only a small proportion of the historical allusions in the work refers to events after 7 BC, and that the later references concern mainly the eastern provinces and are clustered around the years AD 17 and 18.[85]

---

[85] E. Pais, *Ancient Italy*, (trans. C. D. Curtis) (Chicago, 1908), 407. Pais never states what he envisaged happening to the work between 7 BC and the

But Diller favours the view that Strabo's *Geography* was unfinished at the time of his death.[86] This provides an explanation for the various disjunctions in the text, as being the result of inaccurately inserted marginalia, which Strabo did not live long enough to work into the text himself. While I am not convinced by this picture of Strabo's practice of composition, it is in Diller's favour that his study reveals the futility of identifying different phases of writing, rewriting, and emendation. In any case, late references (for which see pp. 288–9) are not confined to a sudden last-minute interest in Asia Minor (Pais's picture), nor do they appear to be the result of hasty or unpolished emendations. Rather, they concern all three continents described in the *Geography*, covering a wide range of topics, both military and political, and are integral to the work as it stands.

The enormous time-span to which an apparently restricted phrase such as 'recently' is applied in the *Geography* suggests various possibilities concerning both the method of composition and the author's self-presentation. In terms of composition, the fact that a span of sixty years could be seen as recent suggests a process of accumulation of data and writing which was gradual and long-lasting. Or, even if the work was finally put together in a relatively short period, the author speaks *as though* events from the whole of the mid-first century BC onwards formed the backdrop to his composition, and I shall discuss this further in chapter VI.

The first century BC and early first century AD must be considered Strabo's 'present', but what dominated his view of this age, and to what extent did it complement and continue his interests in the 'past', as discussed in the previous section? I have already mentioned the ambivalence of Strabo's attitude to the transformation of the Greek East by Roman generals, such as Lucullus and Pompey, during the second quarter of the first century BC. The final suppression of piracy and brigandage was bound up with the defeat of the Mithridatic dynasty with which Strabo's family was closely connected; given this link

revised version of AD 17/18. Was it published, and then republished, or stored unread for a quarter of a century?

[86] A. Diller, *The Textual Tradition of Strabo's Geography* (Amsterdam, 1975), 6.

and Strabo's own involvement in the cultural and political life of Asia Minor, it would be remarkable if he showed no interest in the events which changed his world.

Less close to home is the figure of Julius Caesar, who links the period of Pompey's predominance and the time of the second triumvirate, which led to Actium and the birth of the principate. He is mentioned as having defeated the generals of Pompey at Ilerda, and for his struggle against Sextus Pompey (3. 4. 10). By no means as prominent as Pompey in the *Geography*, nevertheless he appears unsurprisingly in the description of Gaul and Britain, and for his wars against the Veneti and the Salassi.[87] Caesar is, however, not confined to the descriptions of the West. He appears as the restorer of treasures to Corinth, looted by Lucullus, and as Sulla's successor in the restoration of Ilium following its destruction by Fimbria (8. 6. 23; 13. 1. 27). Strabo notes that Caesar's assistance was far greater than that given by Sulla. Thus Caesar appears in a very positive light, righting the wrongs of a previous generation of Romans.[88] We shall see later how Augustus too was given this role.

As I have discussed earlier, one of the crucial chronological markers used by Strabo was the battle of Actium.[89] Not only the defeat of Antonius, but also the celebrations of Octavian and his foundation of the victory city of Nicopolis, feature in the text. The references to Sextus Pompey naturally focus on his Sicilian exploits of the mid-30s BC (5. 4. 4; 6. 1. 6; 6. 2. 4). However, we also hear about the consequences of that war for the character of Sicily in the aftermath. Octavian repopulated the city of Rhegium with an expeditionary force, after ejecting Sextus Pompey from the island (6. 1. 6). He also restored Syracuse, which had been damaged by Pompey, and rewarded parts of Ortygia with assistance for their part in overthrowing

---

[87] For the Veneti 4. 4. 1; the Salassi 4. 6. 7. Strabo here mentions the foundation of Augusta Praetoria in 24 BC to mark the final subjugation of this tribe.

[88] His assassination is deplored at 14. 1. 37. As F. Lasserre, 'Strabon devant l'Empire romain', *ANRW* II 30.1, 874, points out, the use of the same verb for the death of Pompey as for that of Caesar (δολοφονεῖν: 'murder by treachery') is particularly striking.

[89] See above, pp. 254–5, for the use of this landmark in the history of the Roman empire as a means of anchoring other events in time.

Pompey (6. 2. 4). Here we see Octavian beginning to take on the role that Caesar had played, that of putting right the injustices enacted by earlier Romans.

This comes out most clearly with regard to Antonius. Strabo mentions a statue of Aias, which Antonius had carried off from Rhoeteium to Egypt, and which Augustus later returned to its rightful owners. He takes the opportunity to remark that this was the standard pattern: that Antonius 'took away the finest dedications from the most famous sacred places to please the Egyptian woman; but Augustus gave them back to the gods' (13. 1. 30).[90] Given the negative picture that Strabo creates for Antonius, it is worth noting that Antonius actually appears in the work roughly as often as the much more positively portrayed Julius Caesar. His contacts with the Parthians and betrayal by Artavasdes (11. 13. 3; 11. 14. 9; 11. 14. 15; 16. 1. 28), the support he enjoyed from Cleon until Cleon's defection to Octavian (12. 8. 9), his promotion of Polemon I (12. 8. 16), his various dispositions of land (14. 5. 3; 14. 5. 10), and the story of his defeat (17. 1. 9–10) all receive some degree of coverage. As with events in Asia Minor in the 60s, Strabo's concern here too seems to be with periods of geographical transformation.

The important point about Actium was its significance for the changing face of the world. In removing the final obstacle to one-man rule, the battle had serious spatial consequences. No longer would the world be divided into the spheres of influence of the triumvirs, however flexible these might have been.[91] Strabo himself makes clear the advantage of having a single ruler in charge of the empire, claiming that 'it would be difficult to govern such an empire in any other way than by entrusting it to one man, as to a father' (6. 4. 2).[92]

<hr />

[90] See 14. 1. 14 for an example of this process. A more unusual instance is the case of the asylum at Ephesus, which Antonius enlarged to include part of the city. This was reversed by Augustus, since it had resulted in the city falling into criminal hands (14. 1. 23).

[91] The extent to which the triumvirs were actually restricted to their respective areas of command has been seriously challenged by the triumviral documents from Aphrodisias. See the edition of the documents by J. Reynolds, *Aphrodisias and Rome* (London, 1982), which include letters from Octavian to cities in Antonius' sphere of influence, such as Plarasa, and a decree issued jointly by Antonius and Octavian to cities of the Greek East.

[92] Note the clear reference to Augustus' adoption of the title *pater patriae* in

So, the events surrounding Pompey and Lucullus in the East
and the consequences of Actium were important to Strabo not
because they were specifically linked to his spatial or temporal
viewpoint, indicating when or where he wrote, but because
they had severe implications for the transformation of the
world. At the other extreme of Strabo's life-span, the *Geography* contains a large number of references to Tiberius and
events associated with him, especially for a work which some
argue was only emended after 7/6 BC.[93] Indeed the *Suda*
associated Strabo with the reign of Tiberius rather than
Augustus, noting that 'he lived under Tiberius Caesar' (γέγονεν
ἐπὶ Τιβερίου Καίσαρος).[94] In the description of Cantabria, Strabo
says that Tiberius, Augustus' successor, had sent three legions
to the region; Tiberius' continuation of Augustus' assistance
for earthquake-hit cities in Asia Minor receives attention, as
does his decree, in conjunction with the Senate, proclaiming
Cappadocia a Roman province after the death of Archelaus
(3. 3. 8; 12. 8. 18; 12. 1. 4). Most striking of all is the
description of Rome's evolution as a world power whose
empire needs one man at the helm. Tiberius appears at the
end of this as the successor of Augustus, making him his
model, and assisted by his children, Germanicus and Drusus
(6. 4. 2).[95] The passage must have been written between
Tiberius' accession in AD 14 and the death of Germanicus in
19, as the use of the present tense (παρέχει) confirms.

The main region which was undergoing Roman attempts at
transformation towards the end of Strabo's life was northern

2 BC, although by the time of writing, Tiberius had succeeded to the
principate.

[93] Pais, *Ancient Italy*, argues this point at 380–406.

[94] *FGrH* 91 T 1. In direct contradiction, Pais, *Ancient Italy*, 380–1, states
categorically: 'The question as to whether the *Geography* of Strabo is a
product of the age of Tiberius and written between 18 and 19 A. D. should
be answered with a decided "No"!'.

[95] A contrast must be drawn between this passage and the parallel one at
17. 3. 25, in which Tiberius is not mentioned. Nor, however, is it asserted that
Augustus was still in power at the time of writing. We are told simply that the
provinces were 'at the present time as Augustus Caesar arranged them' (ἐν δὲ
τῷ παρόντι, ὡς Καῖσαρ ὁ Σεβαστὸς διέταξεν). This, if anything, implies that
Augustus was by now dead, thus making it noteworthy that the provincial
arrangements had not been altered by his successor.

Europe, and Germany in particular. Strabo mentions several
German campaigns, and denotes some of them as happening
'now'.[96] This does not help in determining the date of writing,
since it is not always clear to which of the campaigns he is
referring, that of Nero Drusus, or of Varus, or of Germanicus.
But as far as the date of composition is concerned, it seems
impossible to conceive of the German description without
these late references. Only four chapters are devoted to the
area, but all except one deals with the Roman campaigns.[97] The
first, in which the death of Nero Drusus appears, could fit with
a completion date for the work of 7/6 BC, but by far the most
extensive German narrative concerns the Varian disaster and a
lengthy description of Germanicus' triumph. Without this, the
whole force of the description of Germany would be lost, as
Strabo is making the point here that the German tribes have
only become known to the Romans through a protracted series
of wars (7. 1. 4).

So, we have a range of references to Strabo's own lifetime
which does not privilege any particular period, but is concerned precisely with the subject of his work, namely, the
transformation of the world into its present state. There is no
bias which might indicate the time of writing or elucidate
biographical details, but this is in perfect accord with the
vague use of temporal phrases so far discussed. Strabo's
Geography is a work reflecting the preoccupations of his
whole life-span, when the world was being altered beyond
recognition.

I have considered how phrases such as 'recently' ($\nu\epsilon\omega\sigma\tau\ell$) and
'shortly before us' ($\mu\iota\kappa\rho\grave{o}\nu$ $\pi\rho\grave{o}$ $\dot{\eta}\mu\hat{\omega}\nu$) refer in the *Geography* to
such wide time-scales as to be useless for the purpose of
determining the author's biography. I turn finally to the
phrases meaning 'in our time'—$\dot{\epsilon}\phi$' $\dot{\eta}\mu\hat{\omega}\nu$ and $\kappa\alpha\theta$' $\dot{\eta}\mu\hat{\alpha}\varsigma$—in
the belief that this will provide the clue as to how references

---

[96] At 7. 1. 3 he relates the victory over the Bructeri on the river Amasias,
and the death of Drusus between the Salas and the Rhine. At 7. 1. 4 he
mentions the disaster that befell Quintilius Varus in AD 9, followed by the
triumph celebrated by Germanicus in May AD 17, after he had defeated the
Cherusci and other tribes.
[97] The exception is 7. 1. 2, which gives details of physique and lifestyle; and
discusses the names Galatae and Germani.

to the present might help our understanding of the *Geography*.
No particular significance seems to be attached to the former.
It is used mainly of political events. The earliest datable event
described by this phrase is C. Antonius' foundation of a city in
Cephallenia. The foundation cannot be dated exactly, but must
have fallen between the year of his exile from Rome after his
consulship with Cicero in 63 BC, and the year of his return, 44
BC (10. 2. 13).[98] The latest event to bear this description is
probably Aelius Catus' transference of some of the Getae into
Thrace from the other side of the Istros (7. 3. 10).[99] Between
these two poles, and all described as ἐφ' ἡμῶν, are Sextus
Pompey's abuse of Syracuse and the rest of Sicily in the
mid-30s BC (6. 2. 4), the foundation of Nicopolis in 29 BC
(10. 2. 2), and Aelius Gallus' Arabian expedition of 25/4 BC
(16. 4. 22). Other applications of the phrase are not to events,
but to ongoing states of affairs, which makes it hard to assign
any particular date to ἐφ' ἡμῶν.[100] So, this phrase includes
anything from the early/mid-40s BC to the later years of
Augustus' reign, making our author a product of the late-
Republic/early principate.

Like ἐφ' ἡμῶν, καθ' ἡμᾶς also gives some idea of events which
fall within Strabo's lifetime, such as the looting of the temple of
Leucothea by Pharnaces (died 47 BC) (11. 2. 17), Julius
Caesar's assistance in the restoration of Ilium after the attempts
of Sulla (13. 1. 27), the rule of King Auletes of Egypt (died 51
BC) (17. 1. 11), and the possession of Siga by Juba I (d. c.46 BC)
(17. 3. 9). All of this suggests that Strabo was alive by the late
40s BC. A few events denoted καθ' ἡμᾶς cluster around the time
of Actium, reinforcing the importance of this event in Strabo's
view of the world: C. Iulius Eurycles, ruler of the Lacedae-
monians καθ' ἡμᾶς, who won this kingdom (as well as Roman
citizenship) after fighting alongside Octavian at Actium (8. 5. 1);

[98] We are told that C. Antonius had not yet completed the synoecism by
the time he was given permission to return, so the foundation was presumably
started not long before that date.

[99] I cannot put a date to this event, but given that Catus was consul in AD 4,
this action is likely at least to postdate the expedition of Aelius Gallus.

[100] Amyntas' control of Derbe and the two Isaurae (12. 6. 3); revolts in
Babylonia (15. 3. 12); and the large size of Laodiceia (12. 8. 16) are all ἐφ' ἡμῶν,
but this does not help greatly in the attempt to pin down a temporal viewpoint
for the author.

the career of Cleon, chief brigand in the mountains of the Troad, whose main anti-Roman activity took place before Actium (12. 8. 8); the establishment of Tarcondimotus as king of the Mount Amanus region (d. 31 BC) (14. 5. 18)—all form part of this group.

But, as I have already mentioned (pp. 242–3), Strabo uses καθ᾽ ἡμᾶς most commonly to refer to the contemporary intellectual life of Asia Minor. If we attempt to put dates to the period of which the phrase was used, we come across the same problems as I identified for the authors who were 'shortly before us', namely, that Strabo might have been referring to any part of whole life-spans. More helpful, and precisely parallel to the way in which Strabo structures the history of cities, are the occasions when he lists famous people in chronological order, leading up to his own day, and breaks into the list to indicate the point at which his contemporaries appear. Tarsus produced Athenodorus, the tutor of Augustus and elevated by Antonius because of a favourable poem he wrote for the victory at Philippi. Strabo then goes on to say that a product of Tarsus 'in his time' was the teacher of Marcellus (14. 5. 14). In other words, the period at which Octavian was being educated does not fall into Strabo's lifetime, unlike the time when the next (or next-but-one) generation was being tutored.

But the curious fact that Strabo describes Posidonius as being καθ᾽ ἡμᾶς should encourage us to abandon the notion that temporal indicators in Strabo can be read as a means to determine precise dates (16. 2. 10).[101] The generally accepted dates for Posidonius are c.135–51/0 BC, but this seems to overlap hardly at all with the possible dates for Strabo, who must have lived until at least the 20s AD, if he wrote the entire work as we have it. This alone should warn us against reading

---

[101] Diller, *Textual Tradition*, 9 dismisses as chronologically impossible the statement at Athen. 14. 657 that Strabo said in Book 7 that he knew Posidonius. I agree with the conclusion, but it does seem strange that two separate pieces of passages suggest contemporaneity, unless Athenaeus was mistaken about the book number, and was referring to the Book 16 passage. In any case, Athenaeus is not casual with the chronological information brought by this remark, but notes that the implication of Strabo knowing Posidonius would be that he was not a very recent authority (ἀνὴρ οὐ πάνυ νεώτερος).

phrases such as 'shortly before us' ($\mu\iota\kappa\rho\grave{o}\nu$ $\pi\rho\grave{o}$ $\mathring{\eta}\mu\hat{\omega}\nu$) and 'in our time' ($\kappa\alpha\theta$' $\mathring{\eta}\mu\hat{\alpha}\varsigma$) with the expectation that they will enable us to determine Strabo's dates, or the time of composition. Rather, they have the effect of creating the impression of a particular intellectual and cultural setting. By describing, say, a historian as $\kappa\alpha\theta$' $\mathring{\eta}\mu\hat{\alpha}\varsigma$, Strabo was not indicating a set of dates, but inserting the historian into his own intellectual milieu, and assigning him an influential role in the development of his own outlook and ideas.

Strabo's present is defined no more precisely than the past which leads to it. The temporal indicators are just as vague, and no clear conclusions emerge from the emphasis placed on certain historical episodes of Strabo's lifetime. The Mithridatic wars, Roman intervention in the East, the events surrounding Actium, and recent activity in Germany all receive a fair amount of attention.

The fact that both past and present appear in the *Geography* qualifies the 'space : time' model of geography and history, and the 'past : present' model. As I have shown, the present identity of places is made up from traditions about the past, denying any strict temporal definition. Such stories could be evoked by aspects of present-day life in the form of religious cult, or physical features of the land- or cityscape.[102] I argued in chapter IV that Strabo was interested in place rather than space, but time is precisely what transforms space into place, and so is an essential ingredient in the *Geography*. Neither past nor present in the *Geography* is set within a coherent time-system. The past is expressed in a whole range of ways; the present is vaguely conceived in chronological terms. However, the patchy, sometimes disorganized histories, which Strabo provides for various places, perfectly reflect the way in which memory and identity work. Just as the whole of the past from the foundation onwards is included in Strabo's descriptions of places, so too is the whole of his own life incorporated in his

---

[102] Camassa, 'Problemi storico-religiosi', 205, notes Strabo's interest in the fact that people would converge on the site of a dead city to perpetuate the rituals associated with the place; at 3. 2. 13 Strabo mentions that there were still traces of the wanderings of Trojan heroes in Iberia. This aspect of Strabo's work makes places into true *monumenta* of the past.

VI

Strabo's Universalism: Geography, History, Rewriting the Roman World

UNITING TIME AND SPACE

In the two preceding chapters I considered Strabo's use of time
and space as two separate matrices. However, as I discussed in
chapter I, such divisions and even the very notions of absolute
entities of time and space are contentious, and both chapters IV
and V exemplify this point. Strabo's concepts and applications
of time and space added up to a single work in which the world
was described, as it existed, against both matrices simultaneously. In this chapter I wish to reunite them and to examine
Strabo's notion of γεωγραφία (geography) as a phenomenon
that confounds the categories of geography and history, and of
time and space. I argue also that Strabo's geographical project
was a fitting product of *his* specific location in time and space.
Firstly, however, I begin the reunion by showing how Strabo's
text reveals the mutually influential nature of geographical and
historical processes; the progress of time affects space, and the
space of the world influences the course of history.

Geography and history: mutual influences
I have already mentioned Strabo's concern with the changing
world, and the problems posed to one following in a literary
tradition that was continually becoming obsolete. But in
addition to the continual evolution of the world under the
progress of time, some phases of history were dominated by
rulers who deliberately altered the appearance of the world by
their manipulation of subject peoples, of whole cities and of
their names. The Romans were such. Aelius Catus moved the
Lusitanians from one side of the river Tagus to the other and
50,000 Getae from the far side of the Istros to Thrace (3. 1. 6;
7. 3. 10). Hipponium in South Italy was renamed Vibo

definition of the present. But within this, his focus in both the past and his present is on periods of geographical change. This accords with the whole framework of the *Geography*, namely, the tradition from Homer to the present day, a framework which itself raises the problem of a changing world, but also again mirrors the way in which the memory of the individual's life and that of the life of a settlement tend to be focused on certain key moments of change.

So the present in the *Geography* acts as a microcosm for the history of the world. Firstly, the description of the world 'as it is now' necessarily involves relating the history of its settlements from their initial foundation onwards, thus allowing the present identity of places to encapsulate their past. However, there is also a sense in which the life of the author, which defines the present in the *Geography*, forms a parallel for the life of the places described in the work. Strabo's 'present' includes his whole life-span, but within that, certain moments of change predominate; so also his biographies of cities and settlements span their entire 'lives', giving us the scope of the past, but within that framework their 'lives', like that of Strabo himself, are structured by periods of transformation. Just as the present identity of a place is made up from memories about its past, so too is Strabo's perspective at the time of writing informed by important memories and events from his entire lifetime. It is to the project as a whole which resulted from that perspective that I now turn.

Valentia and Mithridates' city of Eupatoria was transformed by
Pompey into his own city of Magnopolis (6. 1. 5; 12. 3. 30). If
any justification for this kind of renaming were needed, it is
given by Strabo for Pompey, since Mithridates' city was only
half-finished. Strabo was also fully aware of the linguistic blow
to native culture inflicted by imperialist powers. In his assessment of the Troad, he notes that under Roman rule most of the
people had already lost both their dialects and their names.[1]
The placing of colonies was another way in which Rome
altered the geographical layout of the world. A city which
undergoes all these methods of manipulation is Zelis in Mauretania. It was physically moved to the opposite Iberian coast,
augmented by Roman colonists and renamed Iulia Ioza,
exemplifying precisely the kind of transformation of the landscape through time discussed in chapter V (3. 1. 8).

The opposite process was the power exerted by spaces and
places upon both the progress of history and the process of
historiography. Strabo's belief in the influence of natural
conditions over man's behaviour is to be seen in his description
of the climatic zones of Libya. The Mediterranean coast
offered prosperity, the Atlantic coast a mediocre existence,
and the interior was inhospitable and supported only a
wretched lifestyle, a division which recalls Posidonius' ethnographical zones (2. 5. 33). I discussed in chapters I and IV the
importance of environmental determinism in the Hippocratic
writings and in Herodotus' *Histories*, and indicated that the
hegemonic implications in those authors were rather differently
nuanced from those which we find in Strabo and his near-
contemporary, Vitruvius. In the former texts, fine surroundings led to soft inhabitants and an inability to rule. Vitruvius,
however, explained Rome's rise to power partly in terms of its
privileged and central geographical position which naturally
predisposed it to hegemony.[2] Strabo echoes this sentiment as
regards Italy when he sums up the reasons for the Romans'
present success. Italy, surrounded by sea and mountains, was
like an island with only a few large harbours, offering little
opportunity for attack, but providing every facility for

[1] 12. 4. 6: ἤδη καὶ τὰς διαλέκτους καὶ τὰ ὀνόματα ἀποβεβλήκασιν οἱ πλεῖστοι.
[2] Vitruvius, *De architectura*, 6. 1. 10–11.

commerce.[3] Its varied and temperate climate made the country virtually self-sufficient. It had lakes, the Apennine mountains, rivers, healing springs, and mineral wealth (6. 4. 1).

All of these factors were supplemented by its position with regard to other races. It lay between the largest races (Iberians, Celts, and Germans) to the west and north, Greece to the east, and Libya to the south. Since it was stronger than these races it could exploit their great resources to help itself.[4] Here it is enough to point out that, according to Strabo's analysis, this central geographical location was what made Rome both prone to hegemony over its neighbours and able to exploit their resources.[5] Strabo keeps distinct these two processes, but both were made possible by virtue of Italy's geography. Italy was, however, not the only place to be geographically predisposed to hegemony. Greece had been drawn to leadership not only by the splendour and power of the tribes who lived there, but also by 'the very topography' of the land with its gulfs, capes, and most significantly the large peninsulas such as the Peloponnese (8. 1. 3).

All of this is highly reminiscent of the rhetorical tradition of praising cities and countries, which I mentioned briefly in chapter I. Menander sets out the rules for how to praise a country which involve both its position in relation to land, sea, and sky, and its nature in terms of terrain. For each of these Menander advises that attention be paid to both pleasure and utility. Although Menander's business is naturally to find ways of praising even the most unpromising subject, his list of geographical locations (east, west, south, and north) culminates

---

[3] E. Gabba, 'True History and False History in Classical Antiquity', *JRS* 71 (1981), 55–60, discusses the utopian nature of islands, particularly as the location for a ruling power.

[4] See above, pp. 219–23, for the theme of Rome's function as a drain on the resources of the empire. The whole passage acts as a counter-example to my assertion that Strabo was not concerned with space and relative position. But, in a sense, Strabo *did* have a good idea of how he thought the world as a whole could be conceptualized. What he lacked was any great interest in spatial concepts in between that of the individual place, and that of the whole world.

[5] 6. 4. 1 for the description of Italy: ἐν μέσῳ δὲ . . . οὖσα . . . τῷ μὲν κρατιστεύειν ἐν ἀρετῇ τε καὶ μεγέθει . . . πρὸς ἡγεμονίαν εὐφυῶς ἔχει ('being in the middle . . . and through its superiority in courage and size . . . it is naturally suited to hegemony').

with the most perfect position of all, that of the centre. For a country in this position the orator may claim that 'the whole earth revolves around it, and it is temperate in climate'.[6] When it comes to praising cities, the same issue of location is raised, and the city's position in relation to 'the mainland, the sea, the country in which the city lies, adjacent countries and cities, to mountains and plains' is scrutinized (Men. *Treatise*, 1. 347).

It is clear from this how close Strabo's account of Rome and Italy is to the rhetorical tradition, whose later stages we see in Menander. There are, indeed, many examples of such encomia in literature from the period when Strabo was writing, and it is no surprise to find that these too concern the geographical advantages and blessings of the now firmly established world power.[7] Dionysius of Halicarnassus, in his account of Roman history, devotes two chapters to a description of Italy as the supremely blessed land of Saturn.

In my opinion, the best country not only of Europe, but even of the whole of the rest of the world, is Italy . . . I consider that country the best which is most self-sufficient and generally least in need of imported goods . . . And I believe that Italy possesses this universal fertility and diversity of advantage more than any other land. (*AR* 1. 36)

He goes on, like Strabo, to outline the enormous variety of resources which are found in Italy and which mean that 'it is overflowing with everything both pleasurable and useful', praise which precisely coincides with the two categories of pleasure and utility mentioned by Menander. Dionysius' eulogy culminates with the theme of Italy's temperate climate. 'The finest thing of all is the climate, moderately tempered by the seasons, so that least of anywhere is harm done by extremes of cold or excessive heat to the production of fruits or to the growth of living creatures' (*AR* 1. 37).

The close parallels between Dionysius and Strabo suggest that there was a firmly established tradition for what was appropriate in such encomia. The strength of this tradition is

---

[6] Men. *Treatise*, 1. 345: περὶ αὐτὴν ἡ πᾶσα γῆ κυκλεῖται, καὶ ὥραις ἐστὶν εὔκρατος. It is interesting that Menander picks Greece and Attica, not Rome and Italy, as his example of a region to which this may be applied.

[7] See, for example, Virgil, *Georgics*, 2. 136–76.

particularly evident from the fact that some elements of
Strabo's set piece on Italy seem to contradict the broader
picture which emerges from his work as a whole. It is hard
to reconcile the self-sufficiency of Italy with the flood of
resources towards the centre of power, unless we choose to
argue that Rome and Italy attracted and demanded resources
regardless of the fact that these were superfluous to requirements. We know, in any case, that many of the themes, such as
the avoidance of extremes, which characterize eulogies of Rome
and Italy, had their origins much further back in the thought of
the early Ionian philosophers, the Hippocratic writers, and
Herodotus. The flexibility of such topoi and their varied
deployment for different purposes is clear. The climatologically privileged temperate zone is a movable feature, shifted by
the writers of Strabo's time from Ionia to the centre of power
in Italy, providing, in the same way as Strabo's manipulation of
the periplus tradition, an interesting example of how yet
another strand of the literary tradition could be appropriated
and adapted to suit the altered geographical circumstances of a
new phase in history.

Yet it was not enough for Rome simply to be located in the
most privileged part of the world, since natural advantage must
be combined with human endeavour in order for total success
to be achieved. According to Ephorus, Boeotia was 'naturally
suited to hegemony', but only succeeded in this when its
leaders undertook proper training and education (Str. 9. 2. 2).
The Turdetanians had a country which was 'marvellously
blessed', fertile and with an excellent river network for communications and trade. Yet it was the peoples' initiative in
gaining a good knowledge of the region that enabled them fully
to exploit the natural benefits (3. 2. 4– 5).[8] The Albanians, by
contrast, lived in a land where the earth poured out produce for
the people, without need for toil or 'forethought for war,
government, or farming'.[9] This might seem an ideal situation,
but if we compare it with Strabo's description of Rome we find
that the Albanians lacked all the qualities which made Rome

---

[8] The people of Egypt had mastered the art of controlling nature by hard
work to their own advantage. At 17. 1. 3 Strabo describes how their control of
the Nile went so far as to conquer nature—νικᾶν τὴν φύσιν.

[9] 11. 4. 3–4: πολέμου δὲ καὶ πολιτείας καὶ γεωργίας ἀπρονοήτως ἔχουσιν.

great. It was by valour and toil that the Romans succeeded and the imperfect natural attributes of the city were more than compensated for by its rulers' forethought (πρόνοια) (5. 3. 7– 8). There was a tension between the need for Rome to be seen to have natural strength as geographical determinism demanded, and the need for its inhabitants to be in the position of having to develop their own initiative, avoiding the idleness of the Albanians, who would be ill-suited to responsibility and government.[10]

So the *Geography* provides plenty of examples of how time and space affected each other in the Roman world which Strabo described. But there is another issue, which I discussed in relation to Polybius and Diodorus, namely, how to represent the spatial and temporal aspects of the world in an ordered literary production. I turn now to these literary questions: which periods of history Strabo does privilege in his work, and in particular do spatial considerations determine his choice? How does Strabo deal with representing in a single description the spatial and temporal scopes of the world? Does he allow space precedence over time, so perhaps giving us a means of distinguishing the work from one of universal history?

Temporal and regional variations: juggling time and space

The earliest period is represented not only in the huge wealth of foundation-stories, but also in the many places which are identified as the setting of mythical episodes. Mount Messapius was the scene of the myth of Glaucus, the Anthedonian, who turned into a sea-monster (9. 2. 13); Daulis was famous for the

---

[10] Another obvious problem with a strict theory of environmental determinism was that barbarian peoples must be portrayed as amenable to modification by their future conquerors. The whole question of assimilating potential subjects to the ideals of the conquering nation was not confined to antiquity. L. Bell, 'Artists and Empire: Victorian Representations of Subject People', *Art History*, 5 (1982), 73–86, discusses how this process was applied to visual images of their subjects propagated by British imperialists. The way in which the Roman empire tended to incorporate and absorb peoples, rather than simply to rule over them, made the representation of these peoples as 'not *too* barbarian' all the more imperative. F. Driver, 'Geography's Empire: Histories of Geographical Knowledge', *Environment and Planning D: Society and Space*, 10 (1992), 23–40, points out the pernicious use of environmental determinism to support imperialism by 'innately superior' races.

story of Philomela and Procne (9. 3. 13); the Cappadocian city of Comana was so-called because of its link with Iphigeneia and Orestes, and the lock of hair used in mourning (12. 2. 3).

From the eighth century, we have discussion of Lycurgus, the Bacchiad oligarchy in Corinth, the Lelantine war, and the foundation of Taras (10. 4. 18; 8. 6. 20; 10. 1. 12; 6. 3. 2).[11] The seventh century, except for references to the foundation of Cyrene and to the Cypselid tyranny at Corinth, is largely ignored, as is sixth-century history (17. 3. 21; 8. 6. 20).[12] We might have expected, for example, that Strabo's history of Athens would mention Solon or Cleisthenes, given not only their importance for later Athenian history, but also their specific associations with land reform, and the geographical organization of Attica. However, we hear of only the Peisistratid tyranny from this period. Strabo's history of Athens is predominantly one of a changing constitution: after the synoecism by Theseus, Athens was ruled by kings; next came democracy; then the Peisistratid tyranny; then oligarchy; then back to democracy, broken only twice before the Roman conquest, first by a short time of highly praised Macedonian rule under Cassander, second by the temporary tyranny of Aristion at the time of the Mithridatic war, until Sulla's intervention (9. 1. 20).

The fifth century was more important for Strabo than any other period since the Trojan war and the associated migrations and colonizations. But almost all of the fifth-century material in the *Geography* is focused on Xerxes and the Persian invasions of Europe, and not on Athens and Sparta. A successful Persian invasion would have had serious implications for the way the world looked in all senses—political, urban, and ethnic. Athos is mentioned as the site of Xerxes' intended canal, as is Cape Sestias, the location of the pontoon-bridge (fr. 7. 35; fr. 7. 55).[13] Aegina's history culminated in this period, when it was able to vie with Athens for the role played in the battle of Salamis (8. 6. 16); and Salamis itself, naturally, is dominated by the

[11] The establishment of the Olympic festival should also be seen as part of Strabo's picture of 8th-cent. history.

[12] See 1. 4. 8 on the 6th-cent. border disputes between Thyrea and Oropus; 13. 2. 3 on Pittacus' tyranny on Lesbos.

[13] See also 13. 1. 22.

great battle that took place there (9. 1. 9). Cape Amphiale is noted as the site of Xerxes' attempted mole, forestalled by the naval battle and the flight of the Persians (9. 1. 13); Plataea is famous as the site of yet more Persian and Greek fighting, where Mardonius and 300,000 Persians were killed (9. 2. 31).

The fourth-century material is mainly concentrated on Alexander and his great expedition to the East.[14] Indeed, the whole of the first part of Book 15, on India, is reliant on a fourth-century perspective. Some of the places passed by Alexander along the way are mentioned by Strabo.[15] The river Granicus is noted as the location where Alexander defeated the satraps of Darius, and gained the land from the Taurus to the Euphrates (13. 1. 11); Mount Nicatorium was given its name after Alexander's victory near Arbela (16. 1. 4); Tyre was joined to the mainland by a mole built by Alexander, when he was besieging it (16. 2. 23); Alexandria was developed by Alexander and provided his burial place (17. 1. 6; 17. 1. 8).

The third century was a time of renewed interest in city-foundations and these form the main body of Hellenistic references. Political events are focused on northern Greece, Macedonia and Asia, the Hellenistic kingdoms and the haunts of Alexander's successors. We are told that the stronghold of Cape Tirizis was once used by Lysimachus as a treasury (7. 6. 1); that Potidaea was renamed Cassandreia after the monarch (fr. 7. 25); that the city of Pleuron was abandoned when Demetrius Aetolicus, son of Antigonus Gonatas, laid waste the land (10. 2. 4).

The late third and second centuries are better represented in all areas. Strabo cites Posidonius on M. Marcellus' extraction of tribute from Celtiberia; and Polybius on the destruction of 300 cities in this region by Tiberius Gracchus (3. 4. 13). In Gaul, Massilia was rewarded for its help in the war against the Ambrones and Toÿgeni with a new channel cut by Marius in place of the silted-up Rhône (4. 1. 8). Italy is scattered with

---

[14] Exceptions are 6. 1. 6: Dionysius of Syracuse and the destruction of Rhegium; 13. 1. 59: Mausolus' synoecism of Halicarnassus; 9. 2. 37: the battle of Chaeroneia in 338 BC.

[15] So too are the routes of some of his opponents. Strabo cites Eratosthenes on the path taken by Darius in flight from Gaugamela to the Caspian Gates (2. 1. 24).

references to Hannibal's invasion—Arretium was near the pass
used by Hannibal (5. 2. 9); Casilinum the place where 540
people of Praeneste held out against Hannibal (5. 4. 10).[16] This
theme forms a western counterpart to the invasion of Xerxes.
In the East the wars against Perseus and the final defeat of the
Macedonians in 167 BC had geographical implications in the
form of Aemilius Paulus' destruction of seventy Epeirote cities
(7. 7. 3). The tale of Roman victory recurs in the context of the
descriptions of Pydna, and of the river Hebrus, which formed
the boundary of Macedonia. Strabo tells of how Paulus
annexed the tribes of Epirus to the new province of Macedonia
and divided the country into four for administrative purposes
(fr. 7. 22; fr. 7. 47). The destructive tendencies of the second-
century Romans recurred in the falls of Carthage and Corinth,
which affected the history of the rest of the Mediterranean
(8. 6. 23; 17. 3. 15). In particular, the growth in the slave-trade
via Delos, to satisfy the needs of the now wealthy Romans,
resulted in a bonanza for the Cilician pirates, creating problems
which dominated much of the next century (14. 5. 2).

The history of parts of Asia also changed course dramatically
in this century, again under the Roman influence. The bequest
of the Pergamene kingdom to the Roman people by the last of
the Attalid kings in 133 BC was particularly problematic
(13. 4. 2). Strabo provides a narrative on the revolt incited by
Aristonicus, who wanted to usurp the kingdom of Cappadocia
(14. 1. 38).[17] He gathered together a band of slaves, promising
them freedom in return for their help. The response was swift.
The cities of Asia Minor soon sent troops to counter Aristonicus, as did Nicomedes of Bithynia; five Roman ambassadors
followed, with an army under P. Crassus not far behind in 131
BC. M. Perpernas took over from Crassus and brought the war
to an end. Aristonicus was sent to Rome, and the consul, M'.
Aquillius, went to organize the province.

---

[16] See also 6. 3. 11 on the Apulians, whose land was laid waste by Hannibal
and by later enemies.

[17] For the parallel event in Sicily, organized by Eunus, see 6. 2. 6. The
second century was clearly a period of usurpation. See 16. 2. 10 for the attack
by Diodotus Tryphon on the Syrian throne. He ruled for three years (142–
139), but Strabo cites the incident mainly as proof of the strength of Apameia
at this stage, for this was his base.

With the first century BC we come to Strabo's own lifetime, the historical focus of which I have already discussed. The number of references to events of this period is greater than for any other, partly vindicating Strabo's profession to be concerned with the present, although the cumulative effect of the history of the preceding centuries gives a still stronger sense of the past. In addition to the Mithridatic history and the transformation of Asia Minor which can be explained by Strabo's own background, the history of Parthia and Armenia in the first century also called for attention. The various struggles between the Parthians and Crassus; and Antonius' betrayal by his Armenian assistant, Artavasdes, are noted in Book 16. But Strabo is able to go on to say that Phraates IV was so eager for Roman *amicitia* that he returned the standards captured from Crassus, called meetings with Titius the governor of Syria, and sent four of his legitimate sons as hostages to Rome (16. 1. 28). Gaul and Britain at last come fully into the realm of history in this period. The victory of Q. Fabius Maximus Aemilianus with fewer than 30,000 men over 200,000 Celts was celebrated with a trophy of marble and two temples—to Mars and to Hercules (4. 1. 11).[18] Strabo mentions Caesar's two expeditions to Britain, as well as the subjugation of the Alpine peoples.

The historical events which dominate Strabo's *Geography* have in common their implications for the spatial transformation of the world.[19] The great period of colonization, the Persian invasion of Europe, the conquests of Alexander and the opening-up of the East, the vicissitudes of the Hellenistic

---

[18] The general submission of the Celts to the ways of Rome was signalled by the request of the Aedui for *amicitia* and alliance with the Roman people.

[19] F. Lasserre, 'Histoire de première main dans la *Géographie* de Strabon', in *Strabone I*, 11–26, points out that where Strabo relates Roman failures to change the world, he is quick to provide a reason. In the case of Aelius Gallus in Arabia Felix, the obstacle to Roman conquest is not Roman failing, but the deception by Syllaeus. It is, however, possible to take the argument that Strabo was an apologist for Rome too far. G. Downey, 'Strabo on Antioch: Notes on his Method', *TAPA* 72 (1941), 85–95, proposes that the vagueness in Strabo's account of the various waves of settlement that went to make up the Antiocheian Tetrapolis might have been designed to draw a veil over the original status of the inhabitants of the Greek East, now ruled by Rome. It seems to me more likely that here, as elsewhere, the extreme complication of levels of city history led to genuine confusion.

kingdoms, and the late-third/early-second-century broadening of the geographical scope of history to incorporate the West, introduce Rome's entry on to the stage. Henceforth Strabo's history is dominated by Rome, reflecting the real growth in its influence. One of the questions that I wished to investigate about Strabo's *Geography* was why it was not a history, given that it contains much that we might call 'historical'. Perhaps one simple answer might be that the history in the *Geography* is partly determined by its spatial consequences. Just as Strabo was not interested in the continuous history of each place, but in significant moments of transformation and redefinition which formed part of the place's present identity; just as he denotes time in the *Geography* largely through the chronological markers of the Trojan war, the return of the Heracleidae, and Actium, indicating time through reference to moments of geographical change; so too with the broader history of the world, it is particular phases of global transformation that dominate, giving us a new way of interpreting Prontera's suggestion that geography differs from history 'perché en essa la dimensione dello spazio domina . . . su quella del tempo'.[20]

If we read the *Geography* spatially, as the text dictates, rather than in chronological layers, we gain little sense of coherent phases of history, except perhaps in the case of some early foundations and Strabo's own lifetime. It is notable that this proliferation of references to the most remote and the most recent history perfectly matches the hour-glass structure of the dominant chronological markers in the work, which I identified as the Trojan war and the return of the Heracleidae from the mythological period, and the battle of Actium from Strabo's own time. There is no sense of a steadily increased historical content from the earliest times to Strabo's present, but a sudden drop in level after the mythological period and a near-explosion of interest in the first century BC.

Although a chronological analysis reveals that certain periods throughout the intervening centuries were privileged in their coverage, Strabo was not concerned to create a complete

---

[20] F. Prontera, 'Prima di Strabone: Materiali per uno studio della geografia antica come genere letterario', in *Strabone I*, 252: 'because in it [sc. geography] the dimension of space predominates over that of time'.

synchronic picture out of these. This is wholly consistent with his failure to devise or apply a universal time-system, linking contemporaneous events across the known world. If we consider the question geographically, it is clear that, while almost everywhere has a strong element of foundation history, dealing with the time of its creation, and also a great deal of contemporary history, each area is also characterized by certain formative periods between these two points.[21] As I have argued above, it is almost impossible to gain a coherent sense of these intermediary periods across the scope of Strabo's work. They are different for each place and are patterned by the vicissitudes of individual settlements and peoples, and by the traditions and memories which went to make up their identity. So, apart from certain particularly privileged times in history, which had affected the way the whole world looked, the structuring of historical time in the *Geography* varies place by place, depending on which periods had been formative and which relatively unimportant in the development of a particular city or people, or at least for its history as it was now looked back on. At each new place, we are taken back to the foundation period and shown a unique historical rhythm. India is unusual in lacking such a rhythm; it is the most striking example of a region apparently unaffected by time. Here the account is given in such a way as to suggest that *no* period had significantly altered the place, but this temporal uniformity is hardly surprising, since Strabo confesses to having no new material to add to the Hellenistic accounts, which were themselves concerned with customs, flora, and fauna, rather than with historical or political events.[22]

We are coming slightly closer to one notion of how Strabo's

---

[21] Western Mediterranean: 2nd and 1st cents. BC; Italy: heroic period and 2nd and 1st cents. BC; northern Europe: largely without temporal focus, but historical events tend to be from recent past, especially 1st cent. AD; Greece and Troad: mythical period, heroic age, and some archaic and classical Greek history; Pontus and northern Asia: 1st cent. BC; inland Asia, like northern Europe: timeless world of barbarian customs; eastern Asia: Hellenistic kingdoms; Babylonia: ancient history stretching back to Ninos and Semiramis, and Hellenistic history; Parthia: 1st cent. BC; Arabia and Aethiopia: timeless; Egypt: mostly Ptolemaic, and Antony and Cleopatra; western Libya: timeless, or recent past.

[22] See 15. 1. 1–10, where Strabo sets out his policy on sources for India.

project relates to the matrices of time and space. The past is crucial, but only in so far as it created the present world. Strabo was interested in periods of the past which transformed spaces into places and gave them their present identity. But this interest did not lead him to discuss each formative phase synchronically, because each place was affected individually.[23] Rather, the spatial arrangement predominated and the temporal aspect was introduced place by place, giving space precedence over time and fulfilling one of the possible definitions of geography.

The impossibility of satisfactorily representing in text the simultaneous matrices of time and space was a problem facing all writers of universal accounts. Diodorus is a useful comparand to Strabo, as a contemporary and an author who openly discussed methodological problems. But subtle differences in their introduction of similar material help to clarify the distinction between universal history and universal geography. Both Strabo and Diodorus introduce famous intellectuals into their works. In Diodorus this feature recurs at the end of each year's account. His references to other authors are not confined to 'historians', but range from Philemon to Philistus and Sophocles (23. 6; 13. 103. 3–5). The latter two are introduced at the end of Diodorus' account of the year 406 BC and exemplify the formula perfectly. In summary: 'These are pretty much the events that occurred this year. Philistus' first *History* of Sicily ended with this year and the siege of Acragas, treating 800 years in seven books; and this is the point at which he started his second *History*, written in four books. Sophocles, the tragedian, died now, aged ninety.' As I have discussed, Strabo too introduces intellectual figures to the text, but on a spatial rather than a chronological basis. From Cnidus, for example, came Eudoxus, the mathematician; Agatharchides

---

[23] H. Prince, 'Time and Historical Geography', in *Making Sense of Time*, 17–37, could have been, but was not, describing Strabo's *Geography* when he said that historical geography looks at geographical change; not producing synchronic studies of past geography, but diachronic studies of geography in the course of change through time (p. 25). For the opposite view, see K. W. Butzer's comment in J. N. Entrikin and S. D. Brunn (eds.), *Reflections on Richard Hartshorne's* The Nature of Geography (Washington, 1989), 42, that for Hartshorne geography was 'first and foremost a synchronic discipline'.

and Theopompus, the historians; and Ctesias, the doctor of Artaxerxes and author of works on Assyria and Persia (14. 2. 15). Precisely the same material is used to round off years for Diodorus and places for Strabo—neatly illustrating the temporal and spatial ordering principles respectively. So in some respects Strabo's *Geography* confirms the predominance of space over time in geographical works as opposed to histories; but, as I argued in chapter V, Strabo's interest in inhabited place over abstract space means that time too is crucial to his project, qualifying the 'time : space' model for history and geography.

STRABO'S UNIVERSALISM

The only period of time which is consistently, and even more than the mythological period, part of every place's history is Strabo's present. I have already argued for a spatial conception in the *Geography* which rejected other models—linear, climatic, and continental—in favour of a world created around and tied to a central focus at Rome, in spite of the existence of alternative, even competing, focal points in the Pontic region and the Greek East (pp. 210–28). I have also argued that Strabo's conception of the past was primarily one which might explain the present state of the world and account for the identities of its peoples and places. In both of these senses, Strabo was accurate in stressing that his work was about the present world, one which was specifically Roman. But there is another way in which Strabo's Roman present dominates the *Geography*, namely in its whole conception as a project.

This is the point at which to recall Strabo's use of temporal indicators, which revealed that he regarded the whole of his lifetime as his 'present', regardless of the time of writing, and to recreate the horizons of the age during which he was growing up in Asia Minor. Pompey's dealings in that part of the world achieve some prominence in the *Geography*, as has already been discussed, but Strabo does not fail to include also Pompey's impact on the West. His trophies were, for example, to be seen marking the boundary between Iberia and Celtica. The account of Iberia includes mention of the cities in which the sons of Pompey were defeated—Munda, Ategua, Urso,

Tuccis, Ulia, and Aegua (3. 2. 2).[24] A crucial aspect of
Pompey's image was that of universalism. It was with
Pompey that the idea of Roman rule stretching right across
the known world took on a coherent form. Rome's horizons at
this period were of unprecedented breadth, as authors of the
first century BC attest.

Throughout the extant fragments of Sallust's *Histories* we
catch tantalizing glimpses of these broadened horizons.[25]
Sallust wrote about the source of the Tigris and of the
Euphrates (4. 77), and he compared the Istros and Nile in
size—all great rivers which defined large-scale geography in
ancient thought. The *Histories* incorporated ethnographical
and geographical details on regions as far apart as Scythia
(3. 76), Pontus (3. 62–70), and Spain (2. 5). The latter two areas
bring us more specifically back to Pompey, whose involvement
in the wars against Sertorius and Mithridates contributed to his
global image.

The Homeric all-encircling Ocean, which I argued in
chapter IV was importantly reinstated in Strabo's view of the
world, was also crucial for the image of Pompey and of Rome.
Sallust reveals that Sertorius 'planned a flight to distant
stretches of Ocean' (1. 102): in order to escape from Roman
power, he was forced to flee not only to the edge of the
inhabited world, the Ocean, but even to its remote parts.
The implication is that Roman power itself now extended to
the symbolic edge of the earth.[26] I recall Cicero's suggestion in
the *Pro Murena* (32) that Mithridates aimed to join his forces
with those of Sertorius in Spain and link the Ocean with
Pontus. Sallust's *Letter of Mithridates* (17) turns this around:
Mithridates expresses to King Arsaces his fear that Rome will
turn its attention to Pontus, now that it has reached the Ocean
in the West. The idea that Rome's empire will stretch from the
Atlantic to the Pontus and beyond precisely reflects the power

---

[24] Munda recurs at 3. 4. 9. The trophies of Pompey are mentioned at 3. 4. 7;
3. 4. 9; 4. 1. 3.

[25] All references are to the edition by B. Maurenbrecher, *C. Sallusti Crispi
Historiarum Reliquae* (Leipzig, 1891).

[26] This is confirmed in 1. 11, which states that by 51 BC (in the consulship
of Servius Sulpicius and Marcus Metellus), Roman power was at its height,
having subjugated all of Gaul this side of the Rhine and between the
Mediterranean and Ocean.

given to Pompey by the *lex Gabinia* of 67 BC. Cicero describes Pompey's success in his exercise of this anti-pirate command over the entire Mediterranean world in order to persuade the *populus Romanus* to grant him further powers against Mithridates through the *lex Manilia* (*De imperio*, 33). He does so in terms which stress the fact that Rome's rule reaches as far as the great Ocean itself: whereas the Romans used to see enemy ships at the mouth of the Tiber, now it was unheard of for a single pirate ship to be within the mouth of the Ocean.

The extent of both Pompey's command and his ambition was stressed also by later writers (Appian, *Mith.* 94; Plut. *Pomp.* 25. 2–3). Plutarch relates that Pompey was aiming for world dominion even before his final settlement with Mithridates.

He wanted to recover Syria and march through Arabia to the Red Sea, so that he might bring his glorious career to the ocean which surrounds the world on all sides. For in Africa he had been the first to carry his conquests as far as the outer sea and in Spain he had made the Atlantic ocean the boundary of Roman dominion and in pursuit of the Albanians he had narrowly missed reaching the Hyrcanian sea. (*Pomp.* 38. 2–3)

It is worth comparing this picture with that of Lucullus concerning Roman expansion. Dissent at Rome over Lucullus' handling of the war against Mithridates led to Pompey joining him there in 66 BC under the *lex Manilia*. The troops favoured Pompey, and Lucullus was sent back to Rome. If it had not been for this disruption to the campaign, says Plutarch, the Roman empire would not have been bounded by the Euphrates, but by the outer confines of Asia and the Hyrcanian Sea.[27] Thus Lucullus was seen as a hindrance to Roman expansion, whereas Pompey embodied Roman ambitions for world rule.

These ambitions were summed up in the accounts of Pompey's triumphal procession through Rome in 61 BC. Diodorus describes an inscription set up probably in the temple of Minerva on the day of Pompey's triumph, recalling his achievements (πράξεις) since the campaign against the

---

[27] Plut. *Luc.* 36. 5–6: οὐκ ἂν εἶχεν ἡ Ῥωμαίων ἡγεμονία τὸν Εὐφράτην τῆς Ἀσίας ὅρον, ἀλλὰ τὰ ἔσχατα καὶ τὴν Ὑρκανίαν θάλατταν.

pirates.[28] The victory over the pirates was explicitly linked with the fulfilment of Rome's aim of universal rule. According to Plutarch, inscriptions were carried before the procession listing the nations Pompey had conquered. The triumph was important, says Plutarch, because it involved victory over all three continents—Libya, Europe, and Asia—representing the whole inhabited world (*Pomp.* 45. 5).[29] The boundaries of Roman hegemony after Pompey's exploits now reached from the West to the river Euphrates. The victory in Asia was even more to be admired because Mithridates was a formidable enemy. Appian sets the Mithridatic wars in the context of growing Roman influence throughout the Mediterranean world. He ends his work with a description of the fate of Pontus after the fall of Mithridates Eupator, initially given to Mithridates of Pergamum to rule, but soon linked with Bithynia as a single province governed by a praetor. Appian concludes that the result of the Mithridatic wars was to extend Roman hegemony from Spain and the Pillars of Hercules to the Euxine, Egypt, and the Euphrates (*Mith.* 121).

This desire for world dominion was not confined to Pompey. Plutarch details some of Julius Caesar's plans

to make an expedition against the Parthians; and after subduing these and marching around the Pontus via Hyrcania, the Caspian Sea, and the Caucasus, to invade Scythia; and after overrunning the countries bordering on Germany and Germany itself, to return through Gaul to Italy, and so to complete this circuit of his empire, which would then be bounded on all sides by the Ocean (τῷ πανταχόθεν Ὠκεανῷ περιορισθείσης). (*Caes.* 58. 6–7)

---

[28] Diodorus 40. 4 lists the conquered nations. In Pliny, *NH* 7. 97–8 the same connection between the suppression of piracy and Rome's further victories is present. The link is obvious in practical terms. Thalassocracy, won by Rome through the victory over piracy, had been seen since Thucydides as a step towards empire. At 1. 8 he described the process by which Minos of Crete put down piracy and gained great power as a result of the consequent control of the sea. The foreshadowing in the inscription for Pompey of Augustus' *Res gestae*, set up before his Mausoleum after his death, is brought out by C. Nicolet, *Space, Geography, and Politics in the Early Roman Empire* (Ann Arbor, 1991), 32.

[29] For inscriptions listing conquests see Strabo 4. 3. 2 on the altar to Augustus bearing an inscription listing and depicting visually the sixty tribes of the Galatae, now under Roman rule.

The similarities with the aims expressed in *Pompey*, 38 are striking.

Both Julius Caesar and Pompey were strongly motivated by the desire to emulate the image of Alexander the Great.[30] Plutarch reminds the reader of the fact that, at the time of Pompey's triple triumph, those who would compare him with Alexander claimed that he was less than thirty-four years old, although he was in fact nearly forty (*Pomp.* 46). The fragments of Sallust's *Histories* provide a glimpse of the aspirations attributed to Pompey himself, under the influence of his admirers: 'But Pompey from his early manhood, influenced by what his supporters said, thinking that he would be the equal of King Alexander, sought to rival his deeds and plans.'[31] Caesar was no less eager to align himself with the famous world-conqueror. Plutarch again recounts the anecdote of how, on campaign in Spain, Caesar was reading from the history of Alexander when he suddenly burst into tears. In response to his friends' concerned enquiries, Caesar asked whether they did not think it sad that, while Alexander at his age was already king over so many peoples, Caesar had not yet achieved a brilliant success (*Caes.* 11).

Whatever the degree of truth behind such anecdotes, it seems clear that there was a revival of interest in Alexander's achievements at this period, and an attempt to recreate and even surpass his conquests. If both Pompey and Caesar wanted to make the Outer Ocean the only limit to their conquests, so too had Alexander. According to Justin's epitome of the universal history written by Pompeius Trogus towards the end of the first century BC, Alexander went to India 'intending to establish the Ocean and the furthest limits of the Orient as the boundaries of his empire', and when Alexander reached the Ocean itself, Trogus comments that 'he had established boundaries for his empire as far as the deserts would allow one to advance on land and as far as the sea could be navigated' (12. 7. 4; 12. 10. 5). Either we are seeing the language of

---

[30] I recall the ambitions of Mithridates Eupator to present himself as a new Alexander. See p. 238 n. 100.

[31] Sallust, *Histories*, fr. 3. 88: *sed Pompeius a prima adulescentia sermone fautorum similem fore se credens Alexandro regi, facta consultaque eius quidem aemulus erat.*

Alexander's imperialism applied to Romans of the first century BC, or Trogus is formulating his account of Alexander in the light of his own times. Both possibilities reveal the importance of the connection between Alexander and the first-century expansionism of Rome. As I discussed in chapter I, this is precisely what we should expect; namely, that the new, extended geographical horizons of the first century BC and the attendant re-evaluation of the world would inevitably be formulated, at least in part, against the backdrop of previous periods of such expansion.

Bearing in mind the preoccupations of the time, it is no surprise that Strabo conceived of a universal geography, in which the world would be described as it related to Rome. As far as we know this was the first real attempt to provide an account of the whole Roman world, the first universal geography.[32] Contemporary visual and epigraphic parallels were to be found in Agrippa's map and the *Res gestae divi Augusti*. The world would not be a truly unified whole until the *pax Augusta* had finally taken hold, but the universal ambitions of Pompey and their formulation in various media—sculptural in his theatre, epigraphic, literary, and processional—irrevocably broadened the horizons of first-century BC Romans.[33] Diodorus showed that the project of writing a universal account was as topical in the late 60s as under Augustus and Tiberius, when Nicolaus of Damascus would take the writing of universal history to its limit with an account of world history from the earliest times to the death of Herod in an astounding 144-book

[32] Note, however, the suggestion of A. Luisi, 'Cornelio Nepote geografo', *CISA* 14 (1988), 41–51, that Cornelius Nepos had undertaken a universal geography in 59 BC. Such a work would obviously have serious implications for the originality of Strabo.

[33] See Nicolet, *Space, Geography, and Politics*, 38, for the theatre of Pompey with its representations of subject nations, and 41–7 for the suggestion that similar images adorned the upper galleries of the porticos in the Forum of Augustus. The parallel with the geographical interests of other imperial powers is clear. George, *Historical Geography of the British Empire* (1904) was prefaced with the remark (p. v) that 'My object in writing this little book has been to present a general survey of the British Empire as a whole, with the historical conditions, at least so far as they depend on geography, which have contributed to produce the present state of things.' See R. A. Butlin, *Historical Geography: Through the Gates of Space and Time* (London, 1993), 20.

work. It is impossible to say anything with certainty about the arrangement of Nicolaus' work, since virtually nothing is left from Books 8–95. The first seven books dealt with the history of the Assyrians, Medes, Lydians, Greeks, and Persians until the time of Croesus and Cyrus, and the last ten books must have traced the decade leading up to the accession of Archelaus in 4 BC.[34] Yet, however little we know about the work's organization, two things are clear: firstly, the vastness of the scope, and secondly, the likelihood that it was not hostile to Roman rule, since Nicolaus was also the author of an encomiastic *Life of Augustus*. As I see it, Strabo's *Geography* was a spatial parallel to precisely this kind of pro-Roman universal history.

But, as I discussed in relation to Polybius and Posidonius, 'universalism' is a broad term which requires further definition. The universalism of the late Hellenistic period was connected with the notion of Roman world rule, making it distinctive and internally coherent, however much it may have been reliant on the productions of earlier periods of expansion for some of its formulations. The fact that the Romans were now beginning to claim all, or most, of the inhabited world (οἰκουμένη) as their own must have been a major stimulus to universal writers such as Diodorus and Strabo himself.[35] But neither author restricted his view of the universal to a spatial interpretation. Both, as we have seen, rejected the possibility of taking a synchronic snapshot of their contemporary world, in favour of an account that also had a temporal aspect. I return in the next section to the particular notion of 'historical geography' which resulted from Strabo's interpretation of universalism as both spatial *and* temporal, but for the moment I wish to consider the spatial implications alone.

[34] E. Schürer, *The History of the Jewish People in the Age of Jesus Christ 175 B. C.–A. D. 135*, i rev. G. Vermes and F. Millar (Edinburgh, 1973), 28–32, compiles all the relevant information on Nicolaus. O. Lendle, *Einführung in die griechische Geschichtsschreibung* (Darmstadt, 1992), 245, seems remarkably certain about the organization of the work: 'Klar erkennbar wird aus den Exzerpten die Ökonomie einer synchronistisch angelegten Weltgeschichte' ('From the excerpts there clearly emerges the arrangement of a synchronically organized world history').

[35] Pompeius Trogus' *Historiae Philippicae* were also wide-reaching in both time and space, starting from the first world empire of Ninos and reaching as far as the Augustan present.

One of the main objections to the idea of Strabo's *Geography* as a universal work could be the discrete nature of his account of each place and his lack of a sense of the space between places. But, as I discussed in chapter I and in connection with Polybius, both continuous and discrete notions of space and time could, with equal validity, be used to construct a view of the world. It seems to me that the tension between the part and the whole, which for Strabo meant the individual place and the whole unified Roman world of the late Republic and early principate, is one of the most interesting and enriching features of the work, and worthy of further discussion. I have argued in the two preceding chapters that Strabo's world was based on a unity centred on the present power of Rome, to which each place was bound, both conceptually and by the real flow of resources. In spite of his regional approach, Strabo occasionally hints that he wishes to create a more coherent picture. He tells the history of the Acarnanians in isolation, but then sets it in a more general context. 'So much may be said for the Acarnanians specifically (ἰδίᾳ); I shall now speak of their history generally (κοινῇ), in so far as it is interwoven (ἐπιπλέ-κεται) with that of the Aetolians' (10. 2. 26). The image of weaving is precisely that used by Polybius and Diodorus to describe the way in which they related various pieces of narrative to each other to form a coherent whole.

Strabo's project was explicitly concerned with setting out the whole Roman world, as is made most clear at the end of the work, where he lists the Roman provinces. That this was not exactly commensurate with the whole known inhabited world is conceded in a striking use of μέν . . . δέ, in which the former refers back to the description given in the whole preceding work and the latter forward to just the last two chapters, setting out how Rome came to be in possession of 'the best and most well-known' parts of the inhabited world.[36] Of course, the Romans appear on almost every page of the *Geography*, so

---

[36] 17. 3. 24: τὰ μὲν οὖν μέρη τῆς καθ᾽ ἡμᾶς οἰκουμένης οὕτω διάκειται· ἐπεὶ δ᾽ οἱ Ῥωμαῖοι τὴν ἀρίστην αὐτῆς καὶ γνωριμωτάτην κατέχουσιν . . . ἄξιον καὶ διὰ βραχέων καὶ τὰ τούτων εἰπεῖν ('This then is how the different parts of our inhabited world are laid out; but, since the Romans hold under their sway the most outstanding and well-known part of it . . . it is worth also saying even just a little about their affairs').

the contrast is something of a conceit. The point stands that the work is framed at the start by the image of the colossal statue (κολοσσουργία) and the appeal to view the composition as a whole (1. 1. 23), and at the end by an overview of the world. But this was a world made up of the individual cities and places which Strabo describes, in the main body of the work, as discrete units, with their own individual identities made up of memories from the past. To return to the language of Polybius, 'the overall picture' (τὰ καθόλου) which was Strabo's unified Roman world lay behind the description of it 'piece by piece' (κατὰ μέρος). But the two authors conceived of the relationship between the part and the whole differently. Whereas for Polybius the part could, at times, stand as a microcosm of the whole, as illustrated in his use of geographical 'telescoping', for Strabo the whole was made up of the sum of individual, and different, parts.

But this does not wholly account for Strabo's style of universalism. Later in this chapter I address the issue of how Strabo and his account were caught between the Hellenistic and Roman worlds, but the hypothesis that I should like tentatively to suggest now is that Strabo's attempt to write an account of the entire Roman world necessitated a break from pre-existing regional accounts, because their diverse frames of reference rendered impossible an amalgamation into a coherent description of the world. That is, it is not enough to say that Strabo made up the *Geography* as a whole (καθόλου) simply by adding together disparate regional accounts written individually (κατὰ μέρος).[37]

As I have mentioned, Strabo had relatively little first-hand experience of different parts of the empire, and so must have been reliant on other types of information. In Appendix C I list Strabo's acknowledged sources for the regions he describes. At

---

[37] Note the parallel with Polybius 1. 4. 6: 'we can no more hope to see this [sc. the convergence of world events] from those who write histories dealing with particular events than to get a notion of the form of the whole inhabited world, its disposition and order, by visiting, in turn, the most famous cities, or by looking at separate plans of each' (ὥσπερ ἐκ μὲν τῶν κατὰ μέρος γραφόντων τὰς ἱστορίας οὐχ οἷόν τε συνιδεῖν, εἰ μὴ καὶ τὰς ἐπιφανεστάτας πόλεις τις κατὰ μίαν ἑκάστην ἐπελθὼν ἢ καὶ νὴ Δία γεγραμμένας χωρὶς ἀλλήλων θεασάμενος εὐθέως ὑπολαμβάνει κατανενοηκέναι καὶ τὸ τῆς ὅλης οἰκουμένης σχῆμα καὶ τὴν σύμπασαν αὐτῆς θέσιν καὶ τάξιν).

the start of Book 8 he states his main sources as Homer, periegetic texts, general histories, such as those of Ephorus and Polybius, and scientific treatises, like those by Posidonius and Hipparchus (8. 1. 1). Appendix C reveals that the regional descriptions are indeed dominated by information attributed by Strabo to universal histories, to geographical works of the Hellenistic period, and to Homer. These major sources recur in connection with almost every area treated in the *Geography*, and are sometimes the only ones to be cited explicitly. It is easy to understand why Homer, the founder of Strabo's whole geographical genre, and universal works of a broad scope might be important in Strabo's creation of a unified vision of the world. However, his region-by-region approach might also have been well served by using some of the hundreds of Hellenistic regional histories which we know existed, and I consider now precisely what pattern emerges in his citation of local accounts.

It is first worth noting that any conclusions drawn about source usage must remain to some extent speculative, since it is impossible to be certain how much material was used without acknowledgement. In my discussion I include only those sources named explicitly by Strabo. Secondly, we cannot be sure that Strabo had easy access to sources which we might assume he would use, and access may have been further limited by the practical problems of papyrus consultation. However, local histories should have been relatively easy to consult for a work which was, like Strabo's *Geography*, itself organized spatially. In addition, Strabo was writing at a time when Varro, Pliny the Elder, Diodorus, and Dionysius of Halicarnassus had written, or would soon write, works which betray a substantial use of named sources, in a way that suggests fairly easy access to a wide range of texts. It is hard to show that Strabo himself worked within this context of reference and consultation, but his insertion of himself into the Greek intellectual circles of Asia Minor points in this direction. He certainly spent some years at Rome, and visited Alexandria, although we cannot prove that he used the libraries there. He also gives one clear reference to the consultation of different texts of Thucydides, suggestive of library work, and providing evidence against the idea that he relied solely on his memory of the texts which formed the basis of his Greek education.[38]

There is an additional difficulty in supposing that anyone writing a geography should want to consult regional histories at all. However, the periplus attributed to Scymnus of Chios offers one answer. The author describes his overall project as 'writing in epitome, drawing on several scattered histories, the colonies and city-foundations, and the places across almost all the world which are accessible by sea or land'.[39] This is similar to what we find in Strabo's *Geography*—a geographical description, which is concerned not only with the present, but also with the past. The most important aspect of this poem for my present purpose is that it shows that it is not entirely fanciful to suppose that a potential model for Strabo's work would have been to use the pre-existing local histories, and unite them to form a universal account. I restrict my discussion to texts mostly written in Greek (a few in Latin), which

---

[38] 8. 6. 15: 'In some copies (ἀντιγράφοι) of Thucydides, the name is spelled "Methone" (instead of Methana).' It is, however, possible that the difference in spelling was striking enough to stick in Strabo's memory. I recall C. B. R. Pelling, 'Plutarch's Method of Work in the Roman Lives', *JHS* 99 (1979), 74–96, in which possible research methods are discussed. It is suggested that Plutarch and other authors may have written with just one source open in front of them, but have remembered elements from a wide range of other sources which formed their preliminary reading, as well as drawing on their general knowledge. S. Hornblower develops this picture of variegated research methods, including both oral and written memory, in the Introduction to S. Hornblower (ed.), *Greek Historiography* (Oxford, 1994), 56–64. He stresses, with several illustrative examples, how hard it is to determine an author's knowledge of earlier sources.

[39] *GGM I*, Scymnus ll. 65–8. One striking aspect of the work is its relationship to a history of the Pergamene kings, written in *comic* verse to make the work clearer and more memorable (ibid. ll. 33–5). But in what sense was comic verse appropriate either for a geographical account, or for a history of the Pergamene kings? Perhaps the sense was simply 'light-hearted'; or was there such a thing as 'comic' history as opposed to 'tragic' history? One other possibility suggests itself, although it would necessitate an addition to the entry κωμικός in LSJ. Could a κωμική ἱστορίη be one which was written 'village by village'? I base this suggestion on a fragment cited by Jacoby. Attributed to a certain Protagorides of Cyzicus (*FGrH* 853 F 3) was a work entitled κωμικαί ἱστορίαι referring to a description of Syria, which, like Scymnus' periplus, might favour a geographical interpretation of the adjective, giving another example of discrete units making up an account with universal aspirations.

Strabo either did or did not explicitly cite. While the exclusion of other languages may rule out of consideration various native accounts, it seems likely that, in terms of sources which could possibly have been accessible and useful to Strabo, this restriction will not seriously distort the picture.

From Appendix C it emerges firstly that Strabo's acknowledged use of regional accounts is extremely limited. However, it appears in addition that a pattern of citation can be observed from region to region. For Spain, alongside the predictable sources of geographical works, universal histories, and Homer, Strabo also took his information from the inhabitants of Gades and from Asclepiades of Myrleia, who wrote a regional work on the *Tribes of Turdetania*. We know of no other local sources that might have been available, except possibly the *Iberica* of Sosthenes of Cnidus. For much of northern Europe, Strabo was reliant on general works, supplemented by, for example, Caesar's *Commentarii* on Gaul and the eye-witness accounts of other commanders and travellers. His description of Greece is dominated by Homer and other poets, although he does mention more local works, such as those of Philochorus the Athenian, the Atthidographers as a group, and Pausanias of Sparta's work on Lycurgus. As we move round to Asia Minor, Strabo continues to make some limited use of regional accounts. He mentions the writing of Mithridatic histories (Μιθριδατικά) (11. 2. 14), suggesting that he knew of local histories of the Pontic region; for Bithynia he refers only to Menecrates and Asclepiades of Myrleia, both of whom had written specifically on that area; for Lydia he used Xanthus' fifth-century *Lydiaca*. Armenia is a striking instance where Strabo cites only three sources—one is Metrodorus of Scepsis, the rhetorician, the other two, Theophanes of Mytilene and Artavasdes the Armenian, wrote regional accounts in Strabo's own time. We know of no other local histories for Armenia from this period or before.

However, when we reach Strabo's description of the countries of the Fertile Crescent, the great sweep of land from Persia in the East to Egypt in the West, a quite different pattern emerges. A great number of regional works written in the Hellenistic period in Greek about lands such as Babylonia, Judaea, and Egypt have survived. Berosus of Babylon and

Abydenus; Demetrius, Eupolemus, and Cleodemus-Malchus; and Manetho—all wrote extensive accounts of these areas respectively. But Strabo does not acknowledge his use of a single one of these. It is methodologically dubious to dwell for too long on texts which Strabo did not use, or did not mention by name, especially given that we cannot prove that he actually knew of them at all. However, he *does* refer to several authors who wrote about the countries of the Fertile Crescent: Athenaeus and Diogenes, both from Seleuceia; Baton of Sinope, who wrote a *Persica*; Theodorus of Gadara in Syria; the Phoenician, Mochus; Apollonius Molon, who wrote on Judaea. The fact that Strabo mentions such authors suggests that he was at least aware of regional accounts concerning these lands, but he cites their authors merely as intellectual products of particular places, and does not explicitly use the works as sources for his own account.

This makes the spatial variation in Strabo's use of regional accounts all the more striking, since we cannot simply argue for his ignorance in the case of the Fertile Crescent. I suggest that a brief consideration of the chronological and mythographical frameworks of a range of regional histories from the Hellenistic period might explain the distribution.

Asclepiades of Myrleia's *Tribes of Turdetania*, as attested by Strabo himself, told of the memorials to Trojan heroes, such as Odysseus, Teucer, and Amphilochus, who had sailed to Spain in the great heroic migration following the Trojan war. The area was also, according to this account, colonized by the companions of Hercules. So we catch a glimpse into a work which cast the ethnic make-up of Spain in a framework of Greek heroes and gods, creating a geography of mythical personalities (*FGrH* 697 F 7 = Str. 3. 4. 3).[40]

Justin's epitome of Pompeius Trogus reveals the similar character of accounts concerning parts of Asia Minor, notably Armenia. I have already mentioned (pp. 96–7) Trogus' narrative of the war between Mithridates and the Armenian king, Artoadistes, as an excellent example of the need for flexibility

---

[40] The whole issue of the dispersal of heroes and their contribution to ethnography has been excellently treated by E. Dench, *From Barbarians to New Men: Greek, Roman, and Modern Perceptions of Peoples from the Central Apennines* (Oxford, 1995).

in our approach to ancient geography and history, but the
passage also illustrates my point about accounts written in
Greek terms.[41] The founder of the nation, Armenus, was
bound up in the web of associations which constituted *Greek*
mythology and hero-worship. Trogus' identification of Armenus as a friend of Jason (leading to a digression on the story of
Jason and Medea) linked the foundation of Armenia to the
most prominent Greek myth of the Pontic region. The frame of
reference, within which the Armenian nation was set, was that
of Hercules and the Greek heroes. We are told that Jason was
the first man to subdue that part of the world after Hercules
and Dionysus, and that he made a treaty with the Albanians,
who followed Hercules from the Alban mount, when he was
driving the cattle of Geryon through Italy. So a *Greek* myth
enables us to define the geography of Armenia.[42] It is worth
recalling that Spain and Armenia were both areas for which
Strabo chose to use regional accounts.

Rome and Italy form a slightly special case. Here in the
first century BC, as I argue in the next section, Greek and
Roman elements were curiously juxtaposed. This is clearly
attested by Strabo's *Geography* itself, the work of a man who
was educated in the Greek cities of Asia Minor, but firmly
attached to the Roman élite. The coexistence of these elements is visible already in earlier accounts of the area, by
both native and non-native authors, in their attempts to
reconcile Greek and Roman versions of the early history of
Rome and Italy. The question of language is much at issue,
with A. Postumius Albinus memorably pleading for indulgence in the preface of his Roman history: 'I am a Roman,
born in Latium; the Greek language is totally foreign to

[41] The relevant passage is *FGrH* 679 F 2b = Justin 42. 2. 6–3. 9.

[42] Xanthus the Lydian should not go unmentioned as the first to write in
Greek about non-Greek lands (*FGrH* 765). His work was extremely varied,
ranging from scientific explanations of how sea-fossils were found inland, to
more exotic themes—herbs which cured puppies from snake-bites; the
Amazon custom of gouging out the eyes of male children; the tale of King
Cambles, who ate too much and indeed ate his wife one night, finding her
hand in his mouth in the morning and committing suicide in remorse.
Xanthus used not only the Greek language, but also Greek chronological
markers, such as Xerxes' invasion of Greece and the Trojan war, to describe a
very barbarian world.

me.'[43] According to Polybius, 'he asked in his preface to be excused if, as a Roman, he had not complete mastery of the Greek language and of the Greek method for treating the subject', an indulgence which was not granted.[44] Not only Postumius, a confessed Hellenophile, but also Q. Fabius Pictor and L. Cincius Alimentus were noted for their use of Greek to write the history of Rome.[45]

The foundation of Rome was a source of great dispute. Both Plutarch and Fabius agreed that the best source for the story of Aeneas, Romulus, and the foundation of the city was the version first published among the *Greeks* by Diocles of Peparethus.[46] The foundation-date caused endless trouble for Dionysius, one of the major problems being how to correlate Greek and Roman chronological systems, or more precisely 'to bring Roman times into line with Greek'.[47] L. Cincius gave the date as the fourth year of the twelfth Olympiad; Fabius, the first year of the eighth Olympiad; Porcius Cato, 432 years after the Trojan war.

The assimilation of Roman history to the Greek past, and particularly to the events of the Homeric epics, was a major preoccupation of the writers on early Rome, as seen in both Dionysius and Livy. The great migration of heroes was exemplified for Livy by the fates of Aeneas and Antenor. Aeneas went to Macedonia, Sicily, and Laurentum, where he settled; Antenor and his men populated the land between the

---

[43] *FGrH* 812 F 1b: *homo Romanus natus in Latio, Graeca oratio a nobis alienissima est.*

[44] Ibid. T 7 = Polybius 39. 1, for the whole description of Postumius and his literary aspirations. M. Porcius Cato is reported by Polybius as having replied that there was no excuse for barbarisms, since Postumius had *chosen* to write his history in this manner.

[45] *FGrH* 809 T 4a = Dionysius of Halicarnassus, *AR* 1. 6. 2.

[46] Ibid. F 4a = Plut. *Romulus*, 3. Note the debate in Dionysius about Rome being itself a Greek city. The whole issue of Greekness becomes hopelessly confused at this point. Dionysius adduced as evidence the Greek elements in Roman ceremonies and customs, backing this up with 'native' sources such as Fabius and some intriguing 'ancient local histories' (ἀρχαῖαι καὶ τοπικαὶ ἱστορίαι), but Fabius himself was using Greek sources.

[47] Dionysius 1. 74. 2: πῶς ἄν τις ἀπευθύνοι τοὺς Ῥωμαίων χρόνους πρὸς τοὺς Ἑλληνικούς. Note the precedence given to Greek, although this was a Roman history.

Alps and the Adriatic. The common purpose of such accounts was to explain the ethnographical make-up of Italy.

However, Hellenistic accounts of the countries of the Fertile Crescent present a quite different picture. What I hope to show is that these areas were described using a different frame of reference from the ones discussed above; one which was internally coherent, but not Greek.[48] The story of Judaea was unlike that of any other region, in so far as it was the history of a people and a religion, rather than that of a place. Indeed, one of the most striking features of the sources is the theme of migration—Judaea was wherever the Jews were, giving it a unique geographical instability. Besides migration, the texts on Judaea are characterized by an obsession with chronology. Demetrius' *On the Kings in Judaea* provides a good example of the interest in dates.[49] Throughout the text, the ages in years and months of various rulers were given. But this was a relative dating system. Joseph went to Egypt in the third year of the famine, when x was y years old and z was some other age; from Adam to the time when Joseph's family came to Egypt was 3,624 years; from the great flood to the time when Jacob went to Egypt was 1,360 years. We have no real idea of an absolute date, any more than we do when told that something happened 628 years after the Trojan war or at the time of the Heracleidae. The point is that, given the use of relative dating-systems, the choice of chronological markers is important. In the histories of Judaea, instead of Olympiads and the Trojan war we find the great flood and the exodus from Egypt, events from Jewish history, as chronological markers.

Before leaving Judaea, I should nuance this neat picture of a self-contained Jewish historiography. Alongside Abraham, Moses appeared as an archetypal wise man. His skills knew no bounds—he invented ships, weapons, hieroglyphics, stone-

---

[48] E. J. Bickermann, 'Origines Gentium', *Class. Phil.* 47 (1952), 65–81, offers an analysis of the process by which non-Greek peoples were first written about in Greek terms, then adopted the Greek historiographical tradition as their medium for self-expression, and finally replaced the Hellenocentric world-view with their own frames of reference. The model explains the mixture of Greek and non-Greek, as well as a certain degree of diversity, but does not provide for the possibility that non-Greek peoples formulated their past even before they came into contact with the Greeks.

[49] *FGrH* 722.

laying and water-drawing machines, besides being a philosopher.[50] But Artapanus drew him into a Greek framework—
he was called Musaeus by the Greeks, because he was the
teacher of Orpheus.[51] Therefore the Greek frame of reference
was never wholly absent, but the writings on Judaea have a
distinctive tone, deriving from their internal chronological
system and migration stories, which do not originate at Troy.[52]

An Egyptian parallel for the Jewish historiographical tradition and its interest in chronology is Manetho's account of the
Hyksos dynasty, full of relative dates and lengths of reigns,
rather than an absolute chronology. Eusebius referred to the
work as *On the Egyptian Dynasties after the Flood*, using the
chronological marker from Jewish history. Josephus saw Manetho as an expert on chronology, but he translated Manetho's
dates into a Greek chronological framework for the benefit of
his own readers. So, he concluded, the Jews left Egypt 393
years before Danaus came to Argos, or thousands of years
before the Trojan war. It is interesting that Josephus felt a
translation was necessary, which shows that, chronologically
speaking, even a Hellenized Egyptian like Manetho used a
different language from the Greeks.[53]

Berosus of Babylon furnishes more examples of the use of
non-Greek frameworks. He started his history at the time of
the great flood, and according to Josephus, gave dates for Noah
and his descendants; already the same chronological markers as

---

[50] Ibid. 726 F 3 for Artapanus' account of Moses.

[51] See also Cleodemus-Malchus' tale (*FGrH* 727 F 1) of the sons of
Abraham. A standard migration-story of Afer to Afra, Assur to Assyria,
and Afran to Africa was transformed into a *Greek* story when the three sons
joined Hercules on an expedition to Libya, and Hercules married Afer's
daughter.

[52] Diodorus 1. 96. 2 provides an example of the intrusion of Greeks into
accounts of Egypt. Greek tourists, such as Orpheus, Homer, Solon, and Plato,
eager to learn the wisdom of Egypt, got caught up in the flurry of record-
keeping, became a wonder in their own right, were noted down in the priestly
records, and so became absorbed into the relentless writing of Egyptian
history, for once subsumed in the historiography of another nation.

[53] For Manetho, see *FGrH* 609. Against the view of Bickermann,
D. Mendels, 'The Polemical Character of Manetho's *Aegyptiaca*', in *Purposes
of History*, 91–110, argues that Manetho was deliberately writing in line with
the propaganda of the Ptolemaic court, and was relatively independent of the
Hellenistic tradition on Egypt.

for Judaea and Egypt.[54] His king-list would be unintelligible to a Greek, using 'saroi', 'neroi', and 'sossoi' as units of time-measurement. His dynastic succession, like those of Manetho, was interwoven with the creation story. The story of Babylonia involved sea-creatures who came out at night and gave basic instruction in geometry and architecture, as well as the more standard themes of battles and conquests.

Although all the regional accounts I have mentioned were written in the Greek language, it is clear that some were dominated by Greek frames of reference, both in terms of chronology and through the intrusion of Greek mythology, and some employed quite different ways of formulating the past. There is a difference between accounts in which Jason, Medea, Aeneas, and the Trojan war feature, and those in which dates and places are given by the biblical flood, where the Greek heroes are almost entirely absent and time is marked by king-lists and creation stories. This raised a potential problem for writers of accounts which included all of these areas, namely, how could sources using different frames of reference be successfully combined? It has been argued that the incompatibility of frames of reference, both chronological and otherwise, revealed in these fragmentary texts really only began to be noticed in the later first century BC, that is, precisely when there was a profusion of universal writing.[55] The question is clearly relevant to Strabo and his attempt to assimilate vast quantities of material ranging from Britain to India.[56]

For a possible solution to the problem, I refer back to the

[54] *FGrH* 680.

[55] J. W. Johnson, 'Chronological Writing: Its Concepts and Development', *History and Theory*, 2 (1962–3), 128, notes the preference that tended to be given to Jewish dating for the great flood and other events, even among Gentile authors such as Pompeius.

[56] R. Drews, 'Assyria in Classical Universal Histories', *Historia*, 14 (1965), 129–42, discusses the problem with regard to universal historians such as Diodorus, Pompeius Trogus, and Nicolaus of Damascus, all of whom based the Assyrian material in their works on the account of Ctesias of Cnidus. Drews notes their different responses to the difficulty, which persisted in spite of the various synchronisms that had, by this time, been worked out to link Greek and Assyrian history. Diodorus said that Assyrian and Greek history needed to be treated separately; Pompeius incorporated it better by making the Assyrian empire the first in the succession of empires; Nicolaus, like Diodorus, separated Assyrian history from the rest of his work (pp. 134–5).

pattern of Strabo's use of regional accounts which emerged
from Appendix C, revealing that the countries of the Fertile
Crescent are precisely those for which he does not cite such
local histories. But this is exactly in line with the nature of his
project as I have described it so far. I argued in chapter IV that
Strabo's concern was with the present identity of individual
places, made up of stories about the past, and that this resulted
in a concentration on moments of foundation, migration, and
transformation. I argued further that these preoccupations are
reflected in his use of broad mythological indicators of time,
such as the Trojan war and the migrations of heroes. These are
(while acknowledging the problems involved in using fragmentary sources, as discussed throughout chapter III) apparently the dominant concerns of the extant regional histories
from the Hellenistic period, but they are also precisely the
features which distinguish accounts of the Fertile Crescent
from those based in the Graeco-Roman tradition. The point is
reinforced by the pattern of Strabo's citation of lyric poets and
tragedians (see Appendix C). These are almost always referred
to for a point of mythological detail, and their use, extremely
common in Strabo's description of the Mediterranean world as
far as, and including, Asia Minor, is suddenly abandoned on
reaching the Fertile Crescent, reflecting the fact that the
mythological framework has now changed.

The spatial variations in Strabo's use of regional accounts
and poetic sources can be seen as a consequence of his attempt
to write a united description of his present Roman world. This
world incorporated areas which were in contact with one
another, but which had very different historiographical traditions, whose combination would be extremely difficult. In any
case, there was no need for Strabo to make the attempt, since
the frameworks used by writers on the Fertile Crescent to
formulate the past were of little significance to the experience
and understanding of the world which we might attribute to
Strabo's Graeco-Roman readers. It is easy to explain why
Greek frameworks were kept and others omitted, given Strabo's Greek education and his adherence to the Greek geographical tradition, however much he may have adapted this.
But if the universal account had simply been the sum of all its
individual parts, the disparate nature of the frames of reference

in previous regional histories would have presented no problem. As I have argued before, although Strabo's universalism was conceived of in terms of discrete units, these were crucially linked, not directly to each other, but indirectly through their common ties to Rome, thus necessitating some degree of conceptual coherence, even though this was not translated into the imposition of an overall chronological system.

It would be convenient if the *Geography* were as neatly defined a project as even this, describing the world as it was now in Strabo's time under Roman rule. This is the way in which I have chosen to characterize it, and to a large extent I believe the model works. It explains, at least, why Strabo's interest in the past of places is determined by their present identities and the traditions associated with them; and it is consistent with the recurrent mention of the links between each place and Rome, at the expense of the relationships, spatial, commercial, and cultural, between different places within the empire. I have undertaken to say something about the spatial and temporal construction of Strabo's Roman world, and could, with some justification, omit to deal with those parts of the *Geography* which do not conform to that description.

I must, however, at least acknowledge a disparity between the world of Strabo's *Geography* and his rewriting of the world of Roman power. I recall the contrast which Strabo himself draws between the world he describes (μέν) and the world progressively conquered by Rome (δέ) (17. 3. 24). If Strabo's project were simply to paint a picture of those areas subject to Rome, why did he include, for example, India in his account? The nature of the Indian description gives some clue as to its unusual role in the work. The strongly temporal structure applied to the *Geography* as a whole is almost entirely missing here. India is timeless in the *Geography*; it cannot be incorporated into the historical processes described throughout the work. But that is because, for Rome, India was not historically significant in so far as it had not been conquered. There was no possibility of structuring a description of places in India according to the 'past: present' scheme because Rome had not transformed this landscape, as it had done to most of the rest of the world. In addition, Strabo himself points out the lack of recent information about India, and this is reflected in the fact that, as can be seen in Appendix C, Strabo's account is dominated by the Hellenistic sources, particularly those written in the wake of Alexander (15. 1. 2). But, if there was nothing new to say, and India was one of the few parts of the world not to come under Roman rule, then why did Strabo include it in his description? Strabo's use of Alexander-sources may provide one possible answer. India had fallen within the grasp of Rome's great predecessor in world conquest, whose image was adopted by figures such as Pompey and Caesar. Perhaps Strabo included India in his world because it represented Roman aspirations to go even further in the conquest of the world, to incorporate not only the West, but also the full extent of Alexander's realm.

There was, however, an alternative approach to areas not fully under Roman rule. Parts of the far north-west, notably Ireland, were also non-Roman areas described by Strabo, but, by contrast with India, these unconquered territories are presented as unprofitable and undesirable. Ierne (Ireland) is painted as a place of extreme savagery, cannibalism, and incest (4. 5. 4). Britain was on the way to becoming conquered, and Strabo notes the sending of embassies to Augustus, the British offerings on the Capitolium, and the virtual Romanization of the island (4. 5. 3). However, Britain had not actually succumbed to Roman rule and Strabo is quick to explain this, just as he excused the failure of Aelius Gallus' expedition to Arabia Felix. There is no need, says Strabo, to bring Britain into the tribute-paying part of the empire, since it pays a great deal in export duties (4. 5. 3). In other words, Rome has *chosen* not to conquer Britain.

Dion has discussed the tensions in Strabo's account of the north-western parts of the empire. On the one hand, Strabo saw Britain, in particular, as the next stage in the Roman conquest of the world: 'comme une suite logique de celle de la Gaule'.[57] On the other hand, Strabo defended the Roman failure to conquer this region to date, through geographical misrepresentation. He places Ireland almost in the glacial zone,

[57] R. Dion, *Aspects politiques de la géographie antique* (Paris, 1977), 254: 'as a logical continuation of the conquest of Gaul'.

and discredits Pytheas' account of an island of Thule, even further north, and yet inhabited. For Dion, the political requirements were to the detriment of geographical knowledge: 'C'est principalement en raison de son attitude à l'égard de Pythéas que la géographie romaine, ou du moins une certaine géographie romaine, peut être considérée comme marquant une régression dans l'histoire de la connaissance de la terre.'[58]

The cases of Britain and India may be explained in terms of the aim that, if not yet, they should at some point become part of the 'Roman world'. But we cannot say that of Ireland. I wonder whether this is the moment to invoke the nature of the intended readership and of Strabo himself, the man of state, but at the same time educated and cultured. Places at the extremes of the world were difficult, if not impossible, to incorporate fully into the organizational structures of Strabo's description. But, even if they were not important from the practical point of view of administration and government, the concerns of the man of state (ὁ πολιτικός), they were nevertheless part of the Roman world-view. The impossibility of drawing a line around 'The Roman empire' is reflected in Strabo's *Geography*. Most of what he describes was fully part of the Roman world, in so far as it paid taxes and was ruled by Roman governors, or client kings. But Strabo's Roman world, of interest to the cultured man of learning (ὁ φιλόσοφος), went further, to incorporate areas not yet physically conquered by Rome, but intellectually subsumed into the world of Roman knowledge.

---

[58] Ibid. 275: 'It is principally because of his attitude towards Pytheas that Roman geography, or at least a certain type of Roman geography, could be seen as marking a regression in the history of the knowledge of the world.' The manipulation of geographical knowledge for political ends is, of course, famously illustrated by the use of Mercator's projection to reinforce the Europeans' view of their hegemony. This, and other examples, are discussed by J. B. Harley, 'Maps, Knowledge, and Power', in D. Cosgrove and S. Daniels (eds.), *The Iconography of Landscape* (Cambridge, 1988), 277–312.

THE NATURE OF STRABO'S γεωγραφία
('GEOGRAPHY')

So what kind of a work is the *Geography*? The term 'historical geography' has often been applied, but bears so many interpretations that it will not suffice without further specification.[59] Historical geography may firstly be taken to refer to 'geography concerned with past geographies', in other words attempting a synchronic reconstruction of the world at a moment in the past. Although Strabo does give glimpses of periods at which the world as a whole was being transformed, the synchronic approach is clearly subordinate to other preoccupations. However, he was certainly concerned with past geographies in so far as one of his tasks was to evaluate the preceding geographical tradition and to place his own work within that context.

Alternatively we may see the term as referring to the geography of a place through time, and I have tried to show that this is to a large degree what is 'historical' about Strabo's *Geography*. The past was important for Strabo because it was necessary for understanding the present state of a place. This picture of the individual settlement, together with its memories and the construction of its past, was more important than the relationship between that place and its neighbours. So, Strabo's attitude to time affected his conception of space, and led to a concern with discrete units, each with its own story; or alternatively, his interest in place made time relevant to his view of space, if we accept the suggestion that the passage of time is what transforms space into place. These concerns would enable Strabo to qualify as having written the broadest type of geography possible, as defined by Isaac Watts and cited in Samuel Johnson's *Dictionary*: 'Geography in a strict sense signifies the knowledge of the circles of the earth's globe, and the situation of the various parts of the earth. When it is taken in a little larger sense it includes the knowledge of the seas also;

[59] The various forms of 'historical geography' are discussed in the papers collected by F. Driver et al., 'Geographical Traditions: Rethinking the History of Geography', *TIBG* NS 20 (1995), 403–22. Here the validity of looking at 'the history of geography' at all is challenged, in reaction to the publication of Livingstone's *The Geographical Tradition* in 1992.

and in the largest sense of all it extends to the various customs, habits and governments of nations.'[60]

Strabo's explicit attitude to the past is self-contradictory in the first place. He both denies it as part of his geography, and acknowledges it as necessary for an understanding of the present. The past of different areas varies according to the pattern of settlement. Πόλις-history—the vicissitudes of the cities, their foundations, destructions, refoundations, and changes of status—accounts for a huge proportion of the history in the work. This is hardly surprising, given the importance of cities in structuring the world that Strabo wished to describe. Non-πόλις history—the history of peoples and institutions—is also important, and shares some of the characteristics and vocabulary of city-history, while requiring certain different strategies. The temporal systems adopted by Strabo to describe this past, and its relationship with the present, are complicated and numerous. They include both chronological markers, of the kind used in Hellenistic history, and vaguer, relative time-systems. It appears that, for most of the time, the precise date did not matter to Strabo in the way that it might to a historian such as Diodorus.

The historical events which Strabo includes do not seem to have been chosen at random, but fall into particular phases, affecting different areas at different times. The one uniting factor is that, when Rome begins to rule the world, the events that Strabo mentions similarly cover the whole known world. This is why there is so much more history from the first century BC than from any other period. The history in Strabo's *Geography* confirms that, after the initial period of coherence under the heroes from Troy and their global wanderings, the world did not lend itself to universal history again until the

---

[60] Cited in J. N. L. Baker, *The History of Geography* (Oxford, 1963), 92. For the opposing view that Strabo was *restricted* in the conception of his project, see R. E. Dickinson and O. J. R. Howarth, *The Making of Geography* (Oxford, 1933), 29: 'His main interest lay in political geography and all that that implies. . . . There are limitations worthy of the nineteenth century AD in his view of the scope of geography, as illustrated by examples taken almost at random from his second introductory book.' This seems to me rather a strange way in which to argue, since the style of geography set out in the first two books is quite unlike that adopted by Strabo for his actual description of the world.

Romans reunited it. It was the reunited world that Strabo undertook to describe in a single work. The history of each individual place, which defines its present identity, leads right up to Strabo's own time and to the relationship of the place with Rome. Both spatial and temporal aspects of the text lead in this direction, to the Roman present, which formed the stimulus for the work and united the disparate places through the centre.

The *Geography* could be described as geographical, rather than historical, partly because of its professed concern with the present over the past. Strabo could justifiably make this claim because much of the past encompassed by the work contributes to the present perception of places. However, it was also a geography because a spatial arrangement dominated its composition. There is no real attempt at synchronization; rather each place is treated as a separate entity. But I hope that the preceding chapters have shown that this alone is not satisfactory as a complete definition of geography, since within the narrative of each place, the arrangement of material is temporally determined. In a sense, both of the major models of geography and history which I discussed in chapter I work for Strabo's *Geography*. It is both more spatial than temporal, and more concerned with the present than with the past. But, as I have shown, space, time, present, and past, the defining features of both geography and history, are all part of Strabo's work.

The world of Strabo's *Geography* was still undergoing transformation. This is one of the reasons why it is such a rich and interesting text. Depicting an apparently united world in a universal account, it barely conceals the underlying divisions and tensions. Strabo's *Geography* falls between geography and history because of its universal scope, which necessitated a huge organizational feat of integrating temporal and spatial aspects. But it is more complex even than this, as each element of the formulation is subjected to further fragmentation. The *Geography* is also geographically suspended between the different spatial foci of the Pontic region, the cities of Asia Minor, and Rome, all of which provide different perspectives on the world being described. Still further, the *Geography* is historically suspended between the past world, as found in the Greek literary tradition, and the present Roman world.

The generic issue is a useful starting-point, since it opens up a wide range of practical, philosophical, and literary approaches, but its potential is limited. Strabo was the author of a comprehensive account, which took within its compass the culture, history, and customs of cities and peoples across the whole world known to the Romans, and transformed both geographical and historiographical traditions in order to construct a world-view which was appropriate for the new horizons of the age. The result is both local and universal, interested in the past, but motivated by the present, simultaneously temporal and spatial.

As I indicated in chapter I, the continued importance through the Hellenistic age of the all-embracing Herodotean model, the conviction of Jacoby that generic fluidity was an essential feature of Greek prose writing, and the appropriateness of a geographical and ethnographical *histoire humaine* in depicting new worlds, such as the one faced by Strabo, may offer more illuminating ways of progressing with Strabo's *Geography*, as indeed with the works of Polybius and Posidonius. Just as I would argue that Polybius' *Histories* were far broader in scope than a political narrative, and that Posidonius' fragmentary works can be better understood if we abandon strictly delimited notions of what constitutes geographical and historical writings, so too does Strabo's *Geography* lie at the more capacious end of the spectrum of geographical definitions. Not only does this approach bring these three authors together in terms of literary genre and explain the large degree of overlap in contents and form between what are apparently quite different works, but the notion of a capacious geographical-historical-ethnographical style also offers an appropriate medium in which all of these authors could formulate their various Hellenistic constructions of the Roman world.

Considering the issues of time, space, and literary genre is profitably complemented by an attempt to view the *Geography*, like the works of Polybius and Posidonius, as the product of a particular historical situation. The approach may be exemplified by the third and final meaning that we could give to 'historical geography'; namely as the 'history of geographical ideas'. I discussed in chapter V how Strabo builds up a picture, which starts with Homer and is developed particularly in the first two books, of the tradition in which he was participating. This had a history which ran in parallel to the history of the changing world, reflecting different stages in its development towards the present. It was as essential to understand how geographical knowledge and conceptions of the world had developed through time, as to understand the changes to the world itself. As we have seen, much of the richness of the *Geography* comes from its incorporation of different geographical traditions—both scientific and periegetic—but, as I argued in chapter IV, the geographical tradition of the past relied on spatial models which were at odds with the picture of the Roman world which Strabo wanted to paint. The linear space of the periplus texts and the geometrical space of the mathematical tradition needed to be complemented by a centre–periphery model focused on Rome. So Strabo here spatially, just as temporally in his historical accounts of the cities, created a present which relied on but was transformed from the past and its traditions. Literary genre was forced to evolve into a form that would suit the new age.

The transformation of the tradition brings us back to Strabo, his historical context and his persona as author of the *Geography*. It is striking that self-referential temporal indicators, chronologically related to Strabo himself, are largely restricted to intellectual history. The structured history of cities and the spread of Roman rule and customs also reached the present day, but this was denoted more commonly by the impersonal temporal indicator νῦν ('now'). I argued in chapter IV that Strabo created different spatial focal points, reflected in the use of different, personal or impersonal, temporal indicators to refer to the present (pp. 242–3). What I am suggesting is that Strabo's Roman world might have contained more than one present—a world centred on Rome, and a personal, intellectual base in Asia Minor.

Nicolet has brilliantly demonstrated how Roman power affected geographical conceptions in the first century BC. Very many aspects of Strabo's *Geography* can be explained by reference to the ideas put forward by Nicolet, in particular the notion of Rome as spatial and temporal focus of the world, and the whole concept of providing a comprehensive account of the present state of the world, as paralleled in the map of Agrippa and the *Res Gestae*.[61] Nicolet's stress on the Roman preoccupation with controlling the natural world is, of course, reflected in Strabo's account of how the Romans deliberately transformed the world under their command.[62]

But Nicolet's model of the world of the first century BC only partially accounts for the *Geography* as we have it. Strabo has presented us with a fine example, not only of the Romans' conquest of the world and their geographical conceptions of it, but also of a quite different phenomenon, namely the transition between Greek and Roman worlds. The *Geography* perfectly illustrates that the world which Strabo knew, and was trying to describe, was Roman in name and political power, but could not be conceptualized and depicted except through recourse to the Greek historiographical and geographical traditions, which still dominated mental maps of the world and reflected the reality of the past, which had been transformed into the present.[63] All were required in order to make up Strabo's universal γεωγραφία. The importance of Homer, author of the first and greatest periegetic compositions, mapping out the world by sea through the wanderings of Odysseus, and by land through the provenances of the troops in the *Iliad*, cannot be overemphasized. So the definition of geography as exclusive of the past was unthinkable not only on aetiological grounds, but also because the past literary tradition provided the only framework within which to construct the present Roman

[61] Nicolet, *Space, Geography, and Politics*, devotes ch. 5 to 'Agrippa's Geographical Work' and ch. 8 to 'The "Geographical" Work of Augustus'.

[62] See ibid., chs. 6, 7, and 9, on the Roman census, the cadastres, and the administrative organization of space respectively. G. Traina, *Ambiente e paesaggi di Roma antica* (Rome, 1990), 53, makes the same point about the actual experience of Roman power 'in esigenze amministrative, fiscali, censitarie oltre che culturali e politiche' ('in administrative, fiscal, censorial demands, besides the cultural and political').

[63] C. Jacob, *Géographie et ethnographie en Grèce ancienne* (Paris, 1991), 147, sums up the situation perfectly: 'Strabon vit entre deux mondes: l'Empire romain dont il suit la genèse et l'expansion; le monde grec, dont la culture, la littérature et les traditions l'imprègnent' ('Strabo lived between two worlds: the Roman empire, whose birth and expansion he follows; the Greek world, whose culture, literature, and traditions saturate him').

world, however unsatisfactory that framework was for some areas. The location of Strabo the author in the intellectual circles of the Greek East, set alongside the focus of the world he was describing, Rome, neatly symbolizes the tension that underlies the work, and if we want to maintain a spatial association for geography, then it is appropriate that these two crucial elements should have been spatially distinguished.

But, just as Strabo the author cannot be truly distinguished from the *Geography* which he wrote, so too do the different geographical foci become blurred. Strabo of Amaseia is the same figure as Strabo of the Greek intellectual heartland, and the same as Strabo author of a work which was firmly fixed on the city of Rome and the world of Roman power. In Van Paassen's words, Strabo's was a 'Greek mind in Roman surroundings'.[64] The spatial distinctions are further complicated by the tendency of Greek intellectuals of this period, including Strabo himself, to move to Rome.[65] This is the moment to recall Bowersock's proposed reader, the Roman πολιτικός (man of state) educated in Greek φιλοσοφία (philosophy). And, in parallel with this spatial blurring goes a lack of temporal distinction. As we saw exemplified in the regional accounts of Rome and Italy, Rome and the present were nothing without the Greek world and the past. The tension is neatly encompassed in the *Geography* itself. The work starts with an extensive acknowledgement of the debt to the Greek intellectual tradition, from Homer and his world-view onwards; it ends with a picture of the world in the form of an enumeration of Roman provinces. One might argue that this framing symbolizes the fact that the Greek world of the past has been transformed into and eclipsed by the Roman world of the present. This is the general direction of movement, but

[64] C. Van Paassen, *The Classical Tradition of Geography* (Groningen, 1957), 9.

[65] G. W. Bowersock, *Augustus and the Greek World* (Oxford, 1965), 123–8. A. M. Biraschi, 'Dai "Prolegomena" all'Italia: Premesse teoriche e tradizione', in *Italia Antica*, 127–43, argues further that the circle of intellectuals, of which Strabo and Dionysius of Halicarnassus were part, became involved in the classicistic revival of the Augustan age, with the aim of cultivating the ruling classes through literature that was both political and cultural (p. 131). Thus, the use of the tradition not only authenticated Strabo's work, but also deliberately brought back to prominence the patrimony of knowledge (p. 142).

there is no straightforward progression through the work. We do not get a sense that the world is gradually becoming free of the Greek modes of expression, that places are becoming increasingly liberated from their Greek past to take their place in a fully Roman world. Rather, every time a new place is reached, Strabo goes right back to the earliest period of history again. There is no sense in which the past has been abandoned; rather, just like the Laestrygonians of Bonifacio, the history of each place becomes part of its present.

Epilogue

Herculean was a word I kept wanting to use but never did; the only Herculean part of my trip was every night having to describe how I had spent the day, without leaving anything out; turning all my actions into words. It was like a labor in a myth or an old story. I could not sleep until the work was done.[1]

I started with Theroux's modern-day journey, real and intellectual, around the Mediterranean world, and, in particular, with his identification of the Rock of Gibraltar with one of the Pillars of Hercules. It thus seems appropriate to return to his work at the end of my own periplus around this subject. Theroux still had some distance to go before he reached the end of his voyage, but his description of the daunting nature of his task as 'Herculean' neatly evokes the sense of closure associated with his imminent arrival at the African Pillar of Hercules, setting the seal on a huge undertaking. Here, as elsewhere, both implicitly and explicitly Theroux writes in a way which illustrates the interrelationship between time and space which has been one of the main subjects of this work. His journey through space entails a literary undertaking which is described through direct reference to the mythical past. At the same time, the whole Herculean framework is evocative of a past tradition of writing about space, the periplus text in its most basic form, starting and ending with the Pillars of Hercules. My own return to Theroux and matters Herculean signals that this is the moment for me to recall some of the ideas encapsulated in the intervening space, and also, in the manner of Scylax, to hint at some of the possibilities for future exploration which lie beyond the Pillars.

One of my aims was to explore the problematic overlap

[1] P. Theroux, *The Pillars of Hercules: A Grand Tour of the Mediterranean* (London, 1995), 522.

between geography and history. The difficulty is manifested at various levels. Our problem as readers of ancient texts is that we have certain expectations about what constitutes 'geographical' and 'historical' works, expectations which are the products of a long history of the development of the modern academic subjects known as 'geography' and 'history'. We cannot discard the issue by claiming that geography and history were inseparable in antiquity, making our difficulty simply the result of anachronism. Although we may find it hard to pinpoint what distinguished ancient geography from ancient history, the fact that individual authors, such as Strabo, were responsible for both types of work means that we should at least try to understand what γεωγραφία and ἱστορία were, and how they differed from each other. Restricted modern notions of 'geography' and 'history' may encourage us to abandon these terms altogether in our discussion of ancient denotations, on the grounds that 'geography' is no more akin to γεωγραφία than 'history' is to ἱστορία. But this is an inadequate response, since the modern disciplines of geography and history have been developed consciously against the backdrop of the tradition. In any case, we can profitably exploit some of the debates concerning the modern fields to enrich our range of approaches to the ancient sources.

In chapter I, I considered some of the many arguments which have been raised in relation to the modern subjects, particularly by geographers in an attempt to define their subject against history. Their discussions are formulated largely in terms of the matrices of time and space, both of which I think can be shown to have been conceived of in antiquity, just as in the modern world, not only as abstractions, but also as features of the world as it was experienced. 'Time' and 'space' are useful terms through which to investigate and describe certain features of geographical and historical reality and its literary representation. However, in the case of each of the authors whose works I have discussed, I have argued that we must qualify the straightforward identification of history with time and geography with space.

In particular, I have argued that the key to our interpretation both of well-known works of great length and of more fragmentary texts is the adoption of an inclusive notion of both geography and history. Here the model of Herodotus is of prime importance, both in helping us to move away from generic distinctions towards a more comprehensive history of cultures and civilizations, and in showing how the broad geographical history (or historical geography), of the kind adopted by the adherents to the *Annales* school, was particularly appropriate to periods of change and expansion. Herodotus provides the literary model as well as exemplifying how such an undertaking could be used to rewrite a new world.

The range and complexity of Polybius' spatial conceptions were enormous. His project demanded that he concern himself with history as the transformation of space, but he was also aware of and interested in the role played by geographical space in altering the course of history. Indeed, the main thesis of Pédech's treatment of the geography in Polybius takes the argument even further, claiming that Polybius became increasingly interested in geography as a subject in its own right, rather than as an integral part of political history; that the traveller gradually took over from the man of state.[2] Political and strategic geography thus gave way to wide-scale geographical interests, of the kind which were the subject of much of chapter II. I would, however, argue that Polybius' global geographical conceptions need not be seen in isolation from his historical method, as a later addition to the text; but rather that they were integral to the whole undertaking.

I attempted to show in chapter III how a re-examination of our preconceptions concerning what is 'geographical' and what 'historical' has implications for our understanding of fragmentary works. I have argued not that Posidonius' *On Ocean* and *Histories* were the same as each other in character, but that the blurred boundary between geography and history necessitates flexibility in our approach to assigning fragments to their ancient context, and to reconstructing the nature of the original works themselves.

Strabo has been the main focus of this book. The survival of the *Geography* and the loss of the *History* allow us to study Strabo's world-view through only the former of these two

[2] P. Pédech, *La Méthode historique de Polybe* (Paris, 1964), 555. Pédech sees Polybius' newly found interest in geography as an intellectual preoccupation which resulted directly from his travels.

works. However, I hope to have shown that the *Geography* does
not answer to the description of a purely spatial account of the
world. Even a consideration of space in this work reveals a
strong temporal element, in so far as Strabo treated the
evolution of spatial models which stretched back to Homer
and subjected them to various transformations to make them
relevant to his present Roman world. In addition to this,
Strabo's description of each place is structured by changes
through time, placing city-histories at the heart of a 'geographical' work. But space comes to the fore in so far as it is
moments of geographical transformation which provide Strabo
with his chronological framework, and which dominate his
treatment of the past. The amount of material about the past
which appears in Strabo's *Geography* challenges the identification of history with the past and geography with the present in
a way which seems to contradict even Strabo's own professed
aims; but, as I argued in chapter V, this is because the present
identity of a place comprises both its present and its past.

Dubois complained more than a century ago that our tendency to categorize authors according to literary genre means
that we make Strabo 'moins historien et plus géographe qu'il
ne fut en réalité'.[3] A similar methodological complaint could be
directed at our treatment of Polybius as a historian and of the
fragments of Posidonius' lost works. If nothing else, by
questioning the ease with which we seem able to label ancient
authors and their works as belonging to one genre or another, I
hope to have opened up new possibilities for the interpretation
of relatively well-known texts. Modern debates over the nature
of geography and history, time and space, their separability and
interrelationship, can at the very least make us alert to textual
features which might otherwise be passed over.

But the aim of this book was not only to explore and present
a literary debate which might enrich our reading of some
ancient texts. What starts as a question of genre soon becomes
transformed into an issue of wider significance. If we search
beyond the literary issue of generic classification to the underlying notions of time and space, linked to human experience of

---

[3] 'less a historian and more a geographer than he really was': M. Dubois,
'Strabon et Polybe', *Revue des Études Grecques*, 4 (1891), 349.

the world, and consider ways of conceiving of and depicting that world, we start to unravel a piece of intellectual history. The Roman world as depicted by Strabo has been the main object of that enquiry, but Polybius and Posidonius also provide important examples of attempts to encapsulate in large-scale texts a world which was gradually falling under the sway of a single power. Together, these three authors represent a major and distinctive phase of re-evaluation, when cultural horizons had to be reassessed and a new world constructed. Their responses to this need would be related to, but importantly different from, previous periods of expansion and change. One feature which links the conceptions of all of these authors is their concern to express the unity of the Roman world. Stoic συμπαθεία ('sympathy'), the biographical model of the earth and its individual cities as animate beings with a life-cycle to relate, the notion of fate, and the logic of the natural world all come into play in the attempt to draw together and make sense of the world, in ways which step outside the traditional spatial and temporal patterns of geography and history.

These preoccupations make the works I have studied natural products of their own particular age. The rise of Rome and the unification of almost the whole known world resulted in a wealth of universal accounts. Polybius made explicit the fact that his work was directed towards exploring the way in which Roman power had spread to the extent that world history would cease to be spatially subdivided. His *History* vividly reflects the dynamic changes to geography brought about by the events of the early second century BC. By Strabo's time, the transformation of the world was almost complete. The first century BC was a time of unparalleled production of universal accounts of all kinds—literary, cartographic, and monumental. This is the context in which to read the *Geography*, as an ecumenical representation of the Roman world during the late Republic and early principate.

But how Roman was Strabo's conception of the unified world? It could be argued that his universalism fits perfectly into the context of Pompey's triumphal procession, the *Res gestae*, and the map of Agrippa. Strabo was simply providing another expression of Roman imperialism. But, if the

conception was Roman, the formulation was not. As I have
already discussed, the *Geography* was written firmly and self-
consciously in the Greek literary tradition. I hinted at the need
to move away from literary issues towards the question of how
these works reflected a particular historical period. We may
certainly shift the focus away from generic analysis and the
modern reception of these texts, but the literary contextualization of a work such as the *Geography* tells us as much about
the circumstances of its composition and the world-view of the
author as does a consideration of its factual contents.

We can derive from the information contained in the *Geography* many details of how the Roman empire functioned
under Augustus and the early years of Tiberius' reign. But
we can also draw conclusions about the world of this period
from the manner in which the work was constructed. Strabo's
literary presentation of his own location in time and space,
although oblique, reveals that he was viewing the Roman world
from the perspective of an educated inhabitant of the Greek
East. In this he was not alone, but in the company of figures
such as Dionysius of Halicarnassus. We may recall Dionysius'
call to 'make Roman times conform to the Greek' (*AR* 1. 74. 2).
The world was Roman, but it required a Greek mode of
expression.

A major point of interest to emerge from a consideration of
the *Geography* is the whole first-century BC intellectual milieu,
a world centred on Rome, but comprised of figures from the
Greek East. One of the most fruitful ways in which a study of
Strabo and his work might be developed would, in my opinion,
be to explore further this interaction between Greek and
Roman. Was it simply because of their provenance that these
writers employed Greek traditions and Greek frameworks to
describe a Roman world? Or was it that there existed no
specifically Roman way of conceiving of and writing about
the Roman world? One possible line of enquiry would be to
compare the viewpoint and conceptual framework of other
universal accounts of this period, in order to see whether it is
possible to identify a relatively uniform way of seeing and
describing the Roman world. Of particular interest in this
would be not only accounts written by Roman authors, but
also 'opposition' literature, a category to which the work of, for

example, Pompeius Trogus has been assigned.[4] How different, if at all, was Trogus' spatial and temporal construction of the world from that of Strabo or Dionysius? Was it possible, or even desirable, to escape from the dominant conceptual framework?

The writing of universal accounts was a striking feature of the first century BC, as exemplified by the work of Diodorus, Dionysius, and Nicolaus, and had important predecessors such as Polybius in the preceding century. But time and space were combined in interesting ways not only in these large-scale treatments of the world. I mentioned in chapter VI the possible difficulties faced by an author such as Strabo if he were to try to combine regional accounts into a universal geography. A further area of research lies in shifting the focus from the universal to the local, and considering the extent to which regional accounts were written as representations of isolated fragments of time and space, or whether their authors and readers were consciously aware that they were dealing with 'parts of a whole'.[5] The temporal and spatial limitations of this project have entailed that I largely exclude discussion of Hellenistic regional accounts, but they seem to me perfectly suited to the kind of approach that I have been applying to universal writers. As I mentioned in connection with Pompeius Trogus on Armenia (pp. 96–7), these local accounts regularly define space in terms of the past of the place concerned. Parts of Asia Minor are particularly rich in mythological associations, where past visits by heroes and gods contribute to the distinctive identities of regions and cities. The mythological geography of an area such as Armenia would, it seems, be one possible field for further investigation. A study of the complex relationship between geography, history, time, and space, focused on a restricted area, could be extended beyond the realms of literary texts to include epigraphic, numismatic, monumental, and artistic representations of the region. But

[4] See J. M. Alonso-Núñez, 'L'opposizione contro l'imperialismo romano e contro il principato nella storiografia del tempo di Augusto', *Rivista Storica dell'Antichità*, 12 (1982), 131–41.

[5] See D. S. Levene, 'Sallust's *Jugurtha*: An "Historical Fragment"', *JRS* 82 (1992), 53–70, for Sallust's *Jugurtha* as a self-conscious fragment of a larger history.

how comprehensible would allusions to the appearance of a figure such as Jason be without a knowledge of his wanderings in the wider Mediterranean world? How local could the frame of reference really be?

The fact that this project can be allowed, in all senses, no more time and no more space does not imply that the issues are closed. Rather, I hope to have raised more questions than could be answered, and, with the help of some current debates about the nature of geography and history, to have opened up some new approaches to ancient texts and to their ways of conceptualizing and depicting the world. In particular, I have tried to show that Strabo's *Geography*, which has traditionally been seen as nothing more than a mine of information about the Roman empire in the age of Augustus, deserves study in its own right, as a text of enormous temporal and spatial complexity. The project to write an account of the whole world known to the Romans may be fitted satisfactorily into a context of Roman imperialism, formulated against a Greek literary tradition. However, Strabo's specifically 'geographical' manifestation of this first-century universalism is a unique survival. In a sense, my interests have led me to search in the *Geography* for 'Strabo the historian'. We may indeed wish that we had Strabo's *History*; a comparison of a 'geography' and a 'history' by a single author might bring new insights into what was distinctive about the two styles of writing. But I would not want the *History* to have survived at the expense of the *Geography*, although the former is generally assumed to have been the greater work. We have other universal histories, but only one *Geography* for this period. It provides us with a unique opportunity to see what happened when an intellectual from the periphery of the empire brought the Roman transformation of the world into contact with the richness of the Greek geographical tradition, which had accumulated through time from Homer onwards.

I leave to Defoe the final formulation of the interaction of time and space, illustrated in the constantly changing nature of the subject of his geographical work. His anticipatory apologies will suffice to express my concluding excuses for the imperfect and incomplete state of my own project; but I should like also to adopt his optimism that such imperfection can lead only to improvement and the development of new ideas:[6]

But after all that has been said by others, or can be said here, no description of Great Britain can be what we call a finished account, as no clothes can be made to fit a growing child; no picture carry the likeness of a living face; the size of one, and the countenance of the other always altering with time: so no account of a kingdom thus daily altering its countenance can be perfect. Even while the sheets are in the press, new beauties appear in several places, and almost to every part we are obliged to add appendixes, and supplemental accounts of fine houses, new undertakings, buildings, &c. and thus posterity will be continually adding; every age will find an increase of glory.

[6] D. Defoe, *A Tour through the Whole Island of Great Britain* (London, 1724–6; repr. Harmondsworth, 1986), Preface, p. 46.

APPENDIX A

The Arrangement of Posidonius' *Histories*

This table is designed to provide a convenient overview of the ordering, spatial setting, chronological context, and subject matter of the extant fragments assigned to the *Histories* with a book number. It reveals that these fragments do not adhere to strict chronological order (emendations to F 12, 13, 19, and 24 are clearly intended to dispense with anomalies), and that some regional groupings are prominent.

Book	Fragment	Location	Date (BC)	Subject
2	F 1	Rome and Italy	——	Feasts
3	F 2	Syria	145?	Apamea vs. Larissa
3	F 3	Syria/Arabia	——	Pistachio production
4	F 4	Syria/Egypt	140s?	Hierax of Antioch
4	F 24	Syria	90s	Heracleon's feast
5	F 5	Parthia	——	Dining habits
7	F 6	Egypt	c.144–139	Ptolemy VIII's luxury
8	F 7	Sicily	136–132	Damophilus, slave-leader
11	F 8	Black sea	——	Voluntary slavery
14	F 9	Syria	130s	Antiochus Sidetes' feasts
16	F 10	Syria	——	Luxurious lifestyle
16	F 11	Syria	130s	Antiochus Sidetes' luxury
16	F 12	Parthia/Syria	141/0 or 129	Royal treatment at feasts
22	F 14	Greece	c.325/4	Pythionice's funeral
23	F 15	Celtica	————	Dining habits
23	F 16	Celtica	————	Dining habits
23	F 17	Celtica	————	Bards
23	F 18	Celtica	121? or 150s	Luvernius' wealth
26	F 13	Babylonia/Syria	120s	Lysimachus' feast
27	F 19	Dalmatia	————	Wild produce
28	F 20	Syria	————	·Drinking parties
28	F 21	Syria	121–115?	Feasts and festivals
30	F 22	Germany	————	Dining habits
34	F 23	Syria	121–115?	Parasites
36	F 25	?	————	Drinking measures
47	F 26	Egypt	110–88?	Ptol. X Alex.'s luxury
49	F 27	Rome	92?	Apicius' luxury

APPENDIX B

The Fragments of Posidonius' *Histories*

The purpose of this appendix is to provide a systematic collection of texts and translations of those historical fragments which are securely assigned in the sources to the *Histories*. I also develop some of the arguments put forward in chapter III more fully than is possible within the main text. I first discuss those fragments for which book numbers appear in the sources (according to book numbers rather than to fragment numbers, following the order in Appendix A); then two fragments specifically cited as coming from the *Histories*, but which carry no indication of their position within that work. My aim is not to provide a full historical commentary, nor to do more in this direction than collate some of the views expressed in previously published commentaries.[1] Rather, I argue that the fragments securely assigned to the *Histories* do not justify the assumption that the work followed a rigidly chronological order, that even an annalistic work would have room for temporal flexibility, and that we have no grounds for emending the text of fragments in order to eliminate anomalies.

Fragment 1 (F 53 E–K) Athenaeus 4. 153C–D

ἐν δὲ τῇ β [sc. τῶν Ἱστοριῶν] 'ἐν τῇ Ῥωμαίων', φησίν [sc. ὁ Ποσειδώνιος], "πόλει ὅταν εὐωχῶνται ἐν τῷ τοῦ Ἡρακλέους ἱερῷ, δειπνίζοντος τοῦ κατὰ καιρὸν θριαμβεύοντος, καὶ ἡ παρασκευὴ τῆς εὐωχίας Ἡρακλεωτική ἐστι. διοινοχοεῖται μὲν γὰρ οἰνόμελι, τὰ δὲ βρώματα ἄρτοι μεγάλοι καὶ καπνιστὰ κρέα ἐφθὰ καὶ τῶν προσφάτως καθιερευθέντων ὀπτὰ δαψιλῆ. παρὰ δὲ Τυρρηνοῖς δὶς τῆς ἡμέρας τράπεζαι πολυτελεῖς παρασκευάζονται ἀνθιναί τε στρωμναὶ καὶ ἐκπώματα ἀργυρᾶ παντοδαπά, καὶ δούλων πλῆθος εὐπρεπῶν παρέστηκεν ἐσθήσεσι πολυτελέσι κεκοσμημένων."

In the second book [sc. of the *Histories*] Posidonius says, 'In the city of Rome, whenever they have a feast in the temple of Hercules at the invitation of whoever is celebrating a triumph at the time, the

---

[1] Jacoby = F. Jacoby (ed.), *FGrH*, *Kommentar*; Malitz = J. Malitz, *Die Historien des Poseidonios* (Munich, 1983); Kidd = L. Edelstein and I. G. Kidd (eds.), *Posidonius* (Cambridge, 1972 and 1988); Theiler = W. Theiler, *Poseidonios, Die Fragmente* (2 vols., Berlin, 1982).

preparation of the feast is itself Herculean. For honeyed wine flows, and the food is large loaves, boiled smoked meat, and plenty of roasted portions from the freshly sacrificed victims. Among the Etruscans twice a day costly tables are prepared, and flowered spreads and all kinds of silver cups, and a crowd of fine slaves stands by, adorned with expensive clothes.'

According to Malitz, this passage probably belongs to an ethnography of Rome and Italy. Jacoby too had put forward the possibility of an Italian ethnography at the start of the *Histories*, but, given Athenaeus' failure to indicate the Posidonian context with any accuracy, Jacoby remained uncertain whether the passage was part of a larger ethnography or was rather prompted by a historical event. Kidd suggests that it was possibly prompted by a Roman triumph early in the narrative, possibly that of Scipio Aemilianus over Carthage, of Mummius over Achaea and Corinth, and of Appius Claudius over the Salassi. However, the indefinite ὅταν warns against trying to ascertain a particular historical context; the passage concerns repeated customs. Theiler rejects the idea that a particular triumph in the narrative prompted the discussion, points to the parallel ethnographic passage in Diodorus 5. 40, and concludes that Posidonius is writing in opposition to the day-to-day luxury of the Etruscans.

Fragment 2 (F 54 E–K) Athenaeus 4. 176B–C

Ποσειδώνιος δ' ὁ ἀπὸ τῆς Στοᾶς φιλόσοφος ἐν τῇ τρίτῃ τῶν Ἱστοριῶν διηγούμενος περὶ τοῦ Ἀπαμέων πρὸς Λαρισαίους πολέμου γράφει τάδε· "παραζωνίδια καὶ λογχάρι' ἀνειληφότες ἰῷ καὶ ῥύπῳ κεκρυμμένα, πετάσια δ' ἐπιτεθειμένοι καὶ προσκόπια σκιὰν μὲν ποιοῦντα, καταπνεῖσθαι δ' οὐ κωλύοντα τοὺς τραχήλους, ὄνους ἐφελκόμενοι γέμοντας οἴνου καὶ βρωμάτων παντοδαπῶν, οἷς παρέκειτο φωτίγγια καὶ μοναύλια, κώμων οὐ πολέμων ὄργανα . . ."

Posidonius, the philosopher from the Stoa, relating in the third book of his *Histories* the war between the Apameans and the Larissans, writes as follows: 'Clasping daggers worn at the belt and small spears covered in rust and dirt, and wearing wide-brimmed hats and sun-shields, which provided shade, but did not prevent their throats from being aired, and taking along beakers full of wine and food of all kinds, beside which were flutes and recorders, instruments of festivity not of war . . .'

After the assassination of Alexander Balas in 145 BC and the death of Ptolemy Philometor, the Syrian throne was taken by Demetrius II Nicator. However, his rule was soon opposed by his commander at Apamea, Diodotus Tryphon, who set up Alexander's son, Antiochus

VI Epiphanes, as usurper. The struggle between Demetrius and Tryphon in the ensuing years until Demetrius' disastrous expedition against Parthia in 140 BC, and the attendant inter-city strife, were seen by Jacoby and Kidd as the likely context for this conflict.

However, this particular explanation for the conflict between Larissa and Apamea seems to be motivated simply by the fact that the fragment comes from Book 3 of the *Histories*, which, according to Kidd, 'probably saw the opening of Posidonius' account of Syrian history (ie. from 145 BC)'. So we need a context which will work chronologically. The solution of 145–140 BC may indeed be correct; but its deduction is tenuous and it would be circular to use this fragment as evidence for the start-date of the work.

Fragment 3 (F 55a E–K) Athenaeus 14. 649D

καὶ Ποσειδώνιος δὲ ὁ ἀπὸ τῆς Στοᾶς ἐν τρίτῃ τῶν Ἱστοριῶν γράφει οὕτως·
"φέρει δὲ καὶ τὸ πέρσειον ἡ Ἀραβία καὶ ἡ Συρία καὶ τὸ καλούμενον βιστάκιον· ὃ δὴ βοτρυώδη τὸν καρπὸν ἀφίησι λευκόφαιον ὄντα καὶ μακρόν, παρεμφερῆ τοῖς δακρύοις, ἃ δὴ ῥαγῶν τρόπον ἀλλήλοις ἐπιβάλλει, τὰ δ' ἔνδον ἔγχλωρον καὶ τοῦ κωνίου τῶν στροβίλων ἧττον μὲν εὔχυμον, εὐώδη δὲ μᾶλλον."

Posidonius from the Stoa writes in the third book of his *Histories* as follows: 'Arabia and Syria produce both the "perseion" and the so-called pistachio. The latter sends forth fruit like a bunch of grapes, whitish-grey and large, somewhat like teardrops, which fall upon each other like grapes, but inside it is greenish and less tasty than the seeds of a pine cone, although more fragrant.'

The context in the third book is not known. Kidd's suggestion that exotic fruit may have formed part of an account of Syrian luxury is plausible, but even this may overplay Posidonius' philosophical side; he was not obliged to take a moral stance at every opportunity. This passage may simply be part of a general description of the area. Jacoby went even further than Kidd in linking this with the other fragment from Book 3 (F 2), and placing *both* in the context of Demetrius II Nicator's unbridled rule during the years 145–140 BC. In this case, I favour Kidd's caution.

Fragment 4 (F 56 E–K) Athenaeus 6. 252E

Ποσειδώνιος δ' ὁ Ἀπαμεύς, ὕστερον δὲ Ῥόδιος χρηματίσας, ἐν τῇ τετάρτῃ τῶν Ἱστοριῶν Ἱερακά φησι τὸν Ἀντιοχέα πρότερον λυσιῳδοῖς ὑπαυλοῦντα ὕστερον γενέσθαι κόλακα δεινὸν Πτολεμαίου τοῦ ἑβδόμου βασιλέως τοῦ καὶ Εὐεργέτου ἐπικληθέντος καὶ τὰ μέγιστα δυνηθέντα παρ' αὐτῷ, καθάπερ καὶ παρὰ τῷ Φιλομήτορι, ὕστερον ὑπ' αὐτοῦ διαφθαρῆναι.

Posidonius the Apamean, later involved in public life on Rhodes, says in the fourth book of his *Histories* that Hierax of Antioch firstly played on the flute in accompaniment to the actors who played women dressed as men, and later became a terrible flatterer of Ptolemy VII, called Euergetes, and having obtained the greatest power from him, as also from Ptolemy Philometor, he was later destroyed by him.

Kidd comments that this must be placed after the start date of the *Histories* (*c*.146/5 BC), yet before the year dealt with in the datable fragment which survives from Book 7 (F 6 on the eastern embassy of Scipio in 144–139 BC). There is, however, no compelling reason why a fragment from Book 4 must contain material chronogically prior to that assumed for Book 7. We cannot assume that one incident from a book is characteristic of the 'main' narrative of that book; and this holds true for both F 4 and F 6. The text is problematic in any case, since Ptolemy VII was called Neos Philopator, and Ptolemy VIII Euergetes: it is not certain which is meant here, and the problem recurs in connection with F 6, where it appears that Posidonius' Ptolemy VII Euergetes must be the king to whom we usually refer as Ptolemy VIII Euergetes.[2] Ptolemy VI Philometor reigned from 180 to 164/3 BC; Ptolemy VII Neos Philopator's dates are unclear; Ptolemy VIII Euergetes II Physcon ruled from 145 to 116 BC, giving a wide range of possible dates for the situation described in the fragment.

Fragment 24 (F 75 E–K) Athenaeus 4. 153B–C

Ἱστορῶν δὲ [sc. ὁ Ποσειδώνιος] καὶ περὶ Ἡρακλέωνος τοῦ Βεροιαίου, ὃς ὑπὸ τοῦ Γρυποῦ καλουμένου Ἀντιόχου τοῦ βασιλέως προαχθεὶς μικροῦ δεῖν τῆς βασιλείας ἐξέβαλε τὸν εὐεργέτην, γράφει ἐν τῇ δ τῶν Ἱστοριῶν τάδε· ἐποιεῖτό τε τῶν στρατιωτῶν τὰς κατακλίσεις ἐπὶ τοῦ ἐδάφους ἐν ὑπαίθρῳ ἀνὰ χιλίους δειπνίζων. τὸ δὲ δεῖπνον ἦν ἄρτος μέγας καὶ κρέας, τὸ δὲ ποτὸν κεκραμένος οἶνος οἷος δήποτε ὕδατι ψυχρῷ. διηκόνουν δὲ ἄνδρες μαχαιροφόροι καὶ σιωπὴ ἦν εὔτακτος.

In his account of Heracleon of Beroia, who was promoted by King Antiochus Grypus and then very nearly cast his benefactor out of the kingdom, Posidonius writes in the fourth book of the *Histories* as follows: 'He made the soldiers recline on the ground in the open air, entertaining them to dinner in groups of a thousand. The

---

[2] For the names and reigns of the Ptolemies, see A. K. Bowman, *Egypt after the Pharaohs: 332BC–AD 642 from Alexander to the Arab Conquest* (London, 1986), Appendix 1.

dinner was a huge loaf and meat, and to drink there was wine of any old sort mixed with cold water. It was distributed by men carrying swords and there was an orderly silence.'

According to Kidd, this account of how Heracleon fed his troops probably refers to the period when he was still Grypus' commander. The problem again concerns a book number. The manuscript A gives τετάρτῃ for the book number, which Kidd asserts is 'chronologically impossible', presumably on the grounds that the narrative time in question fell near, but not quite at, the end of the work. For similar reasons, Kidd rejects 14, 24, and 44 as possible emendations, leaving him with Bake's suggestion λδ. Much is at fault with the logic here. The assessment of what constituted the narrative time of each book is based on poor foundations.

On the possibility of Book 14, Kidd refers us to F 11. If Antiochus Sidetes was still alive in Book 16, then it would be surprising to find Antiochus Grypus in Book 14, but see my discussion of F 11 for some arguments against Kidd's characterization of this part of the work. As for Book 24, Kidd points to F 21, concerning the lavish entertainment of Antiochus Grypus at Daphne. The implication is that, if Book 28 dealt with the period 121–115/14 BC, then Book 24 must be too early for F 24, which concerns the end of Antiochus Grypus' reign. Again, problems of fragmentation make this impossible to verify. Müller's suggestion of Book 44 is designated 'rather late' by Kidd, leaving him with no alternative but to accept Bake's λδ.

There is, however, another possibility, which would be to reverse the decision that Book 4 is 'chronologically impossible', and to leave the text as it stands. It seems that, in this case, the spatial context may save the situation. While Antiochus Grypus may seem oddly placed in temporal terms in Book 4, he would fit very well into the Syrian context which Kidd himself (together with Jacoby and Malitz) postulated for the early books of the work.

Fragment 5 (F 57 E–K) Athenaeus 4. 152F–153A

ἐν δὲ τῇ πέμπτῃ περὶ Πάρθων διηγούμενός [sc. ὁ Ποσειδώνιος] φησιν· "ὁ δὲ καλούμενος φίλος τραπέζης μὲν οὐ κοινωνεῖ, χαμαὶ δ' ὑποκαθήμενος ἐφ' ὑψηλῆς κλίνης κατακειμένῳ τῷ βασιλεῖ τὸ παραβληθὲν ὑπ' αὐτοῦ κυνιστὶ σιτεῖται, καί πολλάκις διὰ τὴν τυχοῦσαν αἰτίαν ἀποσπασθεὶς τοῦ χαμαιπετοῦς δείπνου ῥάβδοις καὶ ἱμᾶσιν ἀστραγαλωτοῖς μαστιγοῦται καὶ γενόμενος αἱμόφυρτος τὸν τιμωρησάμενον ὡς εὐεργέτην ἐπὶ τὸ ἔδαφος πρηνὴς προσπεσὼν προσκυνεῖ."

In the fifth book in his account of the Parthians, he [sc. Posidonius] says: 'The so-called friend does not share his table, but, sitting on the ground below the king who reclines on a high couch, he eats what is thrown to him by the king like a dog. And often for no reason in particular, he is dragged away from his dinner on the ground and scourged with rods and whips strung with bones, and once he is covered in blood, he falls prostrate on the floor and does obeisance to the one who has punished him as to a benefactor.'

The lack of names and events make it impossible to date this fragment. Presumably the phenomenon of the 'king's friend' was one which endured over a long period, but even if this is a unique example, we do not know which king is being described. Jacoby suggests that Books 3–5 (6?) contained Syrian history up to the capture of Demetrius by the Parthians, and that the episode came from his account of the war between Demetrius II Nicator and the Parthians, which gave rise to a description of Parthian customs. This is not implausible, but we have no proof in the text as to whether it is right or not.

Fragment 6 (F 58 E–K) Athenaeus 12. 549D–E

τοιοῦτος ἐγεγόνει καὶ Πτολεμαῖος ὁ ἕβδομος Αἰγύπτου βασιλεύσας, ὁ αὐτὸν μὲν Εὐεργέτην ἀνακηρύττων, ὑπὸ δὲ Ἀλεξανδρέων Κακεργέτης ὀνομαζόμενος. Ποσειδώνιος γοῦν ὁ Στωικός, συναποδημήσας Σκιπίωνι τῷ Ἀφρικανῷ κληθέντι εἰς Ἀλεξάνδρειαν καὶ θεασάμενος αὐτόν, γράφει ἐν ἑβδόμῃ τῶν Ἱστοριῶν οὕτως· "διὰ δὲ τρυφὴν διέφθαρτο τὸ σῶμα ὑπὸ παχύτητος καὶ γαστρὸς μεγέθους, ἣν δυσπερίληπτον εἶναι συνέβαινεν· ἐφ' ἧς χιτωνίσκον ἐνδεδυκὼς ποδήρη μέχρι τῶν καρπῶν χειρίδας ἔχοντα ⟨περιῄει⟩. προῄει δέ οὐδέποτε πεζός, εἰ μὴ διὰ Σκιπίωνα."

Like him too was Ptolemy VII, king of Egypt, who announced himself as Euergetes (Benefactor) but was called Kakergetes (Malefactor) by the Alexandrians. At any rate Posidonius the Stoic, who travelled with Scipio Africanus when he was summoned to Alexandria and saw him, writes in the seventh book of his *Histories* as follows: 'Because of a luxurious lifestyle, his body had been totally destroyed by fat and his enormous belly, which it would have been hard to get your arms around; over this belly he put on a little tunic down to his feet with sleeves down to the wrists.[3] He never went out on foot, except because of Scipio.'

[3] The description of this tunic is either deliberately paradoxical or confused. A χιτωνίσκος is, as the diminutive indicates, a 'small' presumably 'short' tunic, but this particular one is then described as coming down to the ground. Presumably the effect is designed to be comic and to stress the ridiculous spectacle provided by Ptolemy.

The reference to Scipio's embassy provides a possible chronological context for the fragment. Although the precise date is the subject of some controversy, the range is restricted to 144–139 BC.[4] Kidd and Theiler see the embassy as providing the context for this discussion of Ptolemy's luxury. However, problems abound. Firstly, we should note the problem of Ptolemy's identification, as discussed in connection with F 4. In addition, Kidd complains that Athenaeus has here, as in T 10b (*FGrH*), confused Posidonius with Panaetius. He points to Cic. *Acad.* 2. 5 and Plut. *Mor.* 200F and 777A in support of Panaetius being Scipio's companion. The issue of whether or not Posidonius, whose rough dates are usually given as being 130–51/0 BC, could possibly be redated so as to allow him to take part in an embassy is problematic in itself. However, Athenaeus' repetition of Posidonius' involvement rules out a careless slip. Justin's epitome of the *Historiae Philippicae* of Pompeius Trogus provides an extremely close parallel for the passage in Athenaeus. 'Ptolemy went out to meet the Roman ambassadors, Scipio Africanus, Spurius Mummius, and Lucius Metellus, who were coming to inspect the condition of the kingdoms of the Roman allies' (38. 8. 8). From the description of Ptolemy which follows, it seems likely that Trogus, like Athenaeus, had direct or indirect access to Posidonius' account. 'To the Romans, however, he was as ludicrous a figure as he was a cruel one to his fellow-citizens. He had an ugly face, and was short in stature; and he had a distended belly more like an animal's than a man's' (38. 8. 9). Trogus, however, does not mention Posidonius in this context. In spite of all these problems, there is relatively little difficulty in determining the period to which the passage refers, namely, 144–139 BC.

Fragment 7 (F 59 E–K) Athenaeus 12. 542B

Ποσειδώνιος δ' ἐν τῇ ὀγδόῃ τῶν Ἱστοριῶν περὶ Δαμοφίλου λέγων τοῦ Σικελιώτου, δι' ὃν ὁ δουλικὸς ἐκινήθη πόλεμος, ὅτι τρυφῆς ἦν οἰκεῖος, γράφει καὶ ταῦτα· "τρυφῆς οὖν δοῦλος ἦν καὶ κακουργίας, διὰ μὲν τῆς χώρας τετρακύκλους ἀπήνας περιαγόμενος καὶ ἵππους καὶ θεράποντας ὡραίους καὶ παραδρομὴν ἀνάγωγον κολάκων τε καὶ παίδων στρατιωτικῶν. ὕστερον δὲ πανοικίᾳ ἐφυβρίστως κατέστρεψε τὸν βίον ὑπὸ τῶν οἰκετῶν περιυβρισθείς."

Posidonius in the eighth book of his *Histories* when speaking about Damophilus the Sicilian Greek, by whom the slave-war was initiated, says that he was possessed by luxury, and he writes in

---

[4] See Kidd (II(i) 291) for the bibliography of discussion over the date of the embassy.

addition as follows: 'So he was a slave of luxury and of evil, dragging round and round the countryside with him four-wheeled chariots, horses, attendants in the prime of life, and a dissolute swarm of flatterers and soldier-slaves. But later he came to a frightful end with all his household, having been treated with extreme violence by his slaves.'

The chronological context is easily determined by the reference to the first slave-war of 136–132 BC.

Fragment 8 (F 60 E–K) Athenaeus 6. 263C–D

Ποσειδώνιος δέ φησιν ὁ ἀπὸ τῆς Στοᾶς ἐν τῇ τῶν Ἱστοριῶν ἐνδεκάτῃ· "πολλούς τινας ἑαυτῶν οὐ δυναμένους προίστασθαι διὰ τὸ τῆς διανοίας ἀσθενὲς ἐπιδοῦναι ἑαυτοὺς εἰς τὴν τῶν συνετωτέρων ὑπηρεσίαν, ὅπως παρ᾽ ἐκείνων τυγχάνοντες τῆς εἰς τὰ ἀναγκαῖα ἐπιμελείας αὐτοὶ πάλιν ἀποδιδῶσιν ἐκείνοις δι᾽ αὑτῶν ἅπερ ἂν ὦσιν ὑπερετεῖν δυνατοί. καὶ τούτῳ τῷ τρόπῳ Μαριανδυνοὶ μὲν Ἡρακλεώταις ὑπετάγησαν, διὰ τέλους ὑποσχόμενοι θητεύσειν παρέχουσιν αὐτοῖς τὰ δέοντα, προσδιαστειλάμενοι μηδενὸς αὐτῶν ἔσεσθαι πρᾶσιν ἔξω τῆς Ἡρακλεωτῶν χώρας, ἀλλ᾽ ἐν αὐτῇ μόνον τῇ ἰδίᾳ χώρᾳ."

Posidonius from the Stoa says in the eleventh book of his *Histories*: 'Many who are not able to stand up for themselves because of their weakness of intellect hand themselves over to the service of the more intelligent, so that they may get from them provision for their needs and give them in return through their own persons whatever service they can manage. In this way the Mariandynians were subordinated to the Heracleots, promising to serve them permanently as long as the Heracleots provided what they needed, and stipulating in addition that none of them would be sold outside the territory of the Heracleots, but only in their own land.'

The lack of any indication as to when this arrangement was established, and the ethnographical nature of the account, make it impossible to give the passage a chronological context. One can imagine the way in which such a passage may have been occasioned by some part of the narrative, but we do not know anything else about Book 11, nor indeed anything about the two books before nor those following, which renders speculative any theory as to the stimulus for this fragment. However, Theiler links the theme of slavery in this fragment with the mention of the Sicilian slave-war in F 7 (Book 8) and concludes that F 8 confirms the extension of the four-year slave-war over Books 8–11 and thus the annalistic structure of the work: a conclusion which is hardly tenable on the basis of this fragment. Jacoby noted the possibility that this fragment may not have been

connected with the first Sicilian slave-war, but may have formed part
of an excursus on the condition of slavery and cultural development.

Fragment 9 (F 61 E–K) Athenaeus 12. 540B–C; 5. 210C–D

(a) ἐν δὲ τῇ τεσσαρεσκαιδεκάτῃ περὶ τοῦ ὁμωνύμου αὐτοῦ Ἀντιόχου [sc.
τοῦ Σιδήτου] λέγων [sc. ὁ Ποσειδώνιος] τοῦ ἐπ' Ἀρσάκην εἰς Μηδίαν
στρατεύσαντός φησιν ὅτι ὑποδοχὰς ἐποιεῖτο καθ' ἡμέραν ὀχλικάς· ἐν αἷς
χωρὶς τῶν ἀναλισκομένων καὶ ἐκφατνιζομένων σωρευμάτων ἕκαστος
ἀπέφερε τῶν ἑστιατόρων ὁλομελῆ κρέα χερσαίων τε καὶ πτηνῶν καὶ
θαλαττίων ζῴων ἀδιαίρετα ἐσκευασμένα, ἅμαξαν πληρῶσαι δυνάμενα·
καὶ μετὰ ταῦτα μελιπήκτων καὶ στεφάνων ἐκ σμύρνης καὶ λιβανατοῦ
⟨σὺν⟩ ἀνδρομήκεσι λημνίσκων χρυσῶν πιλήμασιν πλήθη.

In the fourteenth book speaking of his namesake, Antiochus [sc.
Sidetes], the one who made the expedition against Arsaces in
Media, he [sc. Posidonius] says that he held receptions every day
for the crowds at which, apart from the quantities consumed and
thrown away, each one of the feasters carried away whole meat
joints of land animals, and of birds and of creatures of the sea,
prepared whole and capable of filling a wagon; and after this, great
quantities of honey-cakes and garlands of myrrh and frankincense
with fillets of golden ribbons as long as a man.'

(b) ὁ γὰρ τῷ προειρημένῳ Ἀντιόχῳ ὁμώνυμος βασιλεύς, Δημητρίου δ'
υἱός, ὡς ἱστορεῖ Ποσειδώνιος, κτλ.

For the king called the same as the aforementioned Antiochus, son
of Demetrius, as Posidonius relates, etc.

Antiochus VII Sidetes was in power from the time of the capture of
his brother, Demetrius II Nicator, by the Parthians in 140/39 BC until
his own ill-fated expedition against Parthia in 130/29. We can thus
date the banquets described in these fragments to the decade of the
130s BC. Kidd suggests particular occasions for such lavish public
festivities, namely the collapse of Tryphon in 138 (see F 2) or the
taking of Jerusalem. But we cannot know whether these banquets were
a unique event, and, if so, for what occasion; or whether such lavish
entertainment was a feature of the whole reign. Theiler points out that
Antiochus was the brother, not the son, of Demetrius II, but this
seems an unnecessary interjection as the text asserts only that Antiochus was the son of *a* Demetrius, as he indeed was (Demetrius I).[5]

---

[5] Theiler (II. 103) notes that the same error occurs in Str. 14.5.2, but again
Strabo does not specify which Demetrius he means.

Fragment 10 (F 62 E–K) Athenaeus 12. 527E–F, 5. 210E–F

Ποσειδώνιος δ' ⟨ἐν⟩ ἑκκαιδεκάτῃ ⟨τῶν⟩ Ἱστοριῶν περὶ τῶν κατὰ τὴν
Συρίαν πόλεων λέγων ὡς ἐτρύφων γράφει καὶ ταῦτα· "τῶν γοῦν ἐν ταῖς
πόλεσιν ἀνθρώπων διὰ τὴν εὐβοσίαν τῆς χώρας ἀπὸ τῆς περὶ τὰ ἀναγκαῖα
κακοπαθείας συνόδους νεμόντων πλείονας, ἐν αἷς εὐωχοῦντο συνεχῶς, τοῖς
μὲν γυμνασίοις ὡς βαλανείοις χρώμενοι, ἀλειφόμενοι [δ'] ἐλαίῳ πολυτελεῖ
καὶ μύροις, τοῖς δὲ γραμματείοις—οὕτως γὰρ ἐκάλουν τὰ κοινὰ τῶν
συνδείπνων - ὡς [ἐν] οἰκητηρίοις ἐνδιαιτώμενοι καὶ τὸ πλεῖον ⟨μέρος⟩
τῆς ἡμέρας γαστριζόμενοι ἐν αὐτοῖς οἴνοις καὶ βρώμασιν, ὥστε καὶ
προσαποφέρειν πολλά, καὶ καταυλούμενοι πρὸς χελωνίδος πολυκρότου
ψόφον, ὥστε τὰς πόλεις ὅλας τοιούτοις κελάδοις συνηχεῖσθαι."

Posidonius in the sixteenth book of his *Histories*, when he is saying
about the cities in Syria that they were full of luxury, writes also as
follows: 'The people in the cities, at any rate, because of the fertility
of the land and free from difficulty in procuring the necessities of
life, held many gatherings, at which they would feast continually;
they used the gymnasia as baths, anointing themselves with
expensive olive-oil and myrrh, and the grammateia—for this is
what they used to call the common dining clubs—they lived in as
their homes, and spent the majority of the day stuffing their bellies
there with wine and food, so that they even carried away a great
deal, and they were entertained by the flute played to the beat of the
loud-twanging turtle shell, so that whole cities resounded with such
noises.'[6]

Little can be said in chronological terms about this ethnographical
passage. Kidd determines a temporal context on the basis of the
surrounding fragments. Since F 9 from Book 14 concerns Antiochus
VII Sidetes in the 130s BC and F 11 from Book 16 concerns the death
of the same monarch in 129 BC, Kidd states that 'the date of reference
should be late 130s or early 120s B.C.'. It is, however, impossible to
be certain of the contents of a whole book on the basis of one
fragment. We therefore do not know that either Book 14 or 16 was
focused entirely on this decade.

---

[6] Much difficulty in dealing with this fragment derives from the lack of a
main verb in the Greek, although this may be disguised in translation. The
implication is that Posidonius was going on to discuss something else.

Fragment 11 (F 63 E–K) Athenaeus 10. 439D–E

Φιλόποτης δ' ἦν καὶ ὁμώνυμος αὐτῷ [sc. τῷ Ἀντιόχῳ Ἐπιφάνει] Ἀντίοχος, ὁ ἐν Μηδίᾳ πρὸς Ἀρσάκην πολεμήσας, ὡς ἱστορεῖ Ποσειδώνιος ὁ Ἀπαμεὺς ἐν τῇ ἑκκαιδεκάτῃ τῶν Ἱστοριῶν. ἀναιρεθέντος γοῦν αὐτοῦ τὸν Ἀρσάκην θάπτοντα αὐτὸν λέγειν· "ἔσφηλέν σε, Ἀντίοχε, θάρσος καὶ μέθη· ἤλπιζες γὰρ ἐν μεγάλοις ποτηρίοις τὴν Ἀρσάκου βασιλείαν ἐκπιεῖν."

Antiochus, who fought Arsaces in Media, was fond of a drink and had the same name as him [sc. Antiochus Epiphanes], as Posidonius of Apamea relates in the sixteenth book of the *Histories*. At any rate, when he died, Posidonius relates that Arsaces said as he buried him, 'Audacity and drunkenness caused your fall, Antiochus. For you were hoping to drink dry the kingdom of Arsaces in huge draughts.'

The contents of this passage share the same range of possible dates as F 9 above. Again, Kidd tries to specify the chronological context more precisely. The reference to the death of Antiochus in 129 BC for Kidd 'gives a date point for Bk 16'. However, the fragment assigns to Book 16 only the information that Antiochus was drunken and shared the name of Antiochus Epiphanes. Neither of these remarks require the prompt of Antiochus' death; any point during his life would be plausible. So again, we can be no more specific than to say that the fragment probably concerns the 130s, when Antiochus was in power.

Fragment 12 (F 64 E–K) Athenaeus 4. 153A–B

ἐν δὲ τῇ ιζ περὶ Σελεύκου διηγούμενος τοῦ βασιλέως ὡς εἰς Μηδίαν ἀνελθὼν καὶ πολεμῶν Ἀρσάκει ἠχμαλωτίσθη ὑπὸ τοῦ βαρβάρου καὶ ὡς πολὺν χρόνον παρὰ τῷ Ἀρσάκει διέτριψεν ἀγόμενος βασιλικῶς, γράφει [sc. ὁ Ποσειδώνιος] καὶ ταῦτα· "παρὰ Πάρθοις ἐν τοῖς δείπνοις ὁ βασιλεὺς τήν τε κλίνην ἐφ' ἧς μόνος κατέκειτο μετεωροτέραν τῶν ἄλλων καὶ κεχωρισμένην εἶχε καὶ τὴν τράπεζαν μόνῳ καθάπερ ἥρῳ πλήρη βαρβαρικῶν θοιναμάτων παρακειμένην."

In the sixteenth book, where he relates the story of how Seleucus the king, going up into Media, made war on Arsaces, was taken prisoner by the barbarian, and spent a long time with Arsaces being treated royally, he [sc. Posidonius] writes this as well: 'At Parthian feasts, the king had a couch on which he alone reclined, and which was higher than the others and set apart, and a table laid out for him alone like a hero, laden with barbarian dishes.'

No editor or commentator formally recommends emending the book number given by Athenaeus. However, problems in interpreting the historical content have given rise to the suggestion that the subject matter is incompatible with a location in the sixteenth book. As Kidd

points out, the most famous Seleucid king to invade Media against
Parthia, and to be kept prisoner in regal fashion, was Demetrius II
Nicator, and not Seleucus at all. On the assumption that the name is
incorrect, we might be required to explain the position of the remark
in the context of Demetrius' invasion in 141/0 BC and capture in 140.
However, Kidd argues that 'these are early dates for Bk 16 . . .They
would relate more naturally to Bk 5.'

One may conclude, as indeed Kidd does, that there are no good
grounds for emending the name. However, the argument which
would follow such an emendation, namely that the book number
would be wrong, is in line with Kidd's apparent belief that the extant
fragments of the *Histories* must adhere to a strict chronological order.
His assertion that 'it is of course possible that the book number is
wrong and should be 6 instead of 16', while based on the undeniable
premise that intrusive iotas in numerals are not uncommon, is nevertheless motivated by the desire to neaten up the temporal contents of
the extant fragments. Theiler's comment that the passage may have
been occasioned by the release of Demetrius by Phraates II in 129 BC
seems to me to raise precisely the problem that should settle the issue
of emendation before it even gets going; that is, we simply cannot
contextualize fragments solely on the basis of their contents, and
hence attribute to them a specific place in the chronological layout of
the work.

The major alternative suggestion for dealing with the problematic
identity of the subject of this fragment involves retaining the name
Seleucus, and assuming that this refers to the son of Antiochus VII
Sidetes. Antiochus' invasion of Media in 129 BC (cf. F 9 and 11) ended
in defeat. His son was taken prisoner, but treated royally (Porphry. F
32). Kidd comments that, 'this is more plausible chronologically for
Bk 16', but, as he points out, Seleucus was never king. Jacoby
suggested the emendation τοῦ ⟨υἱοῦ τοῦ⟩ βασίλεως. But Kidd is not
happy with this for two reasons. One objection is the concentration on
a minor character. This can be countered by a reminder that what
looks like such concentration to us, because it features as one among a
small number of glimpses into the text, may have been entirely
subsumed beneath other themes in the original. The fragmentary
nature of the text is sufficiently severe for any decisions about which
were major and which minor characters or themes to be highly
contentious. Kidd's second objection is in direct contradiction to
his own practice with regard to other fragments. He complains that
this is not what fragment says: 'the quotation refers to the King, not
to the son of the King'. In other words, the text should be left alone,
and Athenaeus convicted of a confusion, which we cannot unravel.

This fragment is important for its evocation of particularly unsatisfactory modes of argumentation. A problem in identification, in itself not surprising given our fragmentary knowledge of the whole Hellenistic period and the false logic in assuming that all persons named in fragmentary texts must belong to our list of 'known people', leads to solutions which reveal a deep-seated belief in the chronological ordering of the original text. Book numbers may be altered so as to insert the contents of the fragment into a 'suitable' context; or, alternatively, the text may be changed so as to invent a character who fits the assumed chronological context of the book number as it stands. It seems that the underlying problem of either an error in Athenaeus, or our own imperfect knowledge of Hellenistic history, has given rise to unsatisfactory solutions.

Fragment 14 (F 66 E–K) Athenaeus 13. 594D–E

Ἅρπαλος δ' ὁ Μακεδὼν ὁ τῶν Ἀλεξάνδρου πολλὰ χρημάτων συλήσας καὶ καταφυγὼν εἰς Ἀθήνας ἐρασθεὶς Πυθιονίκης πολλὰ εἰς αὐτὴν κατανάλωσεν ἑταίραν οὖσαν. καὶ ἀποθανούσῃ πολυτάλαντον μνημεῖον κατεσκεύασεν· "ἐκφέρων τε αὐτὴν ἐπὶ τὰς ταφάς", ὥς φησι Ποσειδώνιος ἐν τῇ δευτέρᾳ καὶ εἰκοστῇ τῶν Ἰστοριῶν, "τεχνιτῶν τῶν ἐπισημοτάτων χορῷ μεγάλῳ καὶ παντοίοις ὀργάνοις καὶ συμφωνίαις παρέπεμπε τὸ σῶμα."

Harpalus the Macedonian, having stolen a great deal of Alexander's money and fled to Athens, fell in love with Pythionice and spent a great deal on her, although she was a prostitute. And when she died, he set up a very expensive monument for her. 'And as he brought out her corpse for burial,' as Posidonius says in the twenty-second book of his *Histories*, 'he had the body escorted by a great chorus of the most noted artists and by all kinds of instruments and harmonious bands.'

The date for the event described in this fragment, the funeral of Pythionice, must be soon after 325/4 BC, when Harpalus fled to Athens with much of Alexander's treasure. The case illustrates why we should hesitate before making any assertions about the organization of the *Histories* based on the chronological context of the contents of extant fragments. The funeral of Pythionice clearly lies outside the main chronological framework of a work which followed on from Polybius. Since it is so obviously a case which cannot be emended or renumbered so as to fit the expected pattern, the fragment evokes from Kidd the question: 'Why did he introduce the story?' and the response: 'Presumably it is another of his instances of the inadequate leader corrupted by weakness of character through power and luxury. But it must have been an analogy to a contemporary figure.'

This is perfectly reasonable, but the extremity of the example calls into question Kidd's methodology concerning other fragments which stray outside perfect chronological sequence, and also raises doubts over whether it is legitimate to use *any* fragment to argue for a chronology of the 'main' narrative. It is inconsistent to designate this fragment an analogy; but to emend the book number in others, simply because they could potentially fit *some*where in a narrative starting from 146 BC. Given how little we know about this work, we cannot be sure what is analogy, contrast, parallel, and what is 'mainstream', so that any attempt to reconstruct a chronological framework for the *Histories* is rendered precarious.

I fail to follow the logic of Jacoby's discussion of this fragment. His broad conclusion was that the passage revealed the contents of Book 22 as being Syrian history. The line of thought seems to have been that a narrative concerning the struggle between Antiochus VIII Grypus and Antiochus IX Cyzicenus *c*.117 BC, part of which took place in Cilicia, might have given rise to a mention of Harpalus, who had set up luxurious court in Cilicia until the return of Alexander. Or, another possible explanation is hinted at in Kidd's remark that 'the milieu (sc. for this fragment) would be Babylon or Cilicia, and so probably related to Syrian history'. But both of these possibilities are so tortuously argued and uncertain as to lead us no further towards an understanding of the context of this fragment. As Jacoby gloomily concludes: 'the contents of Books XVII–XXII remain in the dark' ('im Dunkeln').

Fragment 15 (F 67 E–K) Athenaeus 4. 151E–152D

Ποσειδώνιος δὲ ὁ ἀπὸ τῆς Στοᾶς ἐν ταῖς Ἱστορίαις αἷς συνέθηκεν οὐκ ἀλλοτρίως ἧς προῄρητο φιλοσοφίας πολλὰ παρὰ πολλοῖς ἔθιμα καὶ νόμιμα ἀναγράφων "Κελτοί", φησί, "τὰς τροφὰς προτίθενται χόρτον ὑποβάλλοντες καὶ ἐπὶ τραπεζῶν ξυλίνων μικρὸν ἀπὸ τῆς γῆς ἐπηρμένων. ἡ τροφὴ δ᾽ ἐστὶν ἄρτοι μὲν ὀλίγοι, κρέα δὲ πολλὰ ἐν ὕδατι καὶ ὀπτὰ ἐπ᾽ ἀνθράκων ἢ ὀβελίσκων. προσφέρονται δὲ ταῦτα καθαρείως μέν, λεοντώδως δέ, ταῖς χερσὶν ἀμφοτέραις αἴροντες ὅλα μέλη καὶ ἀποδάκνοντες, ἐὰν δὲ ᾖ τι δυσαπόστατον, μαχαιρίῳ μικρῷ παρατέμνοντες, ὃ τοῖς κολεοῖς ἐν ἰδίᾳ θήκῃ παράκειται. προσφέρονται δὲ καὶ ἰχθῦς οἵ τε παρὰ τοὺς ποταμοὺς οἰκοῦντες καὶ παρὰ τὴν ἐντὸς καὶ τὴν ἔξω θάλασσαν, καὶ τούτους δὲ ὀπτοὺς μετὰ ἁλῶν καὶ ὄξους καὶ κυμίνου· τοῦτο δὲ καὶ εἰς τὸ ποτὸν ἐμβάλλουσιν. ἐλαίῳ δ᾽ οὐ χρῶνται διὰ σπάνιν, καὶ διὰ τὸ ἀσύνηθες ἀηδὲς αὐτοῖς φαίνεται.

ὅταν δὲ πλείονες συνδειπνῶσι, κάθηνται μὲν ἐν κύκλῳ, μέσος δὲ ὁ κράτιστος ὡς ἂν κορυφαῖος χοροῦ, διαφέρων τῶν ἄλλων ἢ κατὰ τὴν

πολεμικὴν εὐχέρειαν ἢ κατὰ γένος ἢ κατὰ πλοῦτον. ὁ δ' ὑποδεχόμενος παρ'
αὐτόν, ἐφεξῆς δ' ἑκατέρωθε κατ' ἀξίαν ἧς ἔχουσιν ὑπεροχῆς. καὶ οἱ μὲν τοὺς
θυρεοὺς ὁπλοφοροῦντες ἐκ τῶν ὀπίσω παρεστᾶσιν, οἱ δὲ δορυφόροι κατὰ
τὴν ἀντικρὺ καθήμενοι κύκλῳ καθάπερ οἱ δεσπόται συνευωχοῦνται.

τὸ δὲ ποτὸν οἱ διακονοῦντες ἐν ἀγγείοις περιφέρουσιν ἐοικόσι μὲν
ἀμβίκοις, ἢ κεραμέοις ἢ ἀργυροῖς· καὶ γὰρ τοὺς πίνακας ἐφ' ὧν τὰς
τροφὰς προτίθενται τοιούτους ἔχουσιν· οἳ δὲ χαλκοῦς, οἳ δὲ κάνεα ξύλινα
καὶ πλεκτά.

τὸ δὲ πινόμενόν ἐστι παρὰ μὲν τοῖς πλουτοῦσιν οἶνος ἐξ Ἰταλίας καὶ τῆς
Μασσαλιητῶν χώρας παρακομιζόμενος, ἄκρατος δ' οὗτος· ἐνίοτε δὲ ὀλίγον
ὕδωρ παραμίγνυται· παρὰ δὲ τοῖς ὑποδεεστέροις ζύθος πύρινον μετὰ
μέλιτος ἐσκευασμένον, παρὰ δὲ τοῖς πολλοῖς καθ' αὑτό· καλεῖται δὲ
κόρμα. ἀπορροφοῦσι δὲ ἐκ τοῦ αὐτοῦ ποτηρίου κατὰ μικρόν, οὐ πλεῖον
κυάθου· πυκνότερον δὲ τοῦτο ποιοῦσι. περιφέρει δὲ ὁ παῖς ἐπὶ τὰ δεξιὰ καὶ
τὰ λαιά· οὕτως διακονοῦνται. καὶ τοὺς θεοὺς προσκυνοῦσιν ἐπὶ τὰ δεξιὰ
στρεφόμενοι."

Posidonius from the Stoa in the *Histories* which he put together in a
manner consonant with the philosophy which he had adopted, in
recording many habits and customs from many peoples, says: 'The
Celts serve their food with hay thrown underneath and on wooden
tables which are slightly raised from the ground. The food is a small
amount of bread, a great deal of meat boiled in water and roasted on
charcoal or spits. They eat these cleanly, but with a lion's appetite,
taking whole joints in both hands and gnawing bits off, and if there
is a bit that is hard to tear off, cutting it off with a small knife, which
lies close by with its sheath in its own box. Those who live by rivers
and by the inner and outer sea also eat fish, and these are roasted
with salt and vinegar and cumin. The last they also sprinkle into
their drink. They do not use olive oil because of its scarcity, and
because it seems to them unusual and unpleasant.

Whenever more people dine together, they sit in a circle, and the
mightiest sits in the middle like the leader of a chorus, distinguished from the others either through his coolness in war or
through birth or wealth. The host sits next to him, and the rest
in order according to the value of their rank on either side. And
those who bear the shields stand behind, and the spear-bearers
sitting opposite in a circle feast together like their masters.

Those who serve the drink carry it around in vessels like spouted
cups, made either of pottery or of silver. For truly the platters on
which they serve the food are similar to these, with others bronze
and others baskets of wood or wicker.

The drink among the wealthy is wine brought from Italy and
from the land of Massilia, and this is generally unmixed, but

sometimes a little water is added. Among the poorer people a beer is made from wheat, with honey added, and most drink it on its own. It is called 'corma'. They sip from the same drinking-cup a little at a time, no more than a cyathus; but they do this rather often. The slave-boy carries it round to the right and to the left; and so they distribute it. And they worship the gods turning to the right.'

F 15 is largely concerned with ethnographical material on eating habits, food, seating arrangements, and drink, and so is impossible to date. Kidd links it with F 18 as a single passage. He argues that the ethnography was evoked by the narrative of historical events alluded to in F 18, and that having identified the historical reference, he has provided 'the historical context of Posidonius' ethnography in Bk 23'. I discuss F 18 later, but here note that the Greek makes clear that Posidonius' primary task at this stage was 'recording many habits and customs from many peoples', here the Celts. Even were the two fragments juxtaposed, the topic of Celtic ethnography is treated in its own right and not necessarily as an issue subordinated to the historical narrative.

Fragment 16 (F 68 E–K) Athenaeus 4. 154A–C

Ποσειδώνιος δ' ἐν τρίτῃ καὶ εἰκοστῇ τῶν Ἱστοριῶν "Κελτοί" φησίν "ἐνίοτε παρὰ τὸ δεῖπνον μονομαχοῦσιν. ἐν γὰρ τοῖς ὅπλοις ἀγερθέντες σκιαμαχοῦσι καὶ πρὸς ἀλλήλους ἀκροχειρίζονται, ποτὲ δὲ καὶ μέχρι τραύματος προίασιν καὶ ἐκ τούτου ἐρεθισθέντες, ἐὰν μὴ ἐπισχῶσιν οἱ παρόντες, καὶ ἕως ἀναιρέσεως ἔρχονται. τὸ δὲ παλαιόν", φησίν, "ὅτι παρατεθέντων κωλήνων τὸ μηρίον ὁ κράτιστος ἐλάμβανεν· εἰ δέ τις ἕτερος ἀντιποιήσαιτο, συνίσταντο μονομαχήσοντες μέχρι θανάτου. ἄλλοι δ' ἐν θεάτρῳ λαβόντες ἀργύριον ἢ χρυσίον, οἱ δὲ οἴνου κεραμίων ἀριθμόν τινα, καὶ πιστωσάμενοι τὴν δόσιν καὶ τοῖς ἀναγκαίοις φίλοις διαδωρησάμενοι ὕπτιοι ἐκταθέντες ἐπὶ θυρεῶν κεῖνται, καὶ παραστάς τις ξίφει τὸν λαιμὸν ἀποκόπτει."

Posidonius in the twenty-third book of the *Histories* says: 'The Celts sometimes fight duels during dinner. After gathering in arms they shadow fence and spar with each other, and sometimes they even go so far as to inflict a wound and, provoked by this, even kill, unless the bystanders stop it. But in the past,' he says, 'when whole leg-joints were served, the strongest man took the thigh, and if anyone else made a challenge, they would fight a duel to the death. Others taking silver and gold at the public spectacle, or others a number of jars of wine, and having secured the gift with a pledge and distributed it to those closest to them, lie stretched out on their backs on their shields, while a man stands by and cuts the throat with a sword.'

It is obvious that the contents of this fragment will prove hard to date. It seems that Book 23 contained a significant amount of information on the customs and lifestyle of the Celts. F 16 is interesting in temporal terms in so far as it does distinguish between past and present customs. The implication of 'antiquity' (τὸ παλαιόν) seems to be, according to Kidd, that the earlier part of the fragment deals with customs still practised in Posidonius' own day, but that the text then goes on to detail bygone practices. Kidd translates the fragment using past tenses from τὸ παλαιόν onwards, and draws the conclusion that the 'latter part refers to more barbaric fatal practices of earlier times, perhaps discouraged by later Roman influence, as decapitation was'. However, the tenses of the verbs in Greek do not continue in the past, but rather revert to the present (κεῖνται; ἀποκόπτει) after one sentence about τὸ παλαιόν. If we are to take seriously the choice of tense, the implication must be not that the latter part of the fragment deals with the barbaric practices of the past, now outlawed by Rome, but rather that the contrast with the past concerns only the cause which led to the duelling. The rest of the passage brings us back to the present practice, which is still barbaric. However, such temporal refinements do not tell us anything about the chronological context for the fragment within the work as a whole (although it is incidentally interesting for the thesis of this book that even ethnography had a clear temporal element). Jacoby suggested that the Celtic ethnography was occasioned by the transalpine Celtic war against the Allobroges and the Averni, presumably on the basis of F 18 and the mention of Bituis. I shall argue, however, that such a conclusion is not justified by the text.

Fragment 17 (F 69 E–K) Athenaeus 6. 246c–d

Ποσειδώνιος δ' ὁ Ἀπαμεὺς ἐν τῇ κ καὶ τρίτῃ τῶν Ἱστοριῶν "Κελτοί" φησί, 'περιάγονται μεθ' αὑτῶν καὶ πολεμοῦντες συμβιωτάς, οὓς καλοῦσι παρασίτους. οὗτοι δὲ ἐγκώμια αὐτῶν καὶ πρὸς ἀρθόους λέγουσιν ἀνθρώπους συνεστῶτας καὶ πρὸς ἕκαστον τῶν κατὰ μέρος ἐκείνων ἀκρωμένων. τὰ δὲ ἀκούσματα αὐτῶν εἰσιν οἱ καλούμενοι βάρδοι· ποιηταὶ δὲ οὗτοι τυγχάνουσι μετ' ᾠδῆς ἐπαίνους λέγοντες."

Posidonius of Apamea says in the twenty-third book of the *Histories*: 'The Celts take around with them, even when they are at war, companions, whom they call "parasites". These proclaim eulogies of them both in front of men gathered together and before each of the audience individually. What they listen to are the so-called bards; these poets actually praise them in song.'

There is no indication of temporal context. Rather we have part of an ethnographic section, in which the nature of Celtic society is explored. Kidd takes this fragment as the starting-point for a discussion of Druids, bards, and *vates*, whom Strabo describes as the three honoured classes of Celtic society, and it is quite possible that the passage does concern that issue.

Fragment 18 (F 67 E–K) Athenaeus 4. 152D–F

ἔτι ὁ Ποσειδώνιος διηγούμενος καὶ τὸν Λουερνίου τοῦ Βιτύιτος πατρὸς πλοῦτον τοῦ ὑπὸ Ῥωμαίων καθαιρεθέντος, φησὶ δημαγωγοῦντα αὐτὸν τοὺς ὄχλους ἐν ἅρματι φέρεσθαι διὰ τῶν πεδίων καὶ διασπείρειν χρυσίον καὶ ἀργύριον ταῖς ἀκολουθούσαις τῶν Κελτῶν μυριάσι φράγμα τε ποιεῖν δωδεκαστάδιον τετράγωνον, ἐν ᾧ πληροῦν μὲν ληνοὺς πολυτελοῦς πόμα-τος, παρασκευάζειν δὲ τοσοῦτο βρωμάτων πλῆθος ὥστε ἐφ' ἡμέρας πλείονας ἐξεῖναι τοῖς βουλομένοις εἰσερχομένοις τῶν παρασκευασθέντων ἀπολαύειν ἀδιαλείπτως διακονουμένους. ἀφορίσαντος δ' αὐτοῦ προθεσμίαν ποτὲ τῆς θοίνης ἀφυστερήσαντά τινα τῶν βαρβάρων ποιητὴν ἀφικέσθαι καὶ συναντήσαντα μετὰ ᾠδῆς ὑμνεῖν αὐτοῦ τὴν ὑπεροχήν, ἑαυτὸν δ' ἀποθρηνεῖν ὅτι ὑστέρηκε, τὸν δὲ τερφθέντα θυλάκιον αἰτῆσαι χρυσίου καὶ ῥῖψαι αὐτῷ παρατρέχοντι. ἀνελόμενον δ' ἐκεῖνον πάλιν ὑμνεῖν λέγοντα διότι τὰ ἴχνη τῆς γῆς ἐφ' ἧς ἁρματηλατεῖ χρυσὸν καὶ εὐεργεσίας ἀνθρώποις φέρει. ταῦτα μέν οὖν ἐν τῇ τρίτῃ καὶ εἰκοστῇ ἱστόρησεν.

Furthermore, when Posidonius relates the wealth of Luvernius, the father of Bituis, who was taken from power by the Romans, he says that, attempting to win the favour of the mob, he was carried round in a chariot across the countryside and that he scattered gold and silver to the thousands of Celts who accompanied him, and that he made a square enclosure of twelve stades, in which he filled up vats with expensive drink and prepared such a mountain of food that those who wanted could for several days come in and enjoy what had been prepared with continuous service. And he says that, after he had fixed the closing day of the feast, a native poet came and on meeting him sang a song in honour of his eminence, but lamented his own lateness; and that Luvernius was delighted and asked for a little bag of gold and threw it to him as he ran alongside. The man, when he took it, sang again, saying that the tracks on the ground where his chariot went brought forth gold and benefits for men. This then is what he recounted in the twenty-third book.

The mention of Bituis' removal from power appears to offer a chronological context for this fragment. I have already mentioned and questioned Kidd's assumption that, having identified the historical reference as being to the defeat and annexation of the Averni and Allobroges in 121 BC by Cn. Domitius Ahenobarbus and Q. Fabius Maximus Allobrogicus, he has provided 'the historical context of

Posidonius' ethnography in Bk 23'. Moreover, it is not clear that even this passage should be given a context in 121 BC and the defeat of the Averni and Allobroges. The Greek does not suggest that Posidonius was relating this defeat, when he suddenly decided to include some details on Bituis' father and on his extravagance; rather that Posidonius was at this stage primarily engaged in relating the wealth and luxury of Luvernius, for whatever reason, and that the mention of Bituis was merely incidental to this. The hypothetical question 'who was Luvernius?' is answered with the information that he was the father of the deposed Gallic leader. So, it is not implausible that the 'chronological context' of 121 BC reveals nothing about the organization of this part of the work, but relates only to an incidental piece of information.

Fragment 13 (F 65 E–K) Athenaeus 11. 466B–C

Ποσειδώνιος δ' ἐν κζ τῶν Ἱστοριῶν Λυσίμαχόν φησι τὸν Βαβυλώνιον, καλέσαντα ἐπὶ δεῖπνον Ἵμερον τὸν τυραννήσαντα οὐ μόνον Βαβυλωνίων ἀλλὰ καὶ Σελευκέων μετὰ τριακοσίων, μετὰ τὸ τὰς τραπέζας ἀρθῆναι τετράμνουν ἑκάστῳ τῶν τριακοσίων ἔκπωμα δοῦναι ἀργυροῦν, καὶ σπονδοποιησάμενον προπιεῖν ἅμα πᾶσιν· καὶ ἀποφέρεσθαι ἔδωκε τὰ ποτήρια.

Posidonius in the twenty-sixth book of his *Histories* says that Lysimachus the Babylonian, having invited to dinner Himerus, the tyrant not only of the Babylonians, but also of the people of Seleuceia, with three hundred others, after the tables had been cleared away gave each of the three hundred a four-mina cup made of silver, and made a libation and toasted everyone. And he gave the cups to be taken away.

After the king of Parthia, Phraates II, had defeated Antiochus VII Sidetes in 129 BC, he needed to deal immediately with the Scythians, and left Himerus in charge of Babylonia in his absence. Kidd locates this fragment in the immediate aftermath of F 11, which deals with the drunken ambition of Antiochus VII Sidetes. He thus accepts Müller's emendation of Codex A's κζ to λζ. However, as Kidd himself asserted with regard to the emendation of F 12, this is not what the text says. It must be admitted that Kidd was arguing about the insertion of two words, and not the alteration of one letter in a book number, but the principle remains that emendation must be carefully justified.

Such justification is not easy to maintain in this case. Firstly, the argument that Book 16 dealt with events surrounding the death of Antiochus in 129 BC is based on shaky foundations, as I have argued above in connection with F 11. Even if it could be shown that

Antiochus' death *was* mentioned in Book 16, this would not prove
that it was anything other than a digression or a parallel for some
other such event. It is unlikely that the work was so narrowly
structured as to form a strictly chronological narrative, dealing
exclusively with the events of particular years in each book. Only
such an arrangement could entail the placement of this fragment 'in
the immediate aftermath' of F 11. It seems that a careful reading of F
11 is enough to refute any argument to emend the book number given
by Athenaeus for F 13, to say nothing of the problems of fragmentation and lack of context.

Jacoby suggested a different line of argument for dating the fragment to c.129 BC, not directly based on the link with F 11 and the
death of Antiochus, but simply on the grounds that the appointment
of Himerus as regent and his subsequent debauchery probably
followed soon after the death of Antiochus. However, without
recourse to the connection of the year 129 with Book 16 (F 11), the
need to emend the book numbers in both F 12 and F 13 loses its force.
Jacoby remarked that the number was problematic, because Syrian
history stood awkwardly ('schwerlich') in Book 26, but we have little
evidence for what this book could or could not have included.
Jacoby's comment concerning F 19, namely that Books 22/3 to 27
may have dealt exclusively with the West, would support his argument about the book number in F 13, but seems to be based solely on
the cluster of fragments from Book 23 on the Celts. I thus see no
reason for accepting the emendation and prefer to retain κζ.

Fragment 19 (F 70 E–K) Athenaeus 9. 369C–D

Ποσειδώνιος δ' ὁ ἀπὸ τῆς Στοᾶς ἐν τῇ ἑβδόμῃ καὶ εἰκοστῇ τῶν Ἱστοριῶν
περὶ τὴν Δαλματίαν φησὶ γίγνεσθαι γογγυλίδας ἀκηπεύτους καὶ ἀγρίους
σταφυλίνους.

Posidonius from the Stoa, in the twenty-seventh book of his
Histories, says about Dalmatia that there are uncultivated turnips
and wild carrots.

Kidd starts by commenting: 'This fragment is not much help for
the content of Bk 27.' He finds problematic the absence of a political
context, of any datable event, which might enable him to determine
which years were dealt with in this book. Jacoby and Malitz
speculated that the fragment may have been evoked by the triumph
of L. Caecilius Metellus Delmaticus over the Dalmatians in 117 BC;
Theiler, on the basis of this theory, changed the book number to 24,
κδ. He noted the suggestion that the passage may be linked to either
117 or 119 BC, the year of Metellus' consulship, and so concluded that

the book number must be changed, or that there would be a chronological difficulty.

It seems that this is a prime example of an unnecessary emendation. It is not clear to me why Book 24 should be considered a preferable environment for this fragment than Book 27, when we have no evidence for the contents and arrangement of Books 24–7 other than the contentious F 13. It is, in any case, utterly obscure how a passage on turnips and carrots fitted into the scope of Posidonius' work. It is indeed possible that an account of Metellus' campaign against the Dalmatians gave rise to such a passage as part of a section on the *origines et situs* of an area, newly introduced to the narrative. However, we know nothing like enough about the work to be able to make such assertions, and should certainly not argue on these grounds for emendation of the text. Theiler's additional justification for this emendation, namely that other fragments also require emendation of book numbers (F 13 and F 24), is in danger of circularity.

Fragment 20 (F 71 E–K) Athenaeus 15. 692C–D

ἥδιστον δέ, ἄνδρες φίλοι, ἀναγινώσκων τὴν ὀγδόην καὶ εἰκοστὴν τῶν Ποσειδωνίου Ἱστοριῶν περὶ μύρων τι λεγόμενον ἐτήρησα . . . φησὶ γὰρ ὁ φιλόσοφος· "ἐν Συρίᾳ ἐν τοῖς βασιλικοῖς συμποσίοις ὅταν τοῖς εὐωχουμένοις δοθῶσιν οἱ στέφανοι, εἰσίασίν τινες μύρων Βαβυλωνίων ἔχοντες ἀσκίδια καὶ πόρρωθεν ἐκ τούτων περιπορευόμενοι τοὺς μὲν στεφάνους τῶν κατακειμένων δροσίζουσι τοῖς μύροις, ἄλλο μηδὲν ἔξωθεν παραρραίνοντες."

Dear gentlemen, when reading the twenty-eighth book of the *Histories* of Posidonius I noticed something very sweet that was said about perfumes . . . For the philosopher says: 'In Syria at royal drinking-parties, whenever garlands are given to those feasting, certain men come in with little hide-pouches of Babylonian perfumes, from which, as they go round, they shower with perfumes from a distance the garlands of those reclining, sprinkling nothing else in passing.'

No hint is given in this fragment as to any particular context or temporal setting; this is a custom which presumably carried on for a considerable length of time. However, Kidd suggests that the royal court referred to is 'probably that of Antiochus VIII Grypus between 121–115 B.C.'. The reason given is that F 21, also from Book 28, concerns this monarch and the lavish entertainment at his court. This certainly lends support to Kidd's conclusion; but it by no means compels us to treat F 20 as anything other than a timeless ethnographical passage. Jacoby pointed to the lack of fragments from Books

17 to 22, which make it hard to tell how extensive the Syrian history glimpsed from Book 16 in F 10 really was. However, on a different note, he does suggest on the basis of the present tenses in this fragment that, at the time of writing, the Seleucids were still in power.

Fragment 21 (F 72 E–K) Athenaeus 12. 540A–B; 5. 210E

(a) Ἀντίοχον δὲ τὸν Γρυπὸν ἐπικαλούμενον βασιλέα φησὶ Ποσειδώνιος ἐν τῇ ὀγδόῃ καὶ εἰκοστῇ τῶν Ἱστοριῶν τὰς ἐπὶ Δάφνῃ πανηγύρεις ἐπιτελοῦντα ὑποδοχὰς λαμπρὰς ἐπιτελεῖν. ἐν αἷς τὸ μὲν πρῶτον ἀναδόσεις ἐγίγνοντο ὁλομελῶν βρωμάτων, εἶτ᾽ ἤδη καὶ ζώντων χηνῶν καὶ λαγωῶν καὶ δορκάδων. "ἀνεδίδοντο δέ, φησίν, καὶ χρυσοῖ στέφανοι τοῖς δειπνοῦσιν καὶ ἀργυρωμάτων πλῆθος καὶ θεραπόντων καὶ ἵππων καὶ καμήλων. ἔδει τε ἀναβάντα ἐπὶ τὴν κάμηλον ἕκαστον πιεῖν καὶ λαβεῖν τὴν κάμηλον καὶ τὰ ἐπὶ τὴν κάμηλον καὶ τὸν παρεστῶτα παῖδα."

Posidonius says in the twenty-eighth book of his *Histories* that King Antiochus Grypus held brilliant receptions when he celebrated the festivals at Daphne. During them, there were firstly distributions of uncarved meats; then of live geese, hares, and gazelles. 'And', says Posidonius, 'there were also distributed to the diners golden wreaths and a great number of silver vessels, attendants, horses, and camels. And each man, after mounting his camel, had to have a drink and to take the camel and everything on the camel and the attendant boy.'

(b) "τὸ μὲν γὰρ πρῶτον ἀναδόσεις ἐποιήσατο κατ᾽ ἄνδρα ὁλομελῶν βρωμάτων, μετὰ δὲ καὶ ζώντων κτλ."

'For firstly he made distributions to each man of uncarved meats, and afterwards of live creatures etc.'

The temporal context can be roughly gauged by the reign of Antiochus Grypus. His turbulent accession, after the assassination of his elder brother, Seleucus V, in c.125 BC, was followed by a struggle to defeat the pretender, Alexander II Zabinas, finally accomplished in 123. Grypus was dominated by his grandmother, Cleopatra Thea, until her failed assassination attempt on him in 121 BC. In c.115/14 the next dynastic challenge came from Antiochus IX Cyzicenus. Kidd therefore suggests that this passage can be placed during the peaceful years of 121–115/14. This is a reasonable conclusion, although I reject the further deduction that this gives 'a chronological bracket for Bk 28' for the reason rehearsed many times already, namely that one fragment cannot alone dictate the framework of a whole book.

Fragment 22 (F 73 E–K) Athenaeus 4. 153E

Γερμανοὶ δέ, ὡς ἱστορεῖ Ποσειδώνιος ἐν τῇ τριακοστῇ, ἄριστον προσφέρονται κρέα μεληδὸν ὠπτημένα καὶ ἐπιπίνουσι γάλα καὶ τὸν οἶνον ἄκρατον.

The Germans, as Posidonius relates in the thirtieth book, serve meat roasted in joints for breakfast and drink milk and unmixed wine.

The interest of most commentators in this fragment has sprung not from finding a chronological context, but from the emergent geographical and ethnographical issues of who the Germanoi were and where they lived. Such questions have been discussed at length by Dobesch in his account of Posidonius on northern Europe.[7] However, in terms of the arrangement or οἰκονομία of the work, we are no further forward. The fragment is so small that it could be satisfactorily inserted into a great range of contexts. It could certainly form part of a section on the *origines et situs* of the regions of north-western Europe, perhaps, in the style of Pompeius Trogus, preceding a narrative associated with that area. For Theiler the context is suggested by the fact that we have now arrived at the period of the Cimbrian migrations; for which, however, there is no indication in the text.

Fragment 23 (F 74 E–K) Athenaeus 6. 246D

ἐν δὲ τῇ τετάρτῃ καὶ τριακοστῇ ὁ αὐτὸς συγγραφεὺς [sc. ὁ Ποσειδώνιος] Ἀπολλώνιόν τινα ἀναγράφει παράσιτον γεγονότα Ἀντιόχου τοῦ Γρυποῦ ἐπικαλουμένου τοῦ τῆς Συρίας βασιλέως.

In the thirty-fourth book the same historian [sc. Posidonius] records a certain Apollonius who was a parasite of Antiochus Grypus, the king of Syria.

The same arguments apply as with F 21. The rough contextual date must be the reign of Antiochus Grypus, and probably within that the later, more settled period of 121–115/14 BC. The fragment does, however, reveal how vulnerable is the attempt to discern a regional grouping of material within a broadly chronological framework. Here we find two fragments on Antiochus Grypus interrupted by a fragment (F 22) on German ethnography.

---

[7] See G. Dobesch, *Das europäische 'Barbaricum' und die Zone der Mediterrankultur: Ihre historische Wechselwirkung und das Geschichtsbild des Poseidonios* (Vienna, 1995).

Fragment 25 (F 76 E–K) Athenaeus 11. 494F–495A

ΠΑΝΑΘΗΝΑΙΚΟΝ. Ποσειδώνιος ὁ φιλόσοφος ἐν ἕκτῃ καὶ τριακοστῇ
τῶν Ἱστοριῶν ὡς οὕτω καλουμένων τινῶν ποτηρίων μέμνηται γράφων
οὕτως· "ἦσαν δὲ καὶ ὀνύχινοι σκύφοι καὶ συνδέσεις τούτων μέχρι δικο-
τύλων· καὶ Παναθηναϊκὰ μέγιστα, τὰ μὲν δίχοα, τὰ δὲ καὶ μείζονα."

'PANATHENAIKON. Posidonius the philosopher in the thirty-
sixth book of the *Histories* records the names of some so-called
drinking cups, writing as follows: 'There were also onyx cups and
combinations of these up to two kotyla [around a pint]; and also
some very large Panathenaika, some of two khoes [about 1½ gallons]
and some even larger.'

Although some have wanted to connect this passage with Syria, we
have, as Kidd remarks, no evidence for the Posidonian context.

Fragment 26 (F 77 E–K) Athenaeus 12. 550A–B

εἰς πάχος δ᾽ ἐπεδεδώκει καὶ ὁ υἱὸς αὐτοῦ [sc. τοῦ Πτολεμαίου τοῦ
Φύσκωνος] Ἀλέξανδρος, ὁ τὴν ἑαυτοῦ μητέρα ἀποκτείνας συμβασιλεύου-
σαν αὐτῷ. φησὶ γοῦν περὶ αὐτοῦ Ποσειδώνιος ἐν τῇ ἑβδόμῃ καὶ τεσσαρακοστῇ τῶν Ἱστοριῶν οὕτως· "ὁ δὲ τῆς Αἰγύπτου δυνάστης μισούμενος μὲν
ὑπὸ τῶν ὄχλων, κολακευόμενος δ᾽ ὑπὸ τῶν περὶ αὐτόν, ἐν πολλῇ δὲ τρυφῇ
ζῶν, οὐδὲ ⟨περι⟩πατεῖν οἷός τε ἦν, εἰ μὴ δυσὶν ἐπαπερειδόμενος ἐπορεύετο.
εἰς δὲ τὰς ἐν τοῖς συμποσίοις ὀρχήσεις ἀπὸ μετεώρων κλινῶν καθαλλόμενος
ἀνυπόδητος συντονωτέρας αὐτὰς τῶν ἠσκηκότων ἐποιεῖτο."

Also increased in stoutness was his son [sc. the son of Ptolemy
Physcon], Alexander, who killed his own mother when she was co-
ruler with him. At any rate, Posidonius talks about him in the forty-
seventh book of his *Histories* as follows: 'The ruler of Egypt, hated
by the mob, flattered by those around him, living in great luxury,
was unable to ⟨walk about/relieve himself⟩ unless he went supported by a couple of men. He would jump down barefoot from
lofty couches into the dances at drinking parties and perform them
more energetically than the experts.'

Ptolemy X Alexander I ruled jointly with his mother, Cleopatra
III, until her death in 101 BC. He then co-ruled with his wife,
Cleopatra Berenice, until his death in battle in 88 BC. Kidd suggests
that this passage refers to the later days of his reign, in the late 90s or
early 80s, when he was 'in the gross fruits of power'. However, this
cannot be stated with any degree of certainty. Determining a start
date for Alexander's reign is itself highly problematic. He ruled
jointly with his mother in 110, but soon resigned with the title
'King of Cyprus'; again in 108 he ruled with Cleopatra; and this

second period in power led the way to his third and final co-regency with her, which was ended by her death. So it is difficult to say exactly what the dates of his reign were. The problem is irrelevant if Kidd is correct to place this fragment towards the end of Alexander's reign, but since this is uncertain, the possible chronological span for the passage is rather vague—roughly 110–88 BC.

Fragment 27 (F 78 E–K) Athenaeus 4. 168D–E

παρὰ δὲ Ῥωμαίοις μνημονεύεται, ὥς φησι Ποσειδώνιος ἐν τῇ ἐνάτῃ καὶ τεσσαρακοστῇ τῶν Ἱστοριῶν, Ἀπίκιόν τινα ἐπὶ ἀσωτίᾳ πάντας ἀνθρώπους ὑπερηκοντικέναι. οὗτος δ᾽ ἐστὶν Ἀπίκιος ὁ καὶ τῆς φυγῆς αἴτιος γενόμενος Ῥουτιλίῳ τῷ τὴν Ῥωμαικὴν ἱστορίαν ἐκδεδωκότι τῇ Ἑλλήνων φωνῇ.

Among the Romans there is a tradition, as says Posidonius in the forty-ninth book of his *Histories*, that a certain Apicius had surpassed all men in extravagance. This is the Apicius who was responsible for the exile of Rutilius who published a Roman history in the language of the Greeks.

As a context Kidd suggests the trial of Rutilius in 92 BC, although he does note that the connection between Posidonius' comment on Apicius and the trial of Rutilius is made by Athenaeus and not by Posidonius himself. However, even if we accept Kidd's deduction that Athenaeus probably took the connection from Posidonius, and that Posidonius discussed the trial of Rutilius in Book 49, we do not need to follow him in his further deduction that 'this passage gives a date for the contents of Bk 49'. Theiler remains confused as to the context which may have prompted this passage, since he automatically dates the event to 88 BC and then cannot find a suitable occasion during that year. Jacoby suggested a general survey of Roman morals in the 90s, between the recall from exile of Metellus Numidicus in 99 BC and the governorship of Asia by Q. Mucius Scaevola, whose legate Rutilius was in 94 BC.

Fragment 38 (F 51 E–K) Athenaeus 6. 266E–F

Νικόλαος δ᾽ ὁ Περιπατητικὸς καὶ Ποσειδώνιος ὁ Στωικὸς ἐν ταῖς Ἱστορίαις ἑκάτερος τοὺς Χίους φασὶν ἐξανδραποδισθέντας ὑπὸ Μιθριδάτου τοῦ Καππάδοκος παραδοθῆναι τοῖς ἰδίοις δούλοις δεδεμένους, ἵν᾽ εἰς τὴν Κόλχων γῆν κατοικισθῶσιν· οὕτως αὐτοῖς ἀληθῶς τὸ δαιμόνιον ἐμήνισε πρώτοις χρησαμένοις ὠνητοῖς ἀνδραπόδοις τῶν πολλῶν αὐτουργῶν ὄντων κατὰ τὰς διακονίας.

Nicolaus the Peripatetic and Posidonius the Stoic both say in their *Histories* that the Chians, having been enslaved by Mithridates the Cappadocian, were handed over in chains to their own slaves, so

that they might be settled in the land of Colchis. So truly did the
deity rage against them as the first to make use of bought slaves,
when many men did their own work in carrying out their
business.

In terms of temporal context, this fragment is relatively easy to
place in 86 BC. The Chians were reinstated by Sulla at the end of the
Mithridatic war. From this information much has been derived
about the end-date of the *Histories*. In spite of the lack of a book
number in Athenaeus, Kidd favours a location in the last few books,
dealing with the first Mithridatic war. He rightly rejects the
temptation to link this passage with F 8 on the Mariandynian
slaves and to place F 38 alongside F 8 in Book 11. It is not
improbable that the passage did come from near the end of the
work, and also that the work ended some time during the 80s BC.
However, F 14 should remind us to exercise considerable caution. If
we did not have a book number in Athenaeus for this fragment
concerning Harpalus and dated to *c*.325/4 BC, we might be tempted
to place it, as our earliest datable event, at the start of the *Histories*.
Some might even be led to worry about the start-date of the work.
However, we happen to know that the passage came from the middle
of the work, and we assume that its date lay outside the main scope
of the *Histories*. By analogy, we have no overwhelming reason for
placing F 38 at the end of the work, simply because it contains the
latest datable reference.

Fragment 61 (F 52 E–K) Athenaeus 9. 401A

μνημονεύει δ' αὐτῶν [sc. τῶν κουνίκλων] καὶ Ποσειδώνιος ὁ φιλόσοφος ἐν
τῇ Ἱστορίᾳ· "καὶ ἡμεῖς εἴδομεν πολλοὺς κατὰ τὸν ἀπὸ Δικαιαρχείας πλοῦν
ἐπὶ Νέαν πόλιν. νῆσος γάρ ἐστιν οὐ μακρὸν τῆς γῆς κατὰ τὰ τελευταῖα
μέρη τῆς Δικαιαρχείας ὑπ' ὀλίγων μὲν κατοικουμένη, πολλοὺς δὲ ἔχουσα
τοὺς κουνίκλους τούτους."

Posidonius the philosopher also mentions them [sc. rabbits] in his
History:[8] 'We too saw many on the voyage from Dicaearcheia to
Neapolis. For there is an island not far from the mainland opposite
the most remote areas of Dicaearcheia, which is inhabited by only a
few people, but has many of these rabbits.'

---

[8] The reference to Posidonius' work in the singular is striking. It is the only
occasion in the extant fragments where this title is given. Otherwise, either no
title is given, or it is Ἱστορίαι. It is hard to explain this peculiarity, since this
source, Athenaeus, elsewhere uses the plural of Posidonius' work. This is also
one of only two among Athenaeus' direct references to the *Histories* in which
no book number is mentioned.

Jacoby suggested that this passage may have belonged to Posidonius' Spanish history, since Spanish rabbits were notorious.[9] Kidd
rightly joins Jacoby in noting, however, that the possibilities of
context are endless. The interest in Jacoby's comment lies in the
unspoken methodology of treating the contents of this fragment as a
parallel or an *exemplum*. The arguments deployed by commentators
on the fragments dealt with above indicate the predominant technique
which has been applied; namely, to assume that the contents of a
fragment comply with the subject matter of the 'main narrative'. This
method would lead to the conclusion that the fragment under
discussion came from a part of the *Histories* dealing with events in
southern Italy. A suitable campaign could be found to act as the
stimulus for such a comment, as has been attempted with F 19. It is
indeed possible that the passage was occasioned by the arrival of the
narrative for the first time in this region, resulting in a section on the
origines et situs of the area.

But Jacoby offers an alternative answer, that this fragment came
from a part of the work whose main narrative was located elsewhere
entirely. The implications are far-reaching. Firstly, Jacoby assumes
that a discussion of rabbits could have formed part of a Spanish
history, making details of geography, flora and fauna, or ethnography
integral to Posidonius' *Histories*. Secondly, by acknowledging the
phenomenon of exemplification or of stepping, even momentarily,
outside the strict narrative progression, Jacoby opened up the way for
arguments of the kind that I have used throughout. The positive
correlation between fragment and context, and the consequent deduction that the date and subject matter of a fragment inform us about
the date and subject of the whole surrounding book, is importantly
questioned.

[9] Theiler (p. 89) notes Catullus 37.18: 'cuniculosae Celtiberiae'.

APPENDIX C
Strabo's Acknowledged Sources Arranged Region by Region

The sources in this Appendix are arranged following a broadly generic principle. I have indicated those authors who are known to have produced regional accounts and grouped the poetic sources towards the end of each list.

Spain
Asclepiades of Myrleia—regional
'The people of Gades'—regional
Herodotus
Polybius
Ephorus
Artemidorus
Posidonius
Timosthenes
Pytheas
Anonymous historians
Silanus (the historian?)
Philetas' *Hermenia*
Pherecydes
Homer
Pindar
Anacreon
Athenodorus
Stesichorus
Dicaearchus
Seleucus (Chaldaean astronomer)
Demetrius of Phalerum

Celts and Galatians
Caesar's *Commentarii*—regional
Eyewitness accounts—regional
Ephorus

Posidonius
Artemidorus
Pytheas
Timagenes
Aristotle
Asinius
Aeschylus
'The ancient Greeks'

Britain
Eyewitness accounts—regional
Pytheas

Rome and Italy
Q. Fabius Pictor—regional
Theodorus—regional
Leonides—regional
Aristobulus—regional
Aristocles—regional
Antiochus of Syracuse—regional
L. Coelius Antipater—regional
Atellanae fabulae—regional
The Chorographer—regional
Autopsy—regional
οἱ ἐπιχώριοι—regional
Timaeus
Ephorus
Polybius

Herodotus
Eratosthenes
Posidonius
Artemidorus
Hecataeus
Atthidographers
Aeschylus
Homer
Euripides
Callimachus
Pindar
Ibycus
Sophocles
Tyrtaeus
Asius the poet
Plato
Anticleides
Zoilus the rhetor
Apollodorus *On Ships*
οἱ Ἐνετοι
οἱ παλαιοί
οἱ πρὸ ἡμῶν

German Area

Posidonius
Ephorus
Cleitarchus
'War with Rome'

Northern Europe and Scythia

Hellanicus of Lesbos
Posidonius
Herodotus
Ephorus
Eratosthenes
Pytheas
Homer
Hesiod
Sophocles
Apollodorus' *On Ships*
Socrates' *Phaedrus*
Menander
Chrysippus

Illyria

Eratosthenes
Theopompus
Posidonius
Hecataeus
Plato's *Republic*
Choerilus

Macedonia

Polybius
Ephorus
Herodotus
Demetrius of Scepsis
Eudoxus
Homer

Epirus, Thessaly, and Greece

Autopsy
Atthidographers—regional
Philochorus the Athenian—
    regional
Pausanias of Sparta—regional
Ephorus
Polybius
Posidonius
Eudoxus of Cnidus
Eratosthenes
Theopompus
Hecataeus
Thucydides
Hipparchus
Artemidorus
Periplus texts
Polemon of Ilion
Hesiod
Homer
Pindar
Philochorus
Hipponax
Alcman
Alcaeus
Aeschylus

Antimachus
Stesichorus
Callimachus
Euripides
Sophocles
Tyrtaeus
Callisthenes
Apollodorus
Demetrius of Scepsis
Aristotle's *Politeiai*
Ion
Epicharmus
Philetas
Aratus
Simmias
οἱ τραγικοί
Proverbs
Euphronius
Heracleides of Pontus
Xenophon's *Anabasis*
Hegesias (3rd cent.)
Polemon the Periegete
Demetrius of Phalerum
Zenodotus
Cineas

Pontus

Polybius
Posidonius
Artemidorus
Apollodorus
Demetrius of Scepsis
Polemon of Ilion
Demetrius of Callatis
Pindar
Homer
Apollonides
Hypsicrates

Armenia

Metrodorus of Scepsis
Theophanes of Mytilene—
   regional

Artavasdes the Armenian—
   regional

Bithynia

Asclepiades of Myrleia—regional
Menecrates—regional

*Cappadocia, Lycia, Pamphylia,
and Phrygia*

No sources cited

Cilicia

Athenodorus of Tarsus

Caria

Scylax of Caryanda
Apollonius of Aphrodisias

Lydia

Xanthus the Lydian—regional
Menippus

Cyprus

Hellanicus
Eratosthenes
Palaephatus of Abydus
Damastes

India

Nicolaus of Damascus
Eratosthenes
Artemidorus
Cleitarchus
Megasthenes
Scylax of Caryanda
Ctesias of Cnidus
Nearchus
Patrocles
Orthagoras
Daimachus
Androsthenes of Thasos
Onesicritus
Aristobulus

Homer
Euripides
Sophocles
Pindar
Aristotle
Simonides
Democritus
Timagenes
Apollodorus' *Parthica*
Theodectes
Megillus
Gorgus
Craterus
'Other mythographers'

Babylonia, Assyria, Media,
Persia, Parthia

Charon of Lampsacus—regional
Ctesias of Cnidus—regional
Eratosthenes
Posidonius
Polyclitus
Apollodorus of Artemita
Hellanicus of Lesbos
Juba the Mauretanian
Zeno

Syria

Timaeus

Phoenicia

No sources cited

Judaea

Eratosthenes
Posidonius

Arabia

Eratosthenes
Aristobulus
Nearchus
Artemidorus
Agatharchides

Ctesias of Cnidus
Athenodorus
Metrodorus of Scepsis
Androsthenes the Thasian
Orthagoras
Juba of Mauretania
Homer
Alexander's companions

Egypt

Eudorus of Alexandria—
    regional
Ariston—regional
Eratosthenes
Hellanicus of Lesbos
Polybius
Posidonius
Callisthenes
Herodotus
Artemidorus
Satyrus
Aristotle
Homer
Pindar
Aristobulus
Cicero
Thrasyalces the Thasian
Callimachus
Chaeremon
Sappho
Alexander historians
Nicander's *Theriaca*
Own travels

Aethiopia

Ephorus
Eratosthenes
Posidonius
Charon of Lampsacus
Bion of Soli
Philon
Onesicritus
Homer

Libya

Artemidorus
Eratosthenes
Posidonius
Charon of Lampsacus
Timosthenes

Ophelas of Cyrene
Homer
Callimachus
Iphicrates
Gabinius' *Roman History*

Bibliography

This bibliography lists only works which have been cited in the text or footnotes.

Alonso-Núñez, J. M., 'Les Informations de Posidonius sur la péninsule ibérique', *L'Antiquité Classique*, 48 (1979), 639–46.
—— 'L'opposizione contro l'imperialismo romano e contro il principato nella storiografia del tempo di Augusto', *Rivista Storica dell'Antichità*, 12 (1982), 131–41.
—— 'Die Abfolge der Weltreiche bei Polybios und Dionysios von Halikarnassos', *Historia*, 32 (1983), 411–26.
—— 'Die Weltreichsukzession bei Strabo', *Zeitschrift für Religions- und Geistesgeschichte*, 36 (1984), 53–4.
—— 'Appian and the World Empires', *Athenaeum*, 62 (1984), 640–4.
—— 'An Augustan World History: The *Historiae Philippicae* of Pompeius Trogus', *Greece and Rome*, 34 (1987), 56–72.
—— 'The Emergence of Universal Historiography from the 4th to the 2nd Centuries B. C.', in *Purposes of History*, 173–92.
—— 'Die Weltgeschichte bei Poseidonios', *Grazer Beiträge*, 20 (1994), 87–108.
—— 'Die Weltgeschichte des Nikolaos von Damaskos', *Storia della Storiografia*, 27 (1995), 3–15.
Ambaglio, D., 'Strabone e la storiografia greca frammentaria', in L. Boffo et al. *Studio di storia e storiografia antiche per Emilio Gabba* (Como, New Press, 1988), 73–83.
Amiotti, G., 'Cerne: "ultima terra"', *CISA* 13 (1987), 43–9.
Anderson, J. G. C., 'Some Questions Bearing on the Date and Place of Composition of Strabo's *Geography*', in W. H. Buckler and W. M. Calder (eds.), *Anatolian Studies Presented to Sir William Mitchell Ramsay* (Manchester, Manchester University Press, 1923), 1–13.
Arafat, K. W., *Pausanias' Greece: Ancient Artists and Roman Rulers* (Cambridge, Cambridge University Press, 1996).
Ardener, S. (ed.), *Women and Space: Ground Rules and Social*

Maps (Cross-Cultural Perspectives on Women, 5; Oxford, Berg, 1993).

Auerbach, E., *Mimesis: The Representation of Reality in Western Literature*, trans. W. Trask (Princeton, Princeton University Press, 1953).

Baker, J. N. L., *The History of Geography* (Oxford, Blackwell, 1963).

Bauslaugh, R. A., 'The Text of Thucydides IV 8. 6 and the South Channel at Pylos', *JHS* 99 (1979), 1–6.

Bearzot, C., 'La Grecia di Pausania. Geografia e cultura nella definizione del concetto di Ἑλλάς', *CISA* 14 (1988), 90–112.

Bell, L., 'Artists and Empire: Victorian Representations of Subject People', *Art History*, 5 (1982), 73–86.

Bickermann, E. J., 'Origines Gentium', *Class. Phil.* 47 (1952), 65–81.

—— *Chronology of the Ancient World* (Aspects of Greek and Roman Life; London, Thames and Hudson, 1968).

Biraschi, A. M., 'Dai "Prolegomena" all'Italia: Premesse teoriche e tradizione', in *Italia Antica*, 127–43.

Bosi, F., 'La storia del Bosforo Cimmerio nell'opera di Strabone', in *Strabone II*, 171–88.

Bowersock, G. W., *Augustus and the Greek World* (Oxford, Clarendon Press, 1965).

—— 'Jacoby's Fragments and Two Greek Historians of Pre-Islamic Arabia', in G. W. Most (ed.), *Collecting Fragments. Fragmente sammeln* (Aporemata. Kritische Studien zur Philologiegeschichte, I; Göttingen, Vandenhoeck & Ruprecht, 1997), 173–85.

Bowman, A. K., *Egypt after the Pharaohs: 332 BC–AD 642 from Alexander to the Arab Conquest* (London, British Museum Press, 1986).

Breisach, E., *Historiography: Ancient, Medieval, and Modern* (Chicago, University of Chicago Press, 1983).

Broughton, T. R. S., 'Roman Asia Minor' in T. Frank (ed.), *An Economic Survey of Ancient Rome IV* (Baltimore, John Hopkins, 1938), 499–916 (esp. 'From Attalus to Pompey', 504–34).

Brown, T. S., *Timaeus of Tauromenium* (Berkeley, University of California Press, 1958).

—— 'Suggestions for a Vita of Ctesias of Cnidus', *Historia*, 27 (1978), 1–19.

Brunt, P. A., 'On Historical Fragments and Epitomes', *CQ* NS 30 (1980), 477–94.

Bulhof, I. N., 'Imagination and Interpretation in History', in L. Schulze and W. Wetzels (eds.), *Literature and History* (Boston, University Press of America, 1983), 3–25.

Burstein, S. M., *Agatharchides of Cnidus: On the Erythraean Sea* (London, Hakluyt Society, 1989).

Butlin, R. A., *Historical Geography: Through the Gates of Space and Time* (London, Arnold, 1993).

Butzer, K. W., 'Hartshorne, Hettner, and the *Nature of Geography*', in J. N. Entrikin and S. D. Brunn (eds.), *Reflections on Richard Hartshorne's* The Nature of Geography (Occasional Publications of the Association of American Geographers, 1; Washington, Association of American Geographers, 1989), 35–52.

Camassa, G., 'Problemi storico-religiosi dei libri di Strabone relativi all'Italia', in *Italia Antica*, 191–206.

Cameron, A. (ed.), *History as Text. The Writing of Ancient History* (London, Duckworth, 1989).

Carr, D., *Time, Narrative and History* (Bloomington, Indiana University Press, 1986); rev. N. Carroll, in *History and Theory*, 27 (1988), 297–306.

Cary, M., *The Geographic Background of Greek and Roman History* (Oxford, Clarendon Press, 1949).

Cary, M. and Warmington, E. H., *The Ancient Explorers* (London, Methuen, 1929).

Casson, L., *The Periplus Maris Erythraei* (Princeton, Princeton University Press, 1989).

Chilver, G. E. F., 'Strabo and Cisalpine Gaul: An Anachronism', *JRS* 28 (1938), 126–8.

—— *Cisalpine Gaul: Social and Economic History from 49 B.C. to the Death of Trajan* (Oxford, Clarendon Press, 1941).

Christopherson, S., 'On Being Outside "the Project"', *Antipode*, 21 (1989), 83–9.

Clarke, K. J., 'In Search of the Author of Strabo's *Geography*', *JRS* 87 (1997), 92–110.

—— 'Universal Perspectives in Historiography', in C. Kraus (ed.), *The Limits of Historiography: Genre and Narrative in Ancient Historical Texts* (Leiden, Brill, forthcoming).

Claval, P., 'The Historical Dimension of French Geography', *Journal of Historical Geography*, 10 (1984), 229–45.

Clavel-Lévêque, M., 'Les Gaules et les Gaulois: Pour une analyse du fonctionnement de la *Géographie* de Strabon', *Dialogues d'Histoire Ancienne*, 1 (1974), 75–93.

Coarelli, F., 'Strabone: Roma e il Lazio', in *Italia Antica*, 75–91.

Cordano, F., *La Geografia degli antichi* (Rome, Laterza, 1992).

Cosgrove, D. E., *Social Formation and Symbolic Landscape* (London and Sydney, Croom Helm, 1984).

—— 'The Geometry of Landscape: Practical and Speculative Arts in

Sixteenth-Century Venetian Land Territories', in D. E. Cosgrove
and S. Daniels (eds.), *The Iconography of Landscape* (Cambridge,
Cambridge University Press, 1988), 254–76.
—— 'Power and Place in the Venetian Territories', in J. A. Agnew
and J. S. Duncan (eds.), *The Power of Place: Bringing together
Geographical and Sociological Imaginations* (Boston, Unwin
Hyman, 1989), 104–23.
Cronon, W., 'A Place for Stories: Nature, History, and Narrative',
Journal of American History, 78 (1992), 1347–76.
Darby, H. C., 'On the Relations of Geography and History', *TIBG*
19 (1953), 1–11.
Davidson, J., 'The Gaze in Polybius' *Histories*', *JRS* 81 (1991), 10–
24.
Defoe, D., *A Tour through the Whole Island of Great Britain* (3 vols.;
London, 1724–6; republished and reprinted: Harmondsworth,
Penguin, 1986).
Demeritt, D., 'The Nature of Metaphors in Cultural Geography and
Environmental History', *Progress in Human Geography*, 18 (1994),
163–85.
Dench, E., *From Barbarians to New Men: Greek, Roman, and Modern
Perceptions of Peoples from the Central Apennines* (Oxford, Clar-
endon Press, 1995).
Derow, P. S., 'Polybius, Rome, and the East', *JRS* 69 (1979), 1–15.
Dewald, C., 'Narrative Surface and Authorial Voice in Herodotus'
Histories', *Arethusa*, 20 (1987), 147–70.
Dickinson, R. E. and Howarth, O. J. R., *The Making of Geography*
(Oxford, Clarendon Press, 1933).
Dicks, D. R., *The Geographical Fragments of Hipparchus* (London,
Athlone Press, 1960).
Diller, A., *The Tradition of the Minor Greek Geographers* (Philological
Monographs 14; Lancaster, PA, American Philological Association,
1952).
—— 'Agathemerus, *Sketch of Geography*', *GRBS* 16 (1975), 59–76.
—— *The Textual Tradition of Strabo's Geography* (Amsterdam,
Hakkert, 1975).
Dion, R., *Aspects politiques de la géographie antique* (Paris, Société
d'Édition les Belles Lettres, 1977).
Dobesch, G., *Das europaïsche 'Barbaricum' und die Zone der Medi-
terrankultur: Ihre historische Wechselwirkung und das Geschichtsbild
des Poseidonios* (Tyche Supplement, 2; Vienna, Holzhausen, 1995);
rev. K. J. Clarke, in *JRS* 86 (1996), 190.
Downey, G., 'Strabo on Antioch: Notes on his Method', *TAPA* 72
(1941), 85–95.

Drews, R., 'Ephoros and History Written κατὰ γένος', *AJP* 84 (1963), 244–55.

—— 'Assyria in Classical Universal Histories', *Historia*, 14 (1965), 129–42.

Driver, F., 'Geography's Empire: Histories of Geographical Knowledge', *Environment and Planning D: Society and Space*, 10 (1992), 23–40.

—— et al., 'Geographical Traditions: Rethinking the History of Geography', *TIBG* NS 20 (1995), 403–22.

Dubois, M., 'Strabon et Polybe', *Revue des Études Grecques*, 4 (1891), 343–56.

Dubuisson, M., 'La Vision polybienne de Rome', in *Purposes of History*, 233–43.

Edelstein, L. and Kidd, I. G. (eds.), *Posidonius*, 3 vols.: *I. The Fragments*; *II(i). Testimonia and Fragments 1–149, II(ii). Fragments* (Cambridge Classical Texts and Commentaries, 13 and 14; Cambridge, Cambridge University Press, 1972 and 1988).

Elliott, J. H., *The Old World and the New* (Cambridge, Cambridge University Press, 1970).

Engels, D., 'The Length of Eratosthenes' Stade', *AJP* 106 (1985), 298–311.

Entrikin, J. N. and Brunn, S. D. (eds.), *Reflections on Richard Hartshorne's* The Nature of Geography (Occasional Publications of the Association of American Geographers 1; Washington, Association of American Geographers, 1989).

Evans-Pritchard, E. E., *Essays in Social Anthropology* (London, Faber and Faber, 1962).

Farrington, B., *Diodorus Siculus. Universal Historian* = Inaugural Lecture at Swansea (Swansea, University of Wales Press, 1937).

Fink, C., *Marc Bloch: A Life in History* (Cambridge, Cambridge University Press, 1989).

Finley, M. I. (ed.), *Problèmes de la terre en Grèce ancienne* (Paris, Mouton, 1973).

Fornara, C. W., *The Nature of History in Ancient Greece and Rome* (Berkeley, University of California Press, 1983).

Foucault, M., 'What is an Author?', in P. Rabinow (ed.), *The Foucault Reader* (Harmondsworth, Penguin, 1984), 101–20.

Fowler, D. P., 'Narrate and Describe: The Problem of Ekphrasis', *JRS* 81 (1991), 25–35.

Fowler, R. L., 'Herodotus and his Contemporaries', *JHS* 116 (1996), 62–87.

Fox, M., *Roman Historical Myths: The Regal Period in Augustan Literature* (Oxford, Clarendon Press, 1996).

Fraser, P. M., 'Eratosthenes of Cyrene', *Proceedings of the British Academy*, 56 (1970), 175–207.
—— 'The World of Theophrastus', in S. Hornblower (ed.), *Greek Historiography* (Oxford, Clarendon Press, 1994), 167–91.
Funke, P., 'Strabone, la geografia storica e la struttura etnica della Grecia Nord-Occidentale', in F. Prontera (ed.), *Geografia storica della Grecia antica* (Rome, Laterza, 1991), 174–93.
Gabba, E., 'True History and False History in Classical Antiquity', *JRS* 71 (1981), 50–62.
Gagé, J., 'Hercule-Melqart, Alexandre et les Romains à Gadès', *Revue des Études Anciennes*, 42 (1940), 425–37.
Geertz, C., *The Interpretation of Cultures* (2nd edn.; London, Fontana, 1993; 1st edn. 1973).
Glacken, C., 'Changing Ideas of the Habitable World', in W. L. Thomas (ed.), *Man's Rôle in Changing the Face of the Earth* (Chicago, University of Chicago Press, 1956).
—— *Traces on the Rhodian Shore: Nature and Culture in Western Thought from Ancient Times to the End of the Eighteenth Century* (Berkeley and Los Angeles, University of California Press, 1967).
Godlewska, A., 'Map, Text and Image. The Mentality of Enlightened Conquerors: A New Look at the *Description de l'Egypte*', *TIBG* ns 20 (1995), 5–28.
Gould, P. and White, R., *Mental Maps* (Harmondsworth, Penguin, 1974).
Grafton, A., 'Fragmenta Historicorum Graecorum: Fragments of Some Lost Enterprises', in G. W. Most (ed.), *Collecting Fragments. Fragmente sammeln* (Aporemata. Kritische Studien zur Philologiegeschichte, I; Göttingen, Vandenhoeck & Ruprecht, 1997), 124–43.
Greenblatt, S., *Marvelous Possessions: The Wonder of the New World* (The Clarendon Lectures and the Carpenter Lectures 1988; Oxford, Clarendon Press, 1991).
Grundy, G. B. (ed.), *Murray's Classical Atlas* (London, Murray, 1904).
—— *Fifty-five Years at Oxford: An Unconventional Autobiography* (London, Methuen, 1945).
Guelke, L., *Historical Understanding in Geography: An Idealist Approach* (Cambridge Studies in Historical Geography 3; Cambridge, Cambridge University Press, 1982).
Gurevich, A. J., *Categories of Medieval Culture*, trans. G. L. Campbell (2nd edn., London, Routledge and Kegan Paul, 1985; 1st edn. 1972).
Hahm, D. E., 'Posidonios's Theory of Historical Causation', *ANRW* II 36.3, 1325–63.

Hall, E., *Inventing the Barbarian: Greek Self-Definition through Tragedy* (Oxford, Clarendon Press, 1989).

Hansen, O., 'Did Poseidonios Give Germania her Name?', *Latomus*, 48 (1989), 878–9.

Haraway, D., 'Situated Knowledges: The Science Question in Feminism and the Privilege of Partial Perspective', in D. Haraway (ed.), *Simians, Cyborgs and Women* (London, Free Association Press, 1991), 183–201.

Harley, J. B., 'Maps, Knowledge, and Power', in D. Cosgrove and S. Daniels (eds.), *The Iconography of Landscape* (Cambridge, Cambridge University Press, 1988), 277–312.

Harris, C., 'The Historical Mind and the Practice of Geography', in D. Ley and M. S. Samuels (eds.), *Humanistic Geography: Prospects and Problems* (London, Croom Helm, 1978), 123–37.

Harris, E. E., *The Reality of Time* (Albany, New York State University Press, 1988); rev. G. Allan, in *History and Theory*, 28 (1989), 348–56.

Hartshorne, R., *The Nature of Geography: A Critical Survey of Current Thought in the Light of the Past* (Lancaster, PA, The Association of American Geographers Press, 1939).

Harvey, D., *The Condition of Postmodernity: An Enquiry into the Origins of Cultural Change* (Oxford, Blackwell, 1989).

Hawking, S., *A Brief History of Time: From the Big Bang to Black Holes* (London, Bantam Books, 1988).

Hornblower, J., *Hieronymus of Cardia* (Oxford, Oxford University Press, 1981).

Hornblower, S., *Mausolus* (Oxford, Clarendon Press, 1982).

—— 'Introduction', in S. Hornblower (ed.), *Greek Historiography* (Oxford, Clarendon Press, 1994), 1–72.

—— 'Narratology and Narrative Techniques in Thucydides', in S. Hornblower (ed.), *Greek Historiography* (Oxford, Clarendon Press, 1994), 131–66.

—— (ed.), *Greek Historiography* (Oxford, Clarendon Press, 1994).

Humphreys, S. C., 'Fragments, Fetishes, and Philosophies: Towards a History of Greek Historiography after Thucydides', in G. W. Most (ed.), *Collecting Fragments. Fragmente sammeln* (Aporemata. Kritische Studien zur Philologiegeschichte, I; Göttingen, Vandenhoeck & Ruprecht, 1997), 207–24.

Huntingdon, E. T., *Mainsprings of Civilization* (New York, Wiley; London, Chapman and Hall, 1945).

Hussey, E., *The Presocratics* (London, Duckworth, 1972).

Jacob, C., 'Carte Greche', in F. Prontera (ed.), *Geografia e geografi nel mondo antico: Guida storica e critica* (Rome, Laterza, 1983), 47–67.

—— *Géographie et ethnographie en Grèce ancienne* (Paris, Colin, 1991).

Jacoby, F., 'Über die Entwicklung der griechischen Historiographie und den Plan einer neuen Sammlung der griechischen Historiker-fragmente', *Klio*, 9 (1909), 80–123.

Jakle, J. A., 'Time, Space, and the Geographic Past: A Prospectus for Historical Geography', *American Historical Review*, 76 (1971), 1084–1103.

James, P. E. and Martin, G. J., *All Possible Worlds: A History of Geographical Ideas*, 2nd edn. (New York, Wiley, 1981).

Janni, P., 'L'Italia di Strabone: descrizione e immagine', in *Italia Antica*, 147–59.

—— 'Fernando Colombo e l'INDIKÉ di Arriano', *Geographia Antiqua*, 1 (1992), 161–6.

Johnson, J. W., 'Chronological Writing: Its Concepts and Development', *History and Theory*, 2 (1962–3), 124–45.

Katz, C., 'All the World is Staged: Intellectuals and the Projects of Ethnography', *Environment and Planning D: Society and Space*, 10 (1992), 495–510.

Kern, S., *The Culture of Time and Space: 1880–1910* (London, Weidenfeld and Nicolson, 1983).

Kidd, I. G., 'Posidonius as Philosopher-Historian', in M. T. Griffin and J. Barnes (eds.), *Philosophia Togata: Essays on Philosophy and Roman Society* (Oxford, Clarendon Press, 1989), 38–50.

—— 'What is a Posidonian Fragment?', in G. W. Most (ed.), *Collecting Fragments. Fragmente sammeln* (Aporemata. Kritische Studien zur Philologiegeschichte, I; Göttingen, Vandenhoeck & Ruprecht, 1997), 225–36.

Kimble, G. H. T., *Geography in the Middle Ages* (London, Methuen, 1938).

Kracauer, S., 'Time and History', *History and Theory. Beiheft*, 6 (1966), 65–78.

Lacy, J. R. F. Martinez , 'ἔθη καὶ νόμιμα. Polybius and his Concept of Culture', *Klio*, 73 (1991), 83–92.

Laffranque, M., *Poseidonios d'Apamée: Essai de Mise au Point* (Paris, Presses Universitaires de France, 1964).

Langton, J., 'The Two Traditions of Geography. Historical Geography and the Study of Landscapes', *Geografiska Annaler*, 70B (1988), 17–25.

Lanzillotta, E., 'Geografia e storia da Ecateo a Tucidide', *CISA* 14 (1988), 19–31.

Lasserre, F., 'Strabon devant l'Empire romain', *ANRW* II 30.1, 867–96.

—— 'Histoire de première main dans la *Géographie* de Strabon', in *Strabone I*, 11–26.

Lehmann, G. A., 'The "Ancient" Greek History in Polybios' *Historiae*: Tendencies and Political Objectives', *Scripta Classica Israelica*, 10 (1989/90), 66–77.

Lendle, O., *Einführung in die griechische Geschichtsschreibung* (Darmstadt, Wissenschaftliche Buchgesellschaft, 1992).

Levene, D. S., 'Sallust's *Jugurtha*: An "Historical Fragment"', *JRS* 82 (1992), 53–70.

Lewis, C. S., *The Magician's Nephew* (London, Harper Collins, 1955).

Lewis, D. M., 'The Athenian Rationes Centesimarum', in M. I. Finley (ed.), *Problèmes de la terre en Grèce ancienne* (Paris, Mouton, 1973), 187–212.

Livingstone, D. N., *The Geographical Tradition: Episodes in the History of a Contested Enterprise* (Oxford, Blackwell, 1992).

Luisi, A., 'Cornelio Nepote geografo', *CISA* 14 (1988), 41–51.

Mackie, N. K., 'Augustan Colonies in Mauretania', *Historia*, 32 (1983), 332–58.

Mackintosh-Smith, T., *Yemen: Travels in Dictionary Land* (London, Murray, 1997).

Malitz, J., *Die Historien des Poseidonios* (Zetemata. Monographien zur Klassischen Altertumswissenschaft 79; Munich, Beck, 1983).

Marincola, J., 'Herodotean Narrative and the Narrator's Presence', *Arethusa*, 20 (1987), 121–38.

—— *Authority and Tradition in Ancient Historiography* (Cambridge, Cambridge University Press, 1997).

Massaro, G. D., 'I moduli della narrazione storica nel libri di Strabone sull'Italia meridionale', in *Strabone II*, 81–117.

Maurenbrecher, B., *C. Sallusti Crispi Historiarum Reliquae* (Leipzig, Teubner, 1891).

May, J. A., *Kant's Concept of Geography and its Relation to Recent Geographical Thought* (Toronto, University of Toronto Press, 1970).

McGing, B. C., *The Foreign Policy of Mithridates VI Eupator, King of Pontus* (Mnemosyne Supplement 89; Leiden, Brill, 1986).

Meinig, D. W., 'The Continuous Shaping of America: A Prospectus for Geographers and Historians', *American Historical Review*, 83 (1978), 1186–1213.

Mendels, D., 'The Five Empires: A Note on a Propagandistic *Topos*', *AJP* 102 (1981), 330–7.

—— 'The Polemical Character of Manetho's *Aegyptiaca*', in *Purposes of History*, 91–110.

Merrifield, A., 'Place and Space. A Lefebvrian Reconciliation', *TIBG* NS 18 (1993), 516–31.

―― 'Situated Knowledge through Exploration: Reflections on Bunge's "Geographical Expeditions"', *Antipode*, 27 (1995), 49–70.

Millar, F. G. B., *The Emperor in the Roman World* (London, Duckworth, 1977).

―― 'Polybius between Greece and Rome', in J. T. A. Koumoulides and J. Brademas (eds.), *Greek Connections: Essays on Culture and Diplomacy* (Notre Dame, University of Notre Dame Press, 1987), 1–18.

Mitchell, J. B., *Historical Geography* (London, English Universities Press, 1954).

Mitchell, L. G., *Greeks Bearing Gifts: The Public Use of Private Relationships in the Greek World, 435–323 B.C.* (Cambridge, Cambridge University Press, 1997).

Mitchell, S., *Anatolia: Land, Men, and Gods in Asia Minor, i: The Celts in Anatolia and the Impact of Roman Rule* (Oxford, Clarendon Press, 1993).

Moles, J. L., 'The Interpretation of the "Second Preface" in Arrian's *Anabasis*', *JHS* 105 (1985), 162–8.

―― 'Truth and Untruth in Herodotus and Thucydides', in C. Gill and T. P. Wiseman (eds.), *Lies and Fiction in the Ancient World* (Exeter, University of Exeter Press, 1993), 88–121.

Momigliano, A., *Alien Wisdom: The Limits of Hellenization* (Cambridge, Cambridge University Press, 1975).

―― *Essays in Ancient and Modern Historiography* (Oxford, Blackwell, 1977).

―― 'The Rhetoric of History and the History of Rhetoric: On Hayden White's Tropes', in E. S. Shaffer (ed.), *Comparative Criticism. A Year Book*, iii (Cambridge, Cambridge University Press, 1981), 259–68.

―― *On Pagans, Jews, and Christians* (Connecticut, Wesleyan University Press, 1987).

―― *The Classical Foundations of Modern Historiography* (Sather Classical Lectures 54; Berkeley, University of California Press, 1990).

Morgan, M. G., 'Tacitus on Germany: Roman History or Latin Literature', in L. Schulze and W. Wetzels (eds.), *Literature and History* (Boston, University Press of America, 1983), 87–118.

Most, G. W. (ed.), *Collecting Fragments. Fragmente sammeln* (Aporemata. Kritische Studien zur Philologiegeschichte, I; Göttingen, Vandenhoeck & Ruprecht, 1997).

Moynihan, R., 'Geographical Mythology and Roman Imperial Ideology', in R. Winkes (ed.), *The Age of Augustus* (Providence, Brown University Press, 1985), 149–62.

Müller, C. (ed.), *Fragmenta Historicorum Graecorum* (Paris, Firmin-Didot, 1853).

Murray, O., 'Herodotus and Hellenistic Culture', *CQ* NS 22 (1972), 200–13.

—— 'Omero e l'etnografia', *Κωλακος: Studi pubblicati dall'Istituto di Storia Antica dell'Università di Palermo* (1988–9), 1–13.

—— 'History' in J. Brunschwig and G. Lloyd (eds.), *Le Savoir grec* (Paris, Flammarion, 1996).

Myres, J. L., *Geographical History in Greek Lands* (Oxford, Clarendon Press, 1953).

Nicolai, R., 'Un sistema di localizzazione geografica relativa. Aorsi e Siraci in Strabone XI 5, 7–8', in *Strabone I*, 101–25.

—— 'Scelte critico-testuali e problemi storici nei libri V e VI della *Geografia* di Strabone' in *Italia Antica*, 267–86.

Nicolet, C., *Space, Geography, and Politics in the Early Roman Empire* (Ann Arbor, Michigan University Press, 1991).

Nock, A. D., 'Posidonius', *JRS* 49 (1959), 1–15.

Norden, E., *Germanische Urgeschichte in Tacitus Germania* (Leipzig, Teubner, 1922).

Ogilvie, A. G., 'The Time-Element in Geography', *TIBG* 18 (1952), 1–15.

Paassen, C. Van, *The Classical Tradition of Geography* (Groningen, Wolters, 1957).

Pagden, A., *European Encounters with the New World: From Renaissance to Romanticism* (New Haven, Yale University Press, 1993).

Pais, E., *Ancient Italy*, trans. C. D. Curtis (Chicago, University of Chicago Press, 1908).

Parker, W. H., *Mackinder: Geography as an Aid to Statescraft* (Oxford, Clarendon Press, 1982).

Parkes, D. and Thrift, N., 'Putting Time in its Place', in *Making Sense of Time*, 119–29.

Pédech, P., *La Méthode historique de Polybe* (Paris, Les Belles Lettres, 1964).

—— 'La Géographie urbaine chez Strabon', *Ancient Society*, 2 (1971), 234–53.

Pelling, C. B. R., 'Plutarch's Method of Work in the Roman Lives', *JHS* 99 (1979), 74–96.

—— 'Fun with Fragments: Athenaeus and the Historians', in D. Braund and J. Wilkins (eds.), *Athenaeus and his Philosophers at Supper* (Exeter, University of Exeter Press, 1999).

Podossinov, A. V., 'Die sakrale Orientierung nach Himmelsrichtungen im alten Griechenland', *Acta Antiqua Academiae Scientiarum Hungaricae*, 33 (1990–2), 323–30.

—— 'Die Orientierung der alten Karten von den ältesten Zeiten bis zum frühen Mittelalter', *Cartographica Helvetica*, 7 (1993), 33–43.

Pothecary, S., 'Strabo, Polybios and the Stade', *Phoenix*, 49 (1995), 49–67.

—— 'The Expression "Our Times" in Strabo's *Geography*', *Class. Phil.* 92 (1997), 235–46.

Prandi, L., 'La critica storica di Strabone alla geografia di Erodoto', *CISA* 14 (1988), 52–72.

Prince, H., 'Time and Historical Geography', in *Making Sense of Time*, 17–37.

Prontera, F., 'Prima di Strabone: Materiali per uno studio della geografia antica come genere letterario', in *Strabone I*, 189–256.

—— 'L'Italia meridionale di Strabone. Appunti tra geografia e storia', in *Italia Antica*, 95–109.

Ramin, J., *Le Périple d'Hannon: The Periplus of Hanno* (BAR Supplementary Series, 3; London, British Archaeological Reports, 1976).

Rawson, B. and Weaver, P. (eds.), *The Roman Family in Italy. Status, Sentiment, Space* (Oxford, Clarendon Press, 1997).

Rawson, E., *Intellectual Life in the Late Roman Republic* (London, Duckworth, 1985).

Reynolds, J., *Aphrodisias and Rome* (Journal of Roman Studies Monograph, 1; London, Society for the Promotion of Roman Studies, 1982).

Reinhardt, K., *Poseidonios* (Munich, Beck, 1921).

Rhodes, P. J., 'The Atthidographers', in *Purposes of History*, 73–81.

Ricoeur, P., 'Narrative Time', in W. J. T. Mitchell (ed.), *On Narrative* (Chicago, University of Chicago Press, 1981), 165–86.

Romm, J. S., 'Herodotus and Mythic Geography: The Case of the Hyperboreans', *TAPA* 119 (1989), 97–113.

—— *The Edges of the Earth in Ancient Thought: Geography, Exploration, and Fiction* (Princeton, Princeton University Press, 1992).

Rostovtzeff, M., *Social and Economic History of the Hellenistic World II* (Oxford, Clarendon Press, 1941).

Russell, D. A. and Wilson, N. G. (eds.), *Menander Rhetor* (Oxford, Clarendon Press, 1981).

Scardigli, B., *Die Römerbiographien Plutarchs* (Munich, Beck, 1979).

Schepens, G., 'Polemic and Methodology in Polybius' Book XII', in *Purposes of History*, 39–61.

—— 'Jacoby's *FGrHist*: Problems, Methods, Prospects', in G. W. Most (ed.), *Collecting Fragments. Fragmente sammeln* (Aporemata.

Kritische Studien zur Philologiegeschichte, I; Göttingen, Vandenhoeck & Ruprecht, 1997), 144–72.

Schmidt, K., *Kosmologische Aspekte im Geschichtswerk des Poseidonios* (Hypomnemata, 63; Göttingen, Vandenhoeck & Ruprecht, 1980).

Schubert, F. W. (ed.), *Immanuel Kants Schriften zur physischen Geographie* (I. Kants Sämmtliche Werke VI; Leipzig, Voss, 1839).

Schultze, C. E., 'Dionysius of Halicarnassus and Roman Chronology', *PCPS* 41 (1995), 192–214.

Schürer, E., *The History of the Jewish People in the Age of Jesus Christ 175 B.C.—A.D. 135* i, rev. G. Vermes and F. Millar (Edinburgh, Clark, 1973).

Sechi, M., *La Costruzione della scienza geografica nei pensatori dell'antichità classica* (Memorie della Società Geografica Italiana, 44; Rome, Società Geografica Italiana, 1990), 213–27.

Skar, S. L., 'Andean Women and the Concept of Space/Time', in S. Ardener (ed.), *Women and Space: Ground Rules and Social Maps* (Cross-Cultural Perspectives on Women, 5; Oxford, Berg, 1993), 31–45.

Smalley, B., *Historians in the Middle Ages* (London, Thames and Hudson, 1974).

Smith, N., *Uneven Development: Nature, Capital and the Production of Space* (Oxford, Blackwell, 1984).

—— 'Geography as Museum: Private History and Conservative Idealism in *The Nature of Geography*', in J. N. Entrikin and S. D. Brunn (eds.), *Reflections on Richard Hartshorne's* The Nature of Geography (Washington, Association of American Geographers, 1989), 91–120.

Sordi, M., 'Gli interessi geografici e topografici nella "Elleniche" di Senofonte', *CISA* 14 (1988), 32–40.

Stahl, W. H., 'By Their Maps You Shall Know Them', *Archaeology*, 8 (1955), 146–55.

Starr, C. G., 'Historical and Philosophical Time', *History and Theory. Beiheft*, 6 (1966), 24–35.

Steele, R. B., 'Pompeius and Justinus', *AJP* 38 (1917), 19–41.

Stergiopoulos, C. D., 'Strabon et la division administrative de la Crète', *Revue Archéologique*, 31–2, 6th ser. (1949), 985–92.

Strasburger, H., 'Poseidonios on Problems of the Roman Empire', *JRS* 55 (1965), 40–53.

—— *Die Wesensbestimmung der Geschichte durch die Antike Geschichtsschreibung* 2 (Wiesbaden, Stein, 1966); rev. O. Murray in *Classical Review*, NS 18 (1968), 218–21.

Strout, C., 'Border Crossings: History, Fiction, and *Dead Certainties*', *History and Theory*, 31 (1992), 153–62.

Swain, J. W., 'The Theory of the Four Monarchies: Opposition History under the Roman Empire', *Class. Phil.* 35 (1940), 1–21.

Syme, R., *Anatolica: Studies in Strabo*, ed. A. Birley (Oxford, Clarendon Press, 1995); rev. K. J. Clarke in *Gnomon* (forthcoming).

Theiler, W., *Poseidonios, Die Fragmente* (Berlin, de Gruyter, 1982).

Theroux, P., *The Pillars of Hercules: A Grand Tour of the Mediterranean* (London, Hamilton, 1995).

Thollard, P., *Barbarie et Civilisation chez Strabon: Étude critique des Livres III et IV de la Géographie* (Centre de Recherches d'Histoire Ancienne, 77; Paris, University of Besançon, 1987).

Thomson, J. O., *History of Ancient Geography* (Cambridge, Cambridge University Press, 1948).

Thümmel, H. G., 'Poseidonios und die Geschichte', *Klio*, 66 (1984), 558–61.

Traina, G., *Ambiente e paesaggi di Roma antica* (Rome, La Nuova Italia Scientifica, 1990).

Treggiari, S., *Roman Marriage: Iusti Coniuges from the Time of Cicero to the Time of Ulpian* (Oxford, Clarendon Press, 1991).

Tuan, Y.-F., 'Literature and Geography: Implications for Geographical Research', in D. Ley and M. S. Samuels (eds.), *Humanistic Geography: Prospects and Problems* (London, Croom Helm, 1978), 194–206.

—— 'Space, Time, Place: A Humanistic Frame', in *Making Sense of Time*, 7–16.

Van der Vliet, E. Ch. L., 'L'Ethnographie de Strabon: Idéologie ou Tradition?' in *Strabone I*, 29–86.

Verbrugghe, G. P., 'Narrative Pattern in Posidonius' *History*', *Historia*, 24 (1975), 189–204.

Vercruysse, M., 'À la recherche du mensonge et de la vérité. La fonction des passages méthodologiques chez Polybe', in *Purposes of History*, 17–38.

Vernant, J.-P., *The Origins of Greek Thought* (London, Methuen, 1982).

Waddy, L., 'Did Strabo Visit Athens?', *AJA* 67 (1963), 296–300.

Walbank, F. W., *A Historical Commentary on Polybius* (3 vols.; Oxford, Clarendon Press, 1957–79).

—— *Polybius* (Berkeley, University of California Press, 1972).

Wallace, P. W., 'Strabo on Acrocorinth', *Hesperia*, 38 (1969), 495–9.

Wellek, R. and Warren, A., *Theory of Literature* (2nd edn.; London, Cape, 1966).

White, H., *Metahistory: The Historical Imagination in Nineteenth-Century Europe* (Baltimore, John Hopkins, 1973).

Whitrow, G. J., *Time in History: Views of Time from Prehistory to the Present Day* (Oxford, Oxford University Press, 1988).

Wiedemann, T., *Adults and Children in the Roman Empire* (London, Routledge, 1989).

—— 'Rhetoric in Polybius', in *Purposes of History*, 289–300.

Wiedemann, T. and Gardner, J. F., *The Roman Household: A Sourcebook* (London, Routledge, 1991).

Wilcox, D. J., *The Measure of Times Past: Pre-Newtonian Chronologies and the Rhetoric of Relative Time* (Chicago, University of Chicago Press, 1987); rev. P. Munz, in *History and Theory*, 28 (1989), 236–51.

Winkler, J. J., 'The Mendacity of Kalasiris and the Narrative Strategy of Heliodoros' *Aithiopika*', *Yale Classical Studies*, 27 (1982), 93–158.

Wright, J. K., 'Terrae Incognitae: The Place of the Imagination in Geography', *Annals of the Association of American Geographers*, 37 (1947), 1–15.

—— 'Map Makers are Human. Comments on the Subjective in Maps', in *Human Nature in Geography. Fourteen Papers 1925–1965* (Cambridge, MA, Harvard University Press, 1966), 33–52.

Index of passages

Index of subjects